THE ORIGINS OF CULTURAL DIFFERENCES AND THEIR IMPACT ON MANAGEMENT

Jack Scarborough

QUORUM BOOKS
Westport, Connecticut • London

Library of Congress Cataloging-in-Publication Data

Scarborough, Jack, 1946–
    The origins of cultural differences and their impact on management
    / Jack Scarborough.
        p. cm.
    Includes bibliographical references and index.
    ISBN 1–56720–123–7 (alk. paper)—ISBN 1–56720–439–2 (pbk.: alk. paper)
    1. Diversity in the workplace. I. Title.
    HF5549.5.M5S28   1998
    658.3′008—dc21   97–13404

British Library Cataloguing in Publication Data is available.

Library of Congress Catalog Card Number: 97–13404
ISBN: 1–56720–439–2 (pbk.)

First published in 1998

Quorum Books, 88 Post Road West, Westport, CT 06881
An imprint of Greenwood Publishing Group, Inc.
www.quorumbooks.com

Printed in the United States of America

The paper used in this book complies with the
Permanent Paper Standard issued by the National
Information Standards Organization (Z39.48–1984).

10 9 8 7 6 5 4 3 2 1

To my wife Ellie,
who not only makes all things possible
but makes them fun.

CONTENTS

PREFACE

America is often called a melting pot. My colleague and friend Ivan Blanco says it is a salad. It really is more of a stew. The notion of a melting pot suggests that new arrivals are absorbed and folded into a homogenous, liquid mass—what chemists would call a solution. We are indeed thrown into a common pot where we are subjected to the heat of trying to get along with and understand one another. As we simmer, our essences and flavors intermingle but we still retain our identity. A bit of meat may absorb some of the flavor of a piece of onion, but we still can stick a fork into the pot and pull out morsels we can identify clearly as one or the other. The result then is actually more a mixture than a solution because we retain our essences, that is, our cultural origins. We have no basis to estimate how long this pot must simmer before the mixture really becomes a solution. Perhaps one day it will come to pass.

As one tries to recognize the flavors and the simmering interactions among the ingredients in a pot, one is dealing with the challenge of cultural diversity within the stew. Some stews are more homogenous than others because they have been simmering longer or because there has been little experimentation with new ingredients or seasonings. Some are more flavorful because of a more eclectic mix of ingredients or more-exotic seasonings. Each stew, or culture, has its own recipe of core values. Managers trying to function within a given stew pot may assume, to their regret, conformance with the recipe by each ingredient, that is, each person or cultural group. More-sophisticated managers recognize the potential to be gained by exploiting both the obvious and more-subtle differences among the ingredients even while trying to maintain harmony among them. Added ingredients must conform to the basic recipe, or they may upset a delicate balance.

International managers face the added challenge of being removed from one stew pot and being placed into another with its own recipe, ingredients, and flavors. Cultural stew pots differ most fundamentally at the level of core values and their attendant beliefs and attitudes, those widely-shared drivers of choice, action, and behavior shared by the majority of the members of a culture. These are the meat and potatoes of cultural difference; the foundation not only of what international managers must be aware of but also of what they must understand. Such knowledge enables managers to understand why people of other cultures act, think, believe, and speak as they do. The purpose of this book is in part to develop such understanding but more to deepen it in order to provide readers with an appreciation of the reality that these differences are the result not of aberrant attitudes or faulty character but of unique combinations of historical, economic, social, physical, and religious forces that have shaped the various cultures over many centuries. After we understand the "why" of cultural difference as well as the "what" and the "how," we can apply that understanding while relying on our good will, good judgment, and good intentions and be confident that we can conduct ourselves properly in a different cultural setting.

ACKNOWLEDGMENTS

First I must thank Barry University and Dean Lew Lash for their support in allowing me the opportunity to conduct the research for this book. I am obligated to Professor Ed Locke at the University of Maryland, who made me understand how values drive behavior. My colleagues at Barry—Hugo Hervitz, Ivan Blanco, Luigi Salvaneschi, and especially Chuck Gallagher—kept me on the straight and narrow. My wife Ellie was a terrific editor and, as always, my greatest inspiration.

Chapter 1

THE CULTURAL CONNECTION

The basic premise of this book is that values drive beliefs, attitudes, and actions, that values are in large part culturally derived, and therefore a manager, a negotiator, or a tourist who understands others' cultural background is better able to understand why those people act, think, and speak the way they do, and is better able to predict how those people will react to his or her own words and actions. Rather than try to remember what to expect and how to behave when working or communicating with people of one culture or another, we should instead be able to apply our common sense and good will to act and respond accordingly if we understand the forces driving behavior.

We associate the term culture with nations (or, more correctly and precisely, with ethnic groups) and, more recently, with companies and organizations. Actually, any established, cohesive group has a culture, whether a platoon of soldiers, a Girl Scout troop, the local chapter of the Red Cross, or the Green Bay Packers. *Culture* is simply the set of values, attitudes, and beliefs shared by such a group, which sets the standards of behavior required for continued acceptance and successful participation in that group. Culture is passed on, learned by newcomers from more-experienced predecessors. Children learn their ethnic culture largely from their families and authority figures such as clergy, coaches, and teachers. The new employee learns much of the company culture from more-experienced employees, superiors, and mentors. We tend to look for role models, people who seem to know how to get along in the group, and imitate them. In effect then, members of a culture share common experiences and a heritage that establish and reinforce common values, attitudes, and beliefs. These characteristics define the behaviors members should expect from one another. They not only establish the group's common identity and continuity over time but set it apart from other cultures.

A WORD ABOUT STEREOTYPING

When we generalize about a group of people, as we do in describing a culture, we confront the issue of stereotyping. Despite the negative connotation the term has acquired, we can properly and accurately characterize one group of people as being different from another, and not just in terms of obvious physical differences. The danger comes in assuming uniformity, that each and every member of the group possesses the same traits and conforms to generalizations. Cultural anthropologists have long recognized and used the term *core values* to describe those values that most precisely identify and circumscribe a group. They govern the fundamental beliefs, attitudes, and acceptable behaviors that group holds most deeply and widely, those that define its culture. At the same time, there is no justification to assume that any one individual holds any or all of the values of that person's culture in kind or to the same degree. Every person is a unique *personality*, and we must take time to know each individual we encounter before drawing any conclusions about that person's attitudes and motives. Think of core values, which we address throughout this book, as typical, as values we might expect to find in a person of another culture at the beginning of a relationship but that remain subject to modification as we learn more about that person. Fons Trompenaars (1994) suggests that we think of a core value as lying at the mean of a normal distribution of the population of the culture in question. But keep in mind that a person feels compelled strongly to conform to cultural norms, regardless how much one embraces the underlying values. For example, one need not be a Protestant Christian to succeed in the United States, but one must certainly behave in accordance with the values embodied in the "Protestant work ethic" to do so, even if one has never heard of it.

HOW CULTURE DRIVES BEHAVIOR

Rational behavior, that is, behavior resulting from conscious thought and decision and not from an unthinking emotional response, tends to be goal directed. It is purposeful, intended to accomplish something. That "something" has to do with satisfying some need. Human needs—for example, for survival, security, affection, esteem, or accomplishment—are universal. What is not universal is the *value* we place on various means for satisfying our needs. One kind of cultural difference is well known to all of us—food! I may place more value on chicken soup to satisfy my hunger, whereas you may prefer shark fin soup or *vichyssoise*. Other, culture-based differences in values are of more interest to us here. For example, self-actualization, a need, may be satisfied in one culture by amassing wealth, praise, or other forms of individual recognition, whereas in another it may mean a sense of making a worthy contribution to advancing the processes in one's work-group.

When we judge or prioritize which means of satisfying needs are more acceptable or desirable than others, we are making value judgments, manifesting some deep-seated attitudes and beliefs about what is right and wrong, important and unimportant, acceptable and unacceptable, desirable and undesirable, normal and abnormal. We act then in ways that we believe obtain the most-valuable means of satisfying our needs that we can. In effect, our values motivate our behavior. They are why we do what we do, say what we do, and think like we do. As explained in following chapters, many of the differences in what people value are the result of cultural conditioning.

THE FORCES THAT SHAPE CULTURE (AND CONDITION BEHAVIOR)

Cultures take a long time to develop. Many forces act upon a people to establish their identity, give meaning to their lives, and define what they come to believe and how they should behave. Perhaps no force is stronger in shaping behavioral standards than *religion*. If a culture has a long-standing, dominant religion, active and firm in its teachings of what is right and wrong, those teachings have much to say about that culture's core values. For example, the differences between northern and Mediterranean European cultures, and between the colonies of those respective countries, can be traced in part to differences between Protestantism and Roman Catholicism. These standards are applied to all members of that culture, whether or not one is a believer, actively practices, or is even a member of that religion. The rules are the rules. The sayings of Ben Franklin's *Poor Richard*, which explicated the Protestant work ethic, are as relevant in multicultural, high-tech, twenty-first-century America as they were in the eighteenth-century America of white, Anglo-Saxon, Protestant founding fathers.

How *political power* is distributed and exercised shapes attitudes toward authority, willingness to accept direction, and sense of self-reliance and independence. For example, Americans, lacking the traditions of monarchy and feudalism of Europe and Japan, tend to look more suspiciously upon and circumscribe governmental power, are more resentful of rules, and are more respectful of self-sufficiency or "self-made men." Many strong and/or charismatic *leaders* in both secular (for example, Pericles, Confucius) and spiritual (for example, Martin Luther, Buddha) domains have had dramatic and lasting effects on culture. Historians and storytellers celebrate individuals who exemplify core values, creating *heroes, legends*, and *myths* that reinforce those values and sustain culture through the generations.

Authors create fictional characters to illustrate behavior that complies with or violates cultural norms, or perhaps to modify those norms.

The *physical surroundings* of a people help shape the nature, intensity, and longevity of their values. The degree of isolation or interaction afforded by the geography and topography of their homeland, the amount and kind of natural resource endowments, the felicity or harshness of its climate, and exposure to invasion and natural disasters all can have an effect. Isolation tends to promote cohesiveness and xenophobia and ensures a more homogenous and immutable set of values. A wealth of resources or temperate weather creates a sense of well-being and optimism, whereas rugged terrain, harsh weather, frequent disaster, and a lack of resources can engender pessimism, fear of nature, and a sense of the necessity of interdependence to ensure mutual survival.

The manner in which a people sustains itself *economically*, how it organizes itself to produce or obtain the necessities of life, determines the roles individuals are assigned and the relationships among them, and shapes attitudes toward meaning in life, work, pleasure, and success. A wealth of resources, especially abundant agriculture, facilitates broadening of horizons and the pursuit of education and more technologically advanced endeavors. To a degree, we can associate favorable conditions with a higher standard of living and more-competitive, task-oriented values, whereas we might expect to find a greater value placed on cooperation and relationships in cultures characterized by subsistence economies. This can be said of political and religious circumstances as well. Cultures that have suffered less repression of either form seem to have progressed farther, at least in a material sense. This is not to say that material well-being is necessarily consistent with emotional or spiritual well-being however.

MANIFESTATIONS OF CULTURE

Obviously, we can learn much about a people by studying its history, but there are more-ostensible manifestations that give insight into what people value, especially the arts. Literature opens a window through which the reader can view the kinds of behavior a people accepts or rejects. Fairy tales and fables, proverbs, and aphorisms provide concise object lessons in desirable behavior. As children we learned from the simple lesson "Early to bed, early to rise, makes a man healthy, wealthy, and wise" volumes about what is important in life and that hard work and discipline obtain it. The Japanese learns just as much from "The nail which sticks out will be hammered down." The visual arts do the same. Grant Wood's familiar painting *American Gothic*, depicting a stoic, hardworking farm couple, could have been painted by John Calvin. Japanese woodcuts depict serenity and harmony with nature, and the designs of their products exhibit harmony of form and function. American "rugged individualism" and "the strong, silent type" are depicted in film by the cowboy—lonely, hard-working, and given to righting wrongs and one-word sentences like "Yup" and "Howdy." We grow to admire heroes of "truth, justice, and the American Way" like George Washington, Abraham Lincoln, Martin Luther King, and Superman. Our media create legends of frontier heroes like Davy Crockett and Daniel Boone in one century and Charles Lindbergh, astronaut John Glenn, and President John F. Kennedy (he of "The New Frontier") in another. Contemporary counterparts of these historical trailblazers and independent risk-takers might include entrepreneurs like Ross Perot or Bill Gates, creative wizards such as Steven Spielberg, sports legends like Michael Jordan, or moralists like Billy Graham or Ralph Nader. Every culture celebrates or creates such heroes to reward those who have demonstrated that they know how to behave and to provide role models for its young.

MANAGERIAL IMPLICATIONS

Of more direct interest to us are the even more ostensible manifestations of culture we can observe and understand in workplace behavior. We have discussed how our core values motivate our actions. We work to obtain what we value, beginning with survival and then progressing on toward our ambitions regarding our desired life-style, spanning the range of human needs: affection and affiliation, esteem of self and others, self-actualization, and so forth. We may work because we value the work itself, or because we value it as a means of earning the wherewithal to obtain other kinds of value, which exist in infinite variety. We work at what we enjoy or at what we must, and we exert effort in proportion to the nature and intensity of our felt needs, the cost of the values we believe best satisfy those needs, the magnitude of expected rewards, and our expectation of the likelihood of success and that the desired results will be forthcoming.

Our values shape our attitudes and beliefs about work, success, wealth, authority, equity, competition, and many other such components of the content and context of the work environment. They govern how we wish to be treated and how we treat others; how we communicate, negotiate, process information, and make decisions; the leadership style we like to use; and how and where we want to be led. For managers, whose fundamental challenge is the motivation of others to help achieve desired ends—that is, to behave in productive, cooperative ways—it is difficult to understate the importance of understanding value systems in an increasingly global environment and increasingly diverse work forces. The remainder of this chapter identifies important core values and the attitudinal and behavioral dimensions on which cultures differ, and discusses some managerial implications. Each succeeding chapter addresses a specific culture, discussing how it differs from others and identifying the forces that shaped it.

Much of the research done on cultural differences deals with nations, but nations and cultures are not always congruent. Where they are—Japan, for example—they are addressed as such, but some chapters deal with regional groupings of nations in which cultures cross national boundaries.

CORE VALUE DIMENSIONS

This section identifies core values that can differ across cultures. Each of these variables is continuous; a culture can fall anywhere between the two descriptive poles. Any individual, regardless of cultural origin, can fall anywhere on any continuum. Think of the placement of a culture on a continuum as a starting point for consideration, a cultural tendency that may be modified or even discarded entirely in any individual case. The following value dimensions appear throughout the literature on core values. Others to be discussed later are associated with specific researchers.

Human Nature—Good, Evil, or Neutral?—Changeable or Unchangeable?

Do we believe that people are fundamentally trustworthy until they prove otherwise? Or the reverse? Or should we be open-minded and remain neutral until we have sufficient information to make a judgment? Christianity teaches that people are born with the stigma of original sin and thus are condemned unless saved (that is, changed). In contrast, Shinto makes little distinction between deities and people. To the extent that one is culturally disposed toward one of these positions can affect one's inclination to trust or distrust others, with obvious implications for one's preferred leadership style and how one prefers to negotiate business transactions. Whether one believes that people are changeable can affect how one attempts to motivate them and the importance one places on training.

Purpose in Life—Doing or Being?

Does a person live to work or work to live? Is work a worthwhile and rewarding end in itself, or just a necessary evil pursued only because it provides the wherewithal to obtain what one really needs or what one really enjoys, for example, some form of leisure? Is work primarily a productive activity or a social one? Is life primarily an opportunity to enjoy experiences or to make useful contributions to humanity? Are the most worthwhile endeavors pragmatic or philosophical and emotional? If one values work in and of itself and takes pleasure in a job well done, there is little need to discipline, supervise, or motivate that person. All that is necessary is to teach the person how to perform the task and clarify expectations. The motivational challenge clearly is more difficult in "being" cultures.

Societal Role—Individualist or Collectivist?

Do people prefer to work alone or as part of a group? Do they seek to maximize their individual wealth and well-being and view life as a highly competitive, zero-sum game, or do they see human relationships in terms of win-win possibilities and their own potential maximized in cooperation and contribution to group success? Do they avoid dependence on others and prefer to have their performance measured and be held accountable as individuals rather than as teammates? Do they feel more loyalty to group interests than to personal interests and consider it natural to share with group members? In some cultures, it is news when an individual sacrifices one's own interest for the good of others. In other cultures, it is the norm. In the former, managers worry about the "free rider" problem—what to do about the member of a group who does not pull his or her own weight—and how to get people to work together in teams. In the latter, such behavior is unthinkable and such problems rare.

Nature (and Fate)—Controllable or Controlling?

Can people shape their surroundings and events, or must they submit to nature's whims? Will history unfold as it will and chance drive results, or can people make a difference? Are life's consequences predetermined or subject to human will and technology? People will be more optimistic, inventive, and aggressive to the extent they believe that they can improve their situations as a result of their own actions and ideas, and they will be more interested in developing plans, goals, and budgets and behaving proactively. If not, they will tend toward passiveness and submissiveness, and they will be more inclined to accept whatever fate life deals them.

Time—Precious Resource or Abundant Commodity?— Oriented toward the Past, Present, or Future?

Many readers will have observed that in some places people are driven to make productive use of every available moment and are very punctual, whereas elsewhere it is common to accept with indifference that what does not get done today will get done tomorrow, or someday, and that appointments are mere approximations. In the latter case, the passage of time is something to be appreciated, experienced, and even enjoyed rather than lamented. All cultures have roots in the past, but some put greater emphasis on tradition and traditional ways of doing things, and see the future as but an extension of the past. Some exhibit more flexibility and adaptability and seem to live for the moment, insisting upon an immediate return on invested time, effort, and capital, whereas others sacrifice short-term gratification in favor of maximizing long-term results. Those who value time greatly tend to be more task-oriented and productive and have little patience for socializing in a work setting or relationship building. Those more deeply rooted in the past are more comfortable in highly structured situations and organizations, and they move forward with care and deliberation. Decision making is incremental and mindful of precedents. Those with a strong future orientation are stronger competitors in the long run because they pay more attention to growing people, building assets, and improving skills and processes assiduously and continuously and sacrifice immediate profit in favor of building strength and market power for the future.

Preferred Mode of Communication—High Context or High Content?

High-content communication is complete, straightforward, and direct. The entire message is contained in the words, in the content of the communication. A good, high-content communicator is precise and accurate in the use of language and takes pride in saying exactly what is meant. Much of the message in high-context communication is unspoken; the spoken message is indirect, subtle, and incomplete. The words are complemented by, and perhaps even modified by, facial expression, tone, and posture. The receiver understands the message even though some of it is left unsaid or even contradicted by the spoken words. The ability to decode and understand a vague or incomplete transmission is a result of common bonds and experience, much like those of a long-married couple who can sometimes communicate a paragraph with only a nod or facial expression. The more homogenous the culture, that is, the more commonality of experience and values, the easier it becomes to communicate in a high-context mode. In modern vernacular, people of high-context cultures already know where one another are "coming from" when they speak among themselves. People from high-content cultures must learn that even about one another, not to mention outsiders. It is easy to imagine the difficulties possible when people of high-content and high-context cultures try to communicate. Instead of being appreciated, directness may be seen by the high-context communicator as insulting, overbearing, or condescending overkill (you don't have to explain it to me!). The high-content communicator will miss or misinterpret the subtle cues and signals used by the high-context communicator and may well see indirectness as evasive or even deceptive. High-content people are comfortable with concisely written communications; high-context people prefer to communicate face-to-face so that the entire context can be observed, and they may see written communications as somewhat cold and impersonal. We have come to associate high-content communication in part with collectivist cultures, presumably because the need to maintain harmony within groups favors indirectness and subtlety, and because such cultures tend to be more homogenous, facilitating indirectness and economy of speech. Ferraro (1994) cites research that indicates that high content is most preferred in Germanic, Scandinavian, and Anglo cultures; whereas high context is preferred in southern Europe, China, Japan, and Arabic cultures.

Geert Hofstede (1991), in a comprehensive study of core values, identified three others, power distance, uncertainty avoidance, and masculinity/femininity in addition to individualism/collectivism.

Power Distance—Direction or Consultation?

Power distance represents the degree to which people accept unequal distribution of power. In a large-power-distance culture, people feel dependence on those in authority and expect direction from them. Those in authority exercise power in an autocratic or paternalistic manner. Subordinates avoid crossing the large power distance; they are less willing to challenge or even approach their bosses. They learn strict obedience as children, which carries forward into adulthood. Those in authority are assumed to be there because they have a right to it, either by virtue of inheritance or because of superior expertise. Organizations—beginning with families—are hierarchical, and decision making is centralized. In a low-power-distance culture, people expect to have more control and expect their bosses to involve them in decision making in a consultative or even participatory manner. Young people are treated as equals as soon as they are ready and, as adults, expect to be treated in the same way by their superiors. Managers who seek the advice and participation of subordinates in large-power-distance cultures, particularly those based more on autocracy than paternalism, may find themselves perceived as weak or inept. The reaction is essentially one of "You're the boss, why are you asking me?" Managers trying to employ a highly directive style in a small-power-distance culture will find subordinates resentful or even rebellious.

The source of large power distance typically lies in a tradition of a hierarchical, agrarian society and centralized form of rule. For example, countries under prolonged, direct domination of the Roman Empire and derivative states such as the former Spanish and Portuguese colonies in the Western Hemisphere, or of Confucian bureaucracy such as China, Korea, and Japan, exhibit larger power distances than cultures with more-fragmented, tribal origins such as the Germanic, Scandinavian, or Anglo countries, and much larger than those with more-democratic, egalitarian origins like the United States or Australia. Hofstede found a strong correlation between power distance and latitude (or climate), with cultures in more-temperate climates exhibiting smaller power distances than those in the tropics, which may have some explanation related to agricultural productivity, but one could argue both sides of that proposition. It is possible however, that there is a relationship between power distance and a recurring need for people to organize themselves in order to take collective action for self-preservation, perhaps to fend off powerful enemies or to exploit agricultural resources. Such an organization would require some form of centralized authority and hierarchical structure to function effectively. Over time, this experience would normalize submission to authority. Hofstede also found a correlation between large power distance and larger population, which also could be associated with a need for some form of centralized government to maintain order.

Uncertainty Avoidance—Structured or Unstructured?

Uncertainty avoidance is a measure of tolerance for ambiguity and the unfamiliar. It is not the same as risk avoidance, however. Risks are tolerable in this culture if they are familiar ones for which people have developed a sense of how to cope. People from high-uncertainty-avoidance cultures prefer structured situations, conformance to formal rules and established norms even if apparently unreasonable or impractical to others; tend to have higher levels of anxiety, often manifested in greater emotional expression and aggressiveness; and find it difficult to relax. Such behavior seems compulsive to those from low-uncertainty-avoidance cultures, who appear more controlled and easy-going in comparison. In a high-uncertainty-avoidance workplace, roles must be specified, rules and procedures detailed and enforced, instructions precise, relationships clear, and conflict avoided. Novel situations will cause great stress and can paralyze this organization. The basic rules of bureaucracy, such as unity of command and formality of procedures, have their roots in high uncertainty avoidance. This culture is less inventive and adventurous than the opposite, which is more tolerant of experimentation and deviant ideas, but it is also more diligent and perfectionist in execution. Security is a strong motivator relative to achievement or self-fulfillment. A steady paycheck is preferable to performance-based compensation.

Hofstede's research indicates that cultures with the longest and deepest historical ties to the Roman Empire, the Romance language countries and their former colonies in Latin America and, to a lesser extent, the Germanic countries and Japan were highest in uncertainty avoidance. Other Asian countries with historical ties to China were higher than average. Hofstede suggests that the cause is a long and sustained history of strong, centralized rule. He speculates that the Romance language countries were higher than the Asian countries because Roman rule was based on law, that is, an elaborate system of rules and regulations, whereas centralized rule in China was based on the judgment and wisdom of man, in the Confucian tradition.

This hypothesis seems consistent with the finding that Japan also ranked higher than other East Asian countries because Japan's form of centralized rule and class system were much more structured than China's. The more-detailed moral and behavioral prescriptions of Judeo-Christian religions, as compared to Asian religions, may also have contributed to the difference. Germanic countries were somewhat above the mean, perhaps because their domination by the Roman Empire was not as complete or sustained as were their neighbors to the south and west. Relatively low in uncertainty avoidance were Scandinavian and Anglo countries whose histories were even more removed from the Roman Empire and who, like the Germanic countries, broke away from the highly bureaucratic and politically active Roman Catholic Church in the Protestant Reformation. Lowest in uncertainty avoidance were the former British colonies in the Western Hemisphere and in Asia, including Australia, India, Hong Kong, and Singapore. African countries, lacking a history of centralized rule and institutionalized religions, were just below the mean; Islamic countries were just above it.

Masculinity/Femininity—Tough or Tender?

In Hofstede's usage, a masculine culture is tough, exhibiting aggressiveness, decisiveness, and competitiveness; places great value on achievement outside the home, power, grandeur, and well-defined gender roles; settles conflict by fighting (or arguing) it out; and is task oriented. A feminine culture is tender, exhibiting modesty, reticence, caring for others, and concern for a favorable environment; places great value on nurturing, harmony, and interchangeable gender roles; settles conflict by negotiation and compromise; and is relationship oriented. Masculinity has long been the dominant way of doing business, but relatively recent recognition of the value of cooperation, teamwork, and sustained relationships focuses attention on the feminine side of business and organizations.

There are relatively few feminine cultures, owing to the nearly universal, traditional gender roles of the physically dominant male taking responsibility for providing and protecting and the child-bearing and child-rearing female assuming domestic responsibilities. According to Hofstede, unique circumstances created the handful of feminine cultures, concentrated in Scandinavia and parts of Latin America. In the former case, a lack of resources forced these countries into trading and fishing as primary occupations. The prolonged absences of seafaring men left women to take on more administrative responsibility outside the home. Additionally, the trading profession required the men to cultivate the interpersonal skills necessary to maintain productive relationships with trading partners and among the free trading nations of the Hanseatic League. Differences in Latin America may trace back to the dominant Indian cultures, with feminine cultures appearing to be derived from the artistic and peaceful Inca and Maya, and masculine cultures appearing to be derived from the more warlike Aztecs.

Hofstede also included the individualism/collectivism dimension in his research. He found that generally, collectivism is associated with agriculture. The farther a people are removed from their agrarian roots (and, therefore, from the larger, more-extended families associated with farming and small towns), that is, the more urbanized and industrialized they are, the more individualistic they tend to be. Japan and the newly industrialized countries of Asia are cited as exceptions, attributed to the strong influence of Confucianism, which taught that an individual's highest calling in life was in fulfilling one's obligations to others.

Fons Trompenaars (1994) is another authority on cultural value dimensions. He discusses the following ways in which cultures will differ.

The Universal/The Particular—Absolute or Situational Ethics?

Is the same conduct always right or wrong? Are there absolute moral principles by which all must abide or must standards depend on the circumstances? More specifically, can my obligations to a particular person (or client?) supersede my general or universal duties to society at large? Particularist cultures are more accepting of this proposition. People with universalist values may not cross the street against a Walk signal, even if there is not a vehicle in sight. Trompenaars illustrates the difference with this comparison. The universalist would say of particularists that they cannot be trusted because they will always look out for their friends. The particularist would say of universalists that they cannot be trusted because they cannot be counted on to always help a friend. Realistically, it would be unusual to find anyone who could not think of circumstances under which it would be justified to break a rule or who did not hold certain principles so dear that violating them would be unthinkable. The difference is in degree, not kind. Like Hofstede's "feminist," the particularist places great importance on relationships. Maintaining a relationship may be more important than getting the job done. Harmony may be more important than frankness. Being familiar with someone is more important than familiarity with their products. Trust in another person is more important than a contract; after all, circumstances may require a modification of a contract, but my supplier (and trusted friend) will not let me down. Each situation must be treated on its own merits.

Trompenaars's research found that the universalist view was strongest in the Protestant cultures, the Anglo, Scandinavian, and Germanic countries, and generally weak in Asian and Catholic and Orthodox Catholic cultures, that is, southern Europe and Latin America, and eastern Europe. He attributed this difference to the more-literal teachings of Protestantism compared to Catholicism and Asian religions. He also noted that these same countries are most reliant upon judicial systems to mediate conflicts because universal "truths" are so important that they require institutional protection. Another interpretation is that when business transactions and contracts are engaged in only with known and trusted counterparts, there should be less need to resort to the courts.

Specific/Diffuse—Are Work and Business Separate from the Rest of Life?

In diffuse cultures, everything is related. Business is just another form of social interaction. It is conducted within a larger context of friendship; inquiries and concern about others' families; extensive discussion of extraneous (to those from specific cultures) topics such as politics, books and art, sports, and so on. It is expected that someone from another culture knows something about and appreciates the history and traditions of one's own. It is expected that educated and sophisticated people will have a broad range of interests and knowledge. Conversations and negotiations proceed from the general to the specific and will be very lengthy. General principles and intentions are of more importance and interest than details. Business relationships are seen as and expected to be enduring, like friendships, and therefore are not entered into lightly and without establishing a personal relationship. Contracts and management-by-objectives agreements are seen as relevant only to conditions in place at the time of agreement. Because the relationship is expected to endure, and conditions are certain to change during such prolonged periods, parties must be prepared to modify their agreements and arrangements. It is expected that managers take an interest in the personal lives of their subordinates. (In Japan, managers may get involved in arranging marriages, and weddings sometimes take place in the employer's offices.) Managers from specific cultures will prefer high-content communication, give more-precise instructions, and will be more concerned with reaching goals with rewards attached; their diffuse counterparts will use high-context communication, give more open-ended instructions, and be more concerned with continuous improvement.

Although this distinction is less pronounced geographically than others, and therefore more difficult to attribute to historical or religious forces, diffuseness is predominant in many Asian and Islamic cultures, whereas specificity is strongest in Anglo cultures and predominates in Germanic, Scandinavian, and most other European cultures.

How Status Is Attained—By Ascription or Performance?

We confer status upon people by ascription by virtue of some characteristic of their state of being, for example, their title or position, age, family ties, school ties, social connections, profession, and so on. In other words, we ascribe status to those who seem entitled to it by virtue of who they are. Alternatively, we may confer status upon someone because of what they have achieved, the results they have produced. Cultures that confer status by ascription expect those in authority to act in accordance with their roles; actual performance and results are less important. Unfavorable results are attributed to external and uncontrollable causes. Cultures that confer status by achievement expect those in authority to get things done; appearances are less important. The distinction between form and substance is not a far-fetched analogy. Ascriptive managers deem title and seniority very important and conduct themselves with appropriate ceremony and form, and expect the same from others. Proper respect and deference must be shown regardless of relative capabilities or achievements. Accomplished young managers from achievement cultures find it difficult to wield authority in ascriptive cultures. Senior managers from ascriptive cultures may find it difficult to adjust to the informality and irreverence of achievement cultures. Trompenaars found ascription prevalent in Catholic, Buddhist, Hindu, and Islamic cultures and achievement, like universalist ethics, more dominant in Protestant cultures. The Protestant work ethic and tradition of revolt against both Church and state are at work here.

A POINT OF DEPARTURE—AMERICAN CULTURE

When people of one culture compare themselves to another, they tend to see their own culture as normal and superior and the other as aberrational and inferior. This tendency is called *ethnocentrism*. People have great pride in their own culture; they must, because their culture is their source of identity; they have difficulty understanding why others do not behave as they do, and assume that others would be like them if they could. All such comparisons are relative. I may see your culture as more collective than my own, and consider my own to be individualistic. Yet someone from still another culture may see both of us as collective compared to their own culture. Before we set out to take a look at various cultures, their core values, and the roots of those values, it is useful to see where we stand and how we got there, in order to establish a frame of reference.

With the long-standing and increasingly multicultural character of the United States, it is reasonable to question whether we still embrace universal core values. The short answer is yes. The long answer is that we have experienced successive waves of immigration, each traceable to different geographic (and cultural) origins, who were attracted and subsumed by the core values established by the initial waves originating in the British Isles followed shortly by Dutch, Scandinavian, and German immigrants. Succeeding waves came from Africa (forced), central and southern Europe, Latin America, China, and Japan. In this century, immigration from east

Asia continues, with many more national origins, as does immigration from Latin America and new waves from the Indian subcontinent, the Middle East, and the former Soviet Union. Each succeeding wave, in order to assimilate, had to adapt and embrace American core values, even perhaps while trying to maintain ties to the "old country" in their family lives. Recall that a people's culture is simply the shared values and attendant attitudes and beliefs that prescribe the norms of behavior of that people. Although some tempering or leavening may occur as new values are introduced by immigrants, core values are an enormous force for stability; they give a people its anchor in the winds and seas of change, and they will not yield them. What, then, are core American values?

Of some sixty nations he studied, Hofstede found the United States the most individualistic of all nations, in the first quartile in low uncertainty avoidance, and in the second quartile in masculinity and small power distance. Trompenaars finds us very high in universalist ethics, individualism, specificity in our separation of work from social discourse, achievement orientation, and in a sense of control over nature and our own destiny. Only the German Swiss, Germans, and Scandinavians exceed us in our preference for high-content, low-context communications. We are more willing to express emotions than Asians and northern Europeans, but less so than southern Europeans, Latin Americans, and Arabs.

What does all this mean with respect to our attitudes, beliefs, and behavior? We treasure above all else, and more than anyone else, self-reliance and independence. Anyone who has tried to get two Americans to cooperate with one another, absent a crisis, can attest to this finding. That same person may well then go home and lecture his or her children about the need to stand up on their own two feet and think for themselves! The cottage industry that has developed around promotion of team building and a whole array of other collaborative behaviors is further testimony to our weakness in this area.

Our low uncertainty avoidance allows us to be innovative and experimental—indeed the nation itself was a grand experiment. The combination of low uncertainty avoidance, individualism, masculinity, and high degree of status accorded to achievement makes us very entrepreneurial, aggressive, and intensely competitive, very much a "doing" culture. This drive to succeed puts a great premium on time, and we are impatient not only to avoid wasting any of it but to see the results of our labor. We want immediate results. Specificity and high-content communication cause us to insist on a "no-nonsense–get right to it" approach to work. We get to the point, eschew subtlety, sometimes disregarding the emotional consequences of what we say. We dislike indecisiveness, evasion, and delay. Our universalist ethics, coupled with unparalleled material success that confirms in our minds that we are "right," can cause us to be a bit self-righteous and intolerant (some would say imperialistic!).

Small power distance (but larger than Israel, Australia and New Zealand, Great Britain and Ireland, and Scandinavia, among others) yields egalitarianism, suspicion of power, and belief in individual liberty. Yet we still are somewhat receptive to the notion that some of us will be more powerful than others. Our individualism and achievement orientation cause us to expect power to be exercised democratically, that the powerful are approachable and that relationships between superior and subordinate will be somewhat relaxed and informal, and that power is earned on merit. We admire the earned wealth of the successful entrepreneur (after all, with a bit of luck, that could be me!) much more than inherited wealth, and few things seem to amuse us more than poking fun at British royalty. With relatively small power distance, coupled with low uncertainty avoidance, we do not mind being told what to do, at least not by someone who has accomplished more than we, or having high expectations imposed on us, but we do not want to be told how to do it. We are comfortable with the flexible structure of management by objectives and management by exception. We want to participate in the decision-making process but recognize the ultimate responsibility, authority, and accountability of the boss. Low uncertainty avoidance contributes to optimism and a sense that we can use or even manipulate nature (and, by extension, technology) to serve our needs. Our achievement orientation makes us very goal-driven; we need to see some results and compare them to a standard. Performance-based compensation thus appeals to us. We find breakthroughs exciting, but we have difficulty applying ourselves to undramatic and long-term endeavors like continuous improvement. We are materialistic not just in the value we place on possessions in and of themselves but as evidence of our adherence to and success in pursuing all these values. In this pursuit, we tend to neglect Hofstede's feminine values of quality of life and human relationships. Though informal, open, and approachable—and thus ostensibly friendly—our relationships may be somewhat superficial and shallow. We do business with virtually anyone; if an amicable relationship develops eventually, so much the better. We do not put a premium on familiarity and personal trust, because, as universalists, we trust in the law and rely on the courts to settle our disputes and enforce our contracts. Consequently, we want every detail specified in a contract and look most unfavorably on departures and proposed modifications.

What forces shaped these values? Like children whose values are largely in place by the time they become teenagers, our values were firmly established by the time of the Revolutionary War. They are embodied in *Poor Richard's Almanack*, the *Declaration of Independence*, and the *Constitution* and are chronicled by de Tocqueville in *Democracy in America*. They are the values of the frontier: self-reliance, independence, and adventurousness. The first immigrants were largely misfits, outcasts, and malcontents fleeing religious or political oppression who took on one frontier after another—the Atlantic, the Alleghenies, the great plains and rivers, the Rocky Mountains, and they made the deserts bloom. Just as they fomented the democratic revolution, their descendants were at the forefront of the industrial revolution, the space age, and now the information revolution. The learned among them read John Locke, Jean-Jacques Rousseau, and Edmund Burke and learned of such novel ideas as the supremacy of the individual to the state, the rule of law, and the right to private property. They brought with them the Protestant work ethic, which instilled in them the idea that material success was not evil but evidence of wise and industrious use of God's blessings. Hard work gave meaning to life because it was evidence that one was doing God's work. Later, Adam Smith taught them that as they each pursued their individual self-interest to the best of their ability, society as a whole would benefit from their labors. This economic stimulus was abetted by Social Darwinism, which relieved the successful of any guilt because it was in keeping with the natural order of things that there would be some who would be left behind as others, and society, moved ahead. Thus a new value was added to the inventory of self-reliance, independence, and adventurousness—competitiveness. In effect, we experienced a convergence of intellectual forces that gave us the political freedom to pursue our individual goals and the right to keep the fruits of our labor, taught us that our individual material success was morally worthy, advanced the interest of our community, and was nothing to feel guilty about. The emergence of a new nation, together with its wealth of natural resources, provided the fullest opportunity to experiment with these forces.

Those who first ventured to the new world had to have low uncertainty avoidance and small power distance. They departed from the security of king and Church and made the rules as they went. The rigors of the new world forged their rugged individualism, and the Protestant work ethic, amplified by market-based economics and Social Darwinism, made them very competitive. Initial successes convinced them that they had the right idea, and each succeeding political, military, economic, and technological triumph reinforced these values as they were passed on through the generations.

With this background, we turn our attention to other cultures, other behaviors, other values, and other cultural roots.

ADDITIONAL READING

Readers who wish to study research on cross-cultural differences should examine these two works, cited frequently in this chapter. Readers should not be put off by use of the term "research." These are both highly readable books, well written and interesting, with many practical, real-world examples. They are written for practicing managers, not academic theorists.

Hofstede, Geert. 1991. *Cultures and Organizations: Software of the Mind.* (New York: McGraw-Hill).
Trompenaars, Fons. 1994. *Riding the Waves of Culture: Understanding Diversity in Global Business.* (Burr Ridge, Ill.: Irwin).

An interesting and less formal but more limited treatment of cultural values in the United States, Japan, and several European countries can be found in

Hampden-Turner, Charles, and Alfons Trompenaars. 1993. *The Seven Cultures of Capitalism.* (New York: Doubleday-Currency).

The best works on high-context and high-content communications and attitudes toward time are, respectively:

Hall, Edward T. *Beyond Culture.* 1976. (Garden City, N.Y.: Anchor Press/Doubleday).
———. 1987. *The Dance of Life: The Other Dimension of Time.* (Garden City, N.Y.: Anchor Press/Doubleday).

Readers interested in a general, textbook treatment of the practical implications of cross-cultural differences should consult, in addition to the works cited above, any of the following books, written primarily for international business students.

Adler, Nancy J. 1991. *International Dimensions of Organizational Behavior*, 2nd ed. (Boston: PWS-Kent).
Deresky, Helen. 1996. *International Management*, 2nd ed. (Reading, Mass.: Addison Wesley).
Ferraro, Gary B. 1994. *The Cultural Dimension of International Business*, 2nd ed. (Englewood Cliffs, N.J.).
Lane, Henry W., Joseph J. DiStefano, and Martha C. Moznewski. 1997. *International Management Behavior*, 3rd ed. (Cambridge, Mass.: Blackwell).
Mead, Richard. 1996. *International Management: Cross-Cultural Dimensions.* (Cambridge, Mass.: Blackwell).
Rodrigues, Carl. 1996. *International Management: A Cultural Approach.* (St. Paul: West).
Terpstra, Vern, and Kenneth David. 1991. *The Cultural Environment of International Business*, 3rd ed. (Cincinnati: South-Western).

The most-thorough coverage of adaptation of management practices to specific cultures is found in these two books, written primarily for practicing managers.

Elashmawi, Farid, and Philip R. Harris. 1993. *Multicultural Management: New Skills for Global Success*. (Houston: Gulf).

Harris, Philip R., and Robert T. Moran. 1996. *Managing Cultural Differences*, 4th ed. (Houston: Gulf).

Chapter 2

JAPAN

Many manifestations of Japanese culture have become familiar to western-ers. For example, we know about the Japanese preference for affiliation with groups and loyalty to employers in reciprocity for lifetime employ-ment; for flawless manners, meticulous cleanliness, and indirect and ex-ceedingly polite speech; for very deliberate decision making and long-term thinking; and for great discipline in terms of effort and striving for perfec-tion.

Japan is a unique land, one of contrasts and contradictions when viewed through Western eyes. Using Hofstede's measures of cultural difference, we find that Japan is the most masculine of the cultures he studied. Indeed, Japan's culture is thoroughly male-dominated, highly task-driven, compet-itive, and aggressive. Yet Japan's culture exhibits strong feminine charac-teristics in its compulsive needs for harmonious relationships and indirect, subtle, intuitive communication. There are parallel streams of militarism and a deep and abiding love for beauty and the arts throughout her history. Hofstede also found the Japanese very high in uncertainty avoidance and moderately high in power distance, also confirmed by our observations of Japanese conformity, respect for authority and seniority, and need for se-curity. Yet the Japanese fully expect to participate in decision-making and have been among the world's leaders in creative artistry and process in-novation. Moreover, we associate high uncertainty with more expressive-ness emotionally, but the Japanese, like other Asians, tend to be quite reserved and avoid physical contact. Japan's is the only collective culture among the world's major, fully industrialized nations, a characteristic as-sociated by some with economic backwardness. Clearly Japan defies that characterization. What accounts for Japan's uniqueness and these seeming internal contradictions?

THE CULTURAL SETTING

Japan is an island nation with a largely temperate climate and rugged terrain. Only about one-fifth of its land is level, forcing the population into densely populated pockets, some isolated by highlands and mountain ranges. Japan lacks natural resources, and agriculture is relatively unproductive in yield per labor hour. On its own, then, Japan is a poor country, and the Japanese have always felt great fear of economic deprivation (one reason why the savings rate remains so high). Natural disasters have visited these islands often in the form of earthquakes, tidal waves, typhoons, and volcanic eruptions, and they cause inordinate damage when they strike densely populated areas. The threat of economic deprivation, periodically harsh conditions, and the occasional threat of invasion unite the Japanese in fatalistic stoicism, toughness, interdependence, and a determination to ensure their own survival.

Japan's scenic beauty and intense greenery, much like the U.S. Pacific Northwest, have given its people a deep love for and identification with nature, although its dense population has often caused serious environmental harm since industrialization. The lack of flat land forces the Japanese into very crowded living conditions and makes real estate very expensive. Dwellings were (and still are) very small by U.S. standards. This crowding and somewhat flimsy, open nature of Japanese home construction made privacy difficult and prompted great civility and consideration of others, including meticulous cleanliness and neatness.

No major nation has experienced the isolation of Japan, at first physical and later enforced by its own rulers. Despite ethnic links between Japan and its two nearest neighbors, China and Korea, its culture has evolved without the constant interaction and mingling typical of other ancient civilizations. This isolation has produced the most unique and homogenous culture among the world's large nations. There have been no successful invasions or colonization, no revolutions, and no immigration of any significance. As a result, the Japanese have a very strong sense of unique cultural identity and "we-they" world view and are acutely aware of anything foreign. What for much of its history was a belief that foreigners were meddlesome barbarians at best and xenophobia (foreigners and barbarians are both called *gaijin*) at worst has evolved, for the most part, into mere curiosity and, sometimes, admiration.

This isolation has not been total, however. Japanese traders and scholars, and missionaries from Korea and China, introduced Buddhism and Confucianism as well as China's science, arts, alphabet, and crafts such as silk weaving and pottery during the fifth and sixth centuries. These imports, applied in uniquely Japanese ways to be sure, have had significant effects on Japanese politics and society. Primitive Japan benefited enormously by adapting so much from China, then perhaps the world's most sophisticated people. Japan's practice of learning from other cultures and adapting what it learns to its own culture persists to this day.

Rice

It is difficult to overstate the importance of rice in Japan; the Japanese term for rice, *gohan*, also means meal. Agricultural land is in short supply, and this highly bountiful crop both supports and requires densely packed populations because its cultivation is very labor-intensive. Each step from the transfer of seedlings between nursery and irrigated field to harvesting requires extensive, prompt, and, hence, cooperative effort. Agrarian Japan was essentially a subsistence economy, and entire villages participated in the cultivation of rice, thereby developing a strong sense of shared fate and interdependence. A general lack of resources other than the riches in protein offered by the surrounding seas ensured that this condition persisted throughout the nation's history. Many scholars consider this "rice culture" to be the very heart of the collective nature of the Japanese. Moreover, the traditional importance of rice helps explain the inordinate political power of farmers in contemporary Japan and the very strong protection afforded them, as well as the readiness of the Japanese to absorb the resulting high prices. Foreigners are often skeptical when Japan claims that rice is a national security issue, but many Japanese see it just that way.

HISTORICAL FORCES

Ancient Japan was a land of primitive, semiautonomous tribes and little order and organization. There were two classes: nobility who controlled the land and peasants who worked it. Some nobles claimed descent from deities, thereby establishing a link between divine and political power that persisted in Japan until officially ended by the American occupation after World War II. Chief among them was the emperor who presided over an elaborate court at the traditional capital of Kyoto. Meanwhile, an administrative establishment emerged at Kyoto, later at Kamakura and eventually at Edo, now Tokyo. Whereas the imperial court amused itself with artistic pursuits imported from China, the *daimyo* began learning administrative skills. They enthusiastically adopted Confucian bureaucracy (the *bakufu*), developing a code of law and creating a government, much overdeveloped given the primitive state of Japanese civilization, complete with a supreme council, a prime minister, an array of cabinet ministers, and even a shadow cabinet. Japan had a constitution by the seventh century and, in effect, followed China (third century) as the second of the world's nation-states. This constitution did not prescribe a rule of law as much as an elaborate bureaucracy (it established twelve ranks or "caps" just within the imperial court) and a set of idealized virtues governing everyday behavior. Given the close relationship between government and deity established by Shinto (discussed later), these ideals took on the power of commandments. Supplemented by many rules developed since, called *kata* (which means "form") they address every aspect of behavior and transform ordinary activities like arranging furniture, handling money, or wrapping a package into rituals, which must always be performed in the one correct manner. When the westerner might say "I don't care how you get it done, just do it," the Japanese might say "Don't do it unless you can do it the right way" (De Mente 1993, 11). To violate a *kata* is unacceptable and is tolerated, even if grudgingly, only of non-Japanese. Frequent violation, even by non-Japanese, is uncivilized. This preference for form over substance is difficult for westerners to understand, but it helps explain why the Japanese refuse to produce or buy a product that does not look and perform as well as it possibly can.

This government presided quite loosely over a decentralized network of local warlords. Accumulation of territorial rights through tribal or clan warfare evolved into a totally feudal society by the twelfth century. The emperor became a largely ceremonial figurehead and nominal chief of state. The warlords, or daimyo, controlled large estates, even though the land remained in the hands of the emperor, which were defended by retainers, *samurai* warriors, who in turn were supported by taxes paid in rice to the daimyo by serfs. A four-class system evolved with farmers then artisans and finally merchants all ranking well behind the samurai, who wielded absolute power over subordinate classes to the extent that an unintended insult could bring instant death. With feudalism lasting well into the nineteenth century, it can be readily understood then how the Japanese became thoroughly conditioned to sparse and indirect speech, modesty, and deference to authority. The farmers' higher rank reflected the "rice culture," whereas merchants ranked at the bottom because they were seen as unproductive parasites. There was also a class of untouchables, the *burakumin,* who worked in what were seen as dirty trades such as butchering and tanning. There remains considerable prejudice against these people in Japan.

It is important to recognize however that the nobility and samurai generally wielded power with considerable benevolence, as long as their subjects conformed to the vast array of rules governing proper behavior, and the relationship between them and the lower classes was quite paternalistic. The daimyo's fortunes depended heavily on the rice crop, the only real source of wealth, so they shared the fate of the farmers and samurai, who were paid in rice by the daimyo. Earning relatively little themselves, then, the samurai's loyalty was drawn primarily by the moral power and leadership ability of the daimyo. Thus a sense of shared fate, or mutual dependence, and a highly paternalistic and loyal leadership style emerged quite early in Japanese history. Incidentally, the relatively impoverished life-styles of the samurai, and of the Japanese generally, and the delicate balance between the population that could be supported by rice and that needed to cultivate it kept birth rates well below levels common elsewhere.

The samurai, analogous to European knights, occupied themselves with two primary pursuits when not actually engaged in combat: constant honing of military skills, described by samurai Miyamoto Musashi in the fifteenth-century classic, *A Book of Five Rings*; and pursuit of mental discipline through arts such as calligraphy and painting and Zen Buddhist meditation. This duality still remains evident in *Kendo* (*ken*, sword; *-do*, a Confucian Chinese suffix meaning "the way of the . . .") and other martial art forms. The samurai were totally loyal to their lords, and took intense pride in their discipline, both mental and physical, and asceticism. No punishment or hardship was too great to bear. They carried two swords as symbols of their rank: a long sword used for combat; and a short sword for *seppuku*, or ritual suicide, which symbolized their commitment to their code of honor, *Bushido* (*bushi* are samurai warriors; *-do*, again, from the Chinese for "the way"), and to their lord, who could order or expect suicide for any transgression, real or perceived. Their commitment, discipline, and skills earned the samurai great respect, and this tradition has passed on not only to militarists who plunged Japan into wars of conquest but to Japanese managers who apply much the same code and discipline in more-peaceful arenas.

A modern manifestation of Bushido is the expectation that a Japanese official or executive will resign without prompting upon revelation of some scandal, even though the executive had no involvement. A more common, indeed universal, manifestation is the paternalism and bidirectional loyalty evident in relationships between Japanese managers and subordinates, despite well-defined and entrenched hierarchies. In a broader sense, the samurai's simultaneous pursuit of artistry and military skill, a tradition spanning a millennium, explains in part the seemingly dichotomous juxtaposition of the Japan of peaceful landscape gardens, tea ceremonies, *origami*, and *bonsai* with the Japan capable at times of unspeakable brutality. Ruth Benedict wrote eloquently on this apparent conundrum in *The Chrysanthemum and the Sword*.

Japanese feudalism bore many similarities to the European version, but with important differences with significant cultural implications. Loyalty of samurai and vassals to lords was a moral obligation, total and absolute, not contractual, and superseded all other emotions and obligations, including those to one's family. The daimyo were administrators of feudal fiefs, not a landed aristocracy. As we have seen, warriors were expected to pursue learning and to become accomplished in gentler arts. There was no code of chivalry; women were expected to be as tough as men. (In this most masculine of cultures, the subordinate role of women typical of feudal societies not only survived the demise of feudalism but has persisted and apparently will persist for some time to come.) Struggles for power and wealth were not grounded in religious or ethnic differences as they often were in Europe and the Middle East. The Japanese did not conform entirely to Chinese notions of government. Confucius envisioned rule by a bureaucracy of scholars whose power was justified by great wisdom and learning. Indeed, the Chinese were administering civil service examinations over fourteen hundred years ago. The Japanese, again adapting, maintained power in a European-like hereditary system, more consistent with their origins and tracing lineages directly back to Shinto deities, and forward to the current occupants of the "chrysanthemum throne."

The Tokugawa Period

Feudal warfare and subterfuge among rivals and rebellious lords eventually evolved into a loosely centralized rule under the *shogun* (literally, a barbarian-conquering generalissimo), who presided over a nationwide federation of daimyo. Unification culminated in the Tokugawa shogunate that ruled Japan from the sixteenth century until the Meiji (imperial) Restoration in 1868. Some historians suggest that this unification was precipitated by the arrival of the first of the "meddlesome foreigners," European traders and Jesuit missionaries. As unification proceeded, the shogun and the still powerless emperor, who still retained moral authority, became quite adept at arranging negotiations and compromises among rival daimyo. To minimize the potential for conflict or loss of face, and to avoid the ritual of the elaborate court bureaucracy, it became a common practice for the powerful to remain behind the scenes, even retiring early, or to allow underlings to speak for them and clarify respective positions and interests. They would then continue to make final decisions privately after thorough discussion and evaluation. These practices are the same seen today in negotiating techniques and as the Japanese deftly manage relationships among companies and between the private and public sectors.

The feudal system in Japan outlasted those in Europe and China by several centuries, as it persisted until just after the American Civil War. It is most notable for the stability and unification it produced and for the attendant opportunity to cement transplanted Chinese notions in place. To preserve the Japanese way of life, the Tokugawa issued a series of edicts in the 1630s that closed Japan to foreigners—except for carefully controlled access for Chinese and European traders, primarily Dutch, and emissaries at the port of Nagasaki—and even forbade Japanese living abroad from returning home. The forced isolation greatly retarded technological progress and prolonged the militaristic nature of the ruling class, but it also created the foundation of a stable and powerful Japan.

Merchants took advantage of this relative tranquility to amass considerable wealth as moneylenders and by trading in rice, arms, and various domestic and imported goods well beyond their lowly station in the class system. Meanwhile, stability brought redundancy to many samurai. Many became administrators of the daimyo's estates, setting a precedent of co-operation between public and private sectors. Some newly unaffiliated samurai, or *ronin,* became bandits and others mercenaries. The story of the forty-seven *ronin* who committed seppuku after avenging the murder of their lord in 1703 attained the status of those legends that help define a culture, like those of Daniel Boone and Davy Crockett in America. In this case, the lesson was the unswerving loyalty of Bushido. The forty-seven *ronin* remain buried side by side in an honored and much visited Tokyo graveyard. Some samurai began to turn to the merchants to learn commercial skills. Some borrowed money from the merchants. Arranged marriages between their children raised the social status of merchants and the economic status of samurai. These new skills and alliances created a new arena for samurai discipline and leadership skills and formed the basis for the industrial *zaibatsu* of pre-WWII Japan and, eventually, the *keiretsu* of contemporary Japan.

Although Confucianism had penetrated Japan a millennium beforehand, it had less influence than did Buddhism. The prolonged peace and stability and unity established during the Tokugawa period created the opportunity and need for a test of Confucius's teachings regarding the maintenance of social order.

Confucianism

Confucius is perhaps the most influential individual in Asian history, not so much for his views on government as for his teachings on the proper relationships and conduct among people. Seeking to bring social order to China during a period of great internal strife, he believed in political unity under one just ruler but not necessarily in religious unity, unlike his counterparts in the West. Making no pretenses to divine guidance, he was a social reformer and administrator who taught around 500 B.C. that man is inherently good, unlike Christianity, and that all that is necessary to establish a good life on earth (that is, one characterized by order and stability) is some guidance as to the "right way to live," that right way being prescribed through the Japanese notion of *kata.* Society works best when individuals are loyal to those more learned and experienced and live up to their obligations to one another. Loyalty and obligations are arranged in a hierarchy based on filial piety (son to father) and obedience to the ruler (subject to lord) who exemplifies the "right way" of thinking and living. Other key relationships include those between older and younger brother, between husband and wife, and between friends. The wisdom and advice of elders are held in great esteem; the family unit is highly extended, typically with three generations living in the same dwelling. Public good takes precedence over private good, and matters of "face" and etiquette take on grave importance. The "loss of face" so dreaded in Asia is, in essence, an occasion of some public recognition that one has failed to live up to one's Confucian duty. This sense of duty, combined with a relative lack of moral absolutes in Japanese religion, makes shame before others a much more powerful emotion and deterrent to misconduct than guilt, which resides in one's own mind. This explains the common negotiating ploy of using shame to coerce desired behavior.

The teachings of Confucius were recorded by his disciples primarily in *The Analects of Confucius* and *The Mencius*. Familiarity with these teachings goes far in enhancing one's understanding of East Asian thinking and behavior. In addition to the strong sense of obligation and duty necessary to maintain social order, they addressed the importance of hard work and frugality, legitimacy of one powerful but benevolent ruler, a learned bureaucracy to serve the people, puritanical asceticism, and the importance of education necessary to train leaders and to teach the "right way." Confucianism did not address the afterlife, ritual, the clergy, or other religious ideas and is thus more of a secular philosophy of ethics and life. His influence was so pervasive, however, that many consider Confucianism as a religion.

The Japanese, unwilling to surrender their view of leaders as an embodiment of ancestors and mythical heroes, did not allow Confucian ideas regarding government by the learned to disturb the existing system of hereditary, quasi-divine power, or the supremacy of loyalty to the lord over all others, including family. They did however find his teachings regarding loyalty and the duty to uphold one's obligations to others quite consistent with their own traditional values. Another departure was Japan's rejection of the puritanism advocated by Confucius. The Japanese take great joy in the personal pleasures of life but do not let pleasure interfere in carrying out one's responsibilities. One's family life was to be kept separate and subordinate to one's personal affairs, sometimes including those of a most personal nature. This tradition persists to this day in expectations of after-hours socializing and the limited family life allowed *sarirymen*. Life at home was to be kept separate from one's occupation, and Japanese homes still remain essentially off limits to professional acquaintances and colleagues. One concession to Confucian puritanism is the rarity of public displays of affection, even between happily married spouses, and the relative lack of emotion displayed in everyday life.

Even though feudalism is not Confucian, which takes a much more liberal view of political power, Confucianism remained at the center of Japanese thought until western technology made its way into Japan after the Meiji Restoration. Its primary impacts were to imbue the Japanese with a strong sense of nationhood—no longer would Japan be a smaller, backward China—and the values of decorum, duty, loyalty, and rigid but paternalistic and benevolent hierarchy. It left the heretofore warlike Japanese a docile and highly regimented people quite content to seek direction from above with complete trust. It compelled each Japanese to find what Ruth Benedict called "one's proper station" and act accordingly, to execute the obligations of that role toward others. She points out that this value was so widely held that it took on a national character, citing as an example the Tripartite Pact that formed the WWII Axis alliance among Japan, Germany, and Italy. This pact proclaimed that these nations, to ensure peace, must be given their "proper station" in the world. The eminent Japanologist Edwin Reischauer suggests in *Japan Past and Present* that Japan's imperialism was a result of a national bursting of the bonds of docility in the face of unfamiliar and powerful external forces. For readers interested in an entertaining approach to Japanese history, two sequential novels by James Clavell, *Shogun* and *Gai-Jin,* offer a very insightful account of the Tokugawa period, emphasizing interaction with westerners.

The Meiji Restoration

In 1868 an alliance of daimyo overthrew the shogunate and restored royal rule, assumed by the Meiji family. After seven centuries of military rule, the new government abolished the class system, opened Japan to travel and commerce, and embarked upon a period of rapid and comprehensive learning from other cultures, which continues unabated. Although militarism remained a powerful force, as illustrated by Japan's war with Russia at the turn of the century, its imperialism in China and Korea in the 1930s, and its role in World War II, the transition from feudalism to a democratic government, a more liberal and egalitarian society, an industrialized economy, and status as a world power began in earnest with the Meiji Restoration.

The daimyo and samurai were at first put on pension, then paid off with lump sums. Accelerating what had begun at the end of the shogunate, these sums often were invested in enterprise, and the real and imposed distinctions between samurai and merchant began to disappear. Some samurai of course sought to preserve their tradition and power more ostensibly and formed the kernel of a professional military, but the samurai of earlier centuries was more likely to become the executive or manager of the twentieth. The impact of the twentieth century on Japanese culture has yet to be determined and may not be discernible until well into the twenty-first. It will be interesting to observe the degree to which Japanese and Western cultures converge, and whether the West will influence Japan to any degree approaching the impact of China.

RELIGION

Japan is very much a secular society. Kata and concrete relationships among people and within organized groups hold much more meaning for the Japanese than do universal laws and religious abstractions like a single, omnipotent God or sin. Ethical standards are relative, and generalized values, such as fairness, are difficult for the Japanese to grasp. Consider the implications when westerners insist that the Japanese engage in "fair" trade! Clerics and ceremonial ritual do not play a major role in everyday life, except for special occasions. Shrines and temples abound but are places primarily of beauty and tranquility frequented more for reflection and meditation than for worship. Many Japanese do not avow any one faith, and most are at once Buddhist and Shinto and perhaps one or more others such as Tao or Christian. Even though Confucianism's domain is essentially secular, it remains one of, if not the, primary sources of ethical standards. The Japanese do not hold to absolute standards as much as they focus on their respective network of relationships to others and work diligently to uphold their Confucian obligations in each one. In effect, then, rules of conduct are relative, applied to particular relationships in ways most likely to preserve that relationship. If there are moral absolutes governing Japanese behavior, they are loyalty, filial piety broadly interpreted, and living up to one's obligations to others.

Shinto

Shinto is a prehistoric, uniquely Japanese religion notable for its lack of ethical content, ceremonial ritual, or concern for any afterlife. It involves the worship of nature in many manifestations, called *kami,* and ancestors. *Kami* are deities found in natural objects and living things, including people. There is a reverence for the purity of nature and man's connection to it and a celebration of the past, a kind of folklore enabling legendary heroes to find their way into deity. Man and kami all descend from the Sun Goddess, and some kami are embodied as men. Hence, the boundaries between man and nature or deity are permeable. Shinto embodies the continuity of Japanese culture and nationhood. The Sun Goddess is symbolized by the fiery red disk on the national flag. In Shinto lies the deity of the emperor and an unbroken line of succession to the present day. The Japanese words for shrine and place are the same, as are the words for worship and government. Shinto (and Buddhist) shrines have long been major landholders and have had a long and close relationship with the emperor's court.

When a storm sank a Mongol invasion fleet sent by Kublai Khan to conquer Japan in 1281, the Japanese saw divine intervention in this event, a fortuitous one not only for Japan but for the early shogun in that it invested this new form of government with a degree of divine favor, thereby solidifying its legitimacy. The Japanese called this divine wind *kamikaze*, which readers recognize as the name given to suicide pilots who crashed their planes into U.S. Navy ships to prevent what would have been the first outright invasion of Japan. These pilots perhaps expected to become *kami*, or at least to become honored as legendary heroes for the ages as their reward for dying for the emperor. In these two events we see the Shintoist convergence between human and deity, and government and religion, precipitated by actions of heroic or mythic proportions performed in the interest of the Japanese people.

When combined with the Confucian emphasis on education, Shinto becomes a vehicle for study of the past and the preservation of heroic history and tradition. Following Confucius's teaching, the Japanese built a monolithic, centrally controlled system of public education, under which the same lessons are taught in the same way nationwide. Such a system can and has been used to great effect to homogenize a society. The linkage between religion and government has been strong, then, and Japanese leaders have used Shinto to their own ends. Indeed, Shinto eventually became the official state religion and an instrument of intense nationalism until the U.S. occupation after World War II abolished both "state Shinto" and the divinity of the emperor. Of course Shinto is still a major religion, and many Japanese retain great reverence for the emperor.

Zen Buddhism

The Japanese adapted Buddhism to their own culture, as they did Confucianism, essentially disregarding its rituals and much of its content regarding the afterlife and reincarnation, seeking of enlightenment, and *nirvana*, but seizing upon the Buddhist practices of meditation, self-discipline, and mastery over one's own will. The discipline in this uniquely Japanese version, *Zen* Buddhism, lies in profound appreciation of harmony, simplicity, and beauty in nature; in the quest for insight into the true meaning of simple everyday objects and events; and in achieving oneness with the cosmos. It eschews reason in favor of emotion and intuition and demands an appreciation of subtlety and a willingness to accept things as they are and events as they unfold, change being inevitable. To the Japanese, total reliance on logical argument and objective reality, including financial measures and contractual conditions, seems cold. These must be complemented by harmonious feelings, personal trust and familiarity, and a sense of well-being in the business relationship.

Zen is a very difficult concept for westerners to understand and is one of the greatest differences between Western and Japanese cultures. As an example, compare the formal garden traditionally seen in the West with a Japanese garden. The Western garden will be laid out symmetrically. Plantings will be dense and occupy almost all the space, will be complementary in color and foliage, and appear in regular or even repetitive patterns. In a Japanese garden one finds asymmetry in the overall shape and layout; apparently random arrangements; much open space; many disparate items such as pebbles, rocks, bridges, lanterns, ponds occupied by colorful fish, sculptures, and relatively sparse plantings. Yet, even to the Western eye, the overall effect is pleasing and at least as harmonious and beautiful as the more familiar design. Where the westerner wants to impose order on nature, the Japanese accepts and appreciates it as is. The westerner examines and admires each planting, whereas the Japanese takes in the totality of the setting and the interesting visual relationships among the disparate elements. Another manifestation of Zen is *haiku*, the traditional seventeen-syllable poem (once a wordy thirty-one!). The meaning typically is difficult to grasp and may not exist; the intent is to create a thought upon which the reader may reflect and meditate and interpret in one's own way. Some may describe Western poetry similarly, but the difference is more in degree of ambiguity. In effect, the haiku is more an occasion to provoke meditation than a piece of literature, that is, an opportunity to exercise and perfect one's ability to concentrate. Another manifestation of Zen is the tea ceremony, which has much more to do with prolonged appreciation of grace and simplicity of movement of beautiful objects in a peaceful and pleasant setting than it does with drinking tea. The mental discipline involved in appreciating these art forms is one of intense concentration while remaining open-minded and alert to nuance, alternative meanings, and change. Serenity, harmony, and beauty are common to all. Wordiness, noise, and talking are not.

The dialog between a Zen master and disciple typically involves a question posed by the master that is impossible to answer rationally, called *koan*, such as "What is the sound of one hand clapping?" Reason and logic are irrelevant, and the responses that the disciple brings to the master as they occur—perhaps after thinking about the question for days at a time—will arise more from intuition, insight, and emotion experienced by the student while concentrating on the question. The master is less interested in the response than in evidence of profound thought and intellectual growth. Zen meditation, landscaping, haiku, and other traditional art forms such as *ikebana* (flower arranging), origami (paper folding), and bonsai all emphasize simplicity and striving for perfection. Simplicity facilitates concentration, and pursuit of perfection provides the incentive to maintain discipline. This sort of discipline would serve Japan well when it entered competition in the international marketplace.

Intense concentration was seen as a tool for mastery of the will. Herein lies the attraction of Zen for the samurai who had to endure the rigors of Bushido. Learning from Zen masters and appreciation and practice of art forms in the Zen tradition became an important part of their martial training. By extension, Zen appeals to all Japanese who must master their individual wills and seek perfection in what they do in order to live up to the array of Confucian obligations imposed upon them by each and every personal relationship. The discipline of continuous improvement, especially as applied to manufacturing, is well known to westerners as *kaizen*. The Japanese insistence on the harmonious appearance of products and the quality of form as well as function is grounded in Zen as well. It is much more common to actually practice as well as appreciate the arts in Japan than in the West not only because it disciplines the mind and will, but also (and perhaps even more so) because it is one of the few outlets for individual self-expression. It is not surprising then that the Japanese expect the same discipline of others.

CORE VALUES AND BEHAVIOR

Japanese management practices as we know them today emerged largely since World War II, sometimes arising from pragmatic considerations. For example, promises of lifetime employment were in large part concessions to the realities of labor shortages caused by rapid industrialization, a traditionally low birth rate, and tremendous wartime losses. Nevertheless, these familiar behaviors spring directly from core values that have deep cultural roots.

Collectivism

The isolation and homogeneity of Japan has produced a unique sense of cohesion and separateness from others among the Japanese. The persistent demands of rice culture, lack of resources, and the threats of economic deprivation, natural disaster, and foreign invasion created a strong sense of interdependence. Confucian teaching of individual obligations and duty to others became the dominant ethical standard. The long-lived, highly stratified feudal society created strong horizontal bonds within classes. The emergent social structure was in effect a hierarchy of groups. Rather than cause frustration and bad manners, the density of population and crowding of extended families into small and flimsy dwellings instead forced the Japanese to treat one another with great civility in accordance with Confucian teaching.

Group Identity and Affiliation

The result of these forces was a culture in which the needs of the group take precedence over those of the individual, and one's identity is established by one's affiliation with groups, beginning with Japanese citizenship itself, then cascading downward in priority, typically in a hierarchy through employer, school, school class, hometown, and family. Readers may be familiar with the often-quoted Japanese proverb "The nail which sticks out will be hammered down." Each group in which one holds membership imposes its norms, creating multiple sets of obligations for the individual and, sometimes then, stress and anxiety. Japanese prefer group activities to individual activities and draw great pleasure and comfort in being part of something larger than themselves. They dislike being singled out, whether for criticism or praise. Even groups organized for recreational purposes have formal procedures and, often, uniforms. Participation in group activity provides the Japanese stability, order, and pride. Conversely, loneliness is a great burden, privacy is not desirable, and independence is not admired. Togetherness is the normal state of the Japanese. Consider, for example, how westerners often arrange furniture in their homes against the walls, which tends to disperse people to the edges of the room. The Japanese tend to place furniture and *tatami* mats in the center of the room, as if to draw people together. The Japanese have long understood the productivity of groups and the creative as well as social and functional benefits of teamwork, as illustrated by another proverb cited by Yatsutaka Sai (p. 5): "Three ordinary people can think of a better plan than one *manjushiri* (wise priest)." Clearly, the quality circle is not a novel idea!

Japanese introduce themselves first by the company they represent not by name or professional occupation. They take great pride in their employer affiliation and would be dumbfounded to hear someone criticize one's own employer. They are assigned to work groups rather than to individual positions. Individual job descriptions are nonexistent or vague. Titles indicate rank rather than specific responsibilities, which are assigned to groups rather than to individuals. One's personal worth or achievement is measured, evaluated, and rewarded in terms of what one contributes to one's work group. Personal achievement and merit are recognized and valued only to the extent that they advance the work group's purpose.

Modern Japanese society is a honeycomb of organizations from the *Keidanren,* a sort of quasi-governmental, national chamber of commerce, to keiretsu and agricultural co-ops, to neighborhood PTAs and youth groups—and the Japanese are inveterate joiners. Large companies hire, train, and groom new managers as a class that retains its identity and cohesiveness. Readers may recall seeing Japanese tourists traveling in groups almost seeming to be marching together. The individual feels a great need to find one's proper place in the organization and maintain its harmony, therefore defers to seniors, acts modestly and with restraint, speaks politely and sparingly, and always places group needs and aspirations first. Intense loyalty to the boss (even a new and unknown one), modesty (*enryo*), humility, and concern and sympathy for others govern behavior. Assertiveness and directness are foreign, and any self-promoting behavior is seen as boorish. Acting capriciously or freely violates *shikitari* or "the way things are done around here," an elaborate set of behavioral norms typical of most Japanese organizations. Necessary actions beyond what is prescribed, or in response to unforeseen circumstances, must comply with *atar-amae* (common sense), which is remarkably common in this homogenous culture (Kang 1990, 121). The "free-rider" problem, which so troubles group function in the individualistic West, is unthinkable in Japan. Competition in Japan is intense but is between teams rather than individuals. *Keiretsu* are in effect teams of companies that compete against other *keiretsu* and *gaishi,* or foreign companies.

External Relationships

Intense group solidarity is complemented by discomfort in the presence of non-Japanese. It is tempting to attribute this discomfort to xenophobia or even hubris grounded in Japanese pride in uniqueness and a sense of superiority engendered by military, economic, and artistic sophistication and accomplishment, impeccable manners, and the orderliness of Japanese society. Boye De Mente suggests that a more likely explanation is the Japanese's realization that outsiders do not know, appreciate, or conform to *kata,* which causes much unease because the Japanese anticipate an inability to know how to react to these transgressions. There are no *kata* for dealing with foreigners. The expectation of impending disharmony and lack of *kata* guidance are very threatening and stressful for the Japanese.

The Japanese divide the world into people with whom they have a relationship (the inner circle—*uchi* or "house") and those with whom they do not (the outer circle—*soto* or "outside"). Whereas warmth and respect typically characterize attitudes toward *uchi,* Japanese can be indifferent or quite cold toward *soto* and tend to be uncomfortable around them. There remain vestiges of the xenophobia traditional in Japan and intensified by the Tokugawa isolation. Although the degree of personal familiarity expected in say, Latin America, is not necessary, the Japanese do not do business with strangers in order to avoid the risk of conflict inherent in dealing with them (and also because they prefer to be well prepared for any serious discussion). Therefore, it is usually necessary to use a go-between to establish connections. The Japanese prefer to engage in long-term relationships with familiar suppliers in order to take advantage of the benefits of trust and reliability necessary, for example, to make just-in-time inventory management feasible. A strong reputation (signifying a company that can be trusted) helps overcome these barriers. This familiarity gives the Japanese the same kind of comfort, if not the degree, experienced in one's own organization (see the discussion of *anshinkan* later). This is why the *keiretsu* system fits Japanese culture so well.

Japanese carefully develop networks of contacts and relationships both inside and outside their organizations, especially with suppliers, government officials, and anyone with the potential to provide useful information. This network (or *jinmyaku*), accumulated and cultivated over a lifetime, becomes one's most valuable asset, more so than any individual skill. One's university affiliation is more important than what was studied or the grades earned, not only from the standpoint of prestige but more so for the contacts developed. One's entering class of new hires is another major step in the foundation, to be exploited as that class disperses throughout the company, rotates laterally making many new contacts, and rises in lockstep in the seniority system. The Japanese builds his *jinmyaku* incrementally but steadily from induction onward and maintains it with frequent phone calls and visits, entertainment, and gifts.

Harmony and High-Context Communication

The traditional and intense needs for group affiliation, and thus for preservation of intragroup relationships, and the more contemporary need for maintaining a network of contacts create an equally intense need in the Japanese to maintain harmony (*wa*) in these relationships. It is difficult to overstate its importance. An early Japanese constitution stated in its first article that "Harmony is the greatest treasure" (Sai, p. 28). An early kata, dating from that same period, was that merit and self-advancement must be avoided in order to prevent envy, which in turn would be a severe threat to harmony. Herein lies the root of a culture that awards status by ascription rather than achievement. An important manifestation of the need for harmony is the dominance of high-context communication. More-direct, high-content communication carries too much risk of disappointment, disagreement, confrontation, and therefore disharmony. The tone of voice tends to be flat and unemotional. Too much talking also raises the risk of disharmony and is perceived as disruptive. The Japanese scrupulously avoid sensitive topics like politics and religion and personal matters, beyond simple inquiries about family well-being. They also are very unlikely to express dissatisfaction or discontent in the workplace. The desire to avoid giving offense or creating disharmony is so strong that it apparently suppresses the emotionalism and physical contact found in other cultures high in uncertainty avoidance.

A common value set arising from cultural homogeneity and continuity and from common experience and education facilitates indirect, intuitive, and subtle communication, just as it does between long-married couples, thereby reducing the potential for conflict. Japanese conversation involves much suggestion and implication, testing for mood and reaction, and alertness for any hint of conflict. Oral communication is much preferred because it affords the opportunity to observe the effect of the message and adjust accordingly. The Japanese consider written communication cold and brief or terse letters rude. The need to preserve harmony requires an indirectness that causes the Japanese to say "maybe" or "later" (the ostensible message or *tatemae*) when the actual message (or *honne*) is "no" or "never." Actually, there is no direct equivalent for "no" in Japanese. When a Japanese means to say that something is absolutely impossible, he might say "It will be difficult" or "There are some problems." When the Japanese interjects *hai*, or literally, yes, into the conversation, as is done often, the meaning is "Yes, I hear you" or "Yes, I understand you," not "Yes, I agree with you." Hai really means "uh-huh" rather than yes.

Because westerners place great value on directness and frankness of speech, they may perceive Japanese indirectness as evasive or deceptive. It is not intended as such, and westerners must recognize this. If a Japanese senses that the indirect reply will be misunderstood or resented as misleading or evasive, he may simply remain silent, change the subject, or even walk away. The Japanese, through centuries of cultural conditioning, whether out of respect for elders, fear of beheading by an offended samurai, or concern for sleeping family members on the other side of a paper partition, understand the true meaning of very parsimonious and subtle speech naturally; the westerner must learn to do so. Another practice that troubles westerners is the silence that follows a statement or question. As a sign of respect to the speaker, the Japanese remains silent while thinking about what was just said and how to respond. Thus, westerners must resist the temptation to jump into the temporary void of silence—as they most surely will when speaking to one another—or risk the appearance of failing to render the same courtesy.

Indirectness can take extreme forms. For an example, a superior may chastise a subordinate with words of extreme politeness or praise on his face, but the Japanese interprets them correctly as harsh criticism. The minimization of argument and debate (which normally occurs after hours in a much less formal setting) and the reliance on subtle and often unspoken communication lessen the importance of verbal skills, one reason why the Japanese find it difficult to learn foreign languages. It is not surprising, then, that the Japanese find it difficult to relate with foreigners, lacking the commonality of culture to support the preferred methods of indirect communication and the verbal skills to engage in more-direct communication.

Ritual behavior is another means of maintaining harmony and order, as well as historical continuity and cultural homogeneity. There is but one way to do things, and that is the way they are to be done, whether serving tea, exchanging business cards (*meishi,*) or bowing to the proper depth upon introduction. Formality and use of proper form are grounded in Confucianism (the right way) and in Zen, which imposes discipline in pursuit of perfection. All activities, even recreational pursuits, require thorough preparation (anything worth doing is worth doing right!).

Hierarchy and Participation

Although postfeudal, postwar Japan has evolved into a classless and highly egalitarian society, there remains a very strong consciousness of rank and title. Final authority is strictly hierarchical, but the boss is expected to achieve consensus beforehand. The seventh-century constitution told each Japanese that "You must never decide great matters on your own. You must discuss them with all kinds of people" (De Mente 1993, 5). Information flows well, in all directions. Work spaces are open, and the supervisor works among the work group so that information and ideas are shared automatically and unconsciously. Bottom-up collaboration is formalized in the well-known *ringi* system, through which ideas and recommendations are circulated laterally at each level to gain widespread acceptance before moving upward through the hierarchy. The internal network of contacts maintained by each manager both demands and lubricates this process. The seeming contradiction between the need for harmony and consensus on one hand and large power distance on the other can best be understood through the analogy of family decision making. The decision process is a more elaborate version of what might go on around the dinner table as a family discusses where to go on summer vacation or whether dad should accept a transfer. Consensus is highly desirable and exhaustively sought, but the parents have the final say. Traditional Japanese paternalism is at work in *ringi,* a kind of benevolent, consultative dictatorship. Compare the process to Western practices: Managers also must achieve consensus to implement their decisions effectively, but traditionally have done so after the fact! Hence, even though the need for consensus prolongs the decision-making process, implementation will proceed much faster and more smoothly than in the West. Japanese managers seek employee involvement or concurrence often enough to justify a label for the practice—*nemawashi,* or "tending the roots" (Chen 1995, 184).

Japanese unfailingly respect and defer to position, experience, and age. The Japanese studies your business card with great care not only because your company affiliation means more than your personal identity, but also because the Japanese must identify any status differential in order to decide which of the many hierarchical forms of address available in Japanese is most appropriate and how deeply to bow. Japanologist John Condon found that there are at least ten ways to say "I" and ten more to say "you" in Japanese. The speaker must decide which to use based on the relationship with the listener. Junior members of discussion groups remain silent until senior members have spoken, expressing disagreement only privately. Nevertheless, subordinates are encouraged to regularly submit reports of analysis and recommendations on strategic issues to their seniors that are given careful study. Senior members of negotiating teams often remain silent, only to exert their authority privately, much like the politically astute daimyo. Subordinates willingly accept their lesser roles, knowing that their time will come via seniority-based promotion from within. There is no need for self-aggrandizing behavior because there is no opportunity for, or threat from, fast-trackers. This is not to say that self-promotion, suboptimization, and organizational politics do not exist in Japan. What differs is that these are employed to advance group, not individual, interests. It is not surprising then that with this attitude, in conjunction with the imperative to put the group's interest first, the cooperation and teamwork sought by westerners so assiduously, but with such difficulty, comes so naturally to the Japanese.

Paternalism, Filial Loyalty, and Obligation

The Japanese feel such intense pressure to live up to their obligations to others that they have developed a kind of internal bookkeeping procedure to keep track of them, mentally accounting for receipt and repayment of concessions, favors, gifts, and the like. These obligations are termed *on* when owed to superiors or elders and *giri* when owed to others. Such obligations must be disposed of, and quickly; failure or inability to do so is a source of intense anxiety, even contributing to Japan's relatively high suicide rate. They arise from the traditional Japanese class system, amplified by Confucian filial piety and prolonged feudalism. Confucianism also prescribes the reciprocal obligation, paternalistic benevolence toward those for whom one bears responsibility. The relationship between vassal and daimyo was governed accordingly, as is that between employer and employee. This relationship has come to mean mutual, long-term commitment, not only in terms of lifelong employment but in promotion from within; promotion and salary based on seniority; extensive horizontal rotation prior to promotion to build a holistic and longer-term view of the firm and its functions and a broad base of experience; and extensive, family-oriented benefit plans. Layoffs mean a serious loss of face for the employer and have been avoided by sloughing off excess employees to suppliers and smaller keiretsu members, across-the-board salary cuts, putting employees "on-call" at home, or tolerating idleness in those excess or less-productive employees relegated to the *madogiwa-zoku* or "window watchers' tribe" (Whitehill 1991, 132).

The sense of shared fate in the face of unfavorable business conditions embodied in across-the-board salary cuts descends directly from the practice of sharing the consequences of a poor rice crop by daimyo, samurai, and farmers. The Japanese speak often of *amae,* or the need for affection, which extends to those under one's care, as a cherished corporate value and managerial trait. The pursuit of amae by superiors and the reciprocal "filial" loyalty of subordinates create the sense of solidarity, warmth, and belonging so important to the Japanese.

The Japanese views customers as an *on* relationship. Thus the customer in Japan truly is the boss. Suppliers and allies take on at least a *giri* relationship. In all cases, the driving value is anshinkan, literally "peace of mind" but which signifies in practical usage meeting expectations (typically, for product quality), upholding obligations, and honoring commitments.

In a nutshell, this important notion means "no surprises." Of course, the level of these expectations, in accordance with the discipline of Zen, is very high. Conversely, unexpected or erratic behavior is a grave error.

Diligence, Perseverance and Perfection

"Industry is fortune's right hand and frugality her left" (Japanese proverb, quoted in Sai, p. 45). One achieves harmony and delivers anshinkan through pursuit of perfection in relationships and results. Driven by the Confucian emphases on hard work, duty, and frugality, by the ageless fear of poverty, and by the discipline of Zen, the Japanese are intensely hardworking people. Their willingness to work until the job is done and not take much of their allowed vacation time are well known, as is the pressure to socialize after work and sacrifice time with their families. There are some important similarities between Confucian precepts and the Protestant work ethic, except that the former is felt more intensely and more commonly. Many of Poor Richard's aphorisms about hard work and frugality apply equally well to the Japanese. One qualitative difference may be the intense emphasis on quality and perfection of form as well as function. To the Japanese, a small chip in the painted finish of a large piece of industrial equipment or a dirty plant are strong signals of inferior products. Contemporary notions like constant improvement and zero defects reflect Zen ideals of replication of the beauty and harmony of nature, a holistic view and appreciation of aesthetics, and constant striving for perfection. Just as relationships require wa (harmony), so do products. A camera must not only be high quality but look and feel like high quality. The overall impression must be like that of the Japanese garden—all elements must be in harmony with one another and with "nature" as manifested in the requirements and expectations of the customer. The expression no missu or "no mistakes" is very common in the workplace and in everyday Japanese life (Kang 1990, 94). It is not surprising, then, that the Japanese themselves are extremely demanding consumers.

Like other collective cultures, the Japanese do not feel that they control their own destiny. Unlike other collective cultures, however, and perhaps because of their isolation and scarcity of resources, the Japanese believe that hard work, not only at their tasks but in ancillary behaviors such as punctuality, removes as much of the uncertainty as possible from their lives. In other words, they are not willing to place their faith in some greater force to look after them. This reflects the relative lack of spirituality of Japanese culture compared to other collective cultures.

The search for perfection has driven the Japanese abroad to learn from whoever seems to be best at something. After the Meiji reopened Japan, the Japanese went abroad to learn from, among others, the British how to build a twentieth-century navy and from the Americans how to manage an industrial corporation. Lessons were applied well enough to build a country not much larger than California into a world power by the end of World War I. In this vein it is not surprising, then, that Edward Deming had such influence in Japan a half century later as the nation sought to rise from the rubble of World War II. What could be more consistent with the discipline of Zen, the pursuit of perfection, and delivery of anshinkan than an effective method for statistical process control?

Preferring to learn and apply rather than to pursue breakthroughs, the Japanese excel at steady, incremental improvement, with perfection as the ultimate achievement and then perfect harmony with man and nature as the ultimate objective. Unlike westerners, the Japanese regard nature as a given; they feel no capacity to control it or divert it from its intended course. To the contrary, Zen teaches the Japanese to emulate nature's perfection. One attitudinal manifestation is a kind of resignation that what will happen will happen, that man is subordinate to nature, that is, to events. Incidentally, this is why the Japanese seem too willing to violate contracts or do not seem particularly concerned with the details of a contract under negotiation. They assume that unforeseen events will require adjustments and that people of good will will do so, in accord with *ataramae* (common sense). Likewise, deadlines are flexible. Having to settle a dispute in court is a serious loss of face in Japan. The contract constitutes little more than a statement of commitment and general intent. An inability to work out differences suggests that one is unworthy of a continuing relationship. Whereas westerners enter into relationships quickly and rely on courts to iron out eventual disagreements, the Japanese seeks to reduce risk before entering into an agreement by building a relationship and getting to know the other party.

For this secular society built on Confucian ethics, hard work in pursuit of group success becomes the primary source of meaning in life. There is no greater accomplishment. Hard work is also an opportunity to learn—another Confucian precept. Participation in groups, we recognize well in the West finally, leverages learning, so we seek to build learning organizations. In Japan, we see a learning culture.

Continuity and the Long Term

The Japanese take great pride in their resiliency, as manifested in their ability to recover from natural disasters. This is in keeping with the samurai's stoicism in enduring hardship. Disaster is but a momentary blip in the continuity of the advance of Japanese culture. More interesting perhaps is the Japanese predilection to think and act for the long term. Japanese history and tradition, kept vital and current through Shinto, and cultural homogeneity provide the Japanese with a deep sense of continuity; the future is an extension of the past.

Much is made of the willingness of Japanese companies to forego profit in the short run in the interest of the long-term benefits of increased market share. Taking the long view is consistent with the sense of continuity but is also another manifestation of paternalism and constant fear of losing their competitive edge in world markets, thereby jeopardizing the very survival of this resource-poor nation. Japanese firms know that in order to fulfill their obligations to their employees, they must manage themselves first for long-term survival, then for long-term growth, and lastly for short-term profit. Many companies elsewhere seek to maximize short-term profits but do little to build robustness and staying power, and thus find themselves forced to lay off workers in response even to momentary (at least in the Japanese view of time!) setbacks. Just as the samurai worked to perfect their competitive skills and resilience slowly but surely, just as the Japanese improve their products and their personal artistic skills slowly but surely, just as frugal people who nonetheless feel threatened by deprivation feel compelled to save for the future, so do Japanese firms work slowly but surely to continuously drive product quality up and costs down, to build volume and market share sufficient to achieve the robustness and resilience of samurai. After all, where and who are the samurai now?

Looking at it another way, Japanese companies believe that profit is an inevitable result of treating employees and customers well (by delivering anshinkan). Meanwhile, providing for the security of the work force remains the first priority. Confucian preference for strong direction by those in authority and for order and stability and more than a millennium of kata have built a culture high in uncertainty avoidance, so Japanese workers are well satisfied with this practice, as they have been with the very slow promotions allowed by the seniority system and the need to accumulate a broad experience base before each promotion. Japanese companies build robustness, in part, by treating employees as capital investments rather than as variable costs. This attitude reflects not only moral commitment and paternalism but the more-tangible realities of large investments of time and money in training and rotational accumulation of experience.

CONVERGENCE?

Culture is a force for stability; people are not prone to change the value system that defines their group identity easily or quickly. If those values serve the culture well, this is a strength; if not, culture can be a hindrance. Japan's unique culture served her well while in isolation, but it has been under severe pressure since the Meiji restoration opened Japan to the West. This will continue as the increasingly global community enfolds the Japanese and as the Japanese themselves seek their "rightful place" in the world.

It is unlikely that the preference for group activity and affiliation, harmony and collective success will change in the foreseeable future. However, globalization will require more convergence of high-content and high-context styles of communicating. It is also unlikely that intense feelings of obligation and loyalty will diminish. However, the harsh realities of global competition are already limiting some paternalistic practices with regard to redundant and nonperforming employees and will require greater use of performance-based compensation. Merit and skill have already begun to take on more significance in promotion decisions. The shift away from lifetime employment and seniority will cause great anguish for Japanese managers, especially those at the top who deem maintenance of employee security as a major, or perhaps the major part of their responsibility, and will not be received well by employees. The relentless pursuit of perfection, the importance of form and ritual, and long-term thinking will persist. These highly pragmatic people, who have demonstrated repeatedly the willingness and ability to adapt, will make whatever adjustments become necessary to maintain Japan's competitiveness and seek her "proper place" in the world, but only those necessary adjustments.

The hardworking Japanese do not enjoy the same standard of living as their counterparts in the West. There is already evidence of growing dissatisfaction in this regard. The young in particular wonder what the payoff is for all their parents' hard work and whether they want to follow the same path. Increased travel to the West has made more Japanese aware of the disparity between them and their supposedly less-skilled or less-productive counterparts in North America and Europe. A concerned older generation has labeled these young skeptics *shinjinrui*, that is, the "new breed" (Kang 1990, 176). It remains to be seen whether the new breed signals a substantive change or whether, like younger generations elsewhere, they will grow more conservative. The bargaining power of younger workers could increase as the population ages, the birth rate remains low, and the skills of older workers become obsolete. Offsetting this trend however is the increasing relocation of production offshore in response to the continuously strong yen, high labor costs at home, and concern about trade barriers as Japan's trade balance remains high despite the strength of the yen. One might expect employees to insist on shorter working hours and more time with their families, but many are resisting government efforts to encourage shorter work weeks, perhaps sensing that productivity must remain the primary concern. Foreign firms have found it difficult to recruit Japanese managers in the past, partly due to lifetime employment keeping a lid on the employment market, and partly due to Japanese discomfort with these *soto* (outsiders) and the attendant fear of loss of face before their countrymen for joining the soto. Japanese women were a convenient solution to this problem. This is changing as more Japanese men seek employment with gaishi (foreign companies), particularly in high-technology and high-growth industries, and as Japanese women are now beginning to join Japanese companies as something more than tea ladies.

SUMMARY

The primary forces that shaped Japanese culture include the following:

- Agrarian origins, which grounded Japanese national and organizational culture in the family and the village
- Shinto, which served as the foundation for a secular value system, engendered a deep respect for elders and heroic figures and legends, a strong connection with nature, and a strong sense of nationhood and continuity
- Isolation, both physical and political, producing a unique and homogenous, unified, and somewhat xenophobic culture
- Natural features, including lack of resources, causing a continuing sense and fear of economic deprivation; a lack of arable, livable land, and frequent natural disasters
- The rice culture, which requires and supports cooperative, group effort
- Confucianism, which legitimized a unified, strong central rule and bureaucratic hierarchy, and amplified and expanded the definition of filial loyalty
- (Zen) Buddhism, which instilled discipline, aesthetics, and holistic thinking
- Feudalism, extending deeply into the nineteenth century, which froze Confucian and Zen Buddhist values in place and created a very stable, orderly, masculine, hierarchical society

The core values developed by these forces include

- **Collectivism**—driven by isolation; a sense of uniqueness and difference from others; fear of deprivation, invasion, and disaster; rice culture; a rigid class system; Shinto-based nationalism; and Confucian teachings regarding the value of order and duty and obligations to others
- **Harmony**—made necessary by the powerful sense of collectivism but also caused by Confucian teaching regarding the need for social order and by crowded living conditions, which demand politeness and consideration
- **High-context communications**—necessary to maintain harmony but also caused by hierarchical power and facilitated by homogeneity of culture and commonality of values and experience

- **Hierarchy**—with status accorded through hereditary **ascription**, a result of a typical, prehistoric, agrarian class system; Shinto-based respect for elders and heroic figures; Confucian teachings regarding the appropriateness of centralized power; and long-lived feudalism
- **Strong uncertainty avoidance**—atypical of Asian cultures, due to isolation and fear of external threat, the comfortable familiarity of ethnic homogeneity, and the pervasive tradition of *kata*
- **Participation**—based on each individual's desire and felt obligation to contribute to the advancement of the collective group, encouraged by paternalism and by the Confucian teaching regarding the importance of education
- **Paternalism**—extension of the agrarian family and village-based leadership style of rice culture to larger entities and Confucian teaching regarding the wisdom and benevolence that ought to be attached to the exercise of centralized power on behalf of the masses
- **Filial loyalty**—an extension of agrarian tradition, Shinto-based respect for elders, being the essence of Confucian obligation, reciprocity for paternalism, and a need for strong leadership when threatened by external forces
- **Obligation**—made necessary by collectivism and rice culture but amplified by Confucian teaching
- **Diligence and Persistence**—obligation to others, a strong need for security caused by fear of deprivation, demands of rice culture, Confucian teachings regarding hard work as the primary source of meaning in life and frugality, and Zen Buddhist-based discipline
- **Perfection**—Zen-based discipline and holistic emulation of the perfection of nature
- **Continuity and a Long-Term View**—the need for security, an "earthquake (survivor) mentality," Zen-based discipline, and the Shinto-based perception of the longevity and superiority of the Japanese nation.

ADDITIONAL READING

Japanese Management Practices

Chen, Min. 1995. *Asian Management Systems*. (New York: Routledge).
Durlabhi, Subhash, and Norton E. Marks, eds. 1993. *Japanese Business: Cultural Perspectives*. (Albany: State University of New York Press).

Elashmawi, Farid, and Philip R. Harris. 1993. *Multicultural Management: New Skills for Global Success.* (Houston: Gulf).

Harris, Philip R., and Robert T. Moran. 1996. *Managing Cultural Differences,* 4th ed. (Houston: Gulf).

Hirschmeier, J., and T. Yui. 1981. *The Development of Japanese Business,* 2nd ed. (London: Allen and Unwin).

Kang, T. W. 1990. *Gaishi: The Foreign Company in Japan.* (New York: Basic-Books).

Lee, Sang M., and Gary Schwendiman. 1982. *Japanese Management: Cultural and Environmental Considerations.* (New York: Praeger).

Ouchi, William G. 1981. *Theory Z.* (New York: Avon).

Pascale, Richard T., and Anthony G. Amos. 1981. *The Art of Japanese Management: Applications for American Executives.* (New York: Simon and Schuster).

Sai, Yatsutaka. 1995. *The Eight Core Values of the Japanese Businessman.* (New York: International Business Press).

Whitehill, Arthur M. 1991. *Japanese Management.* (New York: Routledge).

Japanese History and Culture

Benedict, Ruth. 1946. *The Chrysanthemum and the Sword.* (Boston: Houghton-Mifflin).

De Mente, Boye Lafayette. 1993. *Behind the Japanese Bow.* (Chicago: Passport).

Condon, John C. 1984. *With Respect to the Japanese.* (Yarmouth, Maine: Intercultural Press).

Fairbank, John K., Edwin O. Reischauer, and Albert M. Craig. 1973. *East Asia: Tradition and Transition.* (Boston: Houghton-Mifflin).

Hall, John W., and Richard K. Beasley. 1965. *Twelve Doors to Japan.* (New York: McGraw-Hill).

Hardon, John A. 1970. *Religions of the Orient.* (Chicago: Loyola University Press).

Lebra, S. T. 1976. Japanese Patterns of Behavior. (Honolulu: University of Hawaii Press).

Musashi, Miyamoto. 1974. *A Book of Five Rings.* Translated by Victor Harris. (Woodstock, N.Y.: Overlook).

Nakane, Chie. 1970. *Japanese Society.* (Berkeley: University of California Press).

Reischauer, Edwin O. 1965. *Japan Past and Present,* 3rd ed. (New York: Knopf).

———. 1977. *The Japanese.* (Cambridge, Mass.: Belknap).

Fiction

Clavell, James 1993. *Gai-Jin.* (New York: Delacorte).

———. 1975. *Shogun.* (New York: Atheneum).

Chapter 3

CHINA

China is less complex, less of a contradictory enigma than Japan, yet the Chinese still can personify to the westerner the "inscrutable East" or the "mysterious Orient." We see the Chinese as very industrious, frugal, respectful of their elders, deeply concerned for their children, and holding education very dear. Such characteristics differ in degree more than kind. But at the same time, we sense that the Chinese, by our standards, seem subservient to their superiors, overly regimented and concerned with something called "saving face," seem to speak too indirectly and perhaps with a bit much "false" modesty (Oh no, our factory is clearly much inferior to yours!), sometimes very demanding as negotiators, sometimes trying to shame us into making concessions, and too willing to value connections and appearances more than objective merit. They seem to put the interest of the state ahead of any other, insist on access to the most-advanced knowledge and technology available and to the highest-level officials and executives. They may seem overly eager to avoid controversy and criticism and, at times, somewhat humorless or to laugh at inappropriate times. Western teachers try mightily but often ineffectively to encourage participation by Chinese students in classroom discussions. We may more readily identify a Chinese with a small family business or some state-owned enterprise than we would a Japanese whom we might guess to be an employee of Toyota or Sony. Like the Japanese, the Chinese take great pride in their culture and consider themselves so unique that they presume that no foreigner can truly understand them.

Chinese behaviors and attitudes are shaped by a unique set of core values that differ substantially from ours. Hofstede's research did not extend to mainland China. However, we can infer something of Chinese values from commonalities among Hofstede's findings for Hong Kong, Taiwan, and the expatriate "overseas" Chinese of Singapore (not a Chinese culture per se, but heavily influenced, particularly in business, by Chinese expatriates), keeping in mind that these Chinese are essentially free of Communist influence and, in Singapore and Hong Kong, have been subject to extended British influence. Hofstede found all three countries highly collectivist, despite their strong commitment to capitalism, and moderately high in power distance. Direct observations of Chinese behavior by Hu and Grove (1991) confirm these findings and add maintenance of intragroup harmony and its corollary, avoidance of overt conflict, as a third key value. The greatest deviation in Hofstede's findings was in uncertainty avoidance, for which Taiwan ranked somewhat on the high side, whereas Hong Kong and Singapore were quite low, perhaps due to prolonged British influence. Taiwan thus may be more representative of mainland China on this dimension, but its aversion to uncertainty may also reflect a sense of isolation and military insecurity. Taiwan and Singapore fell slightly to the feminine side, perhaps reflecting the centrality of family in Chinese culture, whereas Hong Kong took a more masculine posture, very much in keeping with its reputation for aggressive entrepreneurship.

Trompenaars found that the Chinese tend to (a) view an organization more as a means of clarifying roles than performing functions, (b) prefer the leader to act more as a father figure than a task driver, (c) be flexible and comfortable with respect to change and deadlines, (d) be strongly oriented toward the past, (e) prefer form to substance, (f) believe most strongly, along with the former East Germany, in an external locus of control, (g) assign status more through achievement than ascription, (h) believe that an enterprise ought to care for its members in a paternalistic way, (i) take a diffuse, holistic view of work, life, and relationships rather than a narrow, analytical, specific view, and (j) take a very particularistic view of ethical standards. His findings for Singapore and Hong Kong were quite similar.

THE CULTURAL SETTING

The vast steppes of central Asia and rugged mountain ranges in central and western China separate her from Europe, the Indian Subcontinent, and the Middle East. Though not as geographically isolated as Japan, China's relative inaccessibility, self-sufficiency in resources, and dominance of her much smaller neighbors have allowed a unique culture to remain largely free of foreign influence. The major exception was the introduction of Buddhism by missionaries and perhaps Chinese envoys to India in the first century A.D. Periodic intrusions into northern China by Mongols, including periods of occupation and outright rule, may have altered the Chinese character somewhat with infusions of the stoic discipline and ferocity of those aggressive warriors. With the exception of the transition from feudalism to imperial rule in the third century B.C., China's history was essentially linear until encountering Western colonialism and Japanese imperialism in the nineteenth century, and World War and Communism in the twentieth. The Han, the principal Chinese tribe, has occupied its lands longer than any other known tribe (Laaksonen, 1988). With a government and culture established well before the Roman Empire, the Chinese have long thought of themselves as the center of the world, the Middle Kingdom, and it is not much of a leap to argue that all the cultures of East Asia are but variations of China's. The contiguous and nearby peoples of Southeast Asia, Korea, Mongolia, Manchuria, and Japan have drawn much more from Chinese culture than they have given. The nearby Mongols and Manchus each achieved temporary hegemony over China but eventually found themselves absorbed by it. Japan occupied much of China during World War II and defeated China in a battle over Korea several centuries earlier but, as we have seen, adopted much of China's culture as her own.

China is the world's most populous country and, despite its immense physical dimensions, has long been very densely populated because so much of its land is mountainous. Ninety percent of the population lives in the eastern third of the country. The cultivation of grain—wheat, millet, and sorghum in the north; rice in the south—has occupied the vast majority of Chinese throughout its history. Unlike Japan, China is largely self-sufficient in most resources including energy and basic minerals. Strong ties to the land, and its limited supply relative to the large population, the extent of east-west-oriented mountain ranges and major rivers, and economic backwardness have limited the mobility of China's people. Trade and commerce arose primarily in the south due to a milder climate, the accessibility of ports such as Shanghai and Canton (Guangdong in current usage) serving inland river navigation, and freedom from the rigors of continual conflict with the Mongols along the northern frontier and construction of the Great Wall.

The family has always been the primary economic and social unit, and family roots in the soil and the clan's home village still remain an important source of individual identity, even for modern city dwellers and factory workers. The typical Chinese is the peasant who answers first and foremost to the patriarchal family and clan that farms their typically rented land collectively. Sharing within extended families is the normal sense of property ownership. Nonagricultural enterprises, even large ones, are usually based on the family unit as well, and thus tend to be somewhat simple in organization and scope, even if quite large. The diversified company or even an extended product line is not the Chinese way.

HISTORICAL FORCES

Life for ordinary Chinese peasants, historically some 90 percent of the population, has remained basically unchanged since antiquity. It consists largely of farming the family leasehold, often rented from the communally-owned land of the clan; a bare-subsistence standard of living; frequent hardship both natural and man-made; strict obedience to the patriarchal family, clan, and state; and frequent conscription to fight in wars of feudal rivalry, imperial conquest and consolidation, rebellion against one imperial dynasty or another, and defense against foreign invaders, most often the Mongols. Droughts caused by hot, dry winds blowing in from the Mongolian plains, recurring plagues of disease and locusts, and floods caused by tropical rains and destruction of levees as a military tactic brought frequent famine. The combined effects of natural hardship and warfare kept life expectancy below thirty even as China entered the twentieth century. Even as change accelerated beginning with exposure to the West in recent centuries, and in the face of major upheavals in the twentieth century, most Chinese were relatively unaffected. China is unique among the world's major cultures in the longevity and uninterrupted constancy of its history. Consider the continuity of Chinese history relative to the tumult of European history, an area of roughly equal size (LaTourette, 1964).

China emerged as a nation through the violent consolidation of a highly fragmented feudal system in the most densely populated regions under the Ch'in, the first of China's imperial dynasties, in the third century B.C. Consolidation of remaining outlying regions was essentially completed under the Han dynasty, which ruled from the third century B.C. into the third century A.D. The imperial system persisted fundamentally unchanged in practice through various dynasties, sometimes replaced peacefully, more often violently, until the establishment of a republic under Western-educated Sun Yat-Sen, leader of the nationalist Kuomintang Party (Guomindong) in 1912. The Republic had little opportunity to impact China due to the immediate onset of World War I, followed shortly thereafter and in rapid succession by invasion and occupation by Japan, World War II, and the civil war between the Nationalists and Communists that culminated in the triumph of Communism in 1949. Change in China since 1949, such as it is, is more a matter of very current events than of history.

Confucianism

The feudal period is remarkable primarily for the life of Confucius, during the sixth century B.C., who certainly belongs among the highest rank of the most influential people ever to walk this planet. Confucius regarded himself primarily as a scholar and teacher, though others have come to consider him a philosopher and ethicist and an administrative theorist of the first order. His primary purpose was to find a way to bring order out of the chaos of the feudal system that had dominated China from prehistoric times. As noted in our discussion of Japan, his most fundamental belief was in the principle of filial piety. He believed that an orderly society required peace and harmony, which, in turn, depended ultimately on the absolute right of parents, especially the father, to exert total control over and to expect total obedience and respect from their children in return for paternal benevolence and teaching of virtue and proper behavior, which would continue until the children's marriage. At that point husbands would assume, at least ostensibly, the same kind of power over their wives. By extension, all relationships among people could be structured along hierarchical lines based on age, gender, and learning. Confucius believed that human beings were born good and required only proper teaching to remain so. Education in proper behavior was thus thought to be man's highest calling, the bedrock of an orderly society, and the first obligation of government and family. Those most worthy of respect and authority were those who exhibited virtue and who had acquired sufficient wisdom and experience to teach proper behavior to the young.

Confucius's basic concept of virtue was *jen,* or humanity, manifested in sincerity and in the "golden rule" of treating others only as one would wish to be treated, and *i* or righteousness, construed by Confucius as meaning propriety, duty, a sense of obligation, rather than the Western meaning of conformance to some absolute moral standard. Proper behavior demonstrated healthy respect for age and learning and a sense of decorum; conduct that promotes harmony and avoids even an appearance of potential conflict or embarrassment. Proper behavior was predictable behavior, the result of conforming to formal ritual and ceremony. Its roots lie in a strict hierarchy within the family based first on age and second on generation. Accordingly, the father (or grandfather if living) would exercise literal life-and-death power over children, and his word was law. Day-to-day administration of family affairs was normally the responsibility of the eldest adult male sibling of active, working age. Responsibility for the family's work was distributed through a functional division of labor. Younger siblings would address older siblings using such honorifics as "esteemed elder brother." Indeed, given names in China often reflect the child's standing in the family hierarchy. Confucius considered the family to be the basic building block of society. If families would conduct themselves properly and teach proper behavior to their fundamentally good children, he taught, then an orderly society must follow. An indicator of the importance of family ties, and the primacy of family over individual, is the practice of using the family name first, as in *Sun* Yat-sen. (It is becoming more common today for Chinese to change to the Western practice, causing some confusion. If in doubt, remember that the family name is normally only one syllable and that there are relatively few of them. Any hyphenated name normally is a given name. This applies to Korean names as well.)

The basic purpose of marriage was procreation not romantic fulfillment, and marriages were arranged (and desirable spouses sometimes paid for) by elders. Female children often were considered a burden, and infanticide was not rare. There was intense solidarity within the family, and it was the ultimate refuge and source of security. As an example, Bodde (1957) cites the great fire that nearly destroyed Hong Kong in 1842, after which all survivors were cared for by kin, not by any governmental or charitable agency. Fulfilling obligations to one's family was always the primary duty. The potential loss of face for the entire family was an enormous deterrent to individual wrongdoing. Under the Confucian system, magistrates would hold accountable an entire family for the conduct and debts of any of its members. The tradition of commercial integrity of Chinese businesses, typically organized around a family, has its roots here. The Communists would try mightily to break down the family system, substituting loyalty to state and party for filial piety, with little discernible success. They had more success with women, who often were badly suppressed and mistreated by Confucian thinking and practice. A very entertaining and insightful portrayal of Chinese family life and Confucian values is Pearl Buck's classic novel *The Good Earth*.

To Confucius, society was analogous to the family and the ruler to the father and should also then be arranged in a hierarchy. Scholars, from whose ranks rulers ought to emerge, occupied the highest rung followed by farmers or peasants, workers or artisans, and last, the merchants. There was no room for nobility, military, or clergy. The people owed loyalty and obedience to the ruler, who should be the wisest and ablest among men, who must reciprocate with paternalistic benevolence in the exercise of authority and demonstrate by example virtue and proper behavior. The authority to rule was moral, not force, heredity, or wealth, a function of *jen* and learning, the kind and degree of learning necessary to acquire wisdom and to appreciate the wisdom of benevolence.

The most learned were thus deemed the most fit to rule. The conflict with feudal views of authority is clear, but Confucius believed that governance was too important to be left to accidents of birth, that power ought to be exercised by nontitled scholars appointed by the worthy monarch on merit. He accepted the inevitability of hereditary accession to power only grudgingly, taking relief in his belief that the ruler's instruments of power would be learned officials rising to authority by virtue of demonstrated achievement and benevolence. The emperor, the Son of Heaven (but, unlike Japan, not considered divine), represented and drew his authority from the will of Heaven, a kind of collective wisdom of the revered ancestors, especially family founders, who resided there. Should the ruler fall short of rigid standards of virtue and benevolence, Heaven was expected to indicate its displeasure through a signal such as some natural disaster. In such circumstances, according to Mencius, the most influential of Confucius's disciples, the people had the right to rise up and replace the emperor. Meanwhile, according to Mencius, it was the proper role of the learned to lead and for the uneducated to feed and sustain them. The best leaders were thought to be placid, modest, reserved, and self-controlled. Passion was thought to be the source of conflict and ought to be contained. Accordingly, Confucius thought that rigid training was necessary to overcome the overindulgence of children by their families. The most effective instrument of leadership was example, not fear of punishment, and shame was the most effective control device. The extension of familial respect into society is seen when Chinese address non-family members as "brother" or "sister" and older strangers as "aunt" or "uncle." So certain was Confucius of the power of example that he believed that the demonstration of virtue by the ruler was powerful enough not only to establish internal tranquility but to pacify external enemies as well.

Another important element of Confucian thinking is the Doctrine of the Golden Mean (from the classic *The Mean*), which teaches the worthiness of moderation, of balance, of avoiding extremes. Implicit in this doctrine is the suggestion that being reasonable is more important than reason, that practical compromises are more useful than elegant theories, resolute principle, and excesses of logic. To believe and behave otherwise would be disharmonious and not in keeping with the inherent flexibility of Chinese cosmology (discussed later). This doctrine also embodies Confucian disdain for science. Confucian humanism and concern with relationships and welfare left little room for more-mundane matters like scientific inquiry, technology, and commerce.

Although it may be tempting to compare the benevolent and righteous Confucius with Pericles, Rousseau, and Jefferson, he and his followers were no democrats. Notions such as individual rights and due process did not enter their lexicon and remain foreign concepts to most Chinese. There are no linguistic equivalents to the terms freedom, individual, or even privacy in classical Chinese. Duty and harmony are the organizing principles of Chinese society. In essence Confucius envisioned an orderly, harmonious society based on a strict hierarchical, reciprocal relationship in which loyalty and obedience flowed upward and paternalistic benevolence flowed downward. Within these parameters, all citizens had the right of education and self-improvement, however, with equality of opportunity afforded, at least in theory, by the civil service examination system. Of course the wealthy had more time to prepare and could hire tutors, and nepotism was common as obligations to family superseded all others. Standards and law were a matter of local practice, tradition, and custom as interpreted by officials and heads of clans and guilds according to principles of equity, reflecting the view of government as an extension of the family.

Confucius accomplished little during his lifetime by way of implementing his theories. He wandered from one feudal court to another seeking acceptance of his ideas with little success. Much of the remainder of his time he devoted to teaching disciples who recorded his teachings, elaborated upon them, and disseminated them throughout China (and eventually throughout

East and Southeast Asia). Several centuries passed before Confucius's ideas reached full acceptance during the enlightened Han dynasty. These generally benevolent but always politically astute rulers were eager to seize upon a philosophy that legitimized their rule. Once established, these ideas acquired the strength of a national creed. A people beset by tyranny and the fallout from political intrigue, disorder caused by frequent warfare and disaster and overcrowding were hungry for a system that offered to bring about stability, tranquility and righteousness. Confucius's teachings, recorded as aphorisms and snippets of dialogue in *The Analects* and in the works of principal disciples, would come to be memorized by schoolchildren, much like the sayings in Benjamin Franklin's *Poor Richard's Almanack*. They would become the primary subject matter for universities, beginning under the Han, a civil service training academy, and a system of examinations for prospective civil servants to assess their fitness for service as public officials.

Confucius's vision of government eventually was realized in an elaborate bureaucracy of ministries replete with nine levels of officials, chiefs of staff and cabinet meetings, line and staff organizations, plans (Sun Tzu was a contemporary of Confucius), policies, codes and procedures—all managed by highly trained professionals who had demonstrated their merit-based qualifications to exercise authority in these highly competitive examinations. Their primary duties were to maintain order and to promote the well-being of the people, which Confucius had recognized as essential to maintaining order and harmony. Nevertheless, there was at least as much concern for form as substance in their labors. (Confucius might well have been quite comfortable in contemporary Washington, Paris, London, or Tokyo!) The system proliferated through provinces and prefectures down to the local level, where family patriarchs served as advisors and local officials. Although the benevolence of ensuing dynasties generally failed Confucius's expectations, the bureaucrats went about their work throughout the imperial period. These officials would one day be labeled Mandarins by the Portuguese, apparently from the Latin verb *mandare*, to command (Bodde 1957). Although Confucius imagined these positions to be accessible to all, and many did rise from poverty to high positions, the vast majority of Chinese had long been illiterate and the wealthy thus had a clear advantage. Thus even though merchants ranked at the bottom of Confucius's social hierarchy and were forbidden to hold public office, their children were much more likely to enter civil service than were the children of the more "noble" tillers of the soil. The content of Confucian education was strictly humanistic and ethical. Consistent with ranking merchants at the bottom of the social scale, Confucianists thought education and training in commercial or occupational pursuits a waste of time for the most-talented Chinese and had little interest in the more-mundane, practical matters of life. Indeed it is only in the late twentieth century that the Chinese seem to have recognized that science is something more than superstition and alchemy.

The Mandarins controlled labor and agriculture and coordinated the production and distribution of goods. It was not the Communists who introduced state monopolies, confiscation and redistribution of wealth, forced labor, and price controls to China. These measures have been in the toolkit of Confucian bureaucrats for over two thousand years. When invasion from the north prompted construction of the Great Wall, begun well before the birth of Christ, one result was the debasement of money due to the need for capital and conscription of labor, which tightened the overall supply. As the currency inflated, hoarding of basic commodities began, and great fortunes were built. The Confucian reaction to this disharmonious conduct was to seize control of the commodities salt, iron, copper, and grains; create state monopolies; and impose strict regulation and reprisals upon the miscreant and already lightly-regarded and distrusted merchants.

The Confucian system was much admired by visitors to China such as Arab traders in the first millennium A.D. and Marco Polo and Jesuit and Franciscan missionaries in the second. Marco Polo was especially impressed with the open-mindedness and tolerance of Mongol emperor Kublai Khan, who employed a diversity of people including Muslims and Christians in his thirteenth-century bureaucracy. Confucian ideals of filial piety, obedience and respect for elders, orderliness of hierarchy, benevolence, harmony, and formalized, ritualistic behavior permeated all of Chinese culture. Conceived as a solution to the very worldly problems of disorder and conflict, Confucianism became the only universal system of behavioral norms and ethical standards in China and all of Oriental Asia. As mentioned earlier, this very universality and strong ethical content suggest to some that Confucianism is a religion. In favor of that argument one should consider that if the Chinese were to identify their most ubiquitous religious belief, it is very likely that the most common answer would be the veneration of ancestors. It is left to the reader to make this judgment.

The impact of Confucianism cannot be overstated. It was an enormous force for conservatism as ancient, highly ritualized behaviors, norms, and beliefs are passed on from one generation to another. It produced a highly regimented society where unquestioning obedience can stifle individual expression and creativity among the masses while it establishes as normal an activist and perhaps obtrusive state. The strong anchor in the past and aversion to science, commerce, and economics probably has had much to do with China's technological backwardness and poor standard of living. Certainly its ill effects were intensified by the Communists. Consequently, its goals of tranquility and harmony may well have been achieved, but at a great price in terms of the human spirit and material well-being. Nevertheless, it is easy to see how belief and pride in these fundamentally enlightened and humanistic ideals, first articulated more than two thousand years ago—the longest-lived, continuously sustained system of government, complemented by impressive achievements in the arts and humanities (as they suited the state) and noteworthy contributions to science and commerce, such as the invention of paper—can cause the Chinese to view themselves as the Middle Kingdom and others as barbarians.

Rival Schools of Thought

The violent tumult of the feudal period provoked many to think about how order and tranquility might be achieved. This period eventually came to be known as the time of the "One Hundred Schools of Thought," which calls to mind Mao Zedong's entreaty to "Let a hundred flowers bloom and a hundred schools of thought," although his motive, to lure his enemies into self-incrimination, had the opposite intent. The most significant school was Legalism, which held that people were not born good, and therefore order depended on strict rules and harsh punishment. Rulers, then, must be stern and harsh disciplinarians. The Legalists' primary qualification for leadership was demonstration of military prowess on the battlefield. The care of the people amounted to ensuring that they were tough enough to fight and that they would remain loyal soldiers. Legalism was much more influential than Confucianism during the feudal and very early imperial periods. Indeed it provided the rationale for the imperial consolidation that ended feudalism. As Confucianism gained ground, however, the formal teaching and writings of Legalism dwindled into obscurity. Yet, whether it was because of Legalism or the arrogance that almost inevitably seems to accrue to power anywhere, or a combination of the two, the governance of China has always had a harder edge than Confucius envisioned, often much harder. As one examines China's history, it is difficult to avoid the conclusion that there has been much more loyalty and obedience flowing upward than paternal benevolence flowing downward.

At the opposite extreme was Moism, named for its founder, Mo Tzu, who was repelled by the regimentation and reactionary nature of Confucianism and the waste he saw in elaborate funerals and extended mourning periods attendant to ancestor worship. Instead, he taught, order was a function of the people's universal love and concern for one another. Orderliness based on loyalty to princes and fathers was too restrictive and Taoism too contemplative. Mo Tzu believed that relationships among people ought to be based on indiscriminate, universal love. All that was required for a harmonious society was for people to be left alone so that they could act in accord with their own natural inclinations. This conflicted with the Confucian view that relationships between any two people were contingent upon their relative hierarchical positions. Moism holds that time spent in contemplation and study was wasted and better spent on feeding, housing, and clothing others. Clearly difficult to implement in any significant way, Moism appealed to many emotionally. The Chinese tendency to be good-natured, gregarious, very mild-mannered, peaceful people may be attributable to Moist idealism, but Moism as a formal system of thought faded quite early because the Chinese also tend toward practicality and worldliness. Moist precepts can be discerned, however, in the more-idealistic aspects of Communism.

Exposure to the West

European traders, led by the Portuguese, began visiting China regularly in the sixteenth century. In keeping with the practices of Iberian explorers elsewhere, the Portuguese, unable to accept China's multiple, peacefully coexisting religions, considered the Chinese to be heathens to be converted and little more than savages, and acted accordingly. This did not sit well with the people of the Middle Kingdom who, it will be remembered, thought quite highly of themselves, considered all others to be barbarians and, moreover, were quite satisfied with their own religions. The British, Dutch, and others to follow conducted themselves in much the same manner. The Chinese considered them uncivilized plunderers and pirates. Consequently, like the Japanese, the Chinese confined the Europeans to coastal enclaves and prohibited any interaction except that necessary to conduct business, even refusing to allow Chinese to be taught to any Europeans. This was a significant change as traders from Japan, Arabia, Persia, ancient Greece, and India, among others, had been allowed access to the entire country for many centuries prior to the western Europeans' arrival. They sometimes fought among themselves in China as religious warfare in Europe spilled over into their foreign enclaves, thereby confirming to the Chinese their barbarian nature (not to mention the unworthiness of merchants generally). Nevertheless China, largely self-sufficient economically, benefited greatly from this trade, receiving hard currency, gold, and silver in return for her tea, spices, and silk. Because the Confucian Mandarins benefited as much as anyone, levying a fee on all transactions, they allowed trade with the barbarians to continue. The British, who had achieved the dominant position among the European traders, eventually tired of laying out cash and sought some product they could introduce to China. They chose opium grown in India and began a three-legged trade analogous to the slave trade in the west. The Mandarins objected, and the result was the Opium War of 1839–42.

At this point the Confucian system began to fall apart. The Chinese were defeated soundly by Western military technology, and the British remained, opium and all, until the great upheavals of the twentieth century occupied their attention elsewhere. Further humiliation by Western powers took many forms, and the defeat would be repeated during the Boxer Rebellion.

Ironically, Confucian suspicion of science and the hubris that prevented the Chinese from learning anything from the Europeans had much to do with these defeats, which came about despite China's huge advantage in numbers. More significantly, these same factors, along with the coming isolation of the Cold War, would prevent the Chinese from learning much about industrial technology from the Europeans, Japanese, or Americans until very recently. It became common practice to refer to Caucasians as "foreign devils," and this antipathy may well be the only lasting cultural impact of this initial interaction between China and the West. Worthwhile fictional accounts of this period are the novels of Robert Elegant: *Manchu* deals with the seventeenth century, *Mandarin* the nineteenth, and *Dynasty* the twentieth.

The Nationalists and Communists

Contact with Westerners, especially Christian missionary schools, exposed the Chinese to new ways of thinking about the world. Some industrialization and urbanization was underway at the end of the nineteenth century. Emigration to the West had begun as well, and some mandarins were educated there, most notably Sun Yat-Sen. Sun led a largely peaceful uprising by republican nationalists, the *Guomindong* Party, which ended the last of the imperial dynasties, the Manchus, in 1911–12. Causes included discontent with internal corruption and the humiliation of defeat by Britain in the Opium War and the Boxer Rebellion, resentment against harsh reparations exacted as a result of those conflicts, an increasing Western presence generally, and the loss of Korea for the second time as a result of the Sino-Japanese War of the 1890s. Inherent in this movement was a sense that China, despite all her accomplishments and size, was too weak and too dominated by barbarians, including Westerners and the Japanese, the "devils of the eastern sea," and ought to assert itself. Indicative of this impotency was the Russo-Japanese War of 1904–1905, which was fought primarily in Chinese Manchuria! Moreover, a growing sense of laxity and lack of discipline, thought to be caused largely by external influence, suggested to many a re-emphasis of Confucian values. Sun wanted a government similar to the socialist democracies that would dominate western Europe during most of the twentieth century with a strong Confucian bureaucracy looking after the peoples' economic welfare.

The Communist Party, founded by Mao in 1921, allied itself with the nationalists until Chiang Kai-shek succeeded Sun in 1925. A military man not educated in the west, Chiang was much more interested in nationalism than in republicanism and the welfare of the people. The Communists then broke with the Nationalists, and civil war between the two began shortly thereafter. Nonetheless, they soon found it necessary again to ally themselves against the Japanese invasion of Manchuria, which began in 1931, and eventual occupation of much of China. The civil war resumed immediately upon the end of World War II and ended in Communist victory in 1949 and isolation of the Nationalists on Taiwan (then called Formosa). A highly regimented, collectivist, and secular people, often oppressed and deprived and long accustomed to communal ownership of property and state intervention in the most minute detail, most Chinese found little reason to resist the idealistic promise of Communism (no more landlords or exploitation of peasants, equality for all including women, no opium or prostitution) even if accompanied by totalitarianism. What did not sit so well with the masses was Mao's attempt to supplant filial piety with loyalty to the Party. Confucian values proved too resilient. Communism differed little in its effect on ordinary Chinese from the imperial dynasties. The party meddled in every detail of everyday life—for example, identifying and ridiculing publicly poorly performing employees. Mao's bloody purges and famines induced by his misguided policies accounted for the deaths of more than one hundred million people. For example, during the "Great Leap Forward" when Mao tried to mobilize the entire population to produce steel—every village was to have its own small furnace—the people were forced to leave their lands unattended; the result was an immense famine. Another occurred when Mao decided to mobilize the population to exterminate sparrows, which he believed to be eating too much seed grain, leaving insects free to attack crops without threat from their primary natural foe. Though the political label may be different, Mao's leadership differed little from the most tyrannical of China's emperors in kind and very likely exceeded them in degree. It remains to be seen what lasting impact Communism has on Chinese culture. It seems safe to conclude that it expanded the collectivist horizons of the elite from the family to the state, and that its harsh treatment of its own people prolonged its isolation and retarded further China's industrial and commercial development and full participation in the community of nations. It also may have honed the harder edges of China's rulers and bureaucrats sharpened first by the Legalists and then the Mongols. On the other hand, assuming the end of Communism with the passing of the current generation of leaders, it may well turn out that a mere half-century or so of Communist rule becomes but an insignificant blip in the grand sweep and continuity of Chinese history.

RELIGION

China's Cosmology

Another influential and long-lived product of the feudal period was a common view of the world and how it works. The ancient Chinese came to view nature as an array of opposing but complementary and interdependent forces such as male and female or day and night. Each force was balanced by and needed its complement. For example, there cannot be a high tide in one location without a corresponding low tide in another. These balanced, interrelated, complementary pairs of parts and forces of nature, called *yin* and *yang*, are represented by this familiar symbol shown in the accompanying figure.

Change was thus viewed as cyclical, not linear, as first one force rose and then yielded to its mate, only to rise then yield again, and so on. A corollary to cyclicality was that time had no beginning or end. To the Chinese a fine balance of such primal forces indicated a powerful unity in nature, a harmoniously functioning organism, to which man must concede their destiny and adapt. Man must replicate this harmony, not disrupt it. Recurring famines, plagues of disease or locusts, earthquakes, and typhoons reinforced this belief. Worship of and tribute and sacrifice to ancestors in heaven were in part intended to seek relief from the ravages of nature. These notions, set forth in the ancient classic *I Ching* or *Book of Changes*, are consistent with Confucian striving for order and conservatism in its expectation of continual recurrence of familiar patterns and its aversion to disruption and departure from orthodoxy. Cyclical change and dominance by nature did not accommodate notions such as progress. Subordination of humanity to nature also is consistent with Confucian suspicion and derogation of science.

The Role of Religion

Like Japan, China is a secular society, at least in a Western sense, in that most Chinese do not "belong" to any one faith and there is no monotheistic concept of duty. The Chinese term for religion is *chiao*, which means a system of teaching, not worship, which can be either secular or religious (Bodde 1957). The Chinese feel quite comfortable embracing any of three such systems, or "three paths to one goal," more or less religious depending on one's point of view, that might seem most appropriate for any given need or in any given circumstances. The three systems are Confucianism, for its normative ethical prescriptions; Taoism, for its promise of mystical escape from the rigor and misery of everyday life; and Buddhism, for its promise of a better, more enlightened life in the hereafter. Despite its ethical content, Confucianism is rational rather than spiritual. It seeks order and harmony on earth, not salvation of souls. Taoism seeks health, longevity, and immortality of man, not closeness to a supreme being. Buddhism deals with the hereafter but in terms of making progress toward happiness and enlightenment engendered by overcoming dependence on desires and wants. It calls for an exemplary life but not necessarily a holy or heavenly one. It is common for the Chinese to consider themselves as believers in all three, with perhaps a bit of polytheism and animism added to the mix as well. Again, the only universal and constant religious belief is the veneration of ancestors. One result of this syncretic approach to religion is the open-minded tolerance observed by Marco Polo. Islam, Christianity, Judaism, and many less-prominent faiths all have long and benign histories in China, although Christianity came to symbolize Western colonialism in the last century, thereby arousing some antipathy and suppression. Another is the willingness of the Chinese to believe in or at least accept conflicting ideas, to view questions and issues from various perspectives, and to seek compromise (Fitzgerald 1961).

Taoism

Taoism (pronounced "dowism") is China's principle indigenous religion. Tao, or "the way" (notice the similarity between "dow" and the Japanese suffix "-do" that has the same meaning, as in Bushido, the way of the warrior), seeks long and enlightened life and earthly immortality. Whereas Confucianism focuses on human relationships, Taoism's focus is on the relationship between man and nature. Consistent with China's cosmology, nature is a given, not for meddling by man and disturbances in nature are a consequence of humanity's failures. Chinese art represents the beauty of nature free of man's intervention or even presence. There are no still-life compositions of arranged fruit or flowers in Chinese painting; they are portrayed only in their natural state.

We already know from our discussion of Japan that Confucius made no pretense of theological wisdom. He asked in the *Analects*, "We do not know yet about life, how can we know about death?" and "How can we know how to serve the spirits when we still do not know how to serve man?" As Confucianism took on the character of state orthodoxy, its omission of spiritual content and rigorous regulation of behavior left a void in the Chinese soul. Taoism calls for a departure from the pragmatic concerns and drudgery of everyday life and the substitution of simplicity, inaction, and noninvolvement. It thus offered an alternative to the structure and worldliness of Confucianism and became the religion of the masses until the arrival of Buddhism. It not only accommodated man's spiritual inclinations but added bits of spirit, paradox, mysticism, whimsy, and freedom of individual expression to an otherwise drab, highly conformist existence. The highest praise an artist could expect from a Confucianist was to recognize the fidelity of a copy of an ancient classic, not the creation of a new work (Fitzgerald 1961). The pursuit of immortality generated a kind of alchemy in search of an elixir that would provide everlasting life. The educated and worldly Confucianists considered Taoism as gross superstition suitable only for the uneducated and simple-minded, an unorthodox, popular cult. As far as the elite were concerned, Taoist attempts at medicine gave all science a bad name. Consequently, many of China's technological innovations including gunpowder, developed for ceremonial purposes, and the magnetic compass, used for laying out graveyards, were the work of Taoist priests (Fitzgerald 1961). The Taoists saw little need for a leader but would expect a leader to be passive and quiet; to minimize strife; to minimize meddling in peoples' lives; to avoid warfare, material pursuits, or any act that would impose complications. Simplicity was the ultimate ideal. Simplicity would in turn foster unity and equality, whereas too much knowledge would make people ungovernable.

Buddhism

The only significant foreign force shaping China's culture arrived in the first century B.C. and, as in Japan, was adapted to China's practical, secular leanings. It had spread throughout China and to all levels of society by the fifth century. The essentially secular Chinese had strong reasons to resist Buddhism, including its asceticism and mendicancy (foreign to Confucian humanism, order, and propriety), advocacy of celibacy (which threatens the basic building block of Chinese society, the family), and its disdain for ancestor worship. It had an enormous appeal nonetheless because, unlike Confucianism (which benefited only the elite), or Taoism (an unaffordable luxury for most), Buddhism offered the promise of relief from the meager existence and misery of everyday life so familiar to the vast majority of Chinese. This was particularly so for the more inclusive, optimistic *Mahayana* interpretation of Buddhism that predominated in China, Korea, Japan, and Vietnam. Its appeal lay in Buddhism's four fundamental truths:

1. Life is pain.
2. Pain is the result of desire.
3. Relief from pain could come only with the end of desire, thus reaching *nirvana*.
4. The end of desire depends upon disciplined and moral conduct, culminating in a life of concentration and meditation.

Buddha prescribed an eightfold path to a disciplined and moral life (see the discussion of Buddhism in chapter six) that, to the ordinary Chinese whose life was indeed filled with pain, offered a way out, a source of hope, and a sense of some control. Buddha demanded not worship or prayer but allowed each person to work out his or her own path to nirvana. Buddhism thus encouraged introspection and accommodated some individual flexibility, but considered ideas of self and ego and soul as transient and meaningless (LaTourette 1964).

CORE VALUES AND BEHAVIOR

Hierarchy and Power Distance

The dominance of Confucian hierarchy and traditional, ritual behavior explains Hofstede's findings of large power distance in the various expatriate Chinese populations, even as moderated by Western influences, and Trompenaars's findings regarding the preferences for role clarification and structure, paternalism, status through achievement, form over substance, and a strong orientation toward the past.

Living one's assigned role in the family and social hierarchy is the essence of Chinese culture. There is greater expectation of top-down direction and less involvement of subordinates than in Japan, as exemplified by the life-and-death power of the patriarch who demands lifelong obedience and loyalty. The manager holds much the same authority. Like the Japanese, the Chinese will not challenge superiors publicly but, unlike the Japanese, may be unwilling to do so privately as well. Rank in the hierarchy depends on age, a proxy for wisdom, which the Chinese see as a product of learning, in contrast to the Japanese who see wisdom as a product of experience. Although feudal, imperial, and Communist governments seldom have met the Confucian ideal, the exchange on an individual level of obedience and loyalty for paternal benevolence tends to be asymmetrical in favor of the weaker party. Just as Chinese parents tend to dote excessively on their children, the weaker party in any relationship expects a disproportionately large benefit. This is why negotiators for Chinese enterprises (or for China!) feel free to ask for large concessions from more-technologically-advanced or financially stronger firms. They will use shaming tactics to coerce the "stronger" party into such concessions.

All the usual trappings of a highly autocratic management style—close supervision, tight controls, explicit direction, high formality—are the norm. Much like the clan, Chinese enterprises organize themselves very simply, by function with highly centralized, top-down decision-making authority and vertical information flows. Managers tend to value loyalty more than objective contributions, and disagreement with the boss, at least publicly, is to be avoided. Information is held closely and shared only when necessary to teach or make a point to subordinates (Chen 1995).

Collectivism

Western demands upon China to improve individual rights fall not upon deaf ears but uncomprehending minds. It is with one's duties to others, not one's rights, that one should concern oneself. Among the very last of major nations to industrialize, collectivism has persisted much longer and on a greater scale in China than elsewhere. This does not mean that the individual Chinese lacks a sense of personal dignity and worth, but that those feelings are measured in terms of fulfilling one's role in the family and the broader Confucian hierarchy. The forces for collectivism in China have been very powerful. As is the case in all agrarian, subsistence economies, especially those in which rice is important, the Chinese had to cooperate to survive. Tao demanded submission to the natural and spiritual forces that provided or denied sustenance. Confucius taught that the individual is deeply subordinate to the family and to society. Consequently, individual behavior was regulated in great detail by ancient ritual, the state, the family, and the individual's need to save face. Even Chinese theater is essentially didactic. The pressure to conform is intense. Buddhism does not accommodate pursuit of personal ambition and desires, denies individual identity, and minimizes any enduring sense of self. Even Sun Yat-Sen was suspicious of individual liberty, being more concerned with developing a sense of national unity. Whatever individualism may have been emerging with contact with the West the Communists worked very hard to suppress.

Consequently, the Chinese are social beings, very inclined to be socially and psychologically dependent on others. Decision-making is by consensus within hierarchical levels, and responsibility is diffused, untraceable to any one individual. The family remains at the center of life throughout one's lifetime and the ultimate source of security, comfort, and meaning. We have seen that it is China's primary social and economic unit, but through its responsibility for education of youngsters and care of elders, and worship of ancestors, the family also forms the basic unit of moral authority and religion as well. There is no graver insult or curse in China than that directed toward one's lineage and descendants. Senior positions in Chinese family businesses normally are filled by family members or long-time friends. Expert power is seen as a threat to such relationships and may be avoided. Relationships and feelings are more-important decision criteria than objective information (Chen 1995). Other groups such as craft guilds and various secret societies have long been important parts of Chinese life. Nepotism is not unusual. Local government is essentially a family and clan matter. There is little privacy in dwellings accommodating extended families. Indeed, there is no direct translation; the closest Chinese equivalents of the term "privacy" mean loneliness or even something secretive or sinister.

Chinese collectivism differs from the Japanese in the scope of the collective unit. For the Chinese the primary collective is the family and its extensions into the clan and native village. Japanese collectivism encompasses the nation and the company as well as the family, and pretty much in that descending order of priority. This explains why Trompenaars found that the Chinese view an organization as a practical instrument, whereas the Japanese take the opposite view of the organization primarily as a social structure. Even though China has long had a sense of cultural identity and continuity, its sense of national identity is weaker than Japan's. Chinese enterprises remain centered on the family; those that are not are often run like families. Larger enterprises come under the aegis of the state, at least for the time being.

It is appropriate to note at this point, after observing high power distance and strong collectivism in both China and Japan, that coincidence between the two is the typical case. Cause and effect are difficult to establish, however. The individualist westerner might argue that there must be an unequal distribution of power in order to force people to act collectively, which they might otherwise resist. The typical collectivist might argue that a group of people requires strong direction, and that power is of practical benefit to the group and a suitable reward when an individual demonstrates a willingness and ability to work harmoniously and effectively for the collective good. We will also usually find harmony and collectivism coinciding for the simple reason that it seldom escapes people for long that if they are going to work together, they need to do so harmoniously.

Harmony, Face, and *Guanxi*

A large component of the Chinese conception of merit is the ability to maintain harmonious relationships. Research by Sally Stewart and Chang Chung Him (in Shenkar 1991, 57–68) found that 42 percent of successful Chinese managers identified this ability as the primary determinant of their success. Less often mentioned were, in descending order, education, hard work, luck, risk-taking and commitment, professional competence, loyalty and seniority, and aggressiveness. Harmony was Confucius's ultimate objective. In crowded living conditions, harmony takes on even more importance. People who expect and need to participate and function effectively in groups must behave with decorum and in accordance with group norms. Compliance with one's hierarchical roles is essential to maintaining harmony. The ritual behavior so important to Confucius long ago took on the form of an elaborate system of etiquette governing all facets of human interaction that persists today. For example, it is customary to escort a visitor to the door or even the bus stop upon the visitor's departure. Another is to recognize that an invitation to another cup of tea usually means that a meeting is over and one should soon be on one's way (one's cup would normally be filled without asking while the meeting is underway). The subtlety of such signals would certainly cause them to be missed by the unprepared. The customary use of "go-betweens" or intermediaries is a means by which the Chinese avoids such potentially embarrassing situations. Recognizing that (probably uncivilized!) foreigners are unlikely to know such rules, and wishing to avoid creating a situation that will cause a loss of face, even if not recognized as such by the face-losing westerner, the Chinese simply avoids encounters with strangers, especially foreigners.

These rules or *li,* the precedent for Japanese *kata,* are intended to maintain harmony. Familiarity with and practice of *li* are essential to convey one's civility. Failure to do by Western visitors was one major reason why they were considered barbarians. Failure to conform to *li* constitutes loss of face, which is similar to our sense of dignity but is more serious because conformity to ritual is so central to Chinese culture. This form of face, complying with *li* and with one's proper hierarchical role, is called *lian.* One example of *li* that Western businesspeople often violate unknowingly is to speak in ways seen as immodest. One does not boast or promote oneself or one's product. The Chinese go to great lengths to convey a sense of modesty and humility, and a visitor should do the same. For instance, when being offered a seat of honor next to the host, one must refuse graciously several times before finally accepting reluctantly and humbly. Wait until asked before providing information about one's product or company. They will ask when they want to know and, rest assured, they will! Anger, impatience, or any other manifestation of unpleasantness or conflict will always cause loss of face. Instead be persistent.

Out of a sense of cultural and, more recently, national pride, the Chinese very much want access to the best and are willing to pay for it. Likewise, they prefer access to negotiators with sufficient rank to make commitments for their organizations (even though the Chinese counterpart may not be able to do so!). Equivalent rank is essential.

The second form of face is *mianzi,* which is a measure of prestige or status, of skill, knowledge, success, or wealth. *Lian* is a measure of personal reputation or standing, whereas *mianzi* represents professional reputation or standing. Its source can be personal achievement, political power, or bureaucratic position. Efforts to maintain *mianzi* explain the inclination to diffuse decision-making responsibility and avoidance of situations where a mistake will become a public embarrassment. If one is trying to elicit participation by a Chinese student or employee that one does not know well, one is working against both forms of face-saving. Aggressive, praiseworthy participation can cause loss of *lian,* for immodesty, and a mistake or bad idea causes loss of *mianzi;* together a very strong incentive for remaining silent! In such situations it is best to solicit input privately.

Worse than a loss of face is to act in a way that causes another to lose face. Criticism, even if indirect, and any conversational topic in any way likely to be controversial must be avoided because of the discomfort involved for the Chinese in not knowing how to respond to such unfamiliar behavior. The person who creates such a situation loses more face than the ostensible "victim" by revealing the ignorance of the uncivilized. Personal questions (other than the well-being of children), off-color humor, touching other than shaking hands, and even a hint of immodesty are to be avoided. The Chinese may react to such topics with a grin that looks oddly insincere. This grin is an expression of nervous distress and anxiety about how to behave and respond in such an awkward situation, and it expresses a form of resentment at being placed into it. The compelling need to avoid causing loss of face accounts in part for the indirectness and moderation of Chinese speech. On the other hand, moderated praise of another *gives* face to both parties.

The desire to avoid losing or causing loss of face, combined with hierarchical deference, causes the Chinese to speak sparingly, indirectly, and self-effacingly, even to the point of clearly false modesty. Yet face-to-face contact is much preferred to impersonal written or telephone communications that are difficult for a number of reasons. The symbols of the alphabet are graphical representations of concrete objects. For example, if a certain stroke signifies a tree, two such strokes would mean a forest and three would signify a jungle or some other variety of lush foliage. Such an alphabet is quite limited, and written Chinese is, therefore, very concise; a Chinese translation of an English document might be half the length. This sparse language does not lend itself well to precision or abstraction. The lack of mobility in China has produced a proliferation of dialects, further limiting the utility of written documents and limiting speech to a subset of commonalities. Hence there is an inherent bias toward minimalist, and imprecise, speech (Bodde 1957).

An important practice familiar to those who have done business in China is *guanxi*. One's *guanxi* is a network of enduring relationships, very similar to the Japanese practice of *jinmyaku,* which ensures one of continuing access to assistance and to scarce goods, reflecting not only the need for harmony and familiarity but the lack of geographical mobility. *Guanxi* relationships involve mutual dependence and, unlike *jinmyaku,* have an emotional content as well as a practical one, although the latter usually is more important. These relationships are preserved through the accumulation of mutual, reciprocal obligations known as *renqing* (Chen 1995), similar to the Japanese notion of *giri.* The Chinese thus would prefer to do business not only with someone familiar (and thus known to be "civilized") but with a friend. Like the Japanese the Chinese envision any negotiation as part of a continuing, long-term relationship. Hu and Grove (1991) suggest that westerners be alert to a Chinese presumption that they are part of a *guanxi* network in their home country and therefore are also presumed to be in a position to pull whatever strings are necessary to meet Chinese demands. The Chinese see contracts as indicators of favorable intent and commitment to shared benefit and thus prefer them to be brief, general, and subject to change. In effect, the *guanxi* system serves as a substitute for a formal legal system as the primary regulator of Chinese business relationships. Out of obligation to their superiors and to Chinese people generally and, as is usually the case when negotiating with Western companies, because they see themselves as in the learning or child part of the asymmetrical, parental relationship, Chinese negotiators appear very demanding.

At the same time, their flexibility and desire for continuing relationships cause them to seek win-win outcomes. However, this desirable end does not preclude such tactical ploys as overwhelming flattery or shaming. The very high illiteracy rate, persistent at about 90 percent, made a network of personal contacts among ordinary Chinese all the more important. The significance of *guanxi* should not be underestimated. It not only controls access to Chinese contacts and lubricates business transactions, but it also serves as a substitute for law and contracts as a regulator of business behavior. Law may be nonexistent and contracts vague, but a businessperson in China must not violate obligations established within the network of *guanxi* relationships.

Finally, the more comprehensive Japanese emotion of *amae*, a more generalized need for affection, does not seem to be important to the Chinese, reflecting the harder edge of Chinese hierarchy and more-limited horizons of its collectivism.

Fatalism, Submission to Nature, and High Uncertainty Avoidance

The Chinese unfailingly attribute unforeseen or uncontrollable outcomes to *joss* or fortune, either good or bad, and enjoy games of chance. Consistent with the cosmology of yin and yang, Taoist teaching, and agricultural roots, reinforced by many visitations of disaster, the Chinese sense their fates to be highly controlled by nature and the continuous oscillation of cyclical forces. Their Confucian countenances face the past. Decisions are driven by precedent and the merit of all things, behavior and ideas judged by comparison with the past. The future and nature will unfold as they will; hence Trompenaars's findings of strong external attribution and a highly diffuse view of the world and relationships. Events are the results of forces much greater than man and it is not man's place to interfere. Obstacles are to be avoided not overcome; problems are to be worked around not solved. At the same time, the unity of nature and its interrelatedness manifested in the regular ebb and flow of its forces will maintain order. Man (and his contracts and commitments!) must therefore be flexible. The combined effects of natural order and Confucian ritual *li* explain China's high uncertainty avoidance, at least as observed in its Taiwanese wing. Work is an important but not central part of life. Unlike the Japanese who separate work and family, the Chinese believe that they are one and the same.

Particularism

As was the case in Japan, the lack of ethical content and absolute standards in China's primary religions and the need to maintain harmonious relationships lend a particularist cast to Chinese ethics. Highly pragmatic, the Chinese conduct themselves in ways that best serve each of their particular relationships and *guanxi* obligations. Therefore, like the Japanese, they find it difficult to respond to calls to comply with absolute standards and abstractions like "fairness." The one major exception of course is filial loyalty and reverence for ancestors. This universalist standard, because it is embraced throughout East Asia, is perhaps the primary claim of Confucianism as a religion, that is, more for the scale of its impact than the scope of its ethical teachings.

CONVERGENCE?

It seems reasonable that any convergence between Western and Chinese values and behavior, problematic at best considering the gulf between them, would be restrained by strong Confucian conservatism sharpened by the isolation of the Cold War and the repression still dominant in China, even as China strives mightily to join the industrialized world. The momentum of some two billion fairly homogenous people moving in the same direction largely free of external influences for five thousand years and ruled more often than not and until quite lately by tyrants, is a formidable force not easily swayed from its path. Some recent, significant empirical research bears out that conclusion (Ralston et al. 1993). Even our very capitalistic and more or less democratic friends in Taiwan, Singapore, Hong Kong, and South Korea—all with deep cultural roots in China but with considerable Western exposure—differ substantially from our values. Though the expatriate Chinese communities throughout Southeast Asia and elsewhere have had much the same kinds of commercial success as their kin in Hong Kong and Taiwan, it should be remembered that these Chinese, having fled to escape one calamity or another, originated in the coastal enclaves of Guangdong and Fujian provinces, those most exposed to Western influence and commercialization. Even in those communities much credit for commercial success is attributed to Confucian emphasis on strong rulers, obedient workers, and hard work and to the ability of family-based businesses to move quickly unencumbered by bureaucracy and external stakeholders. The expatriate Chinese remain the largest source of capital investment in China.

There have been a number of reports of increasing unrest within China's leadership regarding the instability threatened by economic reform. News of muscle flexing toward Taiwan, toward the United States regarding trade barriers, toward democracy in Hong Kong, and of arms sales to Iran and other rogue states all give pause, despite the good-news stories about the ubiquity of cellular phones and Kentucky Fried Chicken in the more commercially vibrant but still quite small entrepreneurial enclaves in coastal cities. Only a tiny proportion of China's population has participated in this development, and China remains a thoroughly underdeveloped country by Western standards. The immense size of this market will of course continue to draw attention, and good relationships will continue to develop at the level of the individual firm, but these relationships will be largely of an arm's-length nature—all the more reason to study China and learn her values and behaviors. The effort will not be wasted either in usefulness of the knowledge gained or its useful life.

SUMMARY

The primary forces that shaped Chinese culture include the following:

- Attachment to family grounded in agricultural roots and immobility
- Hardship, natural and human imposed
- Confucian filial loyalty, veneration of ancestors, paternalism, authoritarianism, order, and sense of duty
- Confucian emphasis on learning and merit
- Confucian balance and moderation and preference for what is reasonable over reason
- Confucian distrust of science and commercialism
- Submission to nature and a cyclical view of change
- Taoist simplicity and passivity
- Buddhist introspection and suppression of individuality

The core values developed by these forces include

- **Large Power Distance**—caused by Confucianism, amplified by Legalism, and continuous political oppression
- **Collectivism**—centered on the family, communal ownership, agricultural roots, need for unity against hardship, immobility, and Buddhist suppression of individualism
- **High Uncertainty Avoidance/Conservatism**—caused by and Confucian insistence upon order, ritual behavior, predictability, and the value of tradition
- **Middling Masculinity**—a balance between Confucian emphasis on achievement and patriarchy on one hand and the importance of maintaining relationships on the other
- **Harmony, Modesty, and Humility**—ultimate objective of Confucianism, essential to collectivism
- **Fatalism**—caused by cosmological subjugation to nature, Tao-

ist teaching, Confucian disdain of science, and powerlessness against millennia of tyranny

- **Passivity, Placidity**—caused by Taoist and Buddhist teachings, Confucian restraint, and oppression
- **Flexibility, Tolerance, Particularist Ethics**—caused by acceptance of cyclical change and perceived unity, the power of nature, the need to maintain harmonious relationships, and Confucian moderation

ADDITIONAL READING

Chinese Management Practices

Chen, Min. 1995. *Asian Management Systems*. (New York: Routledge).

Harris, Philip R., and Robert T. Moran. 1996. *Managing Cultural Differences*, 4th ed. (Houston: Gulf).

Laaksonen, Oiva. 1988. *Management in China during and after Mao in Enterprises, Government and Party*. (Berlin: De Gruyter).

Ralston, David A., David J. Gustafson, Fanny M. Cheung, and Robert H. Terpstra. 1993. "Differences in Managerial Values: A Study of U.S., Hong Kong and PRC Managers." *Journal of International Business Studies* 24(2): 249–275.

Shenkar, Oded, ed. 1991. *Organization and Management in China 1979–1990*. (Armonk, N.Y.: M. E. Sharpe).

Chinese History and Culture

Bodde, Derk. 1957. *China's Cultural Tradition*. (Hinsdale, Ill.: Dryden).

de Bary, Wm. Theodore, Wing-Tsit Chan, and Burton Watson, eds. 1960. *Sources of Chinese Tradition*. (New York: Columbia University Press).

Fairbank, John K., Edwin O. Reischauer, and Albert M. Craig. 1973. *East Asia: Tradition and Transition*. (Boston: Houghton-Mifflin).

Fitzgerald, C. P. 1961. *China*, 3rd ed. (New York: Praeger).

Fung, Kwok Ying. 1943. *China*. (New York: Henry Holt).

Hardon, John A. 1970. *Religions of the Orient*. (Chicago: Loyola University Press).

LaTourette, Scott. 1964. *The Chinese: Their History and Culture*, 4th ed. (New York: Macmillan).

Hu, Wenzhong, and Cornelius L. Grove. 1991. *Encountering the Chinese: A Guide for Americans*. (Yarmouth, Maine: Intercultural Press).

Fiction

Buck, Pearl S. 1931. *The Good Earth*. (New York: John Day). (Printed in paperback: New York: Washington Square Press/Pocket Books, 1973).

Elegant, Robert. 1977. *Dynasty*. (New York: McGraw-Hill).

———. 1980. *Manchu*. (New York: McGraw-Hill).

———. 1983. *Mandarin*. (New York: Simon and Schuster).

Chapter 4

KOREA AND SOUTHEAST ASIA

This chapter covers the remaining major countries of East Asia, including the five "tigers" or NICs, the newly industrializing countries of South Korea, Hong Kong, Taiwan, Singapore, and Thailand; and three potential NICs: Indonesia, the Philippines, and Vietnam.* It is an extension of the preceding chapter in that, as indicated earlier, most of the cultures of East Asia are essentially variations of China's culture. Taiwan and Hong Kong are of course ethnic Chinese. Common threads elsewhere can include Confucianism, Buddhism, Taoism, some degree of political domination by China or a strong Chinese expatriate community. Chapter 2 discussed the influence China had on Japan.

With some important exceptions, as noted later, these cultures share many key characteristics, some with common origins. Whether of Confucian, Buddhist, Hindu, or merely agrarian roots, paternalism and hierarchical structure are universal and, therefore, so is large power distance. The same can be said for femininity, based on the need for harmonious relationships and attendant behaviors such as avoiding assertiveness and loss of face; low-content, indirect communications; and the use of go-betweens. The agrarian family is the cultural building block, and individual interests are subordinated to the collective interest. Uncertainty avoidance tends to be weak because both Buddhism and Hinduism teach that change is normal and inevitable and, as suggested by Hofstede, because of the ability to refer uncertain situations to the family patriarch for resolution. Moreover, the historical absence of elaborate systems of religious or secular law reduces the likelihood of anxiety created by novel situations not covered by law. Flexibility thus becomes the norm. Status is ascribed to heredity or to po-

*While Hong Kong has since reverted to China, it is treated separately here because it has much more in common with the other NICs.

sition earned as a result of good *karma*, that is, a positive balance of worthy behavior in one's present and previous lives. Ethical standards are particularistic because of the need to maintain relationships and an absence of absolute moral truths in Asian religions.

This chapter introduces a new set of cultural dimensions and the first departures from Confucian cultures represented by Thailand, Indonesia, the Philippines, and southern Vietnam. Other non-Confucian cultures in East Asia are Malaysia, Cambodia, Laos, and Myanmar (formerly Burma). The primary difference is that the Confucian culture is a "doing" culture, whereas the non-Confucian is a "being" culture. The former places more importance on tasks relative to maintaining relationships; has a strong internal locus of control and sees nature as at least somewhat controllable; seeks to bring about change actively to conform to some idealized, abstract, improved state; prefers to think analytically, use objective information, and assign status on merit and achievement; tends to view time as linear and a valuable resource to be conserved (that is, efficiency and punctuality are very important); and takes a more compartmentalized, less holistic view of life (that is, work and social relationships or family are kept separate).

"Doing" cultures are more individualist, are more masculine and competitive, and have smaller power distances. Like "being" cultures they tend to be weak in uncertainty avoidance, but not out of submission to fatalism but rather because they are conditioned to bring about change proactively. They want to build a more perfect world rather than enjoy the world as it is. "Doing" people tend to define themselves according to their occupations and measure themselves by their achievements. "Being" cultures tend to be more relaxed, more holistic in their world view, more relationship-oriented (relationships are part of work), more accustomed to yielding power; view time as a continually recurring cycle; feel less able to control their fate; and want work, which at best can be enjoyed and at worst can be tolerated as a necessary evil. "Being" people define themselves by their collective affiliations. They "work to live," whereas their "doing" counterparts "live to work." "Doing" people see "being" people as lazy, unproductive, and irresponsible. "Being" people see "doing" people as cold, compulsive, and unable to enjoy life. The Confucian countries of Asia are not (yet, anyway) "doing" cultures, relative to most Western cultures; but they are so, relative to the non-Confucian, Asian cultures. Exceptions include Japan and the NICs, which exhibit many of the characteristics of both "doing" and "being" cultures. It is probably more accurate to say that large urban areas throughout Asia with a substantial multinational company presence such as Guangzhou, Shanghai, Seoul, Bangkok, and Manila are now more "doing," whereas their rural neighbors are still "being."

The principal determinants of a "doing" culture in East Asia seem to be strong Confucianism, secular and highly prescriptive, and a relatively harsh and threatening environment. "Being" cultures have deeper spiritual roots in the more-flexible and adaptable teachings of Buddhism and Hinduism, and more benign environments.

KOREA

There may be no better indication of Korea's deep roots in China than the appearance of the familiar yin and yang symbol at the center of South Korea's national flag, surrounded by symbols representing their interaction, taken from the *I Ching*. Hofstede found South Korea very similar to Taiwan in power distance and collectivism, both quite high, slightly feminine, and even higher than Taiwan in uncertainty avoidance. Trompenaars found Korea to be the least individualist of all the cultures he studied. These findings are not surprising, because Korea's historical and cultural development parallels China's very closely, lagging in time but more intense in the impact of Confucianism and Buddhism. Ethnically kin to the Mongoloid Manchurians to the north, the Koreans occupy a mountainous peninsula, extending southward between the Sea of Japan to the east and the Yellow Sea to the west. Peninsular isolation, a more rigorous climate, rugged topography, and more-direct exposure to continual conflict with the Manchus have produced a tough and hardy people and somewhat of a garrison state.

The Chinese began to influence their much smaller neighbor early in China's feudal period with periodic efforts to colonize the peninsula. The Koreans have long paid tribute to China to maintain peace, and China has long considered the peninsula to be within its sphere of influence as evidenced by its repeated efforts to block Japanese occupation and its massive intervention in the Korean War. The Koreans borrowed freely from the Chinese political system, Confucian values, and Buddhism; imitated Chinese language, art, and dress; studied Confucian texts; and eschewed merchants and commercialism.

There is a tradition of ancestor worship in Korea, and, as in China, the family is the primary economic and social unit. Mahayana Buddhism became the state religion in the eleventh century for a short time, but Confucianism was reinstated shortly thereafter. The Koreans built a Confucian bureaucracy and civil service but relied more upon a rigid, hereditary class system and nepotism to maintain power. Merit and learning were less important, so political intrigue, factionalism, and oppression were even more common. The landowning gentry (*Yangban*) assumed the mantle of royalty and used the basic relationships of Confucianism to maintain their distance from the commoners. Violation of Confucian ethics was a crime, not just a loss of face (Nahm 1988). Although the Korean state was seen as an extension of the family ruled by educated gentlemen, in the Confucian tradition, the ruling class was more indolent and much more militaristic than the Chinese mandarins, primarily because of constant conflict with the

Manchus and, less frequently, with the Japanese and the Mongols. Education was reserved for the elite. Unlike China, where even the poorest of families might spare a son for government service, commoners in Korea were excluded from the civil service exams (Cumings 1984). The imposition of Confucian regimentation without the compensation of Confucian humanism produced a culture even more conservative and more rooted in the past than China's.

Promising advances in technology and the arts came to an end when a massive invasion by Japan in the late sixteenth century destroyed much of Korea's civilization, institutions, and agriculture, setting back cultural and economic development substantially. Upon the Japanese's departure, the ruling class took advantage of the ensuing chaos to consolidate power and made defense their first priority. Stability was restored, and this was the state that became exposed to Western traders and missionaries in parallel with similar developments in Japan and China. The impact of this exposure was limited by another invasion by Japan and a brutal occupation that began before the turn of the century and lasted until 1945. The Japanese introduced heavy industry to Korea during the 1930s and built a great deal of infrastructure, giving rise to a middle class of technocrats. There has been a continuous and strong American presence from the end of World War II onward. Thus though management practices in Korea are essentially Confucian, they have been influenced by both the Japanese and Americans.

The author had an occasion to observe the nature of the Confucian relationship between a Korean boss and subordinate when visiting the captain of a South Korean merchant ship. A steward came to serve tea. He knocked at the open door, bowed, and asked permission to enter. After entering, he bowed deeply to the captain and the guest individually while carrying a heavy, silver tea service, placed the service on a coffee table, and then bowed again to each of us before *backing* out of the cabin. He did not turn his back until he had stepped out of the cabin, into the adjoining passageway, and out of view.

Leadership is authoritarian; decision-making centralized, top-down, and formal; organizations hierarchical, bureaucratic, and organized by function; and clannish. Subordinates voice disagreement discreetly and only in informal settings. American influence appears in the practice of compensation based on a combination of merit, education level, and seniority and the use of performance incentives. Although seniority remains the primary criterion for promotion, it is not as important as it is in Japan. Koreans do not uniformly promise lifetime employment, and both layoffs and job mobility are much more common than in Japan—further evidence of U.S. influence. The Japanese influence is seen in paternalism, the use of vague job descriptions, the importance of lateral consensus, open office layouts, intense training and indoctrination, the strategic practice of penetration pricing on low-end products then gradually moving upmarket, and *keiretsu*-like combines called *chaebol*. The Japanese treated their Korean employees, or slaves, quite harshly and set an example of strict and demanding authoritarianism. *Chaebol* differs from *keiretsu* in that they are family-dominated rather than professionally managed. Unlike the family-owned business in China however, *chaebol* obviously grow quite large. They also cannot control a bank and tend to form subsidiaries to serve as suppliers rather than building cross-owned networks of firms.

The Koreans value a form of workplace harmony called *inhwa*, a variation of Japanese *wa*, which, however, is more vertical than horizontal—harmony depends upon maintaining the proper relationship between unequals. *Inhwa* signifies mutual dependence between boss and subordinate—loyalty in exchange for managerial concern for employee well-being—and incorporates the Japanese practice of *nemawashi*, that is, seeking the support of subordinates. *Inwha* requires that each participant in the relationship care for the feelings or *kibun* of the other (Chen 1995; Alston 1989). However, the typical Korean interpretation of harmony is obedience upward and firm direction downward, a kind of enforced peace. There is Confucian idealism embodied in this notion, even if more hard-edged, and many Confucian attitudes and practices are evident including filial piety, a strong work ethic, formal behavior, extreme humility and modesty, indirect speech, and avoidance of any behavior that could cause loss of face.

Though the Korean firm is run like a family, the harsh nature of the Korean setting and history seem to have reduced the benevolent paternalism seen in other Confucian cultures to a kind of "tough love" familism. Indeed, a recent article in *The Wall Street Journal* (Biers, Rose, and Schuman 1996) indicated widespread, at least in a geographic sense, employee dissatisfaction with harsh Korean expatriate managers reported in China, Vietnam, Pakistan, Argentina, the United States, and Europe. As in China, the strong sense of familial kinship and internal loyalty can engender a sense of suspicion and even hostility toward outsiders. This applies to the familylike organizations as well. Oh (1991) discusses how narrowly-focused Confucian loyalty prompts Koreans and indeed managers in all NICs to act more individualistically and competitively toward outsiders, to be very tough negotiators, disdaining cooperation and compromise. Organized labor in Korea is limited and quite weak. Unlike the Japanese practice of enterprise unions, Korean unions are industry-based. Women, traditionally secluded, have moved into the work force in large numbers, and the nuclear family unit is becoming more important (Lie 1990; Chen 1995). This history of hardship, foreign domination and isolation, and continuing threat of civil war with the North has produced a very intense Korean form of Confucianism: a population that is close-knit, comfortable with decisive if not authoritarian leadership, and hardworking in the common cause of self-preservation. These circumstances would explain Hofstede's finding of strong uncertainty avoidance for South Korea, a departure from the norm for most countries in East Asia.

North Korea, still beyond the pale of the international community in all respects, remains an enigma. Unlike the Chinese Communists, who tried but failed to supplant Confucianism and the importance of family with loyalty to the party, the North Korean Communists have succeeded. Although Confucian behavior patterns persist, the driving ideology, ostensibly socialist, is one of intensely fierce nationalism, veneration of the party leader, and a spirit of self-reliance and sacrifice called *chuch'e* (BYU Culturgram). As this is written, there are scattered reports of experimental economic reform and liberalization, but these reports are more than offset by those of continued isolation, demagoguery, bombastic threats, national paranoia, and manifest hostility toward apparently all nations but those few still squarely and firmly planted in the remains of the Second World. Nonetheless, as this is written, North Korea has proffered an unprecedented apology to the South for a recent, murderous incursion of spies by submarine.

TAIWAN, HONG KONG, AND SINGAPORE

Despite their popular appellation as "newly industrializing countries," only Singapore is a recognized state. The island of Taiwan, formerly called Formosa, was occupied by the Nationalist Chinese under Chiang Kai-shek after their defeat by the Chinese Communists. Although Taiwan considers itself the Republic of China, few nations recognize it officially, and China considers Taiwan a wayward province. Hong Kong, on the mainland of China eighty miles down the Pearl River from Guangzhou (Canton), was a British Crown Colony first occupied during the Opium War in 1841. It was returned to China in 1997. Singapore, also once a British Crown Colony, is an independent island city-state in the Malacca Strait, connected by a causeway to the tip of the Malay Peninsula. Their populations are overwhelmingly Chinese, and their cultures share strong Confucian roots tempered, as in China, by Buddhism and Taoism. Individuals practice any or all three systems of belief as circumstances may require. Consequently, the traditional Chinese behavioral patterns and attitudes prevail, except where noted in the following discussion.

Taiwan, named *Ihla Formosa* or Beautiful Island by Portuguese explorers in the sixteenth century, is a rugged, subtropical island lying 100 miles off the southeast coast of China's Fujian Province, midway between Shanghai and Hong Kong, and about 150 miles north of the northernmost Philippines. Taiwan is what remains of Sun Yat-Sen's vision of China and the Kuomintang (see Chapter 3), a republic with a strong central government operating according to Confucian principles. It maintains autonomy by virtue of its geographic separation from China, its strong military combined with China's naval weakness, and strong U.S. support. Though nominally republican in form, it was governed by Chiang until his death in 1975, and then his son until 1987, as a one-party state under martial law, due to the threat posed by China. An official state of war still exists. A multiparty democracy has been developing since 1989. Indicators of the strength of its Confucian heritage include the presence of a fourth branch of government to manage a national examination system (students may study up to sixteen hours a day seven days a week for a year to prepare for university entrance exams), and that Confucius's birthday is a national holiday called Teachers' Day. The island is densely populated and highly industrialized. Only 12 percent of the population of more than twenty-two million is employed in agriculture. Only Japan, Hong Kong, and Singapore have higher per capita incomes in East Asia.

There had been a Chinese presence on the island long before the exiled Nationalists arrived in 1949. The island was occupied for a brief time by the Dutch during the early colonial period and by the Japanese from 1895 to 1945, a consequence of the Sino-Japanese War. Some Japanese descendants and Sino-Japanese remain. More than 90 percent of the population is Chinese, however, either indigenous or descendant from the Nationalists. The predominant value system of Taiwan is essentially that of pre-Communist China, which is to say, more of the original idealist and humanitarian neo-Confucianism that drove the anti-imperial revolt of 1911–12. It conforms to the East Asian "doing" model except that uncertainty avoidance is quite high, reflecting, like Korea, its highly threatening geopolitical situation.

Hong Kong arose from the nineteenth-century opium trade. Its name comes from the Chinese *Heung Keung* meaning fragrant harbor, the fragrance being that of Indian opium awaiting offloading from British bottoms for transshipment up the Pearl River to Canton and beyond. Prior to British occupation it was known primarily for its indigenous pirates. Perhaps all this is a suitable or even logical origin for what has become the most open, capitalistic market in the world, renowned for its low taxes, free trade, minimal regulation, bustling entrepreneurship, and high productivity and as a major exporter of manufactured goods. Hong Kong is of course one of the world's great trading and financial centers and is the gateway to China. There is much speculation about its future—which is beyond the scope of this book—upon its return to China, being highly valuable to the Chinese as a commercial gateway but also highly irritating as an outpost of freewheeling, laissez-faire capitalism. However one known effect is a massive "braindrain" both of individuals and firms, including some of the original trading houses descendant from the old British East India Company, who are voting with their feet and seeking homes elsewhere.

Hong Kong's population is 98 percent Chinese, and its culture is Confucian modified by more than 150 years of British rule and enterprise. It is what remains of the coastal trading enclaves of Western presence allowed by imperial China, which were the sources of the Chinese expatriate communities active in commerce throughout East Asia and elsewhere. Given the British influence, it is not surprising that the research indicates that the Hong Kong Chinese are more masculine, that is, task oriented, unlike the East Asian model, and thus more representative of a "doing" culture. Nevertheless, they remain collectivist despite the task orientation, just as do the "doing" Japanese and Koreans. They expect to be consulted in decision making even though power distance is large. They are paternalistic but less so, more likely to feel some ability to influence nature and an internal locus of control, and less likely to ascribe status to family origin. Ralston et al. (1993) found the Hong Kong Chinese positioned between U.S. and mainland Chinese managers in Confucian values, task orientation, power distance, locus of control, intolerance for ambiguity, and social consciousness. These findings are consistent for a culture with Asian roots but Western gardeners.

The Republic of Singapore has a similar history. As a major trading, financial, and manufacturing center, it is a vestige of the British colonial presence in the former Malaya (now Malaysia). Malaysia became independent in 1963, and significant political and cultural differences caused it to grant independence to Singapore two years later. Its population of three million is less homogenous than Taiwan's or Hong Kong's: It is about 76 percent Chinese, 15 percent Muslim Malay, and 6 percent Hindu Indian. The Chinese, who gravitated to this commercially strategic location, dominate politically as well as economically, however, and Mandarin is the official language. It is a secular state, and its people are known for their religious tolerance. Singapore also is known as a highly regimented society with strong penalties for deviant but seemingly innocuous behavior such as jaywalking and public gum chewing. Readers may recall the widely-publicized case of an American teenager arrested for vandalism and then severely caned as his punishment. To the thoroughly Confucianist Singaporeans, such antisocial behavior is subhuman and worthy of the same kind of punishment one might give an unruly animal. In this same vein, Singapore has avoided the overcrowding of Hong Kong by regulating family size. Singapore had been, under Lee Kuan Yew, essentially a benevolent dictatorship, and elaborate social control makes civil employment prestigious. Confucius and Sun Yat-Sen may have been more at home in Singapore than anywhere else in the contemporary world. A more democratic constitution was adopted after Lee left office in 1990.

Singapore's value system is consistent with the "doing" East Asian model but less so than Hong Kong's. Exceptions are that it is slightly feminine, there is little sense of control over nature, and it sees organizations more as social than functional systems. The likely explanation is that Singapore's somewhat autocratic leaders have kept it more Confucianist and less Western than Hong Kong.

THAILAND

The Kingdom of Thailand, the first of three non-Confucian cultures discussed in this chapter, is largely landlocked among Myanmar, Laos, and Cambodia. An isthmus between the Gulf of Thailand, an arm of the South China Sea, and the Malacca Strait (between the Indonesian Island of Sumatra and the Malay peninsula) connects this tropical, fertile country to Malaysia to the south. An absolute monarchy long known as Siam, this nation took its present name (meaning "free" land) when it became a constitutional monarchy in 1932, after a military coup. The freedom-loving Thais take great pride in never having been colonized by another country, although Thailand was occupied briefly by the Japanese during World War II. It is a military ally of the United States and staunchly anti-Communist. Of its population of fifty-five million, more than 90 percent are Theravada Buddhists (see Chapter 6), and that religion permeates Thai life. The monarch must, constitutionally, be a Buddhist, and a Buddhist temple (*wat*) is the center of religious and civic life in every Thai village. Thai-speaking Chinese, descendant from imported laborers, constitute about 11 percent of the population. About one million Malay-speaking Muslims live in the southern part of the country. This still primarily agricultural economy is shifting rapidly into manufacturing, and its GDP is growing faster than its population.

The Thais, a distinct ethnic group with its own language, migrated down the Mekong valley into Southeast Asia from what is now Yunnan Province in Southern China beginning in the twelfth century A.D. They settled on lands occupied by the Mon and Khmer peoples who had emigrated from China in the ninth century B.C. The Mon and Khmer had been converted to Buddhism by merchants and missionaries from India and Ceylon (now Sri Lanka), which the Thais also adopted. They established a typical Asian wet-rice culture and lived peacefully in a highly benign environment, despite occasional periods of internal instability and the wartime Japanese occupation, until the present day (LePoer 1981).

By 1887 the Thais found themselves surrounded by European colonies with the British in Burma and the Malay Peninsula and the French throughout Indochina. Skillful Thai diplomacy and minor territorial concessions together with the Europeans' wish to maintain a buffer between them allowed Thailand to remain the only country in Southeast Asia, and one of the few anywhere in Asia, not to experience foreign colonization.

The Thais are a content, good-humored, and peaceful people, easy-going, highly pragmatic, and generally unburdened by ideology. Indicative of their nature is the common expression *Mai Pen Rai* (literally—Never mind!) that means life should be enjoyed and unpleasantness minimized (BYU Cultur-gram). They took readily to Buddhism, a pragmatic religion in that it pre-scribes positive actions to reach a sainted state rather than merely proscribing sin. The Thais took this a step further by practicing Buddhism not to achieve nirvana but to perfect life on earth. Over time they came to reject the Noble Eightfold Path (see Chapter 6) to nirvana as too austere, idealistic, and mystical and instead set their own less-demanding standards which prohibited killing, stealing, lying, and avoidance of intoxicating liq-uor and illicit sexual relations, that is, the "path of right behavior" (Fieg 1989; LePoer 1981). Thai Buddhism retains belief in *samsara*, the eternal cycle of birth, death, and rebirth, that is, reincarnation; and karma, the cumulative net effect of merit and demerit over the span of an individual's lives that determines his intermediate and ultimate fates. The notion of karma amplifies the paternalism and large power distance inherent in pas-toral cultures in that it leads to the assumption that anyone occupying a leadership position deserves authority and respect, having earned them through an accumulation of good karma. The Thai king is assumed to have the highest degree of good karma and is highly respected. Deemed a *bo-dhisattva*, an enlightened one who nonetheless has foregone the search for nirvana in order to serve others, he is expected to uphold the religion and to be brave, wise, and compassionate (LePoer 1981; Girling 1981).

Belief in reincarnation allows the Thai to avoid feeling compelled to max-imize their potential in one lifetime or to make decisions quickly and to view the passage of time without anxiety or regret. What position or suc-cess they achieve is determined largely by their karma for deeds or omissions of present and past lives and perhaps some luck. The most fun-damental tenet of Buddhism is that desire and craving are the sources of all human misery. Therefore striving and ambition are seen not only as pointless and as potential sources of conflict but also as sacrilegious. Efforts to plan or to bring about change also are pointless and even presumptuous. Arrogance or pretentious behavior of any kind and excess, public display of emotion, especially anger, also must be avoided. Laws and regulations are applied flexibly and loosely, even by government bureaucrats.

Harmony must be preserved. Thai society is constructed of a web of intricate patron-client relationships and is highly and minutely stratified. Like Japanese, the Thai language includes a wide array of personal pro-nouns to allow appropriate forms of address depending on the nature of the specific relationship. Close family ties, smooth interpersonal relation-ships, and indirect, self-effacing, face-saving speech prevail. The Thais search for *sabaaj*, that is, comfortable and untroubled situations, in all aspects of life, even in the work setting. The Buddhist ideal of moderation in all things or "The Middle Way" dominates daily life (Fieg 1989). The Thais respond to the totality of another person; relationships are not com-partmentalized into social and work for example. Leaders are expected to act like a teacher or older brother, to be decisive but kind and concerned and not necessarily specific about how a job is to be done. They must be sensitive to the context of each personal relationship. Employees are loyal, respectful, and deferential and must be sought out individually to obtain their views (Girling 1981; Fieg 1989). Even though family obligations outweigh individual interests, the Thais value self-reliance in accordance with the Buddhist precept "By oneself one is purified" (LePoer 1981, 32), meaning that one's salvation is solely within one's own hands.

Thailand has a long trading history, much of it with the West. As a result, a middle class of merchants and government bureaucrats began to emerge early in this century. Thai pragmatism makes it difficult for them to deal with abstractions like management, leadership, and organization (for example, they can describe a good boss without any interest in generalization or theoretical explanations). Consequently, organizations have highly specialized, functional structures. When combined with centralized, top-down decision making typical of hierarchical, paternalistic cultures, the result is little delegation and participation and great volumes of vertical, mostly upward, information flow. Thai firms even have a department, the *saraba* section, whose responsibility is monitoring and regulating the flow of paperwork and seeing to it that top management is kept informed fully and in great detail (Fieg 1989). Therefore, cross-functional coordination and speed will not be a competitive strength for Thai firms for some time to come.

Research findings with regard to Thai values are consistent with the East Asian, "being" model with two exceptions. Hofstede found the Thais moderately strong in uncertainty avoidance. This finding is inconsistent with the driving forces of Thai culture, with results obtained in similar cultures, and with Hofstede's own hypothesis of the relationships between cultural forces and uncertainty avoidance in Southeast Asia. His text suggests that Thai uncertainty avoidance is weak relative to some Western cultures but does not explain the apparent anomaly. One possible explanation is a continuing sense of threat. Externally, in addition to Thailand's long struggle to maintain its independence from colonial powers, there is continuing concern about its nearby Communist neighbors. The Thai frontier approaches to within less than one hundred kilometers the borders of China and Vietnam, and both countries resent Thailand's support of the United States during the Vietnam War. Moreover, Vietnam invaded neighboring Cambodia in 1979 and occupied much of that country for ten years, occasionally venturing into Thailand itself in pursuit of their Cambodian enemies. Internally, the Thais have fought their own Communist insurgency through much of the twentieth century. Trompenaars found the Thais in the middle range for internal versus external locus of control. An external locus would be expected in a culture that is fatalistic and believes in predestination. However, as has been said, Buddhism encourages self-reliance, so a middling finding seems reasonable. Trompenaars obtained a similar finding for India, the origin of Buddhism.

INDONESIA

The Portuguese navigator Ferdinand Magellan, following the eastward route to India discovered by Vasco da Gama, continued onward and landed at the elusive Spice Islands in 1511. These islands, now called the Moluccas, were the intended objective of Christopher Columbus nine years earlier and now are part of the archipelago forming the Republic of Indonesia. Consisting of more than 13,000 islands, including many small atolls but several of the world's largest islands, Sumatra, Java, and large portions of Borneo and New Guinea, Indonesia lies largely within the triangle formed by the Malay peninsula on the Southeast Asian mainland, the Philippines, and Australia. This tropical country stretches some 3,300 miles on a northwest-southeast axis and is the maritime crossroads of Asia, separating the Indian Ocean from the Pacific and the South China Sea. It is the world's fifth largest nation with a population of more than 180 million, primarily of Malay origin but including more than three hundred distinct ethnic groups and many languages. A two-class system with aristocracy based on land ownership has prevailed from ancient times. Javanese constitute about half the population and dominate the country politically. The largest minority is Chinese, about four million strong, who dominate commerce. Indonesia is very rich in natural resources including oil, rubber, tin and other minerals, tropical hardwoods, and—of course—spices. Yet the nation remains quite poor, with 80 percent of the population still engaged in agriculture and extractive industries. Its low labor costs have attracted more low-skill, mass-production manufacturing in recent years, however, as political instability and leftist policies diminish and labor costs rise elsewhere.

Despite the diversity of the population, the dominance of Malay-Javanese allows some generalization. Indonesian values are consistent with the East Asian, "being" model, that is, large power distance; collectivist; moderately weak uncertainty avoidance and moderately feminine; particularistic ethics; ascriptive of status, primarily to family background; taking a holistic view of the world; and preferring managers to act like father figures. Historians describe Indonesians as a peaceful, tranquil people, comfortable with rigid hierarchies and strong moral leadership, valuing social harmony, modest and indirect in their speech, and oriented toward the nuclear family. Indonesians say *belum* (not yet) when they mean "no" (BYU Culturgram). This set of values is a product of Indonesia's Malay roots; the typical, two-class agrarian social system; and Buddhist and Hindu influences. Despite the dominance of Chinese-Indonesians in commerce, there is an absence of Confucian influence in Indonesia. Indonesians tend to resent the success of the Chinese and their connections to the Dutch and have excluded them from government.

European explorers sought sources for spices so assiduously because they were a lucrative cargo, very high in value per unit of volume, thus better able to justify the cost in time and money of their long voyages. Most active in this part of the world were the Portuguese, Spanish, English, and Dutch. After some intense rivalry, these colonial powers essentially divided this part of the world, with the Dutch gaining control of most of what is now Indonesia but that was known for some 350 years as the Dutch East Indies. (The Caribbean Islands Columbus mistook for the "East Indies" are now, of course, called the "West Indies!"). The primary instruments of Dutch control were the Dutch East India Company and military power. Another important factor was Royal Dutch Shell (known to Americans as Shell Oil), formed in 1890 by a merger between the Royal Dutch Company for Exploration of Petroleum Sources in the Netherlands East Indies and Britain's Shell Company.

Indian and Chinese traders brought Hinduism and Buddhism to these islands during the third and fourth centuries A.D. The aristocracy used these religions to justify their power, portraying themselves alternatively as enlightened *bodhisattvas* or reincarnations of Hindu deities. Buddhism was accepted by most of the population, whereas Hinduism, with its caste system, appealed more to the aristocrats (Fischer 1959). Arab traders were among the earlier visitors as well, but Islam did not make major inroads until the thirteenth century. Historians speculate that the peaceful and tranquil Indonesians resisted orthodox Islam as too legalistic and ascetic for their easygoing nature but eventually accepted *Sufi* Islam, a sect that emphasizes only Islam's spiritual aspects. Today about 90 percent of Indonesians are Muslims, but most are only nominal believers. Indonesians are comfortable with and tolerant of all three religions and many accept and practice elements of each. The Indonesians tend to be highly mystical, spiritual people, many still guided by traditional beliefs in animist spirits in addition to the beliefs brought by foreigners.

This country, fragmented both physically and ethnically, is difficult to unify and govern. Nationalism has not been a strong force, though traditionally anti-imperialist Muslims and, later, Communists actively opposed Dutch rule, often quite oppressive and exploitive. Having witnessed the Japanese defeat the seemingly invincible Dutch colonialists at the outset of World War II, independence began to seem more attainable. The Japanese had promised as much in return for mobilization of the population in material support of the Japanese war effort. With the end of the war and after some military conflict with the Dutch and the British—applying their Japanese training and abandoned equipment—independence was granted in 1950. The founder of the Republic, President Sukarno (the use of single names is common in Indonesia), devised a strong, central, but secular government based on the principle of "guided democracy" as a unifying theme that could be accepted by all Indonesians of any faith. He exercised legislative as well as executive power. Important elements of guided democracy include social justice and egalitarianism and government by "consensus" rather than by compromise among competing interests.

Departures from the East Asian, "being" norms identified by Trompenaars include a preference for function over relationships in organizations and an internal locus of control. These findings can be attributed to 350 years of rule by the Dutch, who are, as we shall see, among the most western of all nations. An internal locus also is grounded in the Buddhist precept of self-reliance.

THE PHILIPPINES

Having switched his allegiance to Spain, Ferdinand Magellan landed in the Philippines in 1521 during his attempt at the first circumnavigation of the globe—this time from the east, after pioneering the westward route around Cape Horn through what became known as the Straits of Magellan. He was killed in the Philippines after taking sides in a local dispute, and his ships completed the circumnavigation without him. The first sizable Spanish expedition arrived in 1565, and the Philippines, named after King Philip II of Spain, began 333 years as a colony. After another 47 years as a colony of the United States, the Republic of the Philippine Islands became independent on July 4, 1946. It consists of more than seven thousand tropical islands lying east of the Indochina peninsula between Taiwan and Indonesia on a generally north-south axis about one thousand miles long. Most of the population of sixty-two million (fourteenth in the world), largely of Malay and Malay-Indonesian origin, lives on the northern island of Luzon, the most populous and the seat of government, and the southern island of Mindanao. There are more than ninety linguistic groups, with the indigenous Tagalog-Pilipino and English being the two official languages. The largest minority is Chinese, who—again—dominate trade and commerce. Much of the chain is mountainous, and it is subject to every form of natural disaster, including frequent earthquakes and occasional volcanic eruptions. Like Indonesia, its economy still remains at the subsistence level with most of the population employed in agriculture and extractive industries, but with a growing base of manufacturing. It is the only predominantly Roman Catholic country east of the Mediterranean and the only national culture in Asia with a strong western component.

A recent report in the *Financial Times* said that Filipino senior and middle managers are among the best in Asia, much sought after by multinationals both in the Philippines and as expatriates. The reported reason is their unique understanding of both Asian and Western cultures, which makes them very flexible, adaptable, and good team players (Luce 1995).

The Malay migration began well before Buddhism, Hinduism, and Islam made their way into present-day Malaysia and Indonesia. Thus these peace-ful people brought their traditional values of patriarchal hierarchy, veneration of ancestors and deference to elders, a desire for harmonious relationships and consensus, suppression of individual needs to those of the family and clan, as well as their animistic paganism. They settled by clan in autonomous villages called *barangays*, named for the kind of boat used for migration, and established a typical Asian rice culture. Kinship within and among extended families in each clan's *barangay*, typically consisting of thirty to fifty families, was the only meaningful linkage, although some formed loose confederations. Given Malay values and the demanding nature of rice culture, the *barangays*, led by a hereditary chieftain called a *datu*, generally coexisted peacefully and maintained respectfully distant relationships. Common Filipino values and attitudes traceable to Malay roots include: *hiya*, a sense of propriety and the attendant need to avoid shame and loss of face; *pakikisama*, the obligation to avoid anger and get along with others; *utang no loob*, a consciousness of indebtedness to others; and fatalism commonly expressed as *bahala na* (God willing) (Gochenouer 1990). Malay influence is also evident in the Filipino preference for relaxed, friendly, long-term relationships and good humor. The need to maintain face is manifested in the usual ways, including indirect speech, a reluctance to speak up in group settings, and the use of go-betweens to avoid potentially unpleasant situations. Maintenance of harmony and face are at least as important as task performance. The best boss acts like a father figure.

Indonesian and Malay Muslims eventually did make their way into the Philippines, settling in the southern islands during the thirteenth and fourteenth centuries. They began migrating northward just in time to be halted by the newly arrived and well-armed Spanish. The Muslims eventually would be contained to Mindanao and the Sulu Islands, also in the south, and would remain largely outside mainstream (that is, Christian) Philippine society centered on Luzon.

The Spanish colonization was primarily of religious intent, seeking not only to convert the Filipinos but to use the islands as a base for further penetration of Japan and China by the Church, just as Spain used its Caribbean colonies to support penetration of the American mainland. Unlike Japan and China, the absence of any indigenous central government obviated any substantial resistance, and the colonization was quite peaceful, after the Moros (as the Spanish came to call the Muslims) had been contained. Employing Catholicism as a means of social control (as the Arabs used Islam), the Spanish built a political structure on the existing *barangays*, co-opting the *datus*, to establish central control. They were aided greatly by the clergy, who served as grass-roots organizers. The local priest became a powerful figure and was the instrument for the proliferation of Spanish culture to a breadth and depth unequaled by any European power in Asia. Even so, only about 1 percent of the population speaks Spanish, despite the common use of Spanish family and place names.

The islands had little to offer in terms of material resources (undiscovered until the twentieth century), and the colony operated at a loss throughout the occupation. Ruled by the Spanish Viceroy of Mexico, the primary economic value of the colony was to provide a way station at the splendid port of Manila for an annual galleon voyage plying trade in Chinese silks for Mexican silver. The Chinese community dominated this business as well as virtually all professions and trades. The one abundant resource was labor. The Spanish established a system of landholding called *encomiendas,* under which Filipino labor would be employed, often exploited, and taxed by those favored by the viceroy, including religious orders, and individuals being rewarded for service to the crown. This policy was superimposed readily on the existing system of communal land ownership, share cropping, and debt peonage. The *encomiendas* would evolve into the *haciendas* or plantations that would form the basis for the Philippine's still agrarian, two-class economy. The hacienda system would be the target of anticolonialist activities by the Moros, in the twentieth century by Communist guerrillas (the Huks), and of periodic peasant uprisings. The proprietors of the haciendas acquired enormous political power, which they have used to obstruct land reform throughout the colonial and postcolonial periods. Consequently, political instability has been one of the Philippines' greatest handicaps, and it has continued into recent times, despite the adoption of constitutional democracy upon independence in 1946. There have been numerous changes in government since then, sometimes violent, and many readers will recall the scandals of the 1980s involving the martial-law rule of Ferdinand Marcos, including the assassination of rival Benigno Aquino.

More than 90 percent of Filipinos are Christian, mostly Roman Catholic. Catholic virtues have been embraced but coexist with the values of Malay culture, with many Filipinos retaining polytheistic, animistic beliefs. Resentment of the dominance of Spanish clergy gave rise to a uniquely Filipino Catholic sect, *Iglesia ni Christo.* Muslims constitute only about 4 percent of the population, Buddhists but 2 percent. In some ways the Philippines resembles a Latin American culture as much as it does an Asian one. There is a wide gap between rich and poor, and authority is to be respected deeply (and applied excessively to the extent that Filipinos would come to disrespect it and master the art of circumventing it, much like their American cousins to be). Status is derived from wealth, education, and fair skin color, and one is expected to dress according to one's station in life. The literate gentleman of leisure is the ideal. Hard work was expected, but mental exertion much preferred to physical. There was little interest in science or control of the environment, and excessive rationality was suspect. Males were expected to be *macho*—overtly masculine in the stereotypical sense; highly concerned about appearance and image; highly protective of females, who are relegated to traditional roles; and extremely sensitive to slight or insult. The deadly victimization by Spain of indigenous peoples in Latin America was not repeated in the Philippines however. The Spanish did not allow themselves to establish a presence in the countryside, aside from the clergy. Thus, unlike Mexico for example, the Philippines did not become a very *mestizo* (mixed) society, and only about 1 percent of the population learned to speak Spanish. This is why the Spanish did not develop the islands' mineral resources, as that pursuit had been particularly destructive in Latin America (Corpuz 1965). The Spanish presence never exceeded 1 percent of the total population (Cutshall 1964).

Precipitated by a generation of offspring of wealthy families educated in the West, a major revolt erupted in 1896 with Spain already preoccupied by an ongoing revolt in Cuba. The Spanish-American War began in 1898, and in that same year the U.S. Navy defeated a Spanish fleet in Manila Bay, effectively ending Spanish rule. Despite the Filipinos' expectation of independence, the United States decided that it needed an outpost in the western Pacific and waged a violent military campaign, largely against the Moros, to bring the Philippines under U.S. control as a commonwealth by 1899. This last gasp of Western colonialism aroused strong public opposition both in the United States and abroad. Under continual pressure by Filipinos and Americans, the U.S. Congress passed legislation in 1934 setting a ten-year timetable for transition to Philippine independence. World War II delayed this event by two years. The Filipinos established a constitutional democracy modeled on the U.S. Constitution. Unlike most Southeast Asians, they had fought the Japanese invasion and occupation most vigorously and did so again alongside the U.S. Army after General Douglas MacArthur kept his famous vow to return to the Philippines. Many Americans and Filipinos died in this very hard-fought campaign, and the Filipinos still harbor some resentment toward the Japanese. This common experience and the relatively benign nature of the prewar U.S. occupation created a great deal of good will toward the United States. (The author has viewed the Filipinos' memorial dedicated to the U.S. military outside Manila—it is a magnificent monument.) Despite occasional disputes between governments, most recently over the fate of U.S. military bases, the typical Filipino still regards the United States with great favor and eagerly follows U.S. trends and fashions. Just as Spain built the Philippines' churches and cathedrals, the United States built its political, legal, and educational institutions. The adoption of English as an official language is perhaps the most visible manifestation of this relationship.

Departures from the East Asian cultural model include Hofstede's finding of masculinity and Trompenaars' finding of universalist ethics. The former can be attributed to the strength of *machismo*, which apparently more than offsets the importance Filipinos place on maintaining good relationships, and the latter to the highly articulated and absolute ethical standards prescribed by Catholicism.

VIETNAM

The Socialist Republic of Vietnam lies along the eastern shore of the Indochina peninsula on the Gulf of Tonkin and the South China Sea. Its population is about sixty-seven million, thirteenth in the world, and it is rich in natural resources, largely unexploited. Its topography is very rugged; only the narrow coastal plain comprising about 20 percent of its land is level. The rest of the country is mountainous, and about 75 percent is heavily forested. The Annamite Cordillera, a rugged, north-south mountain chain, obstructs communication westward, but the northern border with China is easier to penetrate. Consequently, Vietnam has been influenced more by China and less by India, unlike its neighbors in Southeast Asia—Laos, Cambodia, Myanmar, and Thailand. Its climate is largely tropical, subtropical in the north. The indigenous Vietnamese, an ancient, village-based, rice culture, lived primarily in the Red River delta in the north, site of the present capital city, Hanoi. Migration southward along the coastal plain settled the Mekong River delta, site of present-day Ho Chi Minh City, formerly Saigon. This region was not heavily settled until the nineteenth century and retains more of a frontier mentality than the long-settled north. It is also less prone to flood and drought than is the Red River delta because of natural flood control provided by the Tonle Sap, a large lake drainage in Cambodia, and remains much less densely populated. Nevertheless, throughout Vietnam, the demands of the rice culture and exposure to typhoons, floods, droughts, and tropical pestilence created the same pressure for collectivism we have seen in Japan and China. Vietnam remains a very rural society, heavily militarized (its standing army is third largest in the world after China and Russia) and is one of the world's poorest nations.

Vietnam's history combines persistent resistance to foreign rule with a readiness to learn from its occupiers. Vietnam was conquered by China's Han dynasty in the second century B.C. and was ruled by China until A.D. 969, more than a thousand years. Throughout this period the Vietnamese resisted the Chinese vigorously. Since China's departure, the Vietnamese have repelled numerous attacks by the Chinese and even the Mongols. A short but intense border conflict occurred between the two as recently as 1979, when China sought to punish the Vietnamese for their occupation of Cambodia, and, as this is written, they remain locked in a dispute over Hainan Island and the Spratley and Paracel Island chains in the South China Sea. More recently, Vietnam withstood about one hundred years of French colonial rule, which ended with the famous military defeat at Dien Bien Phu in 1954, after which the country was partitioned into the Communist North and democratic South. It also survived Japanese occupation during World War II and the prolonged guerrilla war with the United States. Vietnam's experiment with Communism (since 1976 as a reunified country) is extremely brief compared to its long-standing tradition of intense nationalism.

The Chinese left behind in what is now northern Vietnam a strongly Confucian state with a highly centralized administration and a landed, mandarinlike aristocracy. This state would build an army and a system for education of civil servants and professional examinations in Confucian principles (established in 1075). All the familiar components of Confucian doctrine, including a disdain for innovation, trade, and commerce, were apparent. (As is the case elsewhere in Southeast Asia, business affairs were largely the concern of expatriate Chinese originating from those coastal regions of China exposed to westerners.) There were no ties stronger than those of kinship and the village. The extended family was the fundamental social and economic unit, and it was expected to be self-sufficient. The Vietnamese lunar new year observance, *têt*, is essentially a celebration of family and ancestors and an occasion for reunion and renewal of family ties. It means more to the Vietnamese than all our holidays combined mean to us. (It was thus a great military opportunity, with many soldiers on leave to visit their families, as well as in keeping with the Communist approach of breaking down family loyalty in favor of Party loyalty, for the Vietcong and North Vietnamese Army to wage a major offensive during *têt*, as they did in 1968.) The familial, patriarchal hierarchy was mirrored in society and government to the extent that no one individual was the exact equal of any other in any setting. The Vietnamese are great joiners of social groups and guilds. Face and social harmony were important values, and it was expected that behavior would be modified (*dieu*) to suit the circumstances of a particular relationship.

The villagers remained indifferent to the central government and took no interest in its ideologies. They were quite content to tend their rice paddies, worship their ancestors, and live in peace without interference. The elongated shape of the country made central rule difficult during this period, and the villages functioned quite autonomously under the guidance of local councils of notables. Excessive interference or threats would cause villagers to side with opposition parties and sects who promised better protection (a tradition later exploited by the Vietcong guerrillas). The villagers owned land granted to them by the state communally but resented the mandarins' feudalistic ownership of the vast majority of the land, further diminishing the peasants' loyalty to the central government. Peasant uprisings over this issue occurred from time to time. Vietnamese nationalism has had much more to do with love of the land, trod by ancestors and providing sustenance, than with loyalty to any form of government, ideology, or leader.

The Chinese had established a way station in the Red River delta on their trade route with Indonesia and India through which Buddhism most likely made its way into Vietnam in the second century. It spread rapidly and became the dominant religion. Like the Chinese and Japanese, the Vietnamese adopted the more inclusive Mahayana Buddhism in a more secularized form emphasizing intellectual insight and awakening rather than religious belief and faith. Nonetheless, again like the Chinese, they took great solace from the promise of a life in the hereafter that would free them from the rigors of their meager existence. Buddhist monks (bonzes) became privileged landholders, and pagodas appeared throughout the country. Fatalism and the promise of eternal life contributed to their strong and persistent martial spirit (grossly underestimated by both the French and Americans!). The Vietnamese saw themselves not only as fierce warriors but noble ones as they defended their country repeatedly against more-powerful invaders (Hammer 1963).

Taoist detachment, noninvolvement, and mysticism were very influential, as was indigenous animism, and the cyclical dominance patterns of mutually interdependent yin and yang forces dominated Vietnamese cosmology. The rigid, moral prescriptions of Confucius's righteous path (nghia in Vietnamese) and duty to others (on) were complemented, especially among less-regimented southerners, by tinh (spontaneity and emotional expressiveness) and nhan (compassion and benevolence) and an appreciation of mysticism. These values, grounded in Taoism, Buddhism, and animism, constituted jointly a way of life that provided refuge from constant strife (Jamieson 1993; Hammer 1963). Roman Catholics, some two million strong in the south, and two quasi-political, nationalist religious sects, the Cao Dai and Hoa Hao, each a million or more strong, contributed to a highly-fragmented society in South Vietnam. Resettlement of various ethnic tribes and large-scale, voluntary migration between North and South following the 1954 partition contributed to the fragmentation, as did the relative autonomy of thousands of villages.

European missionaries began arriving in 1627, and French colonization began in 1857. They invaded and occupied the southern part of the country first and remained most firmly established there. They ruled directly in the south (Cochinchina) but through Vietnamese administrators in central (Annam) and northern (Tonkin) Vietnam. All of Vietnam as well as present-day Cambodia and Laos came under French rule by 1884. The more open, less regimented nature of the southerners made them quite receptive to western influence. It became fashionable to read French novelists and enlightenment philosophers, and ideas like individualism and independence caught on with the elite among the less-Confucian and more-philosophical southerners. Wealthy Vietnamese began sending their children to be educated in Paris. As the French built Western institutions and infrastructure, an urban middle class emerged, and Saigon, the southern capital, became a major metropolis, much more cosmopolitan than Hanoi. The new middle class found itself torn between Western and Asian values with younger males most attracted to Western thinking and older females occupying the opposite pole (Jamieson 1993). However the French colonialists were mercantilist, exploitive, and oppressive, and opposition arose among various nationalist groups, most notably the Communists led by Ho Chi Minh, a disciple of Mao Zedong. Ho began leading resistance to the French in 1940. In the vacuum left by the departure of the defeated Japanese in 1945 and with the French still reeling from the war, the Communists seized power in the North. The French soon returned, however; resistance resumed; and, with the support of the USSR and China, Ho's forces defeated the French in 1954. The most dominant figure in the south following the partition arranged at the Geneva Convention of that year was Ngo Dinh Diem, President of South Vietnam from 1955 until his death in 1963. Diem was a devout Catholic and a strong, neo-Confucianist conservative. His attempts to reimpose Confucian doctrine through strict social legislation and expel ethnic Chinese and his persecution of Buddhist *bonzes* triggered widespread insurrection. This caused U.S. President John F. Kennedy—the United States had taken up support of the South after the French withdrew—to accede to Diem's removal through a military coup in 1963, which led to his execution. Turmoil ensued, and thus began in earnest direct U.S. involvement in yet another war in Vietnam.

The South differed from the North in its more fragmented society, more-intense exposure to the French and to Western ideas, greater distance in both time and space from Confucian roots, and a less rigorous, less crowded environment. Under these conditions we should expect a South Vietnam in which the bonds of Confucian order and collectivism are weakened, a society more open, individualistic, and enterprising but less disciplined and austere, that is, a more "being" culture. Meanwhile the imposition of Communism on the traditionally Confucianist North created an even more regimented, unified, hardier society, just as it did in China. With the defeat of the South in 1975 and subsequent reunification—seemingly inevitable given these differences—the victors attempted to impose discipline through forced re-education and relocation programs as Vietnam essentially removed itself from the community of nations. Their methods would have been much more familiar to some of the more oppressive Chinese emperors than to Confucius. It has been only since the late 1980s that Vietnam has again opened its doors to foreign investment.

Vietnam is a nation of enormous economic potential still trying to recover from the human and material devastation of war. It remains to be seen how well a people who function so well in war can live in peace. To the extent the North persists and succeeds in remaking the South in its own image, then Vietnam becomes a tropical clone of China. Whatever is said about China and whatever works or does not work there will apply to Vietnam as well, as long as one respects Vietnamese nationalism and pride.

Alternatively, the North may recognize the value of the South's familiarity with Western ways and allow it to function as a commercial gateway to the industrious workers of the North, no less industrious than their cultural counterparts in Hong Kong, Shanghai, or on Taiwan.

ADDITIONAL READING

Management Practices

Alston, Jon P. 1989. "Wa, Guanxi, and Inwha: Managerial Principles in Japan, China and Korea." Business Horizons 33, no. 2 (March-April): 20–31.

Biers, Dan, Matthew Rose, and Michael Schuman. 1996. "Korean Bosses Anger Workers Overseas." Wall Street Journal. July 28, p. A19.

Chen, Min. 1995. Asian Management Systems. (New York: Routledge).

Harris, Philip R., and Robert T. Moran. 1996. Managing Cultural Differences, 4th ed. (Houston: Gulf).

Kearney, Robert P. 1981. "Managing Mr. Kim." Across the Board 28, no. 4 (April): 40–46.

Lee, S. M., and S. Yoo. 1987. "The K-Type Management: A Driving Force of Korean Prosperity." Management International Review 27(4): 68–77.

Lie, John. 1990. "Is Korean Management Just Like Japanese Management?" Management International Review 30(2): 113–118.

Luce, Edward. 1995. "Philippine Factor." Financial Times April 28, p. 10.

Oh, Tai K. 1991. "Understanding Managerial Values among the Gang of Four: South Korea, Taiwan, Singapore and Hong Kong." Journal of Management Development 10(2): 46–56.

Ralston, David A., David J. Gustafson, Fanny M. Cheung, and Robert H. Terpstra. 1993. "Differences in Managerial Values: A Study of U.S., Hong Kong and PRC Managers." Journal of International Business Studies 24, no.2 (Second Quarter): 249–275.

Yoo, Sangjin, and Sang M. Lee. 1987. "Management Style and Practice of Korean Chaebols." California Management Review 29, no. 4 (Summer): 95–110.

History and Culture

Brigham Young University Center for International Studies. Culturgram 1994: Indonesia.

Brigham Young University Center for International Studies. Culturgram 1994: North Korea.

Brigham Young University Center for International Studies. Culturgram 1994: Thailand.

Cameron, Nigel. 1991. An Illustrated History of Hong Kong. (New York: Oxford University Press).

Cima, Ronald J., ed. 1989. Vietnam: A Country Study. (Washington: Library of Congress).

Corpuz, O. D. 1965. The Philippines. (Englewood Cliffs, N.J.: Prentice Hall).

Cumings, Bruce. 1984. *The Two Koreas*. (New York: Foreign Policy Association).

Cutshall, Alden. 1964. *The Philippines: Nation of Islands*. (Princeton: Van Nostrand).

Endacott, George B., and A. Hinton. 1962. *Fragrant Harbor: A Short History of Hong Kong*. (Hong Kong: Oxford University Press).

Fairbank, John K., Edwin O. Reischauer, and Albert M. Craig. 1973. *East Asia: Tradition and Transition*. (Boston: Houghton-Mifflin).

Fieg, John Paul (revised by Elizabeth Mortlock). 1989. *A Common Core: Thais and Americans*. (Yarmouth, Maine: Intercultural Press).

Fischer, Louis. 1959. *The Story of Indonesia*. (New York: Harper).

Frederick, William H., and Robert L. Wooden, eds. 1982. *Indonesia: A Country Study*. (Washington: Library of Congress).

Girling, John L. S. 1981. *Thailand: Society and Politics*. (Ithaca: Cornell University Press).

Gochenour, Thomas. 1990. *Considering Filipinos*. (Yarmouth, Maine: Intercultural Press).

Hammer, Ellen. 1966. *Vietnam Yesterday and Today*. (New York: Holt, Rinehart and Winston).

Jamieson, Neil L. 1993. *Understanding Vietnam*. (Berkeley: University of California Press).

Lapidus, Ira M. 1988. *A History of Islamic Societies*. (New York: Cambridge University Press).

LePoer, Barbara Leitch. ed. 1981. *Thailand: A Country Study*. (Washington: Library of Congress).

Nahm, Andrew C. 1988. *Korea: Tradition and Transformation*. (Elizabeth, N.J.: Hollym).

Neill, Wilfred T. 1973. *Twentieth-Century Indonesia*. (New York: Columbia University Press).

Phelan, John Leddy. 1959. *The Hispanization of the Philippines*. (Madison: University of Wisconsin Press).

Ravenholt, Albert. 1962. *The Philippines: A Young Republic on the Move*. (Princeton: Van Nostrand).

Savada, Andrea Matles, and William Shaw, eds. 1992. *South Korea: A Country Study*. (Washington: Library of Congress).

Taylor, Keith Weller. 1983. *The Birth of Vietnam*. (Berkeley: University of California Press).

Turnbull, Constance Mary. 1989. *A History of Singapore 1819–1988*. 2nd ed. (New York: Oxford University Press).

Chapter 5

THE ARAB WORLD AND ISLAM

The stereotypical views of Arabs as terrorists, enemies of Israel and the West, wealthy oil tycoons, too-clever rug merchants lazily smoking *hookahs* in exotic bazaars, and barbaric tyrants who brutalize petty criminals and relegate women to subservience and harems symbolize what is the world's largest cultural gulf, that between the West and the Arab World and Islam. How do we square that stereotype with our knowledge of individual Arabs who dote on all children, are warm and outgoing, gracious and generous hosts, and eager to be helpful and return a favor?

As was found with the Japanese, the research into Arabic values indicates some seeming contradictions. Hofstede found Arabs high in power distance, moderately collectivist, slightly masculine, and moderately high in uncertainty avoidance. Trompenaars limited his research to Egypt and several of the very small states on the Persian Gulf, and his results were mixed in some cases. He found a common preference for highly directive and paternalistic managers, which complements Hofstede's findings on power distance and uncertainty avoidance. Status is ascribed, particularly to family background; achievement is less important. He found external attribution of causation and outcomes to be quite high and particularist ethics predominant. There was an interesting mix of findings on two items associated with the individualist-collectivist scale. First, there was considerable weight placed on collective responsibility but also on individual decision-making. Second, the quality of life was thought to depend more on collective efforts in Kuwait and Egypt but more on individual freedom in the United Arab Emirates (UAE). Egyptians felt little control over nature, unlike the Kuwaitis who did (perhaps because of their oil wealth!). There was also a mix of findings related to task-driven and relationship-driven values. Egyptians and the UAE saw the purpose of an organization as facilitating function, whereas Kuwaitis and Omanis saw the organization as a social group and a system of relationships. Egyptians and Kuwaitis tended to view the world in a more holistic way, whereas the UAE preferred to deal with specificity. Arab culture is much more "being" than "doing."

THE CULTURAL SETTING

Arab lands extend from the Atlantic eastward along the Mediterranean coast of North Africa through the Arabian Peninsula, the Middle East, and to the Fertile Crescent countries of southwest Asia. Below the North African tier of countries, including Morocco, Algeria, Tunisia, Libya, and Egypt, the Arab population extends southward into Mauritania, Chad, and the Sudan, where it abuts the northern edge of Black Africa. On the Arabian Peninsula, between the Red Sea and Persian Gulf, lie Saudi Arabia, Yemen, Oman, Kuwait, and the small oil states of the United Arab Emirates. The Fertile Crescent countries are Iraq, Syria, Lebanon, Jordan, and Israel (both Arab and Jew are Semitic peoples, descendant from the same ethnic stock).

This region includes two ancient and accomplished civilizations established in large, fertile valleys: Egypt on the lower Nile, and Mesopotamia in the valley of the Tigris and Euphrates in what is now Iraq. The remainder of the region consists primarily of forbidding desert or arid steppe and mountain ranges, with isolated pockets of arable land, such as in Yemen where mountains capture rainfall from the moist air of the Indian Ocean. To speak of *the* Arabs is an oversimplification in that they are not a purely homogenous people; they are linked by language and common experience rather than by ethnicity. The Arab world has come to include the Semitic people of the Middle East; the Egyptians; the Berbers of the Maghrib (that is, central and western North Africa); and descendants of the ancient Aramaic, Syriac, Hittite, Babylonian, and Assyrian peoples of the Fertile Crescent, among others. Arabic-speaking Jews have had some influence, and there are substantial Christian communities including the Copts in Egypt and Lebanese and Syrian Catholics. These variations are more than offset by a common language, similar ways of life, and cultural heritage and by the unifying force of Islam.

Arabs have long traded throughout Asia and parts of Europe and interacted, peaceably and otherwise, with the neighboring cultures of Persia (now Iran), the Indian Subcontinent to the east, and the Turks, Kurds, and Hellenic peoples to the north. Yet the sense of Arab identity and, later, the fervor of Islam have driven the direction of influence more outward than inward, despite separate occupation of nearly all Arab lands by the Byzantine and Ottoman Empires. The direction was reversed, at least among the educated and political classes, by Western countries, primarily England and France, beginning in the nineteenth century. Arab armies converted to Islam the peoples of Kurdistan and what are now the countries of Turkey,

Iran, Pakistan, and Afghanistan. Converting largely of their own accord were the southern tier of former Soviet regions and republics (Azerbaijan and those ending in -stan—for example Dagestan, Uzbekistan, Tajikistan, Turkmenistan). There are also substantial Islamic populations among the non-Arabic peoples of Africa, China, and across the southern tier of Asia from India to Indonesia and the Philippines. Arabs even ruled part of India for a time. Though the association of Arabs and Islam obviously is very strong, it should be remembered that even though most Arabs are Muslim, some are not, and that Islam has spread well beyond the geographic and linguistic limits of the Arab world. The existing borders of Arabic and other Middle Eastern countries are largely arbitrary vestiges of colonial rivalries, not of ethnic or topographical boundaries. These nomadic people and their trading caravans knew no internal boundaries until those imposed by foreigners.

The resources of this region were, prior to the comparatively recent discovery of oil of course, among the most meager on the planet. Mere survival was the objective for almost all. The arid land did not support extensive, permanent presence except in the aforementioned river valleys. Hence the most common way of life was that of the nomad, following the rain in search of temporary pasture. As a result of dependence on foreign goods of all kinds, and as a natural extension of the nomadic way of life, the Arabs were among the world's first and foremost traders, ranging as far as China and up the Volga at least two thousand years ago. Exotic spices and handicrafts paid for imports. The migratory life-style precluded development of any industry.

The roots of Arabic culture remain obscured in antiquity but are generally thought to originate with nomadic Bedouin tribes of pastoral shepherds in the Arabian Peninsula. The tribe was led by the *sheik,* a member of the tribe's dominant family who was elected to this nonhereditary position by tribal elders. Although successors might come from the same family, merit was the primary criterion for selection of the specific individual, and age leant status. A council of elders, the *majlis,* advised the sheik and acted as a voice for members of the tribe. Adherence to custom and precedent, as interpreted by the majlis, regulated tribal life. Authority was highly patriarchal and hierarchical, but the sheik lacked coercive power and was expected to act as an arbitrator rather than as a commander. The sheik was obligated to look after widows, orphans, and the poor, and to keep track of the tribe's accounts including blood money owed and due to compensate for insult. The ability to settle disputes fairly and amicably was a valued skill. These pre-Islamic people generally abhorred the exercise of authority beyond the absolute power of the family patriarchy and relished the freedom of nomads unfettered by societal constraints. Indeed, the nomadic way of life obviated the need for or feasibility of institutional development. Land—when privately owned—water rights, and livestock were owned collectively, and the need for mutual defense against the hardships and dangers of desert life created a strong sense of community, solidarity, egalitarian unity, and interdependence within the tribe.

As was the case in China, the extended family was the basic social and economic unit, and an entire family would be held accountable for the conduct and obligations of its members. Parental authority was absolute. Parents sacrificed for and pampered their children, typically lavishing effusive praise upon them, showing heavy favor for male offspring, and they expected to be cared for by their children in old age. Children were not spared shaming or corporal punishment, however. Woman's primary purpose was to serve men, and she was viewed as undisciplined, deceitful, and naturally promiscuous; thus it was necessary to segregate her from all men other than her husband. According to Barakat (1993) this was an Arab attitude that predated Islam. Yet the *Quran* (*Koran*) would not disparage subjugation of women, would allow polygamy, and would encourage the male's somewhat arbitrary use of women to satisfy various needs. Another similarity to China was that marriage was usually arranged and was viewed not as much as a romantic relationship but a practical one, a societal, procreative institution and a vehicle to allow familial retention of property. As was the case in China, concubinage was common.

Business enterprises did and still tend to be centered on the family. Autocratic, hierarchical, patriarchy became the model form of administration of organizations. Large networks of affiliation based on reciprocal obligation would also become the norm. Agreements were informal rather than contractual. Common were strong feelings of belonging and loyalty to family and tribes. The intensity of these feelings could create rivalries and jealousies, however, and the fragmented nature of this society created a sense of alienation and lack of commitment to or participation in anything larger than one's tribe. There was a clear separation between those with whom one had close relationships and all others; even city dwellers built strong affiliations within neighborhoods. There were no individual rights, although there was great pride taken by individuals in their abilities and accomplishments, especially military heroics.

Each tribe worshipped its own god, embodied in an icon carried by the tribe from place to place, but most recognized the supremacy among gods of *Allah,* who brought the rain and guaranteed all oaths. Religion, like real property, was communal. There was no priesthood, and ritual was essentially pagan. Loyalty to the tribe required conformity to the tribal cult and was the principal moral standard so that religious and political loyalty coincided. Although Islam would bring major changes, much of this lifestyle remains the norm or the ideal for many Arabs. *Muhammad* (Mohammed) himself did not consider city dwellers as true Arabs (Lewis 1993), and there remains a schism between the nomad tribes and the city dwellers. The former considered the latter slaves to the land or to landlords; the latter, who had a deep emotional attachment to the land, considered the nomads to be ignorant vagabonds and thieves. The loss of land was deemed an unbearable injury. The neighborliness and mutual support we associate with rural landowners were fully in evidence. There remains some suspicion among city-dwelling Arabs that the nomads have not quite fully surrendered their love of independence and reliance on pre-Islamic, ancestral traditions, that is, that they are not quite true believers in Islamic law.

Some tribes were thought to be more noble than others, and they would acquire wealth through rent paid for land and tribute. The separation of noble tribes from others created a two-class system more Darwinian than the Chinese or Japanese social systems that, in theory, required benevolence of their upper classes. As villages grew into towns and cities, society became stratified into two layers, with merchants and professionals occupying the upper tier. Arabs who would become wealthy, either as landowners or traders, assumed that those of a lower station deserved their fate. Bedouin aversion to physical labor was embraced wholeheartedly by this upper class; reinstitution of another Bedouin belief, egalitarianism, would become one of Mohammed's most important objectives.

Pre-Islamic Arabs placed great value on honor, courage, strength, martial and material power, chivalry, preservation of independence, and readiness to avenge any insult. Men were fiercely possessive and protective of the chastity of women and security of children. A woman's sexual indiscretion brought more shame to her father and brothers than to her husband. Fierce internal rivalries were common. Loss of honor, shame, and debasement before others were unthinkable. But whereas the grievously-shamed Japanese might kill himself, the Arab might kill another who caused him shame. Aggressiveness and appearances established status, but land ownership and family heritage conveyed it. Loyalty demanded of all that they would exact harsh vengeance upon any outsider who harmed a member of one's tribe. Mohammed would seek to harness all this energy in the service of God. There was and still remains a strong sense of brotherhood, and any internal conflict within the tribe was seen as strictly temporary. The nomadic way of life and harsh environment engendered a strong tradition of generosity and lavish hospitality extended to all visitors, guests and passersby, even enemies and even if requiring sacrifice. This tradition, reflecting pride in home and family and to be embodied in one of the five pillars of Islam, still persists in the proclivity for extending elaborate courtesies and gift giving. In more-impersonal, urban settings it persists in intensity if not in scope. It should be noted, however, that Arab generosity and hospitality are offered often with the expectation of reciprocal obligation.

Like the samurai, the Bedouin took great pride in their abilities both as warriors and as poets, celebrating the valor of their heroes and insulting their enemies with equal verbosity and eloquence. Arabic is a highly pictorial and emotional language and lends itself well to rhythm and rhyme.

Skillful use of the language could arouse passion even among the illiterate. Arabs take great pride in their language rich in meaning and synonyms and beautiful in script. Nevertheless, illiteracy is rampant, and education remains the province of the wealthy. Only in the rich oil states has education become commonly accessible, and only then in very recent times.

The medieval period would see a flowering of Arab culture and a great body of literary work, even as Europe plunged into its Dark Ages. The perfection of handicrafts such as rugs and other textiles, metalwork, pottery, tile, perfumes, and soaps paralleled great accomplishments in paintings and architecture still seen throughout the Mediterranean region. Much of the beauty of Spanish architecture lies in its Moorish influences. Various Arab peoples would make enormous advances in mathematics (*algebra* is an Arabic word) and astronomy. Arabs would introduce to Europe the science of irrigation, paper (brought from China), cotton (brought from India), olives, dates, lemons, coffee, and sugar.

These nomadic tribes carried on a symbiotic albeit standoffish relationship with the sedentary tribes living at isolated oases, exchanging animal products for vegetable. Mecca, the first town in the region, arose on the intersection of the north-south spice route between Yemen and the Mediterranean and the east-west trade route between the Red Sea port of Jedda and the Persian Gulf. (Cities generally arise either around good ports or, like Mecca, at trade route crossroads.) Unlike the tribes, Mecca was controlled by an oligarchy of wealthy merchants and traders who exhibited a high degree of organization, cooperation, and discipline unusual among these nomadic people. As in the surrounding tribes and oases, however, the exercise of public authority was unusual. City life centered on the central market (*bazaar*), where merchants and farmers did business in stalls called *souk,* and a place for worship (*kabaa*) of the dominant local deity. This place of worship would one day, of course, be called a mosque, and the *kabaa* of Mecca would one day become the *mecca* of Islamic pilgrims. A culture models its value system in its heroes and villains, both real and mythical. In that regard, the literary classic *The Arabian Nights* provides interesting and entertaining insights into the Arab character.

HISTORICAL FORCES

Mohammed and the Caliphate

Mohammed, the Prophet, is of course the founder of Islam and its most revered figure. In his effort to attract believers to his faith, Mohammed set in motion forces that would bring a degree of unity and order to this society of tribes isolated in mind and spirit as well as in space. Building upon the traditional, dual nature of tribal loyalty, his efforts to establish Islam as a universal faith had the effect of focusing political loyalty as well. Islam thus embodied a sense of Arab nationalism and was a unifying force. Many in this region still consider themselves primarily as Muslims of mixed ethnic origin. The famous Islamic warrior Saladin, for example, scourge of the Crusaders, was not Arab but a Kurd. Mohammed's religious teachings, which prescribed proper behavior in some detail, acquired the force of law, and his followers thus found themselves, for the first time, led in a civil sense as well as a religious one. In effect, Mohammed had begun to establish a form of government where none had existed beforehand, and he became a symbol of Arab unity, despite the lack of any unified Arab state in a geographic sense. Many Arabs still view existing states as temporary and preliminary to creation of a unified pan-Arab, Islamic state. The Islamic government differed from the tribal form primarily in that it provided for the first time for rule of territory, not just of a mobile community, and placed executive and military leadership at the center. Arabs and Muslims thus became accustomed quite early to judging the legitimacy of government by its conformance to religious law. Distinctions such as church and state, spiritual and temporal, or lay and ecclesiastical did not translate into Arabic. The civil authority attached to religious law made a legislature unnecessary; there would be no law but the law of God. The general lack of institutional structure in Arab government would make it very difficult to govern what would become a far-flung empire.

Born in Mecca in 571 and orphaned at an early age, Mohammed would be raised by relatives and manage the trading business of a widow whom he would marry. He was at first a social reformer, much like Confucius, concerned about the plight of Mecca's poor and their oppression by the wealthy. On one of his customary, solitary retreats to a nearby mountain, he received, at age forty, the first of what he said would be a continuing series of revelations from God through the angel Gabriel. Among them was that there is one and only one almighty God, that God's revelations should guide all aspects of thought and behavior, and that man's purpose on Earth was to serve God's will. He began preaching these revelations first to his family and then to a growing number of followers. He condemned idolatry, disturbing greatly Mecca's rulers who profited from worshippers visiting the town's *kabaa*. Mohammed made no pretense of divinity, maintaining that he was nothing more than a mortal messenger of God's word, one among a number of prophets of the same God as Abraham, David, Moses, and Jesus. His proselytizing, militancy, and support for the poor ran afoul of the merchant oligarchy, who saw him as a threat to their commercial and worldly way of life, so he led his followers in flight to the nearby town of Medina in 622. This flight became known as the *hijra* (hegira), which marks year one of the Islamic calendar.

In Medina Mohammed the preacher became the political leader, mobilizing a drive for Arab unity and expansion of the faith. He found in the combative Bedouin fertile ground for creation of a strong army. The remainder of his life was devoted to subduing the Meccans, accomplished in 630, and attracting highly independent, tradition-bound, and thus quite reluctant surrounding tribes to the cause and to the faith. He eventually would convert the entire Arabian Peninsula. His ability to do so successfully remains his most impressive secular achievement. Mohammed built his following in part as a result of a successful campaign of raids upon merchant caravans in the vicinity of Medina. The tribes may well have been drawn to Mohammed more by his success in this traditional Bedouin pursuit than by his proselytizing. He attributed his success to divine will, thereby lending credence to his teachings. Whatever the means and however exemplary Mohammed's life may or may not have been, it can be said that in a relatively brief period of about twenty years, he shaped the life of his people as no human being had ever done (Lafflin 1975).

As the last prophet, Mohammed made no provision for succession. Upon his death in 632 a small group of his lieutenants established a form of rule called the *khalifa* (caliphate). The caliph was considered a kind of deputy prophet who inherited the full authority and power of Mohammed and whose responsibility it was to safeguard and preserve this heritage. Thus, under the caliphs, faith would continue as the primary social bond. Political and religious loyalty would remain one. Religious law would become absolute and replace tribal authority. The *majlis* and public opinion would become irrelevant. Apostasy would be considered treasonous. The caliph, however was a temporal, not spiritual, leader, a commander of the faithful; orthodox Muslims consider Mohammed the last prophet.

The Arab Empire

Among Mohammed's teachings was the doctrine of *din Muhammad bi'l sayf*, which held that every Arab was obligated to spread the faith and word of God, as transmitted by Mohammed, by force of arms. With Mecca subdued, the first caliph, Abu Bakr, Mohammed's father-in-law, turned his attention to expanding Arab reach, employing the executive authority and standing army established by Mohammed. Meanwhile, the Persian and Byzantine Empires had carried on the last of their long series of wars, which ended in 628, leaving both sides exhausted and weak. Abu Bakr's successor, Omar, exploited this opportunity by leading the Arabs out of the Peninsula to conquer the Fertile Crescent region, including non-Arab Persia (now Iraq). Long subject to oppression and heavy taxation by the occupying Byzantines and the Romans before them, many of these peoples, including Jews and Christians, welcomed the Arabs as liberators. Many converts flocked to the faith, and others adopted the Arabic language without converting. It is important to note, however, that this expansion was, at least at first, primarily Arab, not Islamic. Its military leaders were not particularly religious and were much more tolerant of "infidels" than the

Europeans would one day be toward Muslims, whom they would call Saracens. Arab Muslims considered Jews and Christians as followers of a similar, older, but imperfect faith, and therefore not really infidels.

Arab armies turned to the west, absorbing all of North Africa in the seventh century and established a presence in Somalia and Ethiopia to the south, thence northward into Malta, Cyprus, Crete, Sicily, southern Italy, and the Iberian Peninsula in the eighth century. Their empire (the *dar al-Islam* or all lands under Arab rule) eventually would stretch from the Indus River in India, to the foothills of present-day Turkey's Taurus Mountains and, to the west to the Pyrenees, the Bay of Biscay, and the Atlantic coasts of Portugal and Morocco. The Arab tide did not crest until defeat in southern France by Charles Martel at the battles of Poitiers and Tours in 732.

Long beset by internal rivalry and corruption, the empire began to decline in the eleventh century with the onset of the Crusades from the west and continual conflict with Turks, Mongols, Persians, and even the Chinese to the north and east. It suffered from lack of strength and organization at its center and fragmentation of authority and resources, as well as internal schism and civil war. The riches of revenue from taxes imposed on occupied lands and enslavement of infidels eroded internal discipline. Internal tension and strife intensified as highly decentralized, independent tribes increasingly found themselves bound by highly autocratic sultans who freely invoked the word of God to exercise their will, whatever their purpose. All populated Arab lands in the Middle East and North Africa fell first under Byzantine and then Ottoman rule, which would continue through most of the second millennium and into the early twentieth century.

As the Europeans developed direct trade routes between Europe and the Far East both overland and around the Cape of Good Hope, led by the Portuguese navigator Vasco da Gama, Arab traders and middlemen lost much of their market. European shipping came to dominate maritime commerce as well, pushing the Arabs off the Mediterranean, the Indian Ocean, and even the Red Sea. Lacking resources, deprived of their central role in east-west trade and having passed the peak of their military power, the Arab world was effectively contained and, by the fifteenth century, was entering a long period of stagnation dominated by a quasi-feudal, subsistence economy.

The pre-Islamic, two-class system persisted during the empire, but military leaders supplanted merchants in the upper class, which benefited from the riches that accrue to empires everywhere. Absolute, oppressive, and often corrupt rule became the norm, which was tolerated as long as leaders were perceived as brave and magnanimous in the Bedouin tradition. The unquestioned authority of Islam provided an effective if often abused means to exercise absolute power. Lacking the institutional mechanisms of temporal government, assassination (this term is derived from Arabic) and revolt were the only means to remove rivals or tyrants and became commonplace from the outset. These circumstances would continue essentially unchanged even as the twentieth century brought Europeans in force and the exploitation of oil, the latter creating an even larger gulf between rich and poor Arabs. Islam of course remained the unifying force. Judges who applied Islamic law were the only institutional establishment beyond the ruling upper class.

Interaction with the West

From the outset of Arab trading with and expansion into the West, the Arabs considered the Europeans ignorant barbarians. Like the Chinese and Japanese cultures, Arab culture was much advanced relative to first-millennium Europeans. It was not until the emergence of the nation-state from the turmoil of the Middle Ages that the Europeans drove the Arabs from their continent, and it was not until the ensuing Renaissance that European cultural advancement resumed the march begun during the classical period. Indeed it was the Arabs who preserved much of the glory of Greece while Europe struggled after the fall of the Roman Empire and who then reintroduced it to Europe.

Europeans finally began to look to their south with mercantilist ambitions in the sixteenth century. Their interest began in earnest when Napoleon occupied Egypt in 1798 to sever England's trade route to India and China. Later, the English would build a railroad on this route connecting ports on the Mediterranean and Red Seas, the route to the Indian ocean (eventually supplemented by the Suez canal) and thence eastward. The English and French would build railroads throughout the region and would come to dominate commerce. With the dissolution of the Ottoman Empire at the end of World War I, much of the Middle East and North Africa became European colonies with the English established in what is now Egypt, Iraq, Jordan, and Palestine, the French in Syria, Lebanon, Tunisia, Algeria, and, with Spain, in Morocco, and the Italians in Libya.

Western influence has been greatest in these countries and also in Iran, which has long been a focal point for Western interests first for its oil and then for containing the Soviet Union during the Cold War. However, this influence has been limited largely to the wealthy and the educated; the masses answer still only to Islam. The Europeans brought with them the trappings of class, which wealthy upper-class Arabs adopted readily. The Arabs marveled at Western organization and technology and adapted such institutions as the comprehensive university (there had long been universities established to teach Islam), libraries, museums, the press, charities such as the Red Crescent modeled on the Red Cross, and some Western political processes and institutions. The major exception was Western industrial enterprise. Consequently, Arab students had little interest in practical studies, preferring instead to prepare for the learned professions. Whereas upper-class Arabs benefited financially and politically from European ties, intensified Arab nationalism and resentment was by far the more common reaction. This hostility, amplified by a continuing sense of cultural and moral superiority and complemented by aversion to physical labor, illiteracy, and minimalist education based on rote learning of traditional ways, would prevent the Arabs from adopting the skills necessary to build a diversified, industrial economy. The reader will note the similarity here to the circumstances in China and the very different experience in Japan. This economic backwardness also would continue into the twentieth century and remain a matter of great concern and consternation in the Arab world. Britain, in order to induce Arab neutrality during World War I (vitally important because Turkey and the Ottoman Empire already were allied with Germany), promised to establish a unified Arab state after the war. Instead, Britain allowed (the Balfour Declaration) establishment of a Jewish homeland in Palestine and, with France, would carve up the remnants of the Ottoman empire with both remaining in place. This was seen by the Arabs as treachery and only the most egregious indication of Western depravity and imperialism. One outcome was Arab sympathy for the Communists and even with German Nazism to the extent those doctrines represented, accurately or not, anti-imperialism, and anti-Zionism. Another unfortunate result was the division of native Kurdish lands among Turkey, Syria, Iraq, and Iran, and thus the continuing conflict in that region. An overlay to this tendentious political relationship was the continuing gulf between Islam and Christianity, which had coexisted peacefully since the Moors (mixed Arabs and Berbers) were driven from Spain. Muslim and Christian shared a lack of understanding of one another but also mutual forbearance. It is not so much fear of losing converts to Christianity that troubled Muslims about increased exposure to the West as much as fear of diminution of the level of religious fervor to that more typical of the West.

RELIGION

Islam

Islam means submission to the will of God. A Muslim is one who submits. Islam holds that man's purpose is to serve the will of God. One lives to perfect one's faith and earn salvation. All temporal and human concerns are of lesser consequence. All believers are equal before God—a brotherhood, regardless of race or nationality. In keeping with pre-Islamic custom as well as Mohammed's teaching, religious obligations have the force of law, and temporal authority is subsumed by religious authority. All thoughts, events, and consequences are acts of God. To the pagan, essentially hedonistic, pre-Islamic Bedouin, manliness and honor were the only meaningful virtues. The Bedouin recognized no moral authority other than tribal justice and had no conception of any afterlife. The Islamic notion of salvation had great appeal to people used to the hardship of desert life, who carry an overbearing sense of sadness, suffering, deprivation, and fatalism. Patience, resignation, and abnegation were made worthwhile by the prospect of an eternal paradise.

The *Quran* is a collection of God's revelations to Mohammed recorded over a period of some twenty years. Muslims study it in great detail both as a text of religious principles and exhortations and as a way of life. Many commit it to memory. A relatively short work compared to the Bible, it has been supplemented by the recorded sayings of Mohammed, *hadith,* each conveying a moral lesson, and an accumulation of stories and anecdotes, the *sunna,* drawn from accounts of the life of Mohammed recorded as exemplars of proper behavior. The *Quran, hadith, sunna,* and pronouncements by some of Mohammed's successors provide the basis for *sharia* or religious law, which governs the most-minute aspects of behavior. Sharia is a kind of common law interpreted and applied by Islamic judges. Islam then is more than a religion but a way of life based on goodness, charity, justice, peace, and equality. Most Islamic states consider sharia the law of the land, although not all enforce it to the same degree. It speaks to commercial matters only in the prohibition of usury and the exhortation to keep good business records to prevent disputes.

Muslims must abide by two sets of obligations: moral and ceremonial. Moral obligations include love of and obedience to Allah and "right-living," exemplified by filial loyalty and obedience; the virtues of honesty, kindness, charity, gratitude, and mercy; female chastity and modesty; male obligations of brotherhood and solidarity; beneficence toward one's wife; pursuit of social justice; and equality of all people and races. Duties to God and to others are more important than individual rights. Avarice and usury are condemned. Ceremonial obligations include the "five pillars" of Islam:

1. The profession of faith "There is no god but Allah and Mohammed is his messenger." (Exemplifying the centrality of Islam in Arabic life, this statement appears in Arabic script on the Saudi national flag.)

2. Ritual prayer, a reaffirmation of faith, repeated five times daily.

3. Fasting and abstention from other pleasures from sunrise to sunset during the ninth lunar month, Ramadan, which celebrates the occasion of Islamic revelation.

4. Regular almsgiving, typically amounting to 2–3 percent of income or assets, reflecting Mohammed's origins as a social reformer.

5. A one-time pilgrimage to the holy cities of Mecca and Me-

dina, intended to reinforce a sense of Islamic community and brotherhood.

Islam differs from Judeo-Christian religions more in its centrality to everyday life than in its doctrine and teachings. Muslims consider Jews and Christians not infidels but misguided fellow believers in the same God, that is, to be "people of the Book" or "of the same house." They consider idolatry the worship of Christ, the Christian trinity, or any other figure other than the one true God. Any portrayal of God as a human figure is considered sacrilegious as it is in Judaism, and there is no means of intercession between God and man—that is, man worships God directly and prays only to God. Similarities between the *Quran* and the Bible include a belief in heaven and hell, a day of judgment, Satan, the reward of good and punishment of evil, and many common figures and stories. Jesus Christ is recognized as a prophet and miracle worker but not as divine or the son of God.

With a dearth of institutions to maintain order and settle disputes, with the most minute detail of behavior regulated by Islamic law, and with a proclivity for emotional disagreement, it was easy for a dispute regarding interpretation to escalate into factional strife and schism. The most significant faction is *Shia*, which dominates in Iran and southern Iraq. Shiites dispute the rightful succession to Mohammed, believing that the proper line descends through Ali, Mohammed's son-in-law. A somewhat independent caliphate, using the title *imam* (spiritual leader), operated in this more remote (from the West), eastern region of the empire, and the Shiite branch of Islam became more ascetic and stringent than the Sunni majority. Unlike Sunni-dominated countries, a Shiite state is a theocracy and thus more in keeping with the *Quran*, which advocates religious rule and forbids royal or other secular titles, consistent with the ideal of egalitarian brotherhood. The Shiite imam was a religious figure, a kind of prophet, and there remains a substantial clerical establishment in heterodox Shia, unlike the orthodox Sunni form of Islam. In keeping with Persian tradition rather than Arab, Shiite leadership is inherited as a kind of "divine right." Perhaps because of a sense of insecurity as a minority sect, the Shiites were more inclined to use violent means to preserve their independence, often attacking the Sunni establishment, and remain more resistant to Western incursion. The reader will recognize the Shia, led by the Ayatollah Khomeini, for their revolution against the secular rule of the Shah of Iran, holding the American embassy in that country hostage during the Carter administration, their war against the secular rule of Saddam Hussein in Iraq and, more recently, their alleged connections to terrorism in Israel, the United States, Saudi Arabia, Lebanon, and elsewhere. The rise of Shiism seems to be encouraging the emergence of more-intense Islamic consciousness (what westerners often call Islamic fundamentalism) in those parts of the Arab world more exposed to Western influence and dominated by the Sunni, most notably in Algeria and Egypt, and even in Saudi Arabia itself. Some military analysts speculate that one reason the U.S.-led coalition did not remove Saddam Hussein from power in Iraq during the Persian Gulf War was pressure from the Saudis who wanted to maintain Sunni-controlled Iraq as a buffer against further Iranian Shiite incursion into the Arab world, perhaps facilitated by a Shiite uprising in Iraq upon Hussein's demise.

CORE VALUES AND BEHAVIOR

Hierarchy and Power Distance

The now familiar pattern of authoritarian hierarchy based on the absolute power of the patriarch, amplified by the absolutism of Islam and despotic rule, is as evident in Arabic culture as it has been in other Oriental cultures. Filial piety is sacred and a lifelong obligation. This pattern is repeated in all organizations. The adoption of religious law among the faithful as the law of the land left little room for dissent. Nonconformity is a serious and sometimes fatal source of shame. Self-effacement and humility are expected when dealing with superiors. The pre-Islamic recognition of nobility based on heredity and martial or artistic accomplishment has been intensified by the self-aggrandizing behavior of potentates of one form or another throughout the Islamic period, and the result is a rigid class system with great separation between rich and poor and little in the way of a middle class, especially in those countries not endowed with oil.

Yet the Bedouin ideals of fraternal egalitarianism, representational tribal democracy, and rule through mediation have survived to some extent. There is a considerable body of research, summarized by Ali (1993), that indicates a strong preference for a consultative management style among Arab executives. Ali (p. 53) cites a passage in the *Quran* that encourages such behavior: "Consult them in affairs of the moment, then, when you reach a decision, trust God."

Masculinity

No other major culture compares to the Arabs in terms of the high degree of distinction in male and female roles, yet Hofstede's masculinity finding was only moderately high. The gender distinction, as Hofstede defined it, is moderated by the low value placed by Arabs on labor and task accomplishment and the high value placed on strong, emotive relationships and verbal skills. *Sharia* addresses family relationships in great detail and clearly subordinates the female to the male, even though it allows women to hold a job, receive inheritances, and own property despite contrary Arab customs. However, there is considerable difference among Arab countries in the separation of gender roles, and one may find the genders mixing naturally in a work setting even if kept apart socially. An exception is Saudi

Arabia, which does not allow women to drive, to work with men, or to live abroad without male family members. In contrast, women are found in all walks of life in Iraq; Tunisia has outlawed polygamy, made divorce a prerogative of civil courts, and allows intermarriage. Nydell (1996, 1987) offers a wealth of information on Arab family life and social practices.

Collectivism

Islamic law subordinates individual interest to the public interest. Ties of kinship and tribal ties are intense, as is the distrust of outsiders. Arabs will defend the honor of their families without regard for culpability. The Arab man's ties to his parental family are stronger than his obligations to his wife. The wife joins the husband's family and, under traditional Islamic rules, can be divorced with a simple declarative statement. She, however, cannot initiate divorce. The tradition of tribal independence limits collective ties to the extended family, and Arab collectivism thus is much more similar to that of China than Japan. Arabs will put family interests before work. Arab managers will thus tolerate tardiness due to family circumstances.

Arabs divide the world into friends and everyone else; they will not do business with strangers, and the use of intermediaries is essential. The traditional value placed upon the mediating ability of the sheik makes this an honored and important role. Arabs are enthusiastic and highly skilled businesspeople, stemming from their long history as traders and merchants. They admire business acumen and are very good bargainers. It is considered a highly honorable pursuit; after all, the Prophet himself was once a businessman. After contact is made, development of a good personal relationship becomes the next objective. Socializing should be thought of not as a preliminary ritual to be endured before getting down to business but, as is the case in most non-Anglo cultures, *part of* doing business. It is time well spent. The personalization of relationships is such that the Arab thinks of himself as doing business with another individual rather than with the company that individual represents. These relationships are meant to be lasting friendships that could seem intrusive to westerners as Arabs feel free to ask friends highly personal questions and favors, invade one's "personal space" and drop in unexpectedly. One should expect more physical contact by Arabs (less so in Saudi Arabia and the smaller states on the Peninsula). Connections drive many business decisions, with nepotism common. The need for intimate knowledge and familiarity gives rise to endemic gossipmongering, which in turn can generate emotional disputes. Privacy is not important; friends and relatives visit regularly and often for what can be quite lengthy visits. Arabs draw great comfort and security from these relationships solidified by much gift-giving and picking up of restaurant checks to demonstrate their value and commitment. People and relationships are more important than rules and procedures. Typical Western behavior appears to the Arab as impersonal and insensitive and, when coupled with the "understated" Western manner of speech, standoffish, noncommittal and cold. Although hospitality and generosity may be offered with expectations of reciprocity—indeed Arabs will feel obligated to repay obligations disproportionately—it is also common for Arabs to do favors and extend kindnesses selflessly, especially among close friends.

Individualism

It was noted earlier that the research on the collectivism-individualism scale was mixed in its findings. Supplementing tribal collectivism is a vestige of the fierce independence of Bedouin tribes and the high self-esteem of one who earns the respect of peers through heroic deeds, poetic virtuosity, or skilled diplomacy. This heritage creates an internal conflict between the traditional Bedouin, a kind of rugged individualist, who may chafe when given orders but who eventually submits to the will of Allah. Individualism within the context of intense loyalty to the tribal clan also results in a certain lack of social consciousness, unruliness, and assertiveness (Hamady 1960). Islam is a community of the faithful; it does not espouse any sense of social or political unity, other than the common obligation of obedience to God, the only sovereign. Traditionally there has been little evidence of social aims beyond the well-being of the family or of respect for secular leaders (other than that engendered by fear) or strong patriotism or nationalism (recall that most borders were arbitrarily imposed). However, resentment of real and perceived Western imperialism (Communism is considered a Western affliction)—especially as manifested in support of Israel— concern about Western diminution of Islamic faith, and the oil weapon have given rise to some very intense nationalism in recent times.

Uncertainty Avoidance and Fatalism

There is much in Arab history that would tend to create and reinforce fear of the unknown and to deter initiative. Islam teaches that Allah—not one's knowledge, experience, or character—determines one's fate. As a result of the combined effects of tribal rule based on historical precedent, submission to both the will of Allah and to the vicissitudes of life in one of the world's harshest environments, and the inherent conservatism of Islam, Arabs have a strong external locus of control and orientation toward tradition and the past. Faith requires total surrender; this is the very meaning of the term Islam. The Arab rarely discusses the likelihood of an event without interjecting "if God wills" (*Insha' Allah*). Events that do come to pass do so "in the name of God" or because "God is great" and are received with "praise be to God." God controls the Arab's life and time, whereas the Arab's need to maintain face before other Arabs controls behavior and actions. The colloquialism *kismet* is taken from the Arab *qisma*

(Patai 1983). The *Quran* essentially forbids experiment: "Do not follow what you do not know" (Lafflin 1975, 43). However, Ali (1993) argues that the invocation of Allah's name is more an indication of humility before God than an indicator of fatalism. Moreover, religious faith provides a sense of hope and confidence, allowing some tolerance of uncertainty and willingness to take risks. Although high uncertainty avoidance creates a need for structure, Arabs expect one another to circumvent rules and bureaucracy (which usurp the power of Allah) to advance their personal relationships. Thus even though uncertainty avoidance may well be on the high side, it would be incorrect to assume that the Arab is paralyzed by it.

A significant behavioral consequence is the seeming lack of follow-through, of seeing tasks through to completion. With so little sense of control, long-term planning is seen not only as pointless but as presumptuous and even sacrilegious. Solutions are spontaneous and improvised rather than researched and carefully considered. Conformity is more important than creativity, intention more important than accomplishment, wishes and ideation more important than reality, form more important than substance, and rhetoric more persuasive than objective information. Words, including threats, suffice for action. Original thinking is suspect, and innovation carries the threat of subversion. Change is viewed with trepidation, as a gate to sin, and thus is resisted. There is a certain passivity, a disinclination to act, to initiate, to maintain rather than to change or to improve, to preserve rather than to innovate. A once-vibrant intellectual curiosity and artistic creativity have been dulled by more than a millennium of political oppression and harshly conservative religious dogma (at least by Western standards), an intense focus on the past, the attitude that labor causes loss of face, and a sense of helplessness in the face of the rising economic and political power of the West. Only change that restores the simpler life of the past or moves one closer to God is welcome. When the Arab takes pride in composure and stoic calm in the face of adversity, the westerner perceives a disconcerting lack of initiative and motivation. Disregard of the passage of time and punctuality is another result, and patience is an essential attribute when working with Arabs. One may wait for days for what would seem to require only minutes or hours, and one must be tolerant and forbearing when making inquiries about promised but as yet undelivered results. Ali (1993) argues that much of the Arab proclivity toward centralized rule, apparent lack of energy and dynamism, reluctance to act independently, and illiteracy are a result of the oppressive Ottoman Turk occupation that lasted from 1412 to 1918.

Although the foregoing discussion pertains to Arabs generally, exposure to Western technology and its results has attenuated fatalism among educated Arabs. Yet it remains very much more in evidence in the Arab world than in industrialized countries.

Status Consciousness and Good Form

Though the ranking criterion may change—whether it be the perceived nobility of one's tribe, based on its military or polemical virtuosity; the ability to trace one's lineage to Mohammed or to his relatives and colleagues; or the control of oil wealth—the Arab world has long been divided into two widely separated classes (as always, nomadic Bedouins in the hinterlands command the respect of all and remain outside the class system). Exposure to the West and its institutions has spawned a small, professional, somewhat westernized middle class in this century, with the upper class occupied primarily by those with political power. Most oil wealth remains under political control. As one might expect in a high-power-distance culture, rank and appearances carry great weight; one must exercise authority and dress in accordance with one's social station and entertain and conduct oneself with meticulous formality and social grace. The reluctance of the classes to mix socially amplifies power distance, and there is little social mobility. Elegant speech is valued more than tangible effort and accomplishment. Hard work is the unpleasant fate of the unworthy or unfortunate, and nonprofessional or nonsupervisory positions are shunned. One cannot be seen as trying too hard. There is great importance placed on formality of behavior and manners and outward appearance.

Intensity of Emotion and Extremism

Bedouin values, and a deep sense of community, brotherhood, and kinship, and the beauty of the Arabic language can arouse intense emotions and even explosive rivalries and jealousies. Every tribe had its poet, and even illiterate Arabs can recite sometimes inflammatory or coarse poetry, often intended to insult or defame an enemy. Well-executed poetry became communal property and a source of tribal pride. Though Islamic law forbids strife among believers, assassinations and terrorism have been common from pre-Islamic times and Arabs have long fought one another. The cruelty and savagery often exhibited by the Bedouin may have been amplified by frequent conflict and interaction with the equally ferocious Mongols and Turks. Aggressiveness and hostility, sometimes taking the form of savage pitched battles and at other times more of a skirmish or taunting, have persisted into the twentieth century. *Jihad* or holy war is the most common theme in Islamic writing (Lafflin 1975). Although westerners may perceive jihad as aimed at them, any effort to redress an injury, no matter the source, can acquire the force of jihad. The raiding party was a great and common adventure for pre-Islamic Arabs, and looting was the primary means of acquiring material well-being. Women and camels were favored booty. Bedouin life was quite hedonistic featuring every vice. Offenses of all kinds had to be avenged and honor restored. Property and family had to be defended vigorously. All this uproar and adventure created many opportunities for song and poetic celebration of deeds heroic and otherwise with the flamboyant eloquence so loved by speakers of Arabic. The discipline imposed by Islam would impose much strain and tension on this society and require considerable force to subdue it.

With civil strife apparently a permanent condition, oppressive government would provide the only apparent solution (Lafflin 1975). Mohammed found it necessary to declare an annual truce of four months to allow for trading and religious observation (Patai 1983). Victims of assassination have included caliphs, sovereigns, princes, generals, and governors. This century has seen the assassination of Egyptian President Anwar Sadat and a Saudi king. The period 1948 to 1973, when the Arabs won the opening battles of the "oil war," known mostly for Arab-Israeli conflict, has seen twelve civil wars among Arabs, thirty successful revolutions and at least fifty unsuccessful ones, and the assassination of twenty-two heads of state and prime ministers. There were sixteen occasions between 1958 and 1973 when one Arab state severed relations with another (Lafflin 1975, 109–110). The terrorism so feared today began as early as the tenth century. As noted, much of this violence has been directed toward the Sunni majority by the Shia sect. In many instances, demagogues have been able to recruit and manipulate poorly or uneducated Muslims to carry out their violent aims. Arabs euphemize these conflicts as "family squabbles" or "disagreements among allies." Nationalism has joined religion as a generator of conflict, as seen in the recent war between Iran and Iraq, the running and sometimes violent feuds between Libya and the West and Iraq and the West, continuing strife in Lebanon and Bosnia, and the Persian Gulf War.

The Arab has long lived in a world of extremes—of temperature typical of desert and mountain climates even between day and night; a bone-dry *wadi* (an arroyo) that becomes a raging torrent in a brief thunderstorm; the barren desert and the lush oasis; vast wastelands and teeming cities; extremes of tranquility within one's household and tribe compared to frequent conflict and rivalry without; the autocratic family versus an anarchic state, internal egalitarianism versus submission to wealth, the faith, or to despots both Arab and foreign; mild manners and peacefulness coexist with ferocity and bellicosity; intense love alongside fierce jealousy; lethargy versus spasms of vigorous activity; calm conversation interrupted by sharp outbursts of anger and threat that just as quickly subside; blessings and curses delivered with equal vehemence and eloquence; and profound friendships dissolved permanently by momentary arguments. All is black or white. Lafflin (1975, 85) characterizes Arabs as oscillating between volatile emotion and apathetic sullenness and melancholia, often caused by shame.

Vividly expressed emotions of joy and sadness, likes and dislikes, and hope, stress or despair, spontaneity, flowery praise and eloquence, even if boastful or excessively flattering, are much admired. Emoting and impulsiveness and close physical contact are expected; their absence suggests lack of commitment and insincerity. For example, a typical Arab expression of condolences may take the form of a flowery metaphor such as "Life is God's garden out of which, now and then, he plucks the most beautiful flower" (Barakat 1993, 25). A reciprocation of a simple "Good morning" greeting would be considered trite and unimaginative. Courtesies and compliments must be returned in greater degree. Therefore a proper response to "Good morning" might be "May your day be prosperous," which may in turn elicit another escalation such as "May your day be prosperous and blessed" (Patai 1983). Instead of a simple "Thank you" one might hear "May God increase your well-being!" Such speech comes across as overstatement, as pointless exaggeration and rings hollow to westerners, yet speaking in extremes is normal for the Arab. Assertions are stated emphatically, demands tend to be excessive, and statements often repeated in an effort to communicate conviction. Attempts at eloquence through elaborate simile seem like obfuscation to westerners. Because Arabs expect exaggeration, use of tact and understatement will cause difficulties in understanding. The Arab sees moderate speech as an indicator of lack of seriousness, not respect or modesty. This can create an interesting challenge for Western negotiators as an Arab may open with what seems to be a preposterously outrageous demand and will promise more than can be delivered. One eventually will get to a comfortably middling position but only after traversing a longer distance. Arab leaders are expected to speak in such a manner as well—hence Saddam Hussein's empty promise of "the mother of all battles." In this regard, as in many others, form is more important than substance. To the Arab, indicating an intention may be more important than carrying out the promised action. Artistic use of words carries more persuasive power than logical argument, and ideas have more meaning than facts. This expressiveness was constrained of course by religious taboo and by the need to dissemble to avoid political persecution. Just as Bedouin sheiks were expected to mediate intratribal disputes skillfully, the disputatious Arab still ascribes great status to skillful mediators.

Face or *Wajh*

Reputation is everything to the Arab, who senses that every aspect of public behavior is scrutinized and judged. The Arab even deceives and hides weaknesses to protect reputation and aggressively avenges any damage to it. Beginning with Bedouin celebration of great deeds, Arabs treat others and expect to be treated with dignity and respect. As in China, it is extremely important to uphold the honor of one's family and obligations of kinship. Any insult or injury, especially to one's virility (that is, chivalry) or to family, especially women, must be avenged. Even the most tranquil and peaceful of individuals might be driven to violent reprisal under such circumstances. The reaction to perceived condescension, a slight, or slur can be highly aggressive and vigorous. The line between anger and jihad is easily crossed. The saving of wajh for others is an important social skill, and the importance of protecting the honor and wajh of another takes precedence over factual expression. In essence, charity is more important than accuracy or equity, and one must avoid insulting an Arab or even expressing anything negative, even in private and even if the truth must be suppressed. Thus, as is the case in Japan, Arabs find it difficult to state an outright refusal, and a noncommittal response is very likely a negative one.

The use of intermediaries is a face-saving device in that it obviates the need for a direct refusal. Subordinates may use an intermediary to approach the supervisor for the same reason. Arabs often go on in great length before answering a difficult question or getting to the point, if ever. Self-criticism is rare; the Arab will find it very difficult to admit error or accept blame. As in other Eastern cultures, shame, then, is a more important means of social restraint than is guilt, although an Arab sins only when others witness the transgression, which encourages falsehood and obfuscation. "A concealed sin is two-thirds forgiven" is an Arab proverb (Lafflin 1975). One who reveals the sin of another might then become subject to retribution by the sinner. Hamady (1960) suggests that the fear of public shame brought down by a public mistake is another reason why Arabs are reluctant to experiment or innovate. Another important facet of wajh is stoicism, the suppression or denial of suffering and trouble beyond one's capacity to control or avenge. Arabs go to great lengths, even outright falsehood, to put a positive spin on unpleasant or painful realities or to identify scapegoats, in the end shrugging them off as the will of Allah. Stemming from Bedouin disdain of sedentary farmers and agriculture, the abstention from physical labor it requires has become a matter of face as well. One consequence has been a resistance to industry generally. Another is the extensive use of foreign labor (or laborers from Arab countries not endowed with oil!) to perform unpleasant tasks.

CONVERGENCE?

The Arab world is one in which speeding luxury cars on modern expressways encounter shepherds leading camels or goats across the road. It remains with at least one foot planted firmly in the past as it struggles to join the modern world. Nydell (1996, 1987) speaks of a generation gap emerging as Arabs gain exposure to the West through expanded trade and travel and the resultant struggle with tradition. Many younger Arabs adopt Western ways even as some of their elders think about jihad against the West. Western humanism, skepticism, and reliance on reason rather than on faith cause traditionalists grave concern.

Traditionalism still dominates, however, as much of the Arab world continues in stagnation, creating enormous frustration in this intensely proud people, manifested in a sense of increasing marginalization in the world community. A sense of bygone splendor and lost nobility and accomplishment pervades the Arab self-concept. Even though Arabs may consider westerners immoral, untrustworthy, decadent imperialists, and resent Western ascendancy in cultural achievement where Arabs once demonstrated superiority, there is recognition of a need for Western technology in order to obtain freedom from Western influence or even domination. At the same time, there is recognition that the very faith Arabs wish to practice free of Western interference and dilution has much to do with the Arab world's stagnation. Resistance to change and aversion to industry in the larger and individual sense make modernization difficult, and resentment of westerners makes it difficult to learn. The prohibition of usury makes Arabs uncomfortable borrowing or lending money. This belief has constrained capital formation and retarded development, especially in countries that lack oil wealth. Adding insult to injury is the example of the ancient enemy, Turkey. In the tradition of the Ottoman emperor Suleiman the Magnificent, known as "The Lawgiver," Kemal Ataturk abolished the Turkish caliphate in 1924, established a secular republic, and replaced sharia with Western-like laws and democratic institutions. Turkey has moved forthrightly into the modern world, has long been a member of NATO, for example, and has been led by a female prime minister, all with no apparent injury to Islam in that country or elsewhere. The Shah of Iran had been attempting to follow Ataturk's example, but the Shiites would not permit it and overthrew him.

The failed Soviet intervention in Afghanistan, the Persian Gulf War, the Western treatment of Bosnia, the continued Western support for Israel and for what many Arabs consider corrupt, despotic Arab regimes confirm to many Arabs continued imperialism and meddling. Little has happened that would heal the rift caused by the Balfour Declaration, which many Arabs still believe is all that stands between them and a unified state. Although the Organization of Petroleum Exporting Countries and the oil weapon have lost much might, at least for the time being, the potential for tension and even conflict remains. The revolution in Iran seems to have arrested whatever westernization had been underway in the Arab world. Together with the rise of heightened Islamic consciousness, a notion similar to the notion of "Black pride," seen most recently in the Taliban movement in Afghanistan, and continued terrorism, it illustrates the enormous cultural gulf between the West and the Islam, and therefore, the Arab world.

The Arab culture that reached its peak nearly a thousand years ago is still trying to define itself and come to grips with the modern world. It remains to be seen whether a society that may wish to advance in a material sense on a broad front can do so while governed by sharia or even whether it may ever wish to do so. Some six hundred years younger than Christianity, Islam in some ways seems to be enduring the same kind of struggle Christianity did at the corresponding stage of its development. Six hundred and fewer years ago Christians, in the name of God, were burning Jews and heretics, enslaving Native Americans, and meddling in affairs of state from Europe to Japan.

Consider the obstacles to convergence. Islamic doctrine sanctions violence in that it encourages the use of force. Arabs have long sanctioned assassination and terror to an extent unlike any other of the world's sizable cultures. Material well-being is rooted more in looting than in industry. Both Christianity and Judaism arose in part from resistance to an oppressive state, whereas westerners might see Islam *as* an oppressive state. Judeo-Christians consider themselves children of God, whereas Muslims see themselves as God's subjects. This still highly stratified people finds it difficult to understand our economic, political, and managerial practices as well as our values and sense of virtue, and we theirs. Perceptions of one another are mired in stereotype. We fear one another to some extent, and therefore we resent one another.

In many ways the Arab world is a simmering kettle of internal contradictions. There is conflict between the hedonistic, independent values of the Bedouin and the strictures of Islam and a long history of despotic rule. There is conflict between seventh-century values, attitudes, and beliefs and twenty-first-century needs and between the generations as the young become more westernized. There is conflict between their educated parents who adopt Western technology and management practices and the more traditional, inward-looking Arab as well as between the modern city dweller and still rebellious but respected Bedouin. Managers are torn between tribal loyalties and obligations to the modern organization. There is conflict between orthodox (Sunni) and heterodox (Shiite) and fundamentalist Islam. Despite the recent proliferation of university education, often free, there remains a wide gulf between rich and poor. Many devout Muslims resent the imposition of secular rule and royalty, viewed by many as corrupt and by more as defiant of Islamic doctrine. As noted earlier, Western support of these monarchies sustains Arab suspicion of the West.

In conclusion, it ought to be said that despite this wide cultural gulf, the obstacles to mutually beneficial interaction at the level of the individual and the firm are less daunting. Consistent with the imperatives of cultural influences, many Arab managers continue to place the interests of the individual, the family, and the tribe before those of the organization, and authoritarian practices remain common. Conformance to Islam, personal loyalty, and connections still may carry more weight than does merit. Positions will be found for "good" people more readily than will good people be found for the job. Delegation does not come easily, and even trivial matters may be passed up the chain of command. As has been the case elsewhere, continued and intensifying contact with the West has forced some behavioral concessions. Arabs will make decisions, but only after consultation with subordinates. Meetings will take place, even if not on schedule. Bargains will be struck, as long as one understands Arab ways of doing business and communicating and then builds relationships and adjusts expectations accordingly. Arabs will live up to obligations, but one must learn to be flexible. Merit is supplanting nepotism, and modern management practice is supplanting tribalism. Objectivity, logic, and facts carry more weight as university education becomes more accessible at home and abroad. Ali (1995, 24) observes that in keeping with the internal inconsistencies of the Arab world, the Arab in more-democratic work settings is "thoughtful, takes risks, and is courageous and creative," whereas in more-authoritarian settings, the Arab is "dependent, apathetic, conforming, and conservative." Cross-cultural differences can, here as elsewhere, be moderated by understanding and empathy. Thus will the expectations for profitable and pleasant relationships among Arab and Western businesspeople seem much more sanguine than those between our two cultures in the larger sense.

SUMMARY

The primary forces shaping Arab culture include the following:

- An environment of climatic extremes and deprivation that induces a sense of submission to nature and a trading mentality, necessitates strong tribal cohesion, and generates intense emotion and extreme, sometimes hostile behavior
- The nomadic, prideful, and democratic Bedouin life-style
- Islam, which regulates and impels prescribed behavior with great power and in great detail but which also compels a sense of brotherhood and caring for one another
- A long history as traders that instilled a liking and respect for commerce and the role of the intermediary
- A rich language that facilitates artful and effusive communication and serves as a vehicle for emotional expression
- Exposure to the West that has amplified the conflict between medieval and modern values and the internal dichotomy between bedouin independence and tribal loyalty on one hand and submission to Islamic authority and Arab nationalism on the other.

The core values produced by these forces include the following:

- **Large power distance**—a vestige of a long history of oppressive rule, a bipolar, two-class social system and the intense, pervading discipline of Islam

- Collectivism—grounded in the ancient tradition of tribal loyalty and the prevalence of the extended family as the primary social and economic unit
- Individualism—an ideal of the nomadic, bedouin life-style
- Intense masculinity—in the sense of traditional gender roles; a result of chivalric romanticism that reduces the female to inferiority and the role of helpless supplicant
- Femininity—in the sense of being more relationship-oriented than task-oriented and highly and demonstrably communicative; driven by traditions of emoting and verbal eloquence
- Moderate uncertainty avoidance—with confidence in the support of Allah to guide decisions and actions partially offsetting strong inhibitions posed by the perceived dominance of man by God and nature
- Intensity of emotion—and an inclination toward hostility engendered by traditions of rivalry, possessiveness, a very high value placed on personal honor, distrust of others competing for scarce resources and for survival under harsh conditions, constant warfare, and mastery of the art of insult abetted by a language that inflames passions
- Face—an intense drive to maintain one's reputation, even at the expense of honesty and equity, and shaming as the primary means of social control; a result of a tradition of romanticist boasting and high expectation of conformance first to tribal custom and obligations and later to *sharia*
- Great value placed on warmth, hospitality and generosity—a result of Islamic teaching, a feminine emphasis on human relationships, and, ultimately, a long history of shared hardship and the exigencies of a nomadic life-style in a hostile environment
- Ascribed status—based on heredity; a result of a sense of nobility based on tribal superiority or proximity to descent from Mohammed and a lack of importance placed upon achievement
- Particularist ethics—stemming from a need to maintain one's network of social relationships and to maintain face.

ADDITIONAL READING

Arab Management Practices

Al-Faleh, M. 1987. "Cultural Influences in Arab Management Development." *Journal of Management Development* 6(3): 19–33.

Al-Jafary, A., and A. Hollingsworth. 1983. "An Exploratory Study of Managerial Practices in the Arabian Gulf Region." *Journal of International Business Studies* (Fall): 142–152.

Ali, Abbas J. 1995. "Cultural Discontinuity and Arab Management." *International Studies of Management and Organization* 25, no. 3 (Fall): 7–30.

———. 1993. "Decision-Making Style, Individualism and Attitudes toward Risk of Arab Executives." *International Studies of Management and Organization* 23, no. 3 (Fall): 53–73.

Badawy, M. 1980. "Styles of Mideastern Managers." *California Management Review* 22(2): 51–58.

Elashmawi, Farid, and Philip R. Harris. 1993. *Multicultural Management: New Skills for Global Success.* (Houston: Gulf).

Harris, Philip R., and Robert T. Moran. 1996. *Managing Cultural Differences,* 4th ed. (Houston: Gulf).

Muna, F. 1980. *The Arab Executive.* (London: Macmillan).

Wright, P. 1981. "Organizational Behavior in Islamic Firms." *Management International Review* 21(2): 86–93.

Arab and Islamic Culture

Barakat, Halim. 1993. *The Arab World.* (Berkeley: University of California Press).

De Planhol, Xavier. 1959. *The World of Islam.* (Ithaca, Cornell University Press).

Farah, Caesar. 1968. *Islam.* (Woodbury, N.Y.: Barron's).

Guillaume, Alfred. 1956. *Islam.* (Baltimore: Penguin).

Hamady, Sania. 1960. *Temperament and Character of Arabs.* (New York: Twayne).

Holt, P. M., Ann K. S. Lambton, and Bernard Lewis, eds. 1970. *The Cambridge History of Islam,* 4 vols. (Cambridge: Cambridge University Press).

Lafflin, John. 1975. *Rhetoric & Reality: The Arab Mind Considered.* (New York: Taplinger).

Lapidus, Ira M. 1988. *A History of Islamic Societies.* (Cambridge: Cambridge University Press).

Lewis, Bernard. 1993. *The Arabs in History,* 6th ed. (Oxford: Oxford University Press).

Nydell, Margaret K. 1996, 1987. *Understanding Arabs.* (Yarmouth, Maine: Intercultural Press).

Patai, Raphael. 1983. *The Arab Mind.* rev. ed. (New York: Scribner's).

Rodinson, Maxime. 1979. *The Arabs.* (Chicago: University of Chicago Press).

Waines, David. 1995. *An Introduction to Islam.* (Cambridge: Cambridge University Press).

Fiction

The Arabian Nights' Entertainments. 1929. (New York: Tudor).

Chapter 6

THE INDIAN SUBCONTINENT

One-sixth of all the world's people live in India, second only to China in population. It was the first culture in Asia exposed to Western colonialism and the only one dominated by it. India is a federal republic and a member of the British Commonwealth. A highly pluralistic society in ethnic, religious, and linguistic dimensions, it is unified by Hinduism and a caste-based social structure that together form a socioreligious system of belief and behavioral norms sufficiently flexible to accommodate India's diversity. Hinduism in its preliminary form gave way to Buddhism, which was spread by a descendant of a Mongol invader. Buddhism would then nearly disappear under Muslim rule as Indian culture attained a zenith in scientific and artistic accomplishment and even as Buddhism spread throughout East Asia. Finally, India returned to its cultural roots as it became, once again, primarily Hindu, and this renewed unity spawned the nationalist movement that gave India its independence from Britain. In the process, it lost its primarily Muslim eastern and westernmost lands, which became Pakistan and, ultimately, Bangladesh.

It would seem risky to generalize about such a heterogenous population, but Hinduism and the caste system permeate India to a degree similar to that to which the Protestant work ethic and democracy permeate the United States. Just as immigrants to the United States are expected to abide by those values, so too has India assimilated foreign influences and retained its fundamental character. The only foreign influence of significant impact was British colonization, and that has been limited largely to the upper castes in urban centers. Hofstede found India very high in power distance, slightly collectivist, weak in uncertainty avoidance and moderately masculine. Trompenaars found that Indians tend to (1) view the organization as more of a system of relationships than a functional system, (2) lean toward particularist ethics, (3) lean toward individual freedom in decision-making, (4) lean toward individual responsibility, (5) take a more specific than holistic view of the world, and (6) be slightly paternalistic.

THE CULTURAL SETTING

The Indian subcontinent is separated from the rest of Asia by the world's tallest mountain ranges, the Himalayas to the north and northeast and the Hindu Kush to the northwest. Within it lie India in the center; Pakistan to the west; Bangladesh to the east; and the rugged, Himalayan countries of Nepal and Bhutan. The Indus River in the west and the Ganges River in the east drain a region that is largely plain and hilly plateau. Most of the Republic of India is a very large peninsula that protrudes southward into the Indian Ocean between the Arabian Sea to the west and the Bay of Bengal to the east. The island country of Sri Lanka, formerly Ceylon, lies off the southeastern tip of India's coastline. Most of the country has a tropical climate, dry in the northeast where wheat is the primary crop, and wet in the southeast where rice thrives. India is rich in minerals, and its agriculture has recovered during recent decades from a long history of extensive abuse of the land and slash-and-burn deforestation. India had long struggled to feed its always rapidly growing population and teetered on the precipice of starvation. For example, hundreds of thousands died during World War II when the Japanese embargoed rice from Burma. Despite ranking among the world's leading manufacturers in total output, it remains a poor, largely agrarian economy because of its huge population—nearly 900 million people squeezed into an area about the size of the United States east of the Mississippi River, much of it uninhabitable.

In addition to the familiar social building blocks of agricultural societies—the extended patriarchal family, clan, and village—Indians are organized into the world's most elaborate and finely detailed system of social strata. The family, built on mutual dependence and the source of great psychological support, stability, and comfort, commands the first loyalty of all Indians. Authority is vested in the male gender and seniority by age. There are no peers within the strict family hierarchy, and the omnipotent father may remain quite detached from the children. The emotional bond with the mother tends to be very strong, especially for the preferred male children. Traditionally, wives leave their parental homes and join the husband's family where they fall under the dominance of the husband and mother-in-law. Arranged marriages are common, and it is the duty of the traditional Indian wife to fit in to her new family, to obey and even worship her husband and his family. Even in those regions where matrilineal lines prevail by tribal custom, the wife's inherited familial authority is exercised by her eldest brother (Lannoy 1971). Many higher-caste Indians are well educated, but the economy still cannot support the large pool of scientists, highly skilled professionals, and technicians, many of whom have found employment elsewhere. (During the 1990s however, India emerged as a major competitor in computer software, capitalizing on its highly skilled but relatively poorly-compensated work force.) Indian culture had a great deal of influence on Southeast Asian countries as far eastward as Laos and Cambodia.

HISTORICAL FORCES

A relatively sophisticated, urbanized civilization existed in the Indus River valley of what is now Pakistan from the third millennium B.C. There are many indigenous ethnic groups in the subcontinent, most notably the Dravidians in the south who are related to the indigenous peoples of Australia, as are some of the non-Malay ethnic groups of Indonesia. Subsequent incursions of varying duration and scope, often using the historic invasion route through the Khyber Pass from what is now Afghanistan, by the Indo-European Aryans, Persians, Macedonians and Greeks under Alexander the Great, Huns, Arabs, Mongols first under Genghis Khan and then under Tamerlane (*Timur Lenk*), Turks, Afghanis and, finally, the British have added to the extreme heterogeneity of the Indian people. The most-common and most-durable linkages among them, both closely related and rooted in the ancient Indus River and Aryan civilization, are Hinduism and the caste system. Readers will recall the term "aryan" as used by Adolf Hitler and the Nazis to label their supposedly superior race. This was a misuse of the term, which more properly is applied to the indigenous, non-Mongoloid people of southwestern Asia, the area in the vicinity of the Caspian Sea and Caucasus Mountains (origin of the term Caucasian), thought to be the ancestors of all European, Middle Eastern, and North African peoples. Indicative of India's diversity, only about 40 percent of the population speak Hindi, the primary language, and its constitution recognizes fifteen official languages not including English. There are about fifty major languages with many dialects, some differing by caste. Educated Indians may use Sanskrit, the traditional language of Indian literature. Muslims speak Hindustani or Urdu, and there are many local ethnic languages such as Punjabi, Bengali, and Tamil. The diversity is such that English, established during the British *raj* (rule), became a common tongue among the educated. Illiteracy is more than 60 percent, 75 percent among women.

The Caste System

Established, or adopted from the Aryans, as early as 575 B.C. by the Indus River civilization, the caste system is the basic organizing principle of Indian society, a social system that is also an integral part of Hindu religious belief. A caste is a social stratum with its own origin myth, religious practices, typical occupations, and expected behaviors with respect to such matters as kinship and even diet. Members of a caste are born into it, will remain in it, are expected to marry within it and to conform to its norms, especially the upwardly respectful, hierarchical relationships among the castes. It is by such conformance that individuals accrue "good" karma and thereby raise their expectations of being born into a higher caste in their next reincarnation. Thus the caste into which one is born is a function of one's pre-existing karma, the net balance of one's positive and negative behavior in previous lives. Karma, the law of moral consequences, is a fundamental belief of Hinduism and its antecedents and serves as the vehicle by which religious values shape behavior, and by which one rises or falls according to one's willingness to accept one's station in the current life and caste.

Originally there were four principal castes or *varna*s, which actually were once less-rigid social classes of Aryan culture. Highest of the *varna* are the *brahman*s, the religious leaders and priests who historically dominated the learned professions. Second are the protectors of the people, the *kshatriyas*, the warriors, secular rulers, and large landowners. Third are the *vaishyas*, traditionally farmers and husbandmen but more recently businessmen. Fourth are the *shudra*s, all those artisans and laborers who serve the three upper castes. Below the castes are the "untouchables," those who work in unclean occupations, like Japan's *burakumin*. Originally, color had been a determinant of caste with the light-skinned people of the Indus valley looking down upon the darker-skinned Dravidians of the south (Thapar 1965). Upper castes view and treat those below as unsophisticated or dirty children. Castes do not mingle except when necessary. An elaborate system called *jajman* evolved for payment in kind for goods and services. As the primary medium of interaction between castes, conformance to these reciprocal obligations and upholding the *jajman* system took on a strong moral character.

As India's society became more complex and pluralistic, the caste system became more elaborate. Invaders, even relatively egalitarian Muslims, and other newcomers have been assimilated into the caste system thereby contributing to the proliferation of subcastes. Given the specialization of labor that accompanies economic development, there are now in excess of three thousand subcastes or *jatis*, each with its own set of behavioral norms. It is these *jatis*, not the four *varna*s, that are meaningful in day-to-day life. Occupation is the major differentiator of caste, and, therefore, many castes are represented in a village. The individual thus resides at the nexus of the horizontal relationships within his caste that extend beyond the village and the vertical relationships within village, clan, family, and the caste hierarchy. An additional complication is that there are no universal criteria for ranking castes, and the hierarchy thus varies from place to place. Another is that the social ranking of a caste does not necessarily correspond to its relative wealth. The complexity of the modern workplace is such that castes must mix in order to function, but the castes do not mix in social settings. The upper castes tend to congregate in cities, and members develop extensive networks of personal connections within their own castes and the castes with which they do business. Each caste has a local ruling council called a *panchayat* that settles disputes by consensus.

Though individuals are embedded permanently within their castes, the status of a caste relative to other castes can rise with improved education (so-called sanskritization [Farmer 1993, 15]) and greater wealth, and castes typically work very hard to improve their status. Caste mobility would normally require about three generations, however (Nyrop 1985). The individual immobility and rigidity of the caste system has acted as a constraint on enterprise, compounded by the long-standing practice, since reformed, of imperial confiscation of private estates upon the owner's death. This practice impeded capital formation by encouraging profligate spending and hiding of assets. The customary payment of large dowries also retarded capital formation. Business formation typically occurs within castes where skills and capital can converge.

The constitution adopted in 1950 declared that the individual citizen, not the caste, was the basic unit of society and that all Indians were equal before the law (Lannoy 1971). Of course, a system more than three thousand years old and deeply embedded in everyday life is not so easily discarded.

The Early Empires and the Mughals

The first centralized rule in the subcontinent was established in the fourth century B.C. The most important ruler of the quasi-feudal period to follow was Asoka, who unified much of what is now India in the third century B.C. He is better known for renouncing the use of force, having been repelled by the carnage of battle, asserting the ruler's social responsibility and need for compassion and, of most lasting impact, converting to and propagating Buddhism. Arabs arrived in India as early as 711, learning much of their mathematics and astronomy, irrigation, and cultivation of cotton. They arrived in force in the thirteenth century and imposed a sultanate at Delhi. Waves of Muslim Mongol, Turkish, and Afghani invaders culminated in defeat of the Arabs in 1526, and Baber—a descendant of the Uzbek Mongol, Tamerlane—established what came to be called the Mughal (or Mogul) empire. Indian art and science flowered in this period, during which, for example, the Taj Mahal was built, what some consider to be the world's most beautiful building. The Mughal Empire ranks among the greatest Asian civilizations. It reached its peak in the sixteenth century under Akbar, perhaps one of the lesser known of the most important and most capable of historical figures. Akbar was a highly effective military leader and civil administrator who encouraged religious tolerance—by appointing Hindus to high office, for example—and artistic achievement. He even attempted, unsuccessfully, to synthesize Hinduism and Islam. His most lasting contribution was a system of provincial government onto which the British would graft their colonial empire and that remains in place as the basic structure of India's federal system. Descendants of Akbar persecuted the Hindus and consumed the empire's power and wealth in the process. Invaders from what is now Afghanistan brought down the Mughals in 1741.

The British *Raj* and Independence

Vasco da Gama first arrived in India in 1498. The Portuguese would establish a small colony at Goa on India's west coast in 1510, which remained in place until reclaimed by India in 1962 and which remains the primary home of Christianity in India. Their interests lie eastward in the Indies, however, and they used Goa primarily as a trading outpost and way station. The French East India Company established several outposts on the east coast beginning in 1670 but was never able to mount much of an effort in India relative to the British. The only colonial power to take a concerted interest within India itself rather than as a jumping off point, the British established military dominance in 1757. The British East India Company was firmly established and was, in effect, governing India by 1803. Robert Clive would rise from a modest position as a clerk for the British East India Company to knighthood for his prolonged and successful effort to bring India under the crown. After defeating a full-scale, military rebellion in 1857–58, the British government assumed control and declared India a colony, one that stretched from present-day Pakistan to Burma (now Myanmar). Queen Victoria took the title Empress of India in 1876. Apparently the rebellion, which began as a mutiny, was triggered by Sikh and Hindu soldiers in the British army who took exception to a new Enfield rifle bullet, lubricated by cow and pig fat, from which they had to bite off a cap before loading (Nyrop 1985). This was a serious violation of religious prohibitions—Sikhs would not eat pork, and the cow was of course sacred to Hindus—and ranks among the greatest of cross-cultural blunders.

The British brought to India internal peace, infrastructure, governmental institutions, civil service, their own form of education, and decentralized government. Their objectives were trade (that is, wealth), the military security of an expanded empire, and to bring "civilization" to the "wogs." They referred to the last objective as "carrying the white man's burden." Consequently, they also brought a thorough disregard for the Indians who considered the British not only economically exploitive but aloof and snobbish as well. Greed was rampant, most notoriously under the administration of Governor General Lord Cornwallis, perhaps better known for the final and ignominious British surrender to the American colonials at Yorktown in a previous posting. The Indians also resented British social meddling in their family matters and their paternalistic bureaucracy. Imposition of the British judicial system conflicted with the traditional and elaborate array of behavioral norms established by family, clan, and caste. Unwilling to promote competition for their factories at home, the British educated the Indians in literature and philosophy rather than in more-practical matters. Some literary classics that provide insight into the Indian character and their relationship with the British are E. M. Forster's *A Passage to India* and Rudyard Kipling's *The Jungle Book* and *Kim*.

British-style education backfired when a nationalist organization, the Indian National Congress, was formed in 1885 by Indian intellectuals educated in liberal ideals. After practicing law in South Africa as the first "colored man" to do so, Mohandas K. Gandhi, would eventually become the leader of this organization, which was galvanized by Britain's use, though voluntary, of Indian troops in World War I. In response the British Parliament expanded Indian autonomy in 1919. However, the independence movement continued to grow, bolstered by the example of the Bolshevik revolution in Russia, Woodrow Wilson's call for self-determination for all nations among his "Fourteen Points," and the revelation by the war that Britain was not omnipotent. Gandhi was from a vaishya family and a Hindu influenced by Jainism. He became an ardent pacifist, having read Thoreau's *On Civil Disobedience* while in law school at the University of London, among other similar thinkers, and had associated with Quakers. Consequently he concluded that comprehensive "passive noncooperation" with the British *raj* was the best way to gain independence. Convinced that Western society was corrupt and violent, he traveled for many years throughout India to argue his approach and to set an example of single-minded dedication to Indian independence. Eventually called *Mahatma*, or "great soul," he was greatly admired for his persistent, arduous, and self-sacrificing struggle, and many Indians consider him a saint. Gandhi had also become the champion of the untouchables, whom he called *harijan* or God's children. As a result, they are now protected by the constitution and are entitled to favored treatment in education and in seeking political office in order to alleviate their disadvantaged position.

The Indian National Congress or "the Congress" made independence a condition for India's participation alongside Britain in World War II—and, indeed, Britain granted India independence in 1947. It already had granted independence to Burma in 1937. Meanwhile, India's population had continued to grow very rapidly, and the competition for survival became more intense as antiquated agricultural practices depleted the fertility of the land. This struggle, coupled with relentless and substantial population growth, exacerbated frequent sectarian strife, particularly between Hindu and Muslim and Hindu and Sikh. The primarily Muslim areas in the east and west had long sought separation from the much larger Hindu center. The independence process allowed for plebiscites on this issue, and the Muslim regions voted for separation and became East and West Pakistan. The continuing dispute over Kashmir, adjacent to what became West Pakistan, arose when its primarily Muslim population voted for separation but its Hindu governor refused to allow succession. Massive border conflicts amounting to civil war followed independence as large numbers of Hindus left Pakistan, many Muslims left India, and Sikhs migrated into Punjab. Gandhi was assassinated by a Hindu extremist in 1948 in protest of his efforts to end the conflict between Hindus and Muslims. He was mourned by both sides.

His longtime compatriot in the Congress, Jawaharlal Nehru, succeeded Gandhi as its head of the Congress—still India's largest political party— and became India's first Prime Minister. Whereas the ascetic and philosophical Gandhi had envisioned a simple, traditional, village-based, agrarian India, Nehru was more inclined toward industrialization. India has since set the example for the typical, socialist-democratic, nonaligned, Third World nation seeking to exploit the guilt of the colonial powers and to play off one superpower against another. Its long and largely unpleasant experience as a colony made it suspicious of foreign alliances and also of multinational companies, altogether too reminiscent of the British East India Company.

Maintaining domestic stability in this diverse and volatile country is a constant challenge. Periodic sectarian strife and protests by the poor, by idealistic students, and by separatists have continued. India has suffered border incursions by China, most notably in 1962; lost Tibet in 1956; fought Pakistan over Kashmir in 1948 and 1965 and again in 1971 in support of the successful effort of East Pakistan to establish independence as Bangladesh. There remains a very testy peace between India and western-oriented Pakistan, including worries about the use of nuclear weapons. Continuing domestic turmoil led to the assassination of Prime Minister Indira Gandhi, daughter of Nehru, in 1984 and her son and successor, Rajiv Gandhi, apparently by a supporter of Tamil separatists in Sri Lanka (Farmer 1993) in 1991. Massive rioting followed the destruction of an important mosque by Hindus in 1992.

RELIGION

Every major religion and many lesser ones coexist in India, even if not always peacefully. More than 80 percent are Hindu. India has the fourth largest Muslim population in the world—behind Indonesia, Pakistan, and Bangladesh. Only about 11 percent of the huge population, they are politically weak and geographically dispersed. They are a majority only in the disputed state of Kashmir. The Sikhs (2 percent) and Jains (1 percent), though small in number, are very influential in the military, government, and business, but Hinduism is clearly the primary religious force in Indian culture.

Hinduism

Hinduism is not only a religion but a social system that unifies a country equivalent to the entire continent of Europe in its ethnic, linguistic, and religious diversity. Defying straightforward explanation by westerners, it is neither a creed nor an institution, and it includes a vast array of beliefs and deities. It is more spiritual than other religions of East Asia and is more concerned with the worship of deities and the afterlife. There is no known founder or revealer like Moses or Mohammed. Nevertheless, it permeates day-to-day life as no western religion has since the Middle Ages (Nyrop 1985).

Its source is the Indus River civilization around 1500 B.C., which worshipped one world spirit, Brahman, and lesser spirits represented in the natural world and ancestors. Augmented by the beliefs of Aryan invaders, the tenets of Brahmanism, precursor of Hinduism, were handed down in a series of hymns and poems composed between the twelfth and sixth centuries B.C., known as the *Vedas* and expanded upon by the *Upanishads* composed from the fifth to the third centuries B.C., both used primarily for training Hindu priests. Popular scripture (the *Puranas*) takes the form of lengthy, allegorical, epic poetry in which gods instruct mortals in, and set examples of, proper behavior. The most important, recorded during the first two centuries A.D., are the *Mahabharata,* an account of the exploits of the god *Krishna,* and the *Ramayana,* an account of the god *Rama.* These deities were avatars or earthly (and somewhat earthy) incarnations of *Vishnu.* The *Bhagavad Gita* (*The Song of the Lord*), a single book of the *Mahabharata* and the most important piece of Hindu scripture, lays out the essentials of Hindu *dharma* or moral law. Many interpretive instructions called *sutras*—for example, the *Kamasutra*—have been added to Hindu scripture.

Hinduism requires acceptance of the existing, immutable order of the universe represented by *Brahman,* the universal world spirit and creator. He is first among a trinity that includes *Vishnu,* the preserver, and *Siva,* the destroyer of evil, which then gave rise to a pantheon of incarnations now numbering in the thousands if not millions. (*Brahman,* the deity, is distinguished from the brahmans, the highest caste, by pronunciation with the accent on the second syllable for the deity). There were as many as thirty-three major gods even in Vedic times (Lannoy 1971). Hinduism's flexibility is illustrated in its capacity to recognize spirits that can help believers cope with whatever questions and problems they may confront. It accommodates the animism and idolatry of ancient times and encompasses a great diversity of beliefs, practice, and scripture, and there are many sects with little common doctrine (Spear 1965; Hardon 1970). There are some common, fundamental beliefs, though, including *bhakti,* devotion to the gods; karma; samsara; the eternal cycle of birth, death, and rebirth, that is, reincarnation; belief in heaven and hell, and the importance of purity. Purity is the essential distinction among castes in the sense of the physical cleanliness of one's occupation and in the purity of one's knowledge of Hindu ritual. Dharma is the moral law of the universe, manifested primarily in the caste system and its precise regulation of behavior. Adherence to the duties of one's caste, which is considered living a life of righteousness, duty, and virtue, is essential to building karma and making progress toward salvation. Compliance with dharma is one of four rightful "ends of man." Others include *artha,* the pursuit of material gain; *kama,* the pursuit of love, including sexual pleasure, thought to be indicative of a love of god; and *moksha,* the eventual renunciation of *artha* and *kama* in order to dedicate oneself to spiritual activities and liberate oneself from worldly life, man's ultimate end. All four ends are thought to be essential to a balanced and worthwhile life, but the pursuit of *artha* and *kama* must be done in conformance to the dharma (deBary et al. 1958, 211). *Ahimsa* is belief in the sanctity of all life, including veneration of many animals and plants. For example, the cow is venerated for its symbolism of motherhood and fertility and the purity of its milk. Other common themes are a sense of the interrelatedness of all things, which are in a constant state of flux, and, in keeping with the doctrine of samsara, a belief that one's current physical state is temporary and one's identity transient. Time is cyclical, and all motion and change oscillate about a common center, symbolized by a wheel. Hence although change is normal and expected, progressive (that is, linear) change is not. Hindu cosmology is similar to that of the Tao, a kind of dynamic equilibrium, like a spinning gyroscope . There is great value placed in maintaining the traditions of the past, and work is valued more for its contribution to the present than as a means of bringing about change.

Hinduism is remarkable in its appeal to an overwhelming majority of an extremely diverse population. It is its lack of specificity that allows it to do so—India's plurality makes universal standards problematical. Adherence to dharma is, for many, a matter of demonstration for public consumption of one's conformance to societal constraints, whereas moral relativism prevails in personal standards. Hindus are less interested in differentiating good and evil than in transcending both. That is not to say however that Hinduism is content free. Virtues traceable to Brahmanism include ascetic detachment from worldly pursuits, nonviolence (ahimsa), and temperance. Others include *dama,* the restraint of passion; *dana,* the obligation to give others their due and to be charitable; and *daya,* sympathy and understanding.

Given the importance placed on a quiet, contemplative, spiritual life, it is not surprising that Hindus considered government irrelevant to everyday life and are suspicious of commerce, private property, and profit. Consequently, the brahmans regulated and taxed the vaishyas heavily. This would open the door to business for practitioners of other religions such as Buddhism or Jainism. The actions of a Hindu are supposed to be dedicated to God, not to the practical ends that might be achieved. Hindus who were commercially inclined, then, might convert to these religions. Both religions were reformist and arose in part to escape the caste system. They also were less ritualistic, less mystical, and less superstitious than was Hinduism and appealed more to the affluent and educated more interested in self-inquiry than worship (Lannoy 1971). Like Confucianism and Islam, Hinduism is linked to the secular world, in this case by its connection to the caste system and, in effect, serves as the primary instrument for preservation of social harmony in this very diverse culture.

Sikhism and Jainism

Sikhism combines Hindu practices of discipline and meditation and belief in reincarnation with Islamic monotheism. Sikhs seek salvation through renunciation of worldly values. Every male takes the name Singh, meaning lion. They are recognizable by a turban and beard, and are overly represented in the contemporary Indian military services. Traditionally, Sikhs also wear a dagger, a metal amulet, and knee-length breeches. Known for their military prowess, they have been recruited by the British army and employed with great effectiveness, much like the famed Gurkhas. Sikhism arose during the fifteenth century in the northwest in what is now the Indian state of Punjab. Persecuted by the Mughals, the Sikhs became and remain quite militant, and there is a very active and sometimes violent separatist movement in Punjab. Conflict among Hindus and Sikhs reached a peak in 1984 when the Indian army occupied the Golden Temple in Punjab, the principal Sikh holy place. In retaliation, Prime Minister Indira Gandhi was assassinated by her own Sikh body guards.

Jainism is a more ascetic offshoot of Hinduism that practices ahimsa in the extreme, going to great lengths to avoid harming even an insect. The essence of Jainism is to avoid doing harm to any living thing. Its name is derived from the title of its sixth century founder, Jina, meaning conqueror. The object of Jina's conquest was individual dependence on the world and personal needs, which is accomplished by progressing through stages of increasing self-discipline. Yoga is an important means of self-discipline. These differences from Hinduism are more of degree than of kind however; the primary departure from Hinduism is rejection of the caste system. All Jains are equal before God and man. As a result, the Jains are a tiny sect but very influential nonetheless because the lack of social restraint imposed by caste has allowed the Jains to become very active in commerce, trade, and banking, and their discipline and unity have made them very successful. Their refusal to inflict any harm on animals precluded them from occupations in agriculture, thereby driving them into business and trade.

Buddhism

Siddhartha Gautama (or Gotama), who came to be called Buddha, the enlightened or awakened one, lived in the sixth and fifth centuries B.C. Born in Nepal into a well-to-do family, he led an indulged life as a child. As an adult he sought a "middle path" between a pampered, indolent life and one of ascetic self-denial. The form his enlightenment took was a system of belief that involved fulfillment not in the worship of a deity or in salvation but in the pursuit of one's own individual nirvana, a state of indescribable bliss attained when one frees oneself from selfish cravings and passions. Central to his teachings were the Four Noble Truths and the Noble Eightfold Path to nirvana. The first truth is that human life is suffering and sorrow. The second is that suffering and sorrow are caused by unfulfilled cravings and desires. The third is that escape from human suffering is possible, and the fourth is that the avenue for this escape is the eightfold path. The first path is "right knowledge," an understanding of the nature of life, that is, the four truths. The second is "right aspiration," a determined and clear commitment to the eightfold path. Third is "right speech," which is clear, gentle, and kind. Fourth is "right behavior," which proscribes killing, stealing, lying, consumption of intoxicants, and illicit sex. Fifth is "right livelihood," an occupation that keeps one on the path, that promotes life and well-being rather than accumulation of wealth. Sixth is "right effort," training the will to curb passions and wants and to diligently pursue the eightfold path. Seventh is "right mindfulness," continuous self-examination and awareness of one's degree of progress along the path. Eighth is "right concentration," a focus on some element of life or nature so intense as to allow an escape from worldly desires. These teachings constitute the essential Buddhist dharma or system of rules about how one ought to lead one's life. Apparently, Buddha expected that anyone ought to be able to follow paths one, two, and three but that the remaining paths required more of a vocation of faith. Paths four and five would require dedication of one's life as a novice monk. The remaining paths would require a long and highly disciplined, highly ascetic life of mendicancy and meditation feasible only for the most-dedicated monks.

Buddha wrote nothing of his beliefs so that a number of interpretations arose upon his death. Primary among these were the Theravada (or Hinayana) and Mahayana branches of Buddhism. Theravada, meaning "way of the elders" (Hinayana meaning "lesser vehicle"), firmly established by the third century B.C., was the older and more conservative of the two. It would spread eastward into most of southeast Asia. Meanwhile the more inclusive Mahayana, meaning "greater vehicle," would become more dominant within India in the first and second centuries and would spread northeastward into what are now China, Mongolia, Korea, and Japan and then southward from China into Vietnam. Mahayana was less restrictive in several ways, and therefore more widely accepted. In Buddha's original conception, preserved by Theravada Buddhists, the difficulty in reaching nirvana was thought to be such that it was attainable only by monks who had no other concerns. Most believers then were thought to be excluded from ultimate fulfillment, and it was thought necessary that Theravada monks could pursue their difficult, single-minded goal only in cloistered monasteries. This is what is meant by the "lesser vehicle." They considered Buddha as a saint and an historical figure, an example of what could be attained by the very best Buddhists. Mahayana Buddhists, believing in the impracticality of the Eightfold Path for most people, tended to satisfy themselves with something less as allowing progress toward nirvana. Consequently, Mahayana monks lived and worked among the people in order to proselytize and to help them progress toward nirvana. It was their effort and this hope that allowed Buddhism to spread among the generally irreligious but exploited and mostly downtrodden people of East Asia. Eventually, East Asians would tend to forego the pursuit of nirvana altogether and to apply the meditative, contemplative practices of Buddhism for more-secular purposes. These more pragmatic Mahayana came to consider Buddha to be a God and a savior in that he had attained what seemed increasingly unattainable. Even the Theravada Buddhists of Southeast Asia were satisfied with limiting themselves to the fourth path, right behavior. The Theravada used the term bodhisattva for one who had approached but not yet reached ultimate nirvana, a kind of pre-Buddha. Only a cloistered monk could become a bodhisattva, a "wise being." The Mahayana and even the more remote, latter-day Theravada of Southeast Asia thought single-minded pursuit of nirvana somewhat selfish and used the term to describe someone who had reached a high level of enlightenment and then used it in the service of others (see the sections on Thailand and Indonesia in chapter four). Bodhisattva were expected to demonstrate compassion and self-sacrifice and perform great deeds of service. The Mahayana Buddhists believed that any good Buddhist, not just a monk, could become one.

Other important elements of Buddhism include great value placed on peace and serenity; the belief that all things are in a state of flux and that resistance to change leads to sorrow; and that one's individuality and soul are therefore impermanent and transient. Buddhism was consistent with and depended upon the endemic Indian notions of karma and samsara. The egalitarian nature of Buddhism, novel given the dominance of the caste system, apparently accounted for its initial, widespread acceptance where one might otherwise be doomed to an endless cycle of reincarnations

through one *jati* after another, without relief. Some historians suggest however that had it not been for the Mughal King Asoka, who adopted Buddhism and sponsored its proliferation, Buddhism might never have become
significant in India. As it was, Buddhism reached its peak in India between
200 B.C. and A.D. 200, had begun to decline in the fourth century, and all
but disappeared under the Muslims. It appears to have succumbed to a
combination of opposition by later Muslim rulers, the much more spiritual
hold of Hinduism and the resilience of the decidedly non-egalitarian caste
system, made easier by substantial congruence in doctrine. Thus, despite
India being the birthplace of Buddhism and the world's longest-lived, established religious order, Hinduism simply assimilated Buddhism just as it
did so many other potential influences on Indian culture, and Buddha was
reduced to mere membership in the pantheon of Hindu gods. Buddhism
had a lasting impact, however, primarily in reinforcing many Hindu beliefs,
but also by offering a more egalitarian alternative to the caste system. Buddhism and Jainism arose concurrently during a period of great turmoil in
India, and the asceticism advocated by both lent more discipline to Hinduism, unique among major religions for the licentious conduct of some of
its gods, including some major ones. Buddhism has had a bit of a resurgence
in the twentieth century primarily among the untouchables but still accounts for only about 1 percent of the population (Nyrop 1985).

Islam

The strongest Muslim presence is in the north, closest to Pakistan and
the Khyber Pass. The Delhi sultanate was governed according to the *Quran*
and Islamic law, sharia, and at least at the outset was quite conservative.
Even today, however, some Muslims still enforce *purdah,* the seclusion of
women who are required, when in public, to wear the *borka,* a garment
that covers the entire body except for holes for the eyes. But, in keeping
with the tradition established in the Middle East, they tolerated the practice
of indigenous religions, and Hindu brahmans served as advisors to the
sultans throughout a series of quasi-feudal reigns. This peaceful coexistence
continued under the Mughals, and each religion influenced the other somewhat (Thapar 1966). Many Hindus admired the egalitarianism and simplicity of Islam, especially its monotheism, and converted. In more recent
times, however, the fundamental conflict between monotheism and pan-
theism has given rise to frequent and sometimes very bloody conflicts (Nyrop 1985). Although a sizable minority, Islam has had little effect on the
majority. To the contrary, they have had to make concessions to their egalitarian values in order to be assimilated into the caste system and participate in Indian society.

The Sufi sect, which departs from orthodox Islam in the worship of
saints, polytheism, neglect of sharia, and substitution of retreat for the *hajj,*

has much in common with Hinduism. Much more mystical than mainstream Islam, Sufis would even worship at Hindu shrines, paving the way for the formation of Sikhism.

CORE VALUES AND BEHAVIOR

Large Power Distance

There is little that need be said here. The caste system is institutionalized inequality, both deep and wide. Lower castes are dependent upon upper castes; a kind of universal child-parent or servant-patron relationship *en masse*. Seniority is accepted without question as a normal consequence of karma. Social mobility is largely limited to progress within the caste. Patriarchal authoritarianism is the norm in the home and the workplace. Paternal authority is not necessarily benevolent or, at least, not always exercised with warmth but, rather, from an aloof distance, hence Trompenaars's finding of only a middling value placed on paternalism. Teachers are *gurus* (weighty ones) who disseminate their wisdom without question.

Collectivism

Obligations to family, clan, village, and caste cast a powerful web about individual freedom. Urbanization intrudes on these bonds and creates a sense of anxiety and isolation. Although the advent of a market-based, money economy has weakened *jajman* networks, connections remain very important, especially those within the *jati*. Collectivist traditions continue to suppress individuality, at least in public life. However, Hofstede's results indicate that India was only slightly collectivist, less so than for most other Asian cultures or developing countries. What forces temper Indian collectivism?

First, there is a significant difference between Indian religions and other Asian religions and Confucianism in that Hinduism and Buddhism do not demand subordination of self-interest and place more emphasis on individual control of one's destiny and individual accountability. Hinduism goes a step further and endows the individual with an immortality that surpasses individual ties to others. Hinduism holds the individual accountable only to the gods, a very personal relationship, who will judge conduct and reward or punish with an appropriate placement in a new life. Buddhism holds individuals accountable only to themselves, indeed obligating individuals to monitor their own progress toward maximizing the worth of their own life in very personal terms. Consider the contrast with Confucianism, which holds the individual accountable to society at large; with Taoism, which holds man accountable to nature and for harmonious coexistence with others; and with Shinto, which holds the individual accountable to Japanese nationhood. In other words, the Indian religions leave it up to individuals to act in their own self-interest, subject to moral constraints, rather than always acting in the interest of some larger entity. An Indian can live a moral life without subordinating all one's interests to those of others. Although the emphasis is on the spiritual rather than the material and the temporal, the Indian religions do specifically legitimize the pursuit of material gain as well as the pursuit of some elevated state and, in the case of Hinduism, even of earthly personal pleasure.

Second, the scarcity of resources prevalent throughout India's history intensifies with continued, rapid population growth. Though the objective may be shifting from sustenance and survival to the search for suitable employment and job security—recall the imbalance between the number of highly skilled Indians and availability of suitable employment—this scarcity has created a situation in which the pursuit of self-interest has become increasingly competitive but less cooperative without the discipline imposed by Confucian precepts. Moreover, there is plenty of room for competitive maneuver within the framework of one's caste, and the castes themselves constantly seek to enhance their status through the individual's success and achievement. One must also suspect that three centuries of British rule must have served to moderate collectivism somewhat, at least among the urbanized upper castes.

Third, the British presence and example may have served as a catalyst in a situation where the potential for pursuit of self-interest had long existed free of moral proscription and made increasingly necessary by scarcity and overpopulation. This would also explain Trompenaars's findings regarding a moderate preference for individual decision-making and responsibility and support for the view that an organization ought to be considered a functional system rather than as a system of relationships.

Moderate Masculinity

Many of Hofstede's so-called feminine characteristics are evident in Indian culture. Passivity and nonviolence are fundamental tenets of Hinduism, which at the same time is relatively permissive and nonspecific in regulating other aspects of behavior. Harmonious relationships, modesty, and face are important. Task performance and results should have no intrinsic value to Hindus. There is much concern for the needy and helpless. Nevertheless, scarcity has engendered aggressiveness and competitiveness, and vertical relationships can be cold and authoritarian. What clearly pushes Hofstede's findings to the masculine side, however, is the extreme and perhaps unequaled distinction of traditional gender roles, seemingly strong enough to offset any amount of femininity.

There may be no other major country where women have suffered as much as they have in India where "the vast majority . . . live a life of subordination if not subjection" (Farmer 1993, 21). Polygamy and taking of child brides have been common practices. Indians prefer male children for religious and economic reasons: Hindu ritual requires that a male son be present when parents are cremated to ensure their reincarnation, and not only are males the traditional income earners, but it is customary for the bride's family to pay a very large dowry. A family with several daughters and no sons can find itself in great financial distress. One result was the practice of female infanticide. Another was the murder of young brides by mothers-in-law when a bride's family is unable to deliver the promised dowry. The highest suicide rates are among young women, thought to be a result of psychological and physical abuse by mothers-in-law. Wives traditionally had no property rights. Widows were not allowed to remarry. A widow might be burned alive in her husband's funeral pyre, sometimes voluntary, sometimes not. This practice, called suttee (sati), was outlawed by the British in 1829. Traditional couples live somewhat separate lives, with the women and children taking their meals after the males have eaten, and the husband may feel stronger emotional ties to his mother than to his wife. Property rights were established for women, and polygamy and large dowries were banned by the Indian government, but only as recently as the 1950s. Even so, these practices apparently continue, especially in rural areas. Even as late as the 1980s there was a rising mortality rate among young women, especially in the upper castes where higher dowries are expected (Nyrop 1985). It is tempting to attribute these conditions to the Arab and Muslim influence, but historians indicate that these attitudes predated their arrival and, in any case, are in some significant ways more extreme, by western standards, than Arab or Muslim practices.

It is interesting to note the degree of difference between Eastern and Western views of the relationship between the wife and the husband's family. The Biblical exhortation for a man to leave his mother and cleave to his wife is foreign to traditional East Asian, Indian, and Arab cultures. Kipling's familiar refrain, "East is East and West is West and never the twain shall meet," clearly carries great weight. Nevertheless, in spite of all the foregoing, it is quite common to encounter women in very responsible positions in business and government. Trompenaars found that Indians take a more specific than diffuse view of life that indicates, inter alia, a preference for separating work from family life. Thus, just as the separation of castes is accepted in the workplace as a concession to practical reality, than so too can, apparently, the presence of women in positions of authority.

Weak Uncertainty Avoidance and Fatalism

Like other Asian belief systems, Hinduism is deterministic. The universe must be accepted as is and in whatever new configuration Brahman might choose for it. Karma, destiny, and chance govern humanity's fate, at least in this present life. Man is clearly subordinate to the gods and nature, which are really one and the same. Change is normal, accepted, and accommodated. Passivity in the face of threat has a certain nobility. A paucity of absolute standards allows flexibility. Novel but challenging circumstances can be referred to a hierarchy for disposition.

Status by Ascription

The caste system places each individual permanently within a hierarchy based almost entirely on relative status. Karma ascribes precisely and irrevocably the appropriate status, high or low, to each rank and position within that hierarchy. Conversely, task performance and achievement are accorded little weight under Hindu doctrine.

Particularist Ethics

Despite the outward conformance to Hindu dharma and the rigors of caste relationships, there are relatively few truths in Hindu doctrine and relatively little prescriptive content in Hindu teachings. Given the importance of harmonious relationships, still important to Indians despite occasional conflict and violence, behavior is conditioned by the need to maintain relationships within the family, clan, village, and caste, as well as between castes. The *jajman* system and more-contemporary networks must be maintained to ensure survival and well-being. Government and secular law, indeed all worldly authority, are irrelevant to the devout Hindu.

CONVERGENCE?

Davis and Rasool (1988, 18) found that successful managers in India are similar to successful managers elsewhere but that they depart from the "model Indian pattern . . . because they favor pragmatic, dynamic, achievement-oriented values." They add that these managers value organizational stability, but also productivity, efficiency, and pursuit of personal goals including job satisfaction, security, individuality, dignity, prestige and power, but not profit maximization. This sort of mixed bag of values is to be expected in an economy in transition.

By implication, Davis and Rasool suggest that the typical and presumably less successful Indian manager values the theoretical or ideal, stability and, presumably, relationships more than accomplishments. This finding also suggests that convergence is underway as indicated by the presence and characteristics of those successful managers. Other forces are at work here as well, however. Perhaps the strongest is necessity—the need to employ India's extensive talents and energy more effectively in order to improve the lot or, more basically, to ensure the survival, of its burgeoning population in an increasingly competitive world. Any obstacle offered by the spirituality and passivity of Hinduism does not seem great enough to withstand this obvious and overwhelming circumstance. Notwithstanding its disdain for the material world, Hinduism is an infinitely flexible and fundamentally benevolent force that will find a way to accommodate greater industrialization and more-Western practices. Aggressiveness and competitiveness have long existed in India—necessities given the rigors of life in that land—and need only to be released and marshaled in a productive direction.

That proposition focuses attention on the caste system, which is another matter altogether—for if any force will prevent release of Indian talent and energy, this is it. Perhaps the best evidence of its debilitating presence is the large number of those talented and energetic Indians one can find employed all over the globe. One must suppose that many of those individuals would prefer to live and work in their homeland if the same opportunities were available to them there.

Consequently, these remarks should not be construed as indicative of a major cultural transformation in India. It should be recalled that the impact of the British *raj* was limited to urbanized upper castes and that most of India remains as it always has been. Moreover many Indians still remain suspicious of the West, its ways, and its multinational companies. The disaster at Bhopal in 1984 was a major setback in that regard. Even the educated elite who may adopt Western thought processes and life-styles are less likely to adopt Western values. Hinduism is, after all, more than three thousand years old and is not only the primary religion but the very foundation of social order.

SUMMARY

Intuitively it would seem that the forces unifying a highly disparate population would have to be quite strong in order to overcome resistance much as an emergency demands willing cooperation among rivals, that its merits would be so powerful as to be beyond question by any and all. In this case we have the opposite, a force so flexible, Hinduism, that it accommodates extensive pluralism. The corollary of that proposition, however, is that such a flexible standard makes generalizations and predictions about behavior quite risky and that unity is therefore illusory. India's continuing sectarian strife, separatism, and political instability would support that conclusion. That said, it remains that the roots of Indian culture are few in number, a seemingly incongruous circumstance given its diversity. One might argue, then, that the very notion of an Indian culture may be a chimera. On the other hand, one could argue that there is much more commonality of values, attitudes, and beliefs in India than in, say, Europe, a geographic entity similar in size and diversity. These few forces include

- Hinduism—the essence of Indian culture; which provides moral justification for the caste system
- The Caste System—which regulates this disparate society
- The British Colonial Experience—which prompted a still-immature transition from a "being" culture to a "doing" culture
- An agrarian economy—characterized by scarcity of resources and overpopulation

The core values developed by these forces include

- **Large Power Distance**—institutionalized by the caste system and rationalized by karma.
- **Collectivism**—necessitated by the extended family, clan, and village structure typical of agrarian roots, especially a wet-rice culture, and amplified by the need to maintain harmonious relationships within and between castes
- **Individualism**—necessitated by the need to compete for scarce resources, encouraged by religious imperatives for individual responsibility, and amplified by the extended British example
- **Masculinity**—established by extreme separation of traditional gender roles, amplified by aggressiveness required to ensure survival in the face of scarcity
- **Femininity**—attributable to Hindu passivity, nonviolence, spirituality, disdain for worldly and material pursuits, and the need to maintain collective relationships
- **Weak Uncertainty Avoidance**—a result of Hindu beliefs in a universe in constant flux, karma, submission to the will of gods and nature, the lack of absolute standards, and the ability to rely upon hierarchical guidance in anomalous situations
- **Status by Ascription**—determined by caste and justified by karma
- **Particularist Ethics**—a residual of minimal absolute standards and prescriptive content in religious teaching and a tradition of flexible interpretation of existing religious doctrine and, to ensure survival in difficult circumstances, a need for maintenance of a variety of relationships as well as flexibility and adaptability

ADDITIONAL READING

Davis, H. J., and S. A. Rasool. 1988. "Values Research and Managerial Behavior: Implications for Devising Culturally Consistent Managerial Styles. *Management International Review* 28(3): 11–21.

de Bary, Wm. Theodore, Stephen N. Hay, Royal Weiler, and Andrew Yarrow. 1958. *Sources of Indian Tradition.* (New York: Columbia University Press).

Farmer, B. H. 1993. *An Introduction to South Asia,* 2nd ed. (London: Routledge).

Hardon, John A. 1970. *Religions of the Orient.* (Chicago: Loyola University Press).

Lannoy, R. 1971. *The Speaking Tree: A Study of Indian Culture and Society.* (New York: Oxford University Press).

Nyrop, Richard F., ed. 1985. *India: A Country Study.* (Washington: Library of Congress).

Spear, Percival. 1965. *A History of India,* vol. 2. (Baltimore: Penguin).

Thapar, Romila. 1965. *A History of India,* vol. 1. (Baltimore: Penguin).

Fiction

Forster, E. M. 1952. *A Passage to India.* (San Diego: Harcourt Brace Jovanovich).

Kipling, Rudyard. 1948. *The Jungle Book.* (Garden City, N.Y.: Doubleday).

———. 1927. *Kim.* (London: MacMillan).

Chapter 7

MEXICO

We have learned much about Mexico in recent years while debating the North American Free Trade Agreement, immigration, and drug interdiction. If this continues, we may one day know as much about Mexico as Mexicans know about the United States. Consider one knowledgeable observer's claim that any of Mexico City's major dailies prints more news about the United States on any given day than the *New York Times* prints about the rest of the world *in toto* (Condon 1985, xvi). Nevertheless, at least one stereotype has been demolished—if Mexicans really were lazy, there would not be so much concern in the United States about losing jobs to Mexico. Highly competitive, multinational firms cannot afford such workers no matter how low the wage rate.

The Mexicans are a warm, sentimental, philosophical, proud, and creative people. Their value profile is similar to Japan's in content and in its mix of "doing" and "being" characteristics. Like Japan, Mexico departs from both profiles in its strong uncertainty avoidance, which is found in all Catholic countries except the Philippines. Hofstede also found Mexicans high in power distance (being), masculine (doing), and highly collectivist (being). Trompenaars found that Mexicans (a) view organizations more as social than as functional systems, inclined toward (b) moderately collective responsibility and decision making (both "being" characteristics) but (c) taking a more specific than diffuse view of the world and (d) very achievement oriented (both "doing" characteristics), and (e) abiding by particularist ethics.

THE CULTURAL SETTING

The 1,500-mile border between the United States and the United Mexican States is the most frequently crossed in the world. Mexico is not only hot, dry desert but lush jungle, icy mountain peaks, and rugged coastline. There are about ninety-five million Mexicans, about 90 percent *mestizo,* that is, descendants of the Amerinds and Spanish colonists, and 90 percent Catholic. Amerinds are the ubiquitous native American Indians who actually arrived in the Americas from Asia using an ice or then-existing land bridge to cross the Bering Strait perhaps forty thousand to fifty thousand years ago and arrived in Mexico perhaps ten thousand years ago. Miscegenation of the two cultures is largely complete, and the Mexican population is relatively homogenous; the only significant variable for most being the relative proportions of Spanish and Indian blood. Mexico is exceedingly rich in mineral resources, especially precious metals and gems and petroleum, but very limited in arable land and is subject to every form of natural disaster. Mexico is one of the most industrialized countries in Latin America. About 80 percent of its trade is with the United States, in both directions. The great bulk of wealth and industry is concentrated in Mexico City, Guadalajara, and the states adjacent to the U.S. border. Two-thirds of the population live in cities, and Mexico City is the world's largest metropolitan area. Spanish is the primary language, although more than fifty Indian languages are spoken. The literacy rate is still quite low but improving rapidly. Population growth is also still quite high but improving.

The patriarchal, extended family is the basic economic and social unit and commands the Mexican's loyalty above all else. The *parentelas,* the network of close family connections, extends to all descendants of both paternal and maternal great-grandparents. The practice of godparenting (*compadrazco*) extends beyond Baptism and spiritual responsibilities. Additional godparents are selected by the family from among relatives and friends on occasions such as First Communion, Confirmation, and marriage, and also secular events such as graduation, the dedication of a new factory, and even a first haircut. This enlarged circle of godparents, or *compadres* and *comadres,* assumes part responsibility for the material as well as spiritual well-being of the child. A third set of relationships is *cuatismo,* taken from an Indian word for twin brother, *cuate.* Cuates share interests, leisure time, and intimate information in lifelong relationships of deep friendship and expectations of support in times of need (Rudolph 1984). The bonds of affection and support developed among a multitude of relatives by blood and by choice and close friends are instrumental in ensuring one's place, livelihood, and well-being. Mexicans are very protective of their families, and those who do not work in family businesses tend to keep separate their lives at work and at home (Riding 1989; Lafaye 1976). One's network provides employment, promotions, salary increases, and even for externalities such as access to government licenses and permits. This is not to say that merit and personal qualifications are not important but, rather, that they may not be sufficient. Power brokers occupying key positions in these networks command great loyalty (Rudolph 1984).

At the same time, Mexicans take great pride in their individual identities and respect the individuality of others as repositories of an eternal soul. There is great significance attached to one's character and *gravitas,* to power and position, much more so than to one's achievements. According to Condon (1985) for example, when a Mexican says "May the best man win," he or she means, literally, the best person, not the best competitor. The importance of relationships is such that principles and rules will be ignored in order to maintain them. Interpersonal reality need not coincide with objective reality, and one must always find something positive to say (Condon 1985). Mexicans, like many Latin Americans, take great delight in flouting rules of any kind. Condon adds that it is unlikely, for example, that a Mexican driver would comply with a traffic signal in the total absence of traffic and late at night.

Most businesses are run like a family with the proprietor or manager exercising unquestioned authority. There is little delegation or discretion for subordinates, and their authority rarely matches their responsibilities. However, there is an expectation that the workplace will have an agreeable, convivial atmosphere and that there will be an opportunity to set aside at least part of the work day for pleasure or personal business, typically a long lunch break. Family-owned businesses of all sizes are common, and they are run according to the families' traditions and interests, which may well conflict with textbook practices. Decision making is top-down and driven more by intuition than by objective analysis (Rehder 1968; Kras 1995). Preferred leadership behavior is that of a benevolent autocrat (Morris and Pavett 1992; Stephens and Greer 1995). Mexican subordinates are comfortable with direction but expect to be asked, and in a friendly, respectful manner, rather than told what to do and are sensitive to being too closely supervised and checked (Kras 1995). Nepotism is expected, desirable, and standard practice. The presence of women in the workplace still unsettles many Mexicans who prefer to idealize their women in traditional gender roles. The mixing of men and women outside the family bears much the same connotation and anxiety for many Mexicans as it does for Arabs, centering around the expectation that no good can come of it. Hence seclusion of women in the home and separation of genders during social events are common among more-traditional Mexicans.

Despite stereotypes regarding *siestas* and *mañana,* Mexicans are a hardworking and industrious people but dream of a life of leisure. Guided in their individual behavior by widely shared traditions established by the Aztecs and reinforced by the Spanish, Mexicans nevertheless are quite anarchic and independent and thus very difficult to organize. Power, pragmatism, and family loyalty supersede law and principle, and the spiritual supersedes the material. To others and especially to outsiders with a more democratic heritage, Mexicans may seem evasive and distrustful (Riding 1989). Respected Mexican philosopher Samuel Ramos (1962) characterizes his countrymen as highly resistant toward any centralized authority and prohibitions.

A common criticism of Mexican managers is that they much prefer dealing with theories and abstractions and thus have difficulty attending to details and following through on plans and intentions. Consequently, subordinates not only lack sufficient authority to carry out their responsibilities but also may lack adequate understanding of just what must be done because their directives may be too general or vague. In turn, problems are left unsolved, workers become frustrated as projects are abandoned, and superiors lose respect when they seem to back away from commitments and cannot understand why their subordinates are unable to execute elegant plans (Kras 1995). Ramos (1962) attributes such characteristics to insecurity and lack of confidence. Another consequence is that Mexicans are attracted to impressive, conceptual proposals backed by a record of success, but they generally avoid details (Condon 1985).

Although Mexico is comparatively homogenous ethnically, there is a substantial difference in attitude between the north, essentially a "doing" culture, and the south, a more "being" culture. The north lacked a substantial Indian population when the Spanish arrived. As a result, its development followed a pattern of immigration and settlement rather than conquest and exploitation. The region's economy became more broad based, with mining and then industry emerging alongside agriculture; the southern, more-tropical regions remained less developed. The north, now the land of the *maquiladoras,* also came into direct contact with the United States, and much of its population now identifies more with the North American lifestyle (and management style!) than with the traditional Mexican way of life. Criticized as *malinchistas* (a term taken from the name of Cortés's Indian mistress, interpreter, and informer, *Malinche* (Marina), and applied to those who seemingly abandon their Mexican heritage), the *norteños* (northerners) instead claim to be providing a buffer against the United States and to be "Mexicanizing" the adjacent U.S. states at least as fast as U.S. ways penetrate Mexico. Whereas the typical Mexican remains locked in the past, the *norteños* believe that they can adopt North American ways without jeopardizing their heritage (Riding 1989).

HISTORICAL FORCES

A major difference in U.S. and Mexican cultural origins is the nature of their experience with Europeans. The United States was *settled* by European *immigrants* fleeing *from* oppression by government or the Church and seeking a better life *in* the new world. These immigrants displaced the Amerinds and usually kept apart from them. Much the same can be said for

Brazil and the southern cone countries of South America, especially Argentina and Uruguay. Mexico, on the other hand, and much of Central America and northern South America were *conquered* by representatives *of* government and Church seeking to save the natives and to take riches *from* the New World for the benefit of their European patrons. Rather than displacing the Amerinds, the Spanish exploited them and commingled their cultures.

The values brought to Latin America by the Spaniards were not the values of Europe as much as they were the values of the Arabs. The *conquistadores* who led Spain into the New World during the early sixteenth century matured, as did many generations before them, under the influence or outright dominion of the Moors, who had first established a presence in Spain in 711 and remained for much of the ensuing eight centuries until finally being driven out in 1492. As we explore the notion of *machismo*, the reader is invited to compare it to what we know about the prototypical character of the Arab, the bedouin. If one were to substitute Roman Catholicism for Islam, there is not much difference between the objectives and methods of Spain in the New World with those of the Arabs in their empire. Perhaps the most significant is that the Arabs were much more tolerant of those who refused or resisted conversion. Spanish conquest in the Western Hemisphere and elsewhere coincided with the Reformation and the spread of Protestantism in Europe, and Spain saw itself as the last true defender of the Church. Indeed, King Charles I of Spain became King Charles V of the Holy Roman Empire in 1519, the year the conquistadores extended the Spanish Empire from Cuba to Mexico. Mexican poet and Nobel laureate Octavio Paz (1985) points out the Arab origins of the traditional Spanish politico-military strongman (or *caudillo,* a title some readers will associate with the twentieth-century Spanish fascist Francisco Franco), who commands loyalty of a quasi-religious fervor.

The Aztecs

Pre-Columbian Mexico was dominated by high civilizations, particularly the Mayans in the south, surpassing anything seen in Europe. These advanced civilizations began to appear around 1500 B.C. and flourished between 300 B.C. and A.D. 900. Some of their temples and massive pyramids still stand. These were well-organized, urbanized societies accomplished in the arts, science, agriculture, administration, and trade. Teotihuacán was the first urban center in the Western Hemisphere with a population as large as one hundred thousand when it was destroyed by fire around A.D. 800. They organized themselves in hierarchies with priests, intellectuals, scientists, and artists in the upper ranks. Although their descendants remain, these civilizations eventually passed from the scene for unknown reasons and had relatively little impact on modern Mexico in any institutional sense, much like the ancient but then highly-advanced civilizations of Egypt and Babylon. However, much of the value system remains in evidence, perhaps because it had much in common with the values of the conquistadores.

The Mexica, or Aztecs, achieved dominance in Mexico's central plateau by the fourteenth century and consolidated their conquests into an empire with its capital at Tenochtitlán, on the site of present-day Mexico City. This civilization was also highly accomplished and literate, but it was known more for its warlike nature. The Aztecs were skilled in prose, poetry and music, architecture, jewelry, and mosaics. Intellectual achievement, professional education, and training in trades coexisted with human sacrifice and even cannibalism. Aztec cosmology held that the gods provided the sunlight and rain that sustained man's crops, and that they protected man from all-too-common natural disasters. Man, in turn, must complete the cycle by providing sustenance for the gods through the sacrifice of its own, primarily captives from conquered peoples. A break in this cycle would bring cataclysm, which could be prevented only by continued sacrifices and, thus, new conquests.

Militarism, martial skills, and dignity and valor in battle were considered virtues and were the measure of merit required to attain leadership. The emperor would be that individual who most excelled on these dimensions and who had rendered the most-distinguished service within the ruling dynasty. Aztec society was strictly stratified, dominated by a priestly class, with nobility drawn from among military leaders and politicians, followed by the merchants and traders, and then commoners including farmers, skilled workers, vendors, and lower-ranking civil servants. The lowest class lived apart in their respective neighborhoods or barrios, owned their land communally, and rendered military service together under their own leadership. Enemy captives served as slaves. There was an elaborate criminal justice system under which upper classes received more-severe punishment because they were expected to set an example. The Aztecs ruled a loose confederation of surrounding city-states that were required to pay tribute and provide soldiers but were allowed, essentially, to govern themselves. This relative autonomy would make it difficult for the Aztecs to marshal a unified defense against the conquistadores.

New Spain

Hernán Cortés landed at what he would call Veracruz from Cuba in 1519. Aided by Indian enemies of the Aztecs, the European diseases his men brought with them, and the Aztec emperor Moctezuma's belief that Cortés was a manifestation of a legendary god, Cortés's eight hundred-odd Spaniards managed to defeat the Aztecs in 1520. Such expeditions were entitled to all but the *quinto real,* the "royal fifth," of any riches found.

Apparently Cortés did not see this as sufficient incentive for his men because before setting off into the unknown interior from Veracruz, he ordered them to burn all his ships (Lueke 1994).

Several important aspects of Spanish culture coincided with values already in place in Aztec culture: theocratic autocracy, military aggressiveness, and a rigid class system. New Spain was divided into three-classes: first, whites including the Spaniards, called *peninsulares* or those from the Iberian Peninsula, and creoles (*criollos*) or Mexican-born whites; second the *castas* or, later, the *mestizos*, those of mixed blood; and third, the Indians (*indios*). The peninsulares, whether secular or clergy, retained the highest positions, however, and criollos remained in secondary positions. Whites and mestizos could be found at any economic level but had more political rights regardless. Indicative of the Spanish attitude toward the Indians, mestizos were expected to comply with the law, but Indians, being irresponsible children, were not (Cumberland 1968). The Indians of course were accustomed to social stratification but now found themselves at the bottom of the hierarchy as a class. Intermarriage and concubinage began with Cortés, and the two cultures began a complete and thorough commingling. Eventually, with as many as sixteen classes below the still purely Spanish criollos, including Black, Mulato (Black and Spanish), and *Zambo* (Black and Indian) mixtures resulting from a limited attempt at slavery, the Spanish would lump them all together as *las castas* or the castes (Cumberland 1968).

A viceroy ruled New Spain (and the Philippines) with considerable autonomy, supported by the *audiencia*, a combined judicial and legislative body. Envoys from the Spanish crown would visit periodically to protect its interests, and envoys from the Spanish Church would bring the Inquisition. The conquistadores and Church assumed control of all land, with the Church holding as much as one-half. Large parcels of royal land were granted in trust to those who had rendered valuable service to the crown, along with Indian vassals to work the land and pay tribute. This was the encomienda system—land "commended" to a worthy Spaniard to act as a caretaker for both the land and the "childlike" Indians (mentioned in Chapter 4 in connection with the Spanish conquest of the Philippines). In effect, Spain had introduced feudalism to the new world. As Mexico became more autonomous, the encomiendas were transferred to private ownership as haciendas or large, privately-owned estates. This system produced little wealth, however, as European diseases and Spanish oppression took a hideous toll of the Indian population, limiting the number available to work the land. About two-thirds of the indigenous population was wiped out by A.D. 1600, and more than three centuries passed before the population returned to the preconquest level (Rudolph 1984; Riding 1989). As the conquistadores moved northward, they discovered silver, and the feudal system began producing real wealth for the crown, used to finance its various European wars. Relationships between the Spanish and the Indians and then between the Spanish and rural criollos and mestizos became increasingly polarized, with ownership of land a burning issue that would remain so as, for example, the practice of debt peonage persisted well into the twentieth century.

The University of Mexico, established in 1551, was built on the medieval European model. Hence, traditional education in Mexico emphasized broad theoretical knowledge, the humanities, and preparation for the learned professions and the priesthood, but it did little for the masses (Rehder 1968). The man of letters and leisure, accomplished in the arts, facile in conversation on a variety of topics, as well as elegant, immaculately groomed, and polished became the ideal, much as he was in Spain. Gentlemen did not (and still do not, even at home) engage in physical labor and took great pride in eloquence and the ability to speak with flair and drama. Command of the Spanish language remains a primary indicator and discriminator of social class. All matters of appearance—including the use of formalities and titles, dress and grooming, old-world manners, and correct speech—are of great importance. Mexicans take pride in being gracious hosts and will go to great pains to pick up a restaurant check (Riding 1989). Pretention well beyond one's means was and is common (Rudolph 1984). Families of even very modest means will hire live-in housekeepers and gardeners; they will spend lavishly for special events such as *quinceañera,* the traditional celebration of introduction to society of female children at age fifteen. Paz (1985) suggests that the Mexican preference for form is a constraint producing behavior according to formula.

Another Spanish ideal was *machismo,* the notion that a real man must be immensely proud, fearless, authoritative, intelligent, fiercely possessive of his wife while pursuing as many sexual conquests as possible, always prepared to defend his honor and avenge any insult, and somewhat of a dreamy romantic. Moreover, it was expected that one would boast about one's abilities and achievements as a man. Part of the aura of machismo is passion, whether it be expression of love or anger. Many learned students of Mexican culture attribute to machismo a kind of cultural inferiority complex derived from a sense of pressure to demonstrate manly dominance and bravado while under the constraints of poverty and oppression and recognition of the lack of significant accomplishment as a people since the time of the Mayans and Aztecs. Having established the ideal of the learned, virile man of leisure, the typical Mexican finds it difficult to attain and then compensates with bravado and vainglory. An important concept in Mexican culture connected with honor and the relationship between the genders is *la chingada* or the violated woman. In a sense, Mexicans see their country as *una chingada,* exploited and suppressed by foreigners since Cortés. (For an elaboration of these views see Riding 1989, Paz 1985, and Ramos 1962.) This sense of frustration and inferiority is manifested for the masses

by the common caricature of the *pelado,* the "plucked one," as an eternal
victim of fate and the powerful. The *pelado,* lacking manly achievements
and authority over no one but his own family, assumes the role of overbearing lord and master at home (Condon 1985). The upper classes have
sought relief from this syndrome by imitating the ways of influential foreigners, first the Spanish, then the French and, more recently, (North)
Americans (that last distinction is important because Latin Americans also
see themselves as "Americans"). Ramos adds that Mexicans tend to feel
inferior not because they are Mexican but because so many are poor.
Though these attitudes were brought to Mexico by the Spanish, their origins lie farther eastward. The similarities between these attitudes attributed
to the Spanish and those attributed to Arabs are striking. Arabs tend to
prefer form to substance and abstractions and planning in broad strokes
to action and details. They admire theoretical knowledge, broad learning,
and linguistic skill and oratory. Who is more macho or more of a gracious
host than the Bedouin? And what civilization shares more the sense of lost
opportunity as an ancient but highly accomplished people fell victim to
oppression, both external and self-imposed?

Conditions changed little until the nineteenth century, which brought
great upheavals, beginning with a nationalist revolution in 1810, abetted
unintentionally by a French invasion of Spain, stimulated by successful revolutions in the United States, Haiti, and France, and led by a village priest.
Self-rule was established in 1821, which was followed by utter chaos including many coups and rigged elections. During the ensuing fifty years,
Mexico would see some fifty governments and thirty presidents, one on
nine different occasions and three others three times each (Cumberland
1968). The heroes of this century were populists, nationalists, and liberal
reformers, most notably Benito Juarez, a full-blooded Zapotec Indian, and
General Antonio López de Santa Ana. This was the same Santa Ana who
won the Battle of The Alamo in 1836 but was sent to President Andrew
Jackson in handcuffs two years later by Sam Houston after the Battle of
San Jacinto. The century included two full-scale and bloody revolutions or
civil wars, depending on one's perspective (both triggered by the reformers'
efforts to reduce the power of the Church): a war with the United States
in 1845–48 that cost Mexico half its territory (what is now Texas, California, Arizona, New Mexico, Colorado, and parts of Nevada and Utah),
and a military intervention by Spain, Britain, and France invited by conservative descendants of the peninsulares and wealthy criollos seeking help
against the reformers in 1862. This intervention provoked a threat from
President Lincoln to invoke the Monroe Doctrine, which he was unable to
do because of the demands of the U.S. Civil War. Nevertheless, the threat
was enough to convince the Spanish and British to withdraw relatively
quickly, but the French Emperor Napoleon III went so far as to install
Maximilian, brother of Austrian Hapsburg Emperor Franz Joseph, as Em-

peror of Mexico in 1863. After five years of bloody conflict, military assistance from the United States—accommodated by the end of the U.S. Civil War—and military exigencies in Europe forced France to withdraw its troops, leaving Maximilian to be executed by Mexicans in 1867. It was during this century that Mexicans acquired a sense of nationhood and *Mexicanidad*, or unique Mexicanness (Rudolph 1984). One important manifestation was nationalization of the petroleum industry in 1917.

A civil war that began in 1857 produced a constitutional monarchy and transition from an empire to a nominal republic in 1874. Nevertheless, Porfirio Díaz ruled as president and absolute dictator from 1877 until 1910 in an administration that was oppressive, notoriously corrupt, and resented for catering to foreign interests at the expense of most Mexicans. Díaz was determined to restore order and progress and certainly succeeded as he brought the kind of stability needed to attract foreign investment. Mexico's economy, education, and infrastructure grew rapidly during this period, but only to the benefit of the powerful concentrated in the cities. The result was the Mexican Revolution, which began in 1910, triggered by a fraudulent election. Its leaders included populist heroes Emiliano Zapata and Pancho Villa. One million died before the military phase ended in 1917. A new constitution was supposed to create a liberal democracy. However, the presidency of Mexico has since been essentially an appointed position. The leader of the Institutional Revolutionary Party (*Partido Revolucionario Institucional*, or PRI), which was actually a coalition of parties that has been in power since 1929, simply nominates his successor. The local PRI bosses then ensure his election. In reality then, the political phase of the Revolution may only now really be approaching an end as Mexico finally appears to be making the transition to a more pluralistic democracy.

Economic progress during the Díaz regime gave rise to a small middle class and a new social structure differentiated by employment. (After four centuries of intermarriage the ethnic distinction between Spanish and Indian has largely disappeared, as has the term criollo—Mexico is now a country of mestizos in all classes.) Social classes include the upper class "decent people" (*gente decente*), middle-class white-collar workers, professionals, and managers (*empleados*) as well as small-business owners and lower-class and blue-collar workers, the "working class" (la clase obrera) (Rudolph 1984). There is a great status differential between empleados and *obreros*, with the former commanding confianza or confidence in their trustworthiness, character, and educational preparation. Although obreros might be respected for their skills, they might otherwise be treated as irresponsible children (Davis, in Rehder 1968).

The Church

Catholic priests landed with Cortés and set out immediately to save the Aztecs and other tribes in the hinterlands. Church and state acted in concert. Bishops served on the audiencia, priests served as de facto mayors, and government tax collectors would collect the Church tithe of 10 percent on crops, profits, and rent, which would be shared with the crown as well as with local officials. The Church took responsibility for schools, hospitals, the care of orphans, the aged, and the mentally ill and maintained local records. Before long the Church found itself in a contradictory position with its parish priests, many of them criollos, acting as protectors of the Indians and the poor while the priests' superiors, peninsulares all, egged on the conquistadores.

As the nineteenth century got underway, the military authorities came to fear the growing influence of the Church, especially the Jesuits who administered the educational system. The Church was the government at the local level, and the parish priest was the central figure in the village. There was no connection between the people and any central authority, clerical or secular. The first rebellion against Spain, beginning in 1810, was led by a criollo priest. It was in part a reaction to the beginning of more than a century of edicts, laws, and constitutional provisions that suppressed the power of the Jesuits, abolished monastic orders, ordered deportation of non-Mexican clergy, declared marriage to be a civil contract thus allowing divorce, denied that tithing was a civic obligation, and, finally, nationalized all Church land. Many of these reforms were instituted by the same populists and nationalists who sought independence from Spain. Yet many rural Mexicans who felt much closer ties to their local Church, parochial schools, and parish priests than to any government, whether Spanish or Indian, objected. Rebellious parish priests faced the Inquisition, and many were excommunicated. This conflict was at the root of the devastating internal violence that swept the country three times between 1810 and 1929. In 1926 the entire Mexican Church went on strike to protest nationalization of its land, including the churches themselves, refusing to hold Mass or administer any sacraments, thereby precipitating a three-year rebellion. Relations between Mexico and the Vatican still remain somewhat strained.

The United States

The relationship between the two countries is like that between two very close relatives who nonetheless often get on each other's nerves. As difficult as it may be to understand for North Americans, Mexicans have long identified the United States as the primary threat to their national security. A glance at a map and a cursory review of the historical relationship between the two countries make this attitude quite understandable. Though the fear may have evolved into that of economic or cultural dominance rather than military occupation, it remains no less real (recall that the U.S. Southwest once belonged to Mexico, that the U.S. Army campaigned all the way to Mexico City under Zachary Taylor and occupied much of northern Mexico under Winfield Scott during the Mexican War, that U.S. Marines occupied

Veracruz in 1914, and that General John J. Pershing pursued Pancho Villa across the border in 1916 after Villa tried to loot an armory in New Mexico).

The distinction drawn earlier between northern and southern Mexico is of course due in large part to the influence of the United States. Norteños follow U.S. media and events avidly, like U.S. products, and visit the United States often, but many have never visited Mexico City. U.S. investment, not to mention U.S. negotiators and managers, have a long history in Mexico, accelerated by the advent of the maquiladoras and sure to be accelerated even further by the North American Free Trade Agreement. This process has all been well documented and will be familiar to most readers. A more interesting question is the effect this interaction will have on the United States. Consider, for example, that only Mexico City has a larger population of Mexicans than does Los Angeles.

RELIGION

Three apparitions of the Virgin Mary as a brown-skinned Indian, Our Lady of Guadalupe, in 1531, came to symbolize then and now to all Mexicans and many other Latin Americans the unbreakable bond between Spanish Catholicism and the Mexican Indian. Like the Spanish class system and machismo, Catholicism grafted rather easily onto the Aztec belief system, which included a supreme deity; life after death in heaven or hell; saintlike figures; practices similar to baptism, confession, and penance; days of feasting and fasting; hierarchies of priests; and convents (Herring 1972). Likewise, then, it reinforced the existing value system. However, it was difficult to convince the Indians to give up pagan rituals entirely, and Mexican Catholicism remains tempered a bit by Indian mysticism and animism.

The Catholic Church is one of the world's great conservative forces and perhaps reached its zenith as such during the Spanish colonial period and the Inquisition. It remains a bastion of centralized authority, bureaucracy, and uniformity. Paz (1985) sees as the primary difference between North and Latin America the divergence between Catholic orthodoxy, with its face toward the past, and the reformist nature of Protestantism. Spain not only avoided the Reformation but also the revival of classical humanism, the Enlightenment, that followed. As other Europeans moved from feudalism and empire to the more liberal nation-state and religious tolerance, Spain remained locked in the Middle Ages and was quite willing to use force to preserve the status quo. Indeed, even an autonomous Mexico remained officially an empire until 1874. Catholic doctrine holds that man is essentially fallen and weak, stained with original sin, and that only the Church holds the key to salvation, that is, achieving a state of grace through faith and receiving the sacraments. Backed by the might of the Spanish empire, coupled with its own sense of infallibility and single-mindedness of doctrine, the Church presented a highly authoritative and authoritarian posture. Preaching reliance upon the cardinal virtues of faith, hope, and charity, the Church encouraged the faithful to rely upon it for their salvation rather than upon themselves. In effect, all significant events were acts of God, not man.

CORE VALUES AND BEHAVIOR

Large Power Distance and Hierarchy

In accordance with both Aztec and Spanish traditions, the Mexican manager wields absolute authority but must not demonstrate weakness, indecisiveness, or even a lack of relevant knowledge. As the *jefe*, the leader, he is entitled to complete respect, just like the Mexican father; there is a parent-child relationship between boss and subordinate. However, the *jefe* should cultivate a warm, personal relationship with subordinates, just as a father is expected to treat his children. A manager who does so is not merely a *jefe* but a *patrón*. A patrón refers to his workers as his *muchachos* (boys) whereas a jefe might refer to workers as obreros or *trabajadores,* which are much less personal terms. Large power distance remains securely in place, however, in that subordinates will not manifestly challenge or question the boss (Stanley M. Davis, in Rehder 1968). Whether imposed by Indian leaders, the Spanish, or the Church, rigid hierarchy is the established means of maintaining order.

Strong Collectivism

In keeping with the now familiar pattern of most long-established cultures, Mexican collectivism is intense but limited to the extended family, to which the Mexican appends his compadres (godparents) and cuates ("twins" or close friends). There is little sense of community beyond pride in *la raza* (the race) and Mexicanidad (Mexicanness). Relationships beyond the extended family circle may be characterized by suspicion and even hostility, and the Mexican is quite willing and capable of aggressive competition. Even modest homes may be surrounded by garden walls. Businesses are run like families, and nepotism is still common, especially in small companies and more-rural areas. Mexicans expect strong loyalty, trust, and reliability from both directions in the employer-employee relationship. The same is expected from business relationships, hence the preference for doing business with familiar faces.

Strong Masculinity

Combine the aggressiveness and combativeness of the Aztec with machismo, and the effect is like one ocean wave coinciding with another. Little more need be said here, but if one needs more evidence of Mexican masculinity, consider that the constitution requires that the president be male (Rudolph 1984). Even though status is accorded to power and form, Mexicans are hardworking and achievement-oriented. There is a similarity to the Japanese model in the need to work hard in the face of a long history of real and impending hardship. A difference, however, is that the Mexican is working hard of immediate necessity and living for today. There is little sense of status, obligation, or psychic satisfaction in work or building for the future for working class Mexicans.

Ascribed Status

Trompenaars speaks of cultures that interweave ascribed status with status by achievement. Mexico is such a culture in that it ranks relatively low on Trompenaars's ascription scale but clearly places great importance on matters of form and behavior. There is reason to expect such a combination because the Aztecs were a meritocracy and the Spanish assigned class by cosmetic factors such as ethnicity, old-world manners, and appearance.

Femininity, Saving Face, and Mañana

Despite and perhaps because of intense masculinity, there are strong feminine aspects to Mexico's value system, as is usually the case in collectivist cultures where relationships are so important. Sensitivity to insult induces face-saving behavior. Machismo notwithstanding, tact, modesty, and understatement are expected in a business setting. Public criticism is unacceptable in any circumstances. Mutually beneficial consensus is the preferred business arrangement. However, given a long history of external intervention in Mexico and the pelado mentality, Mexicans are loath to do business with strangers, and therefore patience is necessary to establish a personal relationship before doing business.

Mexico's history is filled with hardships of all kinds. One consequence is a determination to enjoy what pleasures life brings. Thus, patience and flexibility are important with respect to appointments and other time commitments. Mexicans will find it difficult to drop what they are doing if it is enjoyable or part of an ongoing relationship in order to be punctual elsewhere, especially if that pending commitment is with someone known less well. The Mexican promises delivery next week knowing that delivery actually will require two weeks not because he is deceitful or lazy but because he wants to avoid unpleasantness and save face. Moreover, there is little felt need to conserve time. It is not viewed as linear and highly segmented as it is in the United States. Instead, several events and relationships can progress in parallel rather than in series. A single conversation may and probably will involve both business and pleasure, just as the work-day is expected to include some pleasurable or at least personal time.

Traditionally, Mexicans have valued a pleasant atmosphere in the work-place at least as much as compensation, have tended to remain with a "good" employer, and have preferred friendly rather than competitive workplace relationships Compensation is becoming more important, how-ever, and Mexicans are becoming more mobile in search of opportunity, but the motivation for greater material rewards is associated more with being able to do more for one's family than with a sense of achievement (Kras 1995).

Strong Uncertainty Avoidance and Fatalism

The past holds much more meaning for the Mexican than does the fu-ture. The Day of the Dead, a national holiday, is an occasion for reflection on one's heritage and celebration of ancestors. The Mexican is much more a romantic and an artistic dreamer than a change agent. The Indian tra-dition is one of close ties to nature, both physical and spiritual, creating a strong sense of external locus of control and fatalism. These attitudes have been amplified by the autocratic rule of the conquistadores and the Church who suppressed initiative and reduced confidence. The Catholic virtues of faith, hope, and charity induce a passive posture. There is a tendency to wait and hope and place one's fate in the hands of God and the saints, and one's family, patrón, and connections; only the patrón has the earthly power to make life better for the poor Mexican (Rehder 1968). A more worldly constraint is a history of boom and bust economic cycles and po-litical instability, which limit the perceived value of planning (Condon 1985).

Particularist Ethics

There is no paucity of absolute, moral standards in Catholic doctrine. According to Trompenaars, however, Catholic cultures tend toward par-ticularist ethics in their assumption that God will accept minor transgres-sions committed for some larger good, such as a lie told only to protect a friend. Maintaining relationships supersedes compliance with abstract prin-ciples and rules that Mexicans normally enjoy circumventing in any case. But Trompenaars also found that Mexicans were less likely to make such compromises in the case where helping an outsider would harm one's em-ployer. Ramos (1962) believes that a general lack of principle causes Mex-icans to distrust others, presumed to suffer the same lack. Nepotism is a reflection of particularist ethics. Whereas a U.S. manager might wonder how to trust a Mexican counterpart who puts the interests of a friend ahead of the apparent interests of the business, the Mexican wonders how to trust someone who would not.

CONVERGENCE?

Defeat by the United States in the Mexican war and the necessity of U.S. assistance to expel the French served to cement in place a sense of inferiority in Mexico (Riding 1989) that only deepened as the two economies and societies diverged economically with the industrial revolution. Despite resentment of U.S. intervention and expansionism and fear of U.S. cultural and economic dominance, Mexicans admire the honesty, efficiency, and freedom of North Americans on an individual level seen as lacking in themselves (Riding 1989). Kras (1995) and Stephens and Greer (1995) report that the attitudes of Mexican managers in larger companies are becoming more competitive, task-oriented, and participative and less authoritarian and paternalistic. This is to be expected, given the increase in foreign investment, especially with respect to the cross-fertilization of the *maquiladoras,* and Mexico's history of imitation of influential foreign powers, most recently the United States. At the same time, Kras finds no change in the high value placed upon warmth and conviviality, appearance, good manners, formality, status, titles and connections, face-saving, and a preference for the broadly educated, the theoretical, and the abstract. She suggests that convergence in such areas as open communication and participative management can be encouraged by taking the time to develop a trusting relationship built on mutual confidence and respect. Stephens and Greer agree that Mexico's business culture will remain "softer" than that of the United States with more emphasis on form than substance, more respect shown for others in speech and manner, and a high value placed on non-work pursuits. They add that U.S. managers must still work hard to elicit participation and encourage initiative and innovation, even though uncertainty avoidance seems to be declining among professionals. They see little change in the avoidance of details in negotiations and contracts, warning that persistence in such matters will signal distrust, and suggest that the warmth of the Mexican character makes them excellent communicators and enhances teamwork and cooperation. Mexicans tend to perceive North Americans as unwilling to listen to and learn from Mexicans. Like most Latin Americans, they see U.S. managers as somewhat cold, insensitive, rigid, impatient, compulsive, and unable to really enjoy life. As one spends more time with Latin Americans, enjoying their warmth and hospitality, one wonders if they may be right.

VARIATIONS

The conquistadores migrated southward and established much the same conditions throughout Central America. The northern regions of South

America, the Andes, the Amazon valley, and northern Chile had parallel experiences. The Spaniard Francisco Pizarro landed in what is now Peru in 1532, and a similar history unfolded from that point forward. These countries have value profiles very similar to Mexico's with the exception of generally lower rankings in masculinity. One explanation is the more peaceful nature of the Incas, much like the Mayans but very much unlike the Aztecs. Another is that the Spaniards did not penetrate these rugged and forbidding regions as deeply as they did in Mexico. Chile in particular came to be dominated by a relatively small influx of Europeans who acquired influence well beyond their numbers (Herring 1972). An exception to this entire pattern is the low power distance and strong femininity found in traditionally democratic and comparatively well-educated Costa Rica, which had a relatively small Indian population and a historical experience much more similar to that of the United States, Brazil, and the southern cone countries. The Europeans (primarily Portuguese and then Italians in Brazil and many Italians and Spanish in the south, but also Germans, Swiss, French, Poles, Austro-Hungarians, Russians, Turks, and Japanese) came as immigrants and settlers not as conquerors and exploiters. Brazil and the southern cone countries of Argentina, Chile, and Uruguay exhibit smaller power distance and tend to be more individualistic than their northern neighbors. Brazil has the most middling value profile of all these countries, perhaps because of the moderating effect of large Black and mulatto populations descendant from African slaves brought by Portuguese colonizers. The African influence was one of geniality, good humor, love of life, and gaiety still evident in Brazil (Herring 1972).

Clearly, it should not be presumed that what is said here regarding Mexico can be applied indiscriminately to other Latin American countries. Many would have their own chapters if length so permitted.

SUMMARY

The primary forces that shaped Mexican culture include the following:

- Indian, particularly Aztec, origins
- Spanish conquest and colonization
- The Roman Catholic Church
- The political and economic power of the United States
- A rugged, infertile land given to climatic extremes and frequent natural disasters

The core values developed by these forces include the following:

- **Large Power Distance** and **Hierarchy**—imposed by the centralized, vertical power structures of the Aztec class system, by Spanish military power and social class ranking, by the bureaucratic Church on which Mexicans came to depend for meaning in their lives, and by the patriarchal family typical of agrarian societies

- **Strong Collectivism**—centered in the highly extended, agricultural family, compadrazco and the cuate network, and grounded in the interdependence engendered by harsh conditions

- **Strong Masculinity**—in terms of traditional gender roles, aggressiveness and competitiveness driven by Aztec militarism and meritocracy, Spanish-Arab machismo and romanticism, the effort required to survive harsh conditions, and, more recently, by the necessity created and example set by the United States

- Emergent **Individualism**—due primarily to the influence of the United States

- **Ascribed Status**—based on power and cosmetic factors attributable to the Spanish, which at least partially supplanted Aztec meritocracy

- **Femininity** and **Face Saving**—required to maintain relationships within the extended family and network and to avoid triggering the machismo defense mechanism

- **Strong Uncertainty Avoidance**—a result of Indian fatalism, which in turn is rooted in dependence on nature, in the inherent conservatism and dependency created by Spanish and Church rule and Catholic doctrines of original sin and reliance upon faith and hope

- **Particularist Ethics**—a result of distrust and dislike of central authority, the need for maintenance of relationships and face, and the expectation of God's forgiveness and Catholic absolution no matter the nature of the transgression

ADDITIONAL READING

Management Practices

Condon, John C. 1985. *Good Neighbors: Communicating with Mexicans.* (Yarmouth, Maine: Intercultural Press).

Kras, Eva S. 1995. *Managing in Two Cultures.* Rev. ed. (Yarmouth, Maine: Intercultural Press).

Morris, Tom, and Cynthia M. Pavett. 1992. "Management Style and Productivity in Two Cultures." *Journal of International Business Studies* 23, no.1 (First Quarter): 169–179.

Rehder, Robert R., ed. 1968. *Latin American Management: Development and Performance*. (Reading, Mass.: Addison-Wesley).

Stephens, Gregory K., and Charles R. Greer. 1995. "Doing Business in Mexico: Understanding Cultural Differences." *Organizational Dynamics* 24, no. 1 (Summer): 39–55.

History and Culture

Cumberland, Charles G. 1968. *Mexico: The Struggle for Modernity*. (New York: Oxford University Press).

Herring, Hubert. 1972. *A History of Latin America*, 3rd ed. (New York: Knopf).

Lafaye, Jacques. 1976. *Quetzacóatl and Guadalupe*. (Chicago: University of Chicago Press).

Lueke, Richard L. 1994. *Scuttle Your Ships before Advancing*. (New York: Oxford University Press).

Miller, Robert Riyal. 1985. *Mexico: A History*. (Norman: University of Oklahoma Press).

Parkes, Henry Bamford. 1970. *A History of Mexico*. (Boston: Houghton Mifflin).

Paz, Octavio. 1985. *The Labyrinth of Solitude*. (New York: Grove).

Ramos, Samuel. 1962. *Profile of Man and Culture in Mexico*. (Austin: University of Texas Press).

Riding, Alan. 1989. *Distant Neighbors*. (New York: Vintage).

Rudolph, James D., ed. 1984. *Mexico: A Country Study*. (Washington: Library of Congress).

Fiction

Fuentes, Carlos. 1982. *Distant Relatives*. (New York: Farrar, Straus and Giroux).

———. 1991. *The Death of Artemio Cruz*. (New York: Farrar, Straus and Giroux).

Chapter 8

RUSSIA

Russia or the Russian Federation is of course the most significant remnant of the Soviet Union that fell apart in 1991. Although the country still extends across nearly half the Northern Hemisphere (and retains twice the area of the United States or China), our focus will be on the much more densely populated European plain west of the Urals. Asiatic Russia, which includes Siberia, remains one of the world's most desolate and inaccessible regions, although rich in mineral resources. It is tempting to think that after Russia shrugs off the effects of Communism, without downplaying the significance of that challenge, that it will be able to join the rest of the developed world. We must recognize however that totalitarian Communism was not much of an aberration in Russian history. For Russia and for many of its former satellites to become more Western will require them not just to embrace some western ideas but to make a major cultural shift. It is by no means a sure thing.

Much has been said about the nature of management within a communist system. We perceive that Russian managers care little about how well a job is done as long as one makes one's quota, that there is no incentive beyond fear of punishment to improve or demonstrate concern for the customer, and that bureaucracy in its worst sense is rampant, preventing risk-taking or initiative. Yet events since the fall of Communism indicate that there is considerable entrepreneurialism in Russia, though not always of a socially responsible nature. Veiga, Yanouzas, and Buchholtz (1995) investigated core Russian management values, using a methodology similar to Hofstede's. They found traditional Russians very high in power distance and uncertainty avoidance, moderately individualistic, very short-term oriented, and very low in entrepreneurialism (risk-taking) and in concern for others. Bollinger (1994) found evidence of high power distance, high uncertainty avoidance, collectivism, and femininity. These findings support common perceptions. There also is evidence of change, however, particularly among younger Russians.

THE CULTURAL SETTING

Russia's land is largely flat and rolling steppe. Its only significant topographical feature is the Urals, the relatively low-lying range that serves as the nominal boundary between Europe and Asia. Only about one-sixth of its land is arable due to the harsh climate and sandy soil, and much of the most fertile land was lost when Ukraine, to Russia's southwest, became independent. Russia remains rich in natural resources, including oil, though much of this wealth lies in Siberia, and much was lost with the departure of the republics around the Caspian Sea. The largely featureless terrain has made Russia vulnerable to foreign invaders, which have come frequently and from many directions. Whereas the invasions by Napoleon and Hitler are the most well known, the most significant in terms of long-term impact was that of the Mongols who pillaged and looted most of Russia and occupied the country for much of the Middle Ages. Russia's huge land mass has allowed it to fall back toward Moscow and absorb invasions while the invader's supply lines grow longer and to buy time until the winter sets in. This was the strategy that defeated both Napoleon and the Germans. It was also employed by the Reds to defeat the Whites in the Civil War that solidified Communist rule after the 1917 Revolution. Russia also has been invaded by Goths, Turks, Magyars (now Hungarians), Bulgars, Poles, Lithuanians, and Swedes, among others. Between invasions, Russia has engaged in continual warfare primarily with the Turks to the south, where an expanding Ottoman Empire and religion were major issues, and with European neighbors over access to the Baltic and the fertile lands of Poland and Ukraine. Russia initiated its own kind of manifest destiny as it eventually stretched its empire to the Pacific.

Russia's population is about 150 million, ranking sixth behind China, India, the United States, Brazil, and Indonesia. Three-quarters of the people, 80 percent ethnic Russians, live in cities. The ethnic Russians are Slavs who apparently originated in the region of the Pripet Marshes in the borderlands of Belarus and Ukraine (since independence it is customary not to say *the* Ukraine) and who populated most of what is now eastern Europe. Approximately two thousand years ago, the so-called East Slavs began settling along the rivers of what is now western or European Russia, displacing indigenous Finnish tribes who then moved northward. They were a tough people who went about settling an enormous, forbidding land even while buffeted continually by invaders. Their settlements, called *mir*, firmly established by the sixth century, were self-governing, agricultural communes widely dispersed by the poor quality of the land but bound by patriarchal, extended families. The central role of these communes in Russian history and culture is illustrated by the very term *mir,* which can mean not only village but world and peace (the last interpretation used for the Russian space station that carries this name).

The traditional peasant commune was led by village elders who wielded absolute but paternalistic power. They sought unanimity and defined whatever consensus seemed to be emerging from open discussions and made recommendations to the chief elder, who would make the final decision. The Communists initially sought to combine the collective and individual aspects of the traditional process into a kind of collegial decision-making until Stalin reimposed individual autocracy in the extreme. What remained unchanged was the unwillingness of subordinates to take any initiative without an explicit directive from above. One result of *perestroika* was a 1987 mandate for participation in decision making by an elected workers' council and election of managers. These were reversed two years later in part because managers complained that workers were electing managers who would demand little of them (Puffer 1994).

Russian work groups are cohesive, building bonds of solidarity and camaraderie (Vlachoutsicos and Lawrence 1990) out of a need for strength in numbers as a defense against hostile external forces, both human and natural. Russians conform to group performance norms, are suspicious of those who depart from them, and tend to resent and envy the successful. These attitudes are grounded in the ethic that everyone should share alike in the generally miserable existence of the Russian peasant. The Russian worker was expected to be tenacious and hardworking but not innovative. The Communists reinforced this ethic by rewarding managers primarily according to their adherence to party rules and principles. Those inclined to innovate and take the initiative could do so only by circumventing the party administrative machinery and at great personal risk (Puffer 1994). In effect, the taking of initiative or risk in itself can be construed as a violation of norms. Likewise, traditional Russian managers are delighted to delegate or otherwise diffuse accountability while remaining unwilling to delegate authority.

Russians often are portrayed as pessimistic and lacking in self-confidence but also as boastful, clever, and grandiose in their ambitions. Throughout their history they have tackled enormous enterprises—whether it be single-handedly wresting Jerusalem from the Ottoman Empire; mobilizing to stop massive invasions; building the world's largest factories, power plants, and rockets; or trying to defeat the West in the Cold War. At the same time they often seem incapable of carrying out the most routine task effectively. Russians traditionally have adhered to strong ethical practices in personal relationships but have had little compunction about deceiving superiors and officials and circumventing the established order. Corruption and bribery have been so widespread that they are presumed to be the norm. Under the Communists, an individual who would not consider stealing from or lying to friends and family might quite willingly steal from or deceive an employer with no shame or guilt. The substantial presence of organized crime in the contemporary business environment is a natural progression of this phenomenon.

Russia has long had a two-class system consisting of a very small and very wealthy nobility (or Communist elite) and a very large (more than 90 percent) and very poor peasantry that was bound to the land and its owners officially until 1861 and de facto since. The former disdained business (Harris 1995), and the latter lacked opportunity, training, and access to capital. The Communists replaced the Romanov nobility with the *nomenklatura* (the 'named ones'), the privileged party officials and bureaucrats. Status in Russia is largely a function of age and learning. There is too much cynicism to respect power, wealth, or class.

HISTORICAL FORCES

Russian history can be summarized in one word—suffering. In this century alone perhaps fifty million Russians died in the World Wars, the Russian Revolution and Civil War, and in other conflicts, another twenty-three million in Stalin's purges, and countless others in the gulags and at the hands of the KGB and its predecessors. No country except China has had so many leaders so cruel to and destructive of its own people, for so long, so massively, and as recently. Consider numerous foreign invasions, some totally devastating, misguided, and wasteful foreign adventures, intense political oppression in peace as well as in war, actual or virtual slavery imposed upon 90 percent of the population until late in the twentieth century, sustained poverty and deprivation, inept economic policy causing enormous squandering of effort and capital, and the debilitating effects of prolonged isolation and a daunting physical environment and one acquires a sense of the distance Russians must traverse to join the modern world. Russia is a Third World nation in every respect save its military and space program. As a result, despite their enormous talents, resources, tenacity, and robustness, the Russians remain a very suspicious and cynical people. The theme of fatalism and submission to authority runs throughout much of Russia's abundant literature. Examples include Turgenev's *Fathers and Sons* and Dostoyevski's *Crime and Punishment*.

The Kievan Rus and the Russian Empire

The rivers of Russia flow primarily northward into the Baltic and White Seas and southward into the Black and Caspian Seas and thus became important trade routes linking what are now Scandinavia and the Baltic countries to the north and northwest with Byzantium and the Middle East to the south. Scandinavian traders became quite familiar to the East Slavs and called them the Rus. A peaceful people content to tend their crops but dispersed and vulnerable and lacking political organization, the Rus endured invasions by Swedes, Lithuanians, Germans, Hungarians, Poles, Turks, and others. Content to pay tribute in return for protection and being left alone to pursue their way of life, they asked for or were forced to accept—the reality is unclear—Scandinavian rule, which was established as the Rurik dynasty at Kiev, the present-day capital of Ukraine, in A.D. 878. The so-called Kievan Rus was the first Slavic state and became a well-ordered, commercial, urban society, free of feudalism unlike its western European counterparts, which thrived until it was crushed and dispersed by the Mongols in 1240. A major (Rus)sian trading center had developed at Novgorod, between present-day Moscow and the Baltic, located at a key river portage. It would go on to become a prosperous and fully European city and a member of the Hanseatic League. Its wealth, enough income to pay handsome tribute to the Mongols, and protection by surrounding marshes allowed it to avoid the fate of Kiev. Meanwhile, Moscow had risen to prominence because it lies at the hub of Russia's network of rivers and roads and it absorbed Novgorod into its domain.

The Muscovite Grand Prince Ivan I, a descendant of the Rurik dynasty, established Moscow's dominance over other Russian princes by inducing the Metropolitan (prelate) of the Russian Church to move to Moscow and by consolidating collection of tribute for the Mongols. Ivan III or Ivan the Great (1462–1505) took advantage of dwindling Mongol power and refused to pay tribute, thereby establishing Russian independence, and began the military unification and expansion that would create the Russian Empire. Ivan IV or Ivan the Terrible (1533–1584) assumed the title czar (Caesar) seeking to assert himself and Moscow as heirs to both Rome and Byzantium. He recaptured the valley of the Volga, the route to Persia and Baghdad via the Caspian Sea, from the Mongols and took much of Siberia, Russia's first venture east of the Urals. He earned his appellation however as one of history's most ruthless despots. For example (among many), angered by Novgorod's Western orientation, he attacked the city and exterminated virtually its entire population (and Russia's only entrepreneurial enclave), many personally and through hideous torture, over a period of only five weeks. He believed that if he treated his people cruelly, they would do the same to Russia's enemies, and only then could he complete the reunification of Russian lands and fulfill the dream of empire (Lourie 1991). Ivan's most lasting innovation was a secret police to carry out his will. This instrument would serve Russia's tyrants well in the centuries to come. The Ruriks died out after Ivan IV, largely because he murdered his son and heir in a fit of rage, and left Russia united and mighty but barbarous and ignorant (Lourie 1991). An important figure who ruled during the unstable period between the passing of the Ruriks and the accession of the Romanovs was Boris Godunov. After drought, plague, and famine sent peasants streaming into the cities around 1600, he decreed that all peasants would henceforth be fixtures of the land on which they were born. In effect, Godunov had enslaved millions of Russians by binding them to the soil and, in effect, to the landowners. Most of the Russian population became serfs virtually overnight.

The Russian Orthodox Church

The trade route from Byzantium, or Constantinople, via the Black Sea and the Dneiper River brought missionaries of the Greek Orthodox Church, who also introduced Greek art, architecture, and the Greek alphabet that would provide the basis for the Russian Cyrillic alphabet. Prince Vladimir of the Kievan Rus led the conversion from paganism—the Rus's primary deity had been Perun, god of thunder and lightning—to Orthodoxy in 988. Legend has it that he chose Orthodoxy because Judaism had no homeland, Islam forbade consumption of alcohol, and the Church of Santa Sophia (Holy Wisdom) in Constantinople impressed his ambassadors with a beauty much more in keeping with the Russian ideal of spiritual majesty and worship of painted, pagan icons than did the churches of Rome. The Orthodox Catholic Churches (the Roman Catholic Church re-emerged from Byzantine control in the Great Schism of 1054) do not recognize the leadership of the Pope and are governed along national lines. Accordingly, as Orthodoxy grew in Russia, it became the Russian Orthodox Church.

The Church became the centerpiece of everyday life in the Russian village, and the Russians took solace and refuge from their meager existence in their faith. The Mongols allowed the Russians to practice their faith and the Church to stand as the only institutional force in Russia. Russian trade, industry, education, arts, and literature dissipated during the occupation, and its leaders answered to the Mongols. The Church thus became the focus of Russian nationalism and the only source of continuity and means of preservation of Russian culture and traditions, much as the Irish monasteries and the Greeks before them preserved classical traditions in the West during Muslim incursions and the Dark Ages of Europe. In effect, the Church became Russia.

The Mongols

The Mongols, called Tatars by the Russians and Huns by other Europeans, crushed all resistance, devastated the cities (except Novgorod), and occupied most of Russia from 1237 to 1480. Attacked from several directions and from much closer strongholds than those of Napoleon and Hitler, the Russians were unable to resist these fierce warriors. Once established, the Mongols sought only tribute, remained apart, and allowed the government, people, and the Church to function normally, intervening only, but brutally, when necessary to collect the rent. Thus they had little direct effect on Russian culture, but their indirect effect was enormous. Given its remoteness in space from much of Europe, especially the more progressive states such as France, Holland, and England, and its association with Byzantium rather than with Rome, Russia had long been insulated from European trends and events. Now, isolated and dominated by the Mongols, the Russians fell further behind western Europeans by another 250 years during a period of great vitality and advance in the west (Acton 1986). For the Russians there would be no emergence from Medieval feudalism, no Reformation or Renaissance or Age of Reason or Scientific Revolution, and consequently no foundation laid for an Enlightenment or industrial revolution. The Russian Orthodoxy of the ninth century would remain the Russian Orthodoxy of the future. Moreover, by the time the Mongol yoke was lifted, the Crusades had opened new trade routes to the Middle East, and various nomadic tribes impeded Russian trade routes to the south. The only means to wealth left for the Russian nobility was to exploit the peasants (Lourie 1991). A second indirect effect was that the Mongols taught the Russians by example how best to extract that wealth—through harsh, centralized, absolute rule.

The Romanovs

Modern Russian history began with Peter the Great (1689–1725), the first major figure of the Romanov dynasty that ruled Russia from 1613 until 1917. Peter took an enormous interest in all things European and was the first czar to travel outside Russia. He defeated Sweden, a major power at the time, at Poltava in 1709 to gain access to the Baltic and established a new capital, St. Petersburg, on land formerly colonized by the Swedes. Facing the Gulf of Finland, the Baltic, and the West, and distinctly Western in its layout, architecture, and canals as compared to the traditional Russian style based on the Greek and the Orthodox "onion dome," it symbolized what was supposed to be a major cultural shift. Peter drove Asians out of Russia, freed southern Russia from the remaining Mongol khans, freed women from domestic seclusion, and suppressed the Church. He abolished the traditional long beards symbolic of Orthodoxy and taxed wearers of Asiatic dress. He built a navy; organized a standing army run by educated, professional officers; reorganized the government's administrative machinery along Western lines; established a uniform calendar and currency, factories, hospitals, a newspaper, and even an academy of science—which he had to staff with western Europeans. Peter made it a practice to learn various crafts and military skills from the bottom up, and he selected and promoted his advisers on merit. In effect, Peter transformed Russia into a modern and powerful European state, at least in a geopolitical sense. All of this made no difference to the ordinary Russian, however, who remained a serf. In reality, Peter's suppression of the Church, his disdain of Russian traditions, and his construction of an elaborate caste system only widened the gulf between the Russian people and their masters, and he imposed his will with whatever force was necessary—he was still a Russian czar at heart despite his progressiveness. Meanwhile, serfdom continued to deprive the people of any incentive and to stifle productivity. The few serfs who could fled to the west, south, and east, and they generally prospered as independent farmers known as cossacks (from the Turkish *kazak* for free man), and Ukraine and Siberia became Russia's frontiers and symbols of freedom (Lourie 1991). The name Ukraine means "on the edge" in Slavonic (Davies 1996, 334).

Catherine the Great (1762–1796), a German princess who married Peter III (and apparently conspired with her lover to kill him), became enthralled with French culture, fashion, and political liberalism, even corresponding with Voltaire and Montesquieu, and French became the language of court. A putative reformer, when informed by the landowners of the likely consequences of any attempt to lift the bonds of serfdom, and having taken notice of the fate of the monarchy after the French Revolution, she quickly lost her enthusiasm for political reform, and serfdom continued. She rationalized her hypocrisy with sophistry, arguing that millions of serfs kept in ignorance could not be freed because of it. Her only lasting contribution, Catherine took Poland and the Crimea (southern Ukraine) into the empire. Alexander I (1801–1875) was contemplating a representative assembly when interrupted by Napoleon. He allied Russia with England, Austria, and Prussia to contain Napoleon but suffered a massive defeat at Austerlitz. He then withdrew from the conflict, conspired with Napoleon to divide Europe between them, and was rewarded by Napoleon's invasion of Russia in 1812 (an eerie precursor of the Molotov-Ribbentrop pact of 1939 between Hitler and Stalin and subsequent events). Aided by the preeminent Russian generals "distance" and "winter," Alexander defeated Napoleon at Borodino and chased the *grand armée* all the way back to Paris in 1814. Only fifty thousand of six hundred thousand invaders left Russia alive. In an apparent reversal of sentiment, Alexander then proposed a Holy Alliance of Russia, Prussia, and Austria to forestall further movement toward representative democracy and revolution in Europe. Alexander also solidified Russian control of Ukraine and Finland. Some Russian officers had observed life in France (where they ordered restaurant food "*bistro!, bistro!*"—Russian for *quick* [Lourie] 1991) and, after comparing it to their own, staged the "Decembrist" uprising in 1825, an important precedent that was quickly suppressed. Russia's first university was established in Moscow in 1755. However, its western European faculty lectured in Latin and German, unintelligible even to the nobility, whose *lingua franca* was still French (Pipes 1974). Meanwhile, serfdom continued. Repressive rule left violence as the only form of expression for the masses, and the numerous local upheavals were put down harshly.

Flirtation with the West and thought of political reform ended under Nicholas I (1825–1855). There was a debate throughout the nineteenth century between Russian intellectuals and writers who thought Russia ought to be left to develop its own unique culture, the Slavophiles, and those who preferred a Western model. This is the theme, for example, of Tolstoy's (an ardent Slavophile) *War and Peace*. Pursuing a dream of Catherine, Nicholas invaded Turkey in 1854 in an attempt to restore Byzantine Christianity and free Jerusalem from Islam. The British, concerned about the threat to their trade route to India posed by a Russian presence in the Middle East, joined Turkey, France, and others to stop the Russians. The scene of Tennyson's *The Charge of the Light Brigade*, the two-year Crimean War was a disaster for the Russians that aroused enormous resentment in the peasantry, who once again had paid the price for the czar's folly. In response to the building turmoil, and convinced that serfs made neither good farmers nor good soldiers, Alexander II (1855–1881) emancipated the serfs, by then some forty million strong, in 1861 and established the right to trial by jury for all. Given the nominal right to buy land, but at the owner's choice of parcel and price, and assessed high tax valuations, they were of course unable to do so (Kirchner 1976; Acton 1986). Alexander II was about to announce a form of limited, representative government when he was assassinated by a terrorist in 1881. Thus serfdom ended, but peasantry resumed. It was a distinction without real difference.

Folly anew was Nicholas II's (1894–1917) attempt to wrest occupied territory from the Japanese in northeast Asia. The Russo-Japanese War of 1904–1905 was another disaster for Russia, defeated soundly on land and sea. Revolutionary activity began in earnest as laborers and peasants joined rebellious soldiers and sailors inspired by a mutiny on the battleship *Potemkin*. Land and factory owners demanded reforms to mollify the workers who staged a massive, general strike in 1905. This was the Octobrist Revolution. Nicholas responded by establishing a representative assembly, the *duma*, and, in effect, a constitutional monarchy that would not survive World War I. Russia entered the war ostensibly to assist its brother Slavs in Serbia who had assassinated Archduke Franz Ferdinand of Austria in Sarajevo, thereby igniting the war, and faced annihilation by the Austro-Hungarians. In reality, Russia still had designs on Constantinople—the Ottoman Turks were allied with Germany and the Central Powers. Russia suffered horrendous losses early in the war due in part to the government's inability to equip its troops properly. Soldiers were sometimes sent into battle unarmed with orders to retrieve weapons from the dead (Lourie 1991). After food shortages caused massive riots in Petrograd (St. Petersburg), the duma called for Nicholas to step down. He abdicated in 1915 and was exiled to Ekaterinburg (that is, Catherineburg, now Sverdlovsk).

The Communists

A rapid attempt to catch up with Western industrialization late in the nineteenth century led to wide-scale abuse of workers, providing fertile ground for Marxists. Radicals, led by Marxists, had demanded a democratic republic rather than Nicholas's constitutional monarchy. With Nicholas in exile, Vladimir Ilyich Lenin seized the opportunity and won power for his Bolsheviks in 1917 by promising immediate peace, a classless society, land reform, and worker control of factories. He delivered on the first promise, signing the Treaty of Brest-Litovsk in 1918, but at the cost of Poland, Ukraine, the Baltic States, and Finland. This cost Russia its most fertile land, a quarter of its total land and population, and three-quarters of its steel production and coal reserves (Acton 1986). A three-year civil war ensued with the so-called Whites, a loose alliance of the nobility, much of the military, reformers who believed the Bolsheviks to be worse than the czars, separatists, Cossacks, and any who stood to suffer under a Marxist regime in opposition to Lenin's Reds. Their only common interest was opposition to the Bolsheviks. To deprive them of the possibility of unified leadership, Lenin arranged for the assassination of Nicholas II and his entire family. This was the storied end of the Romanov dynasty. Lenin did not keep his promises of political reform, he abolished the duma, and his preferred instrument of power became the *cheka* or secret police. By the end of the Civil War in 1921, which had been fought most aggressively throughout Russia, there were twenty million dead, and Russia had lost 80 percent of its industry. The Union of Soviet Socialist Republics, led by Lenin, the first General Secretary of the Communist Party, was established in 1922. The state planning agency, *gosplan,* went into operation immediately. Sailors of the navy's Baltic fleet had rebelled at Kronstad in 1921, demanding reinstatement of the duma and devolution of some power to local councils of workers, farmers, and soldiers. Lenin crushed the rebellion, but to regain favor, he incorporated some perestroika-like reforms called the New Economic Policy that allowed some localized free enterprise but retained government control of major industries. He also dropped the name Bolshevik, meaning "majority" (of the Communist Party), which had by then taken on highly negative connotations. Mindful of Marx's dictum that religion is the opiate of the people, Lenin dismantled the Church and confiscated its property. Nine of every ten Russian churches did not survive Communist rule (Richmond 1992, 157).

Upon Lenin's death, Josef Stalin became General Secretary in 1929 after a power struggle with Leon Trotsky, who had organized the Red Army for Lenin and engineered the Reds' victory in the Civil War. Stalin immediately executed or exiled all those who took advantage of Lenin's New Economic Policy and embarked on the first of the now notorious five-year plans to rebuild Russia's industrial and military might, primarily with slave labor organized by the secret police. He forcibly collectivized agriculture, engineered artificial famines to exterminate *kulaks* ("wealthy" peasants—readily vilified because many were money lenders able to exert some power over their fellow peasants [Vakar 1962]) he did not send to Siberia (some five million disappeared), and through various means purged and killed tens of millions of his countrymen solely to protect his power—no excuses about racial superiority, no rationalizing or scapegoating—just raw, murderous power. Stalin eventually had Trotsky assassinated even though he had long been in exile in Mexico. Yet even though he apparently saw an assassin or rival behind every Russian tree, he badly misjudged the intentions of Adolf Hitler, his only rival in world-class criminality. More tens of millions of Russians would pay the price yet again for that folly, made still worse by Stalin's purge of his own military leaders in 1937, even as German tanks and planes were rolling out of factories *en masse,* as Hitler publicly vilified Communists and Slavs and loudly demanded *lebensraum* (living room), with a clearly covetous eye to the east.

The Cold War followed World War II, and the significant events are too recent and familiar to require recitation here. Despite the onerous nature of the Soviet government and system, the experience of the Great Patriotic War and a long, uninterrupted history of submission to authority sustains in individual Russians a close identification with the state. Nevertheless, the system finally collapsed with the nuclear accident at Chernobyl, a massive earthquake in Armenia that revealed the shoddiness of Soviet construction and an inability to respond to the disaster, the military debacle in Afghanistan, and Mikhail Gorbachev's policy of *glasnost* that allowed Russians and East Europeans to learn not only of these flaws but to compare their countries and life-styles to others. Even then, change in Russia was essentially top-down. In the chaos that has followed, including the rise of organized crime, Russians seem to long for the stability and order of the past. Many Russians still support the Party, and others speak even of restoring the Romanovs.

RELIGION

The Orthodox Catholic Churches differ from Roman Catholicism more in form than in substance. Orthodox means "right belief" or "correct teaching," and the Church considered itself the "custodian of eternal truths" (Pipes 1974, 225). Its believers consider it to be more true to the origins of Catholicism than was the Roman Church and therefore were less willing to tolerate deviation from Church teachings. Its doctrine and sacraments are essentially the same, but Orthodoxy places more emphasis on faith, ceremonial majesty, aesthetic splendor, and elaborate ritual and places little value upon rationality and study of scripture (Acton 1986; Lourie 1991). Ritual traditions were more important than the gospel

(Church scriptures were not translated into Russian until the 1860s–1870s), and the clergy were not particularly learned as they were in the West (Pipes 1974). The Church taught humility, resignation to the will of the almighty, and submission to Church authority, even preaching that the Mongols were sent by God to punish Russians for their sins (Miller 1961). The congregation was an egalitarian community and any effort to raise oneself above the mean was seen as arrogant and greedy. There is a sense that it is morally wrong to get ahead, especially if at the expense of others (Richmond 1992). There persists in Russia a suspicion and even hostility toward those who have done so successfully. Satisfaction in belonging to the congregation (*sobornost*) was the only apparent manifestation of a Russian sense of community (Miller 1961). Quiet suffering and acceptance of one's fate were virtues. Strong faith enabled Russians to withstand the rigors of their environment and deprivation and to give relatively little attention to worldly concerns, other than survival. Russia's remoteness and Mongol-imposed isolation from Roman Catholic Europe made it unnecessary for the Russian Church to make any concessions to reformers or to science (Pipes 1974). It was thus an enormous force not only for conservatism ("All evil comes from opinions"—a Russian proverb [Pipes 1974, 246]) but for acceptance of centralized control. It was not much of a leap for the Russian to accept the czar and, later, the Communist Party, as the one true source of political truth.

Traditionally, the Byzantine Church was subordinate to the state and welcomed its power, which enabled it to propagate and preserve its beliefs. Vladimir took the same stance when he led Russia into Orthodoxy. Being an instrument of the state, Russian submission to the Church amounted to submission to the czar, and apostasy was treason. The Church considered the czar to have divine authority and to be the rightful ruler of Orthodox Christians everywhere, and claimed to trace his roots all the way back to Augustus. More significantly, it did not oppose the depredations of the czars or even Stalin or the institution of serfdom, and as time passed it became less relevant to the ordinary Russian. Therefore, when the Communists sought to supplant the one true faith of Orthodoxy with the one true faith of Marxism, there was scant resistance, and Russia entered a spiritual void.

CORE VALUES AND BEHAVIOR

Large Power Distance

Russians do not merely accept great power distance, they seem to expect and prefer it. Russian leadership is absolutist and brooks no compromise. Its leaders' power is so absolute and their claims of perfection and faultlessness so extreme that the ordinary Russian reacts only with cynicism

(Mead 1951). It is the only kind of leadership Russia has known and, apparently, the only kind thought to be adequate to cope with so many threats. What other outcome is possible given the onerous suppression of the czars, the Mongols, and the Communists as well as the intolerance for dissent inherent in Russian Orthodoxy? This is a land in which Stalin remains much admired, despite his horrific crimes, simply because he led the victory against the Nazis. This is a highly regimented people accustomed to being told even when to turn over while sunbathing or being cited for a dirty car (Richmond 1992). At the same time, Russians will disregard NO SMOKING signs and jaywalk with impunity. They are an essentially lawless people (Smith 1976), in part because there are so many laws that it is impossible to obey them and in part because there is little respect for government. Russians respond to personal authority, not abstract constraints. Nearly universal employment by the state has instilled a bureaucratic mentality in much of the population. The most petty official will not only act with intransigent rigidity but will seek to lord it over any who come under his authority, no matter how few in number or low in position.

Strong Collectivism

The communal spirit was a core value long before the Communists forcibly collectivized agriculture. Mutual dependence was necessitated by the constant threat of invasion, poor soil, and brutal weather. The mir was run collectively by unanimous consensus of heads of households, and Russians took great pride in their contributions to that common good. All members were entitled to an equal share of the mir's production (or deprivation). The mir owned its land and paid tribute and taxes communally. Membership in the Orthodox congregation, the *sobor,* was another source of comfort and satisfaction. Its egalitarian tradition left a seemingly envious penchant for bringing down those who have moved ahead and redistributing their wealth. Performance-based compensation was an alien notion. Upon moving to cities, Russians spontaneously created workers' cooperatives called *artels* that functioned like a mir (Richmond 1992).

The Russians are exceedingly warm people when among friends, but Western visitors will be taken aback by the crowding, physical and inquisitive intrusion, and minimization of personal space (like Chinese, there is no direct translation into Russian of the word privacy). Lacking most other pleasures in life, Russians value intense personal relationships. They are stoic but sentimental, known for their overwhelming hospitality and deep compassion, even for the drunkards so common in this harsh land of pessimists and cynics. Russians rely on their network of coworkers, friends, and family for security—deep trust being essential due to the intrusive and repressive power of the state and its secret police—and personal connections (*blat*) lubricate everyday life (Richmond 1992).

Individualism

Russia can seem hostile and forbidding to visitors, and Russians cold and impersonal. *Nyet,* no, is the automatic, first response to any request (Richmond 1992). Their unpleasant history has made them cynical survivors quite willing to elbow others out of the way for access to newly stocked shelves or a subway car. Russians refuse to form an orderly queue. It is as if there is a strong assertiveness seething just below the surface but exercised in relatively innocuous ways not likely to draw a response from the authorities. Unlike other fundamentally collectivist cultures, Russians have not been well-served by their communal spirit as their leaders have, throughout their history, either taken from them much of what they produce or removed any incentive to produce anything beyond mere subsistence. Consequently, a Darwinian, survival-of-the-fittest and devil-take-the-hindmost mentality has emerged.

Extremes of behavior are typical. Despite their warmth and compassion, Russians can be very aggressive, brusque, and demanding. They can be kind and cruel, friendly and hostile, hardworking and lazy, and seem to love both order and anarchy—Hingley's (1977) observation remains valid today; despite the immense power of Russia's rulers, this nation has never seen an orderly transfer of political rule. Russians compensate for the servility they must demonstrate publicly by insisting upon what Hingley describes as strict equality in personal relationships.

Femininity

Russians value warm, demonstrative, deeply committed, and highly emotional human relationships perhaps more than anything else. Few Russians have had other sources of pleasure or satisfaction in their lives. Absent the choice of material well-being, the Russians have long sought human and spiritual well-being and consider themselves superior in that regard. They are known for prodigious bursts of energy and effort alternating with periods of lethargy, behavior that cultural historians attribute to the very short growing season. Oppression, serfdom, and Communism have certainly removed any external incentives. There is a strong moral imperative to regress to the mean of communal performance. Little value is placed on productivity, time, or punctuality, because none of these has been rewarded, or their lack punished, under the Communist system. Russians will take time to consider the broader implications of a decision or action though neglecting practicalities or urgency. Although women had little formal role to play in the governance of the mir or the Party, they have long held important responsibilities outside the home. This was in part a necessity, especially in the twentieth century, as Russia's male population has been decimated continually by wars and purges, but may also be due to the influence of the highly feminine Scandinavians.

Strong Uncertainty Avoidance and Fatalism

Employment in the state bureaucracy or membership in the Party is the traditional ambition of many Russians—Richmond (1992, 71) cites a Russian economist who found that in 1989 there were three million agricultural officials in the Soviet Union compared with only two million farmers in the United States. Russians have a deep sense of history and continuity. They speak of the Tatar, French, and German invasions as if they happened just recently. There has been little real change in Russian history; the Communists differed little from the czars in terms of their impact on ordinary Russians. Predictability and stability are much preferred to uncertainty and change. Russians seek strong leadership to maintain order and connection to tradition, and to guide them through a hostile world offering little beyond suffering and misery, the only certainties. There is a long tradition of shunning, banning, or exiling innovators, intellectuals, and dissidents. Russians admire the West for its achievements but also see Western pluralism as mystifyingly chaotic and Western self-sufficiency as daunting isolation. Having experienced so much hardship—few Russian families have not been touched directly by death imposed by invaders or Russia's own leaders—Russians tend to expect things to go badly (Richmond 1992). This attitude would explain in large part Russia's long-standing pandemic of corruption and the burgeoning of organized crime since the fall of Communism. It might also explain why Russians admire "big" accomplishments, achievements on a grand scale—big buildings, big missiles, big numbers—because someone has somehow defied the odds.

High Content Communications

Russians speak with directness, sometimes quite bluntly, and expect the same. They are well known for taking extreme bargaining positions and likewise expect the same. Spontaneous and voluble expressions of emotion, including loud and boisterous argument followed by exuberant backslapping and toasts, are the norm. However, though exaggeration and boasting may characterize bargaining or casual conversation, the Russian is deeply proud of "Mother" Russia, or the *rodina*, and will engage in good natured deception (*vranyo*) rather than criticize it. Russians also will promise more than they can deliver, including time commitments, more out of pride and a sense of the grandiose than with any intent to be deceptive.

This is a departure from the typical pattern wherein collectivism and femininity are associated with high-context communication employed to maintain group cohesion and harmonious relationships. It may be that the extremes of deprivation and hardship Russians have experienced have taught them the necessity to speak up forthrightly in order to survive. This would also explain the apparent paradox of aloof, brusque, aggressive public behavior and warm, good-humored private behavior.

Universalist Ethics

Orthodoxy, backed by the state, permits no deviation from the one and only truth. There is little tolerance of deviant behavior. Historical arbitrariness and government lawlessness and corruption diminish respect for civil law in favor of the natural law of equality and fairness. When Russians deal with one another rather than with the state, departures from the law are common when simple fairness suggests an alternative. Consensus within the mir and the congregation regulate behavior, and community interests supersede individual rights and relationships. In a country where social justice is a rare and treasured commodity, it is to be expected that the search for it is a common theme in Soviet literature. A shared love for the rodina makes patriotism a universal and overriding ideal. Ideology drives Russian thought processes and negotiating positions. Ideas, plans, and proposals are evaluated in terms of their moral content and broad impact, and those initially seen as disadvantageous to the Russian interest require lengthy, patient, and persistent persuasion. Adherence to principle as viewed from their perspective makes Russian negotiators seem extreme and rigid; they pursue their positions with skill and tenacity. High in uncertainty avoidance, Russians insist upon detailed, written agreements and may even require more-general, preliminary formal agreements of intent while negotiations are underway. Given the inclination to distrust outsiders, there will be a need to establish a personal relationship prior to entering into negotiations.

CONVERGENCE?

There has not been a people expected to change so dramatically, so fast, and from such a long-established and entrenched tradition as the Russians of the 1990s. Nevertheless, Veiga, Yanouzas, and Buchholtz (1995) suggest that that is exactly what is happening, at least as perceived by younger Russian managers employed in private enterprise. Their research found changes from pre-Perestroika levels of greatly reduced power distance and uncertainty avoidance (from very high levels), sharply increasing long-term orientations (from a very low level) and entrepreneurialism, and moderately increased concern for others (from a very low level) and individualism (from an already moderate level). The young Russian managers attribute these changes to a widely-perceived need for more democracy and competitiveness in order to improve conditions for their businesses and their country. Despite strong collectivist traditions, Trompenaars found considerable individualism in all the former Eastern-bloc countries he studied. Puffer (1994) found a stream of research that indicates that Russian managers increasingly believe in shared power, more delegation, strategic decision making, hard work and seeking opportunity, that it's all right to be a winner, a need for business integrity to complement personal integrity, and free-market competition. She suggests that westerners seeking to cultivate these changes should

- Make it clear to Russians that they will not be held responsible for unforeseen negative outcomes
- Avoid the appearance of exploitation or otherwise harming the Russians' collective interests
- Encourage application of natural Russian energy and tenacity by stressing continuously the need for action
- Build personal relationships on trust, respect, and setting an ethical example
- Encourage cooperation
- Constrain Russian impulsiveness based on bravado, overconfidence, or penchant for "bigness" by developing, jointly, concrete action plans

VARIATIONS

All the newly or once-again independent Slavic countries were part of and comprised much of the former Soviet Bloc. The East Slavs populate what are now Russia, Belarus, and Ukraine; the West Slavs populate Poland, the Czech Republic, and Slovakia; and the South Slavs populate Bulgaria, Yugoslavia (which means "South Slav" and now includes only Serbia and Montenegro) and its former Republics of Slovenia, Croatia, Bosnia, and Macedonia, and the former Soviet Republic of Moldova (formerly called Moldavia and Bessarabia, it lies between Romania and Ukraine). Non-Slavic, former Soviet-Bloc countries include Hungary; the former East Germany; the Baltic countries of Lithuania, Latvia, and Estonia; Romania; and Albania. Hungarians (or Magyars—pronounced "mudyars") originated in the Urals and migrated into Europe during the fifth century, separating the West and South Slavs. Though Trompenaars did not study Russia, he did include a number of the larger among these countries in parts of his research. There was insufficient consistency in his findings to generalize about either Slavic or other former Communist countries, reflecting significant differences in their histories, religions, and geography. A detailed exploration of these differences is beyond the scope of this book, but several are worth mentioning.

Poland, Hungary, the former Czechoslovakia, and the Baltic states are European countries in every respect save about forty-five years as Soviet satellites. Prior to World War II they were industrialized, trading nations (Hungary and Slovakia less so) with largely free-market economies and relatively open societies. They are for the most part Roman Catholic; their capitals, such as Prague, Budapest, Warsaw, and Vilnius, are classic European cities; their contributions to Western science and arts are substantial, as were their roles in European history. The Polish astronomer Copernicus was the first major figure in the Scientific Revolution. Poland was once the largest country in Europe, stretching all the way to the Black Sea. It was the Poles and Hungarians who stopped the westward advance of the Mongols, and it was Polish leadership that stopped the Muslim Ottoman advance from the south at Vienna. Hungary rose to prominence as part of the Austro-Hungarian Empire centered upon the valley of the Danube, which provided for communication and commerce. Both countries have similarities to Germany in their traditions of hard work and discipline, romantic nationalism, courage as warriors, old-world manners, and respect for titles and paternalistic nobility. The Czechs, wedged between Germany and Austria, are heavily Germanized. Readers may recall that it was Hitler's annexation of the heavily German Czech Sudetenland that was the opening shot of World War II. (On a lighter note, consider that the world's most popular type of beer, pilsener, originated in the Czech city of Pilsen, not in Germany.) The Balts have strong historical ties to the Scandinavians across the Baltic Sea. Building on their strong European traditions, these countries, along with Slovenia in the south, are most likely to make a successful transition from the Second World to the First.

The South Slavs settled the rugged Balkan Peninsula and experienced a very different history. Lacking a counterpart to the Danube and its fertile valley, their settlements were more isolated and their resources more limited, generating a fierce territoriality despite the warmth and generosity typical of all Slavic people. They became fragmented as Serbs, Croats, Bosnians et al. More significantly, the Balkans contained what Hupchick (1994) describes as an intricate though fluid system of major cultural fault lines. Here Romans confronted Asian and Germanic "barbarians," the Byzantine Empire confronted the Crusaders and the Holy Roman Empire, Roman Catholicism confronted Orthodoxy, the Habsburgs and then the Austro-Hungarian Empire confronted the Ottoman Turks, and Christianity confronted Islam. Here, in other words, East met West—and often violently. The Ottomans, who advanced as far northward as Vienna in 1683, would occupy much of the peninsula for five hundred years. The fragmented Slavs developed loyalties in numerous directions that were tested and avenged as boundaries shifted to and fro. Rivalries became embittered, and atrocities became common. This was complicated further by the presence of significant minorities of rival groups in every region, prompting the more vicious among the warring parties to prosecute "ethnic cleansing." American and western European military personnel and reporters covering the ongoing Civil War in the former Yugoslavia find themselves frustrated by an inability to identify the "good guys" and unable to determine whether the grievances and descriptions of crimes they hear occurred the preceding day or a century ago. Much as Russia was held in suspension by the Mongol occupation, so too were the Balkans by the Ottomans. Given this history and its current manifestations, it appears that only Slovenia in the far northwest, a part of the Holy Roman, Habsburg, and Austro-Hungarian Empires and with close ties to Austria, is likely to escape the quagmire in the foreseeable future. Croatia has similar ties but is more deeply involved in the civil conflict.

The East Slav Ukrainians and Belarusians have much in common with their Russian brothers but have more of a Western orientation, at least in their western reaches, due to occupations by Lithuania and by Poland from the fourteenth through eighteenth centuries. Ukraine in particular, with its milder climate and fertile soil, is known for sunnier, more outgoing dispositions and greater optimism and Cossack independence. Both republics, along with Poland, were devastated during World War II as the Germans fought their way into Russia and again as they were driven back. This campaign was the bloodiest and most sustained in the history of warfare, and recovery is not yet complete. The nuclear accident at Chernobyl, located in Ukraine, was another major setback for both as most of the fallout fell in Belarus. Their future remains uncertain.

SUMMARY

The forces shaping Russian culture include

- An infertile, defenseless, and environmentally rigorous land
- A long history as a communal, peasant society
- Serfdom
- The highly conservative Russian Orthodox Church
- Extreme oppression by the Mongols, the czars, and the Communists
- Prolonged and extreme material deprivation

The core values developed by these forces include

- **Large Power Distance**—resulting from more than 1,200 years of continuously harsh, autocratic rule and the Orthodox faith, which teaches and venerates submission to authority

- **Strong Collectivism**—a result of a tradition of communal self-government with an ethic of equality in sharing scarce resources and the necessity of mutual interdependence for protection against a hostile environment, despotic rulers, and foreign invaders
- **Individualism** and **High-Content Communication**—products of the survival instinct and a reaction to prolonged and extreme suppression
- **Femininity**—a result of the mutual interdependence required to cope with a hostile physical environment and political oppression, which made essential the cultivation and maintenance of close personal relationships
- **Strong Uncertainty Avoidance** and **Fatalism**—results of frequent foreign invasion; a harsh environment; suppression of individual initiative and ambition by coercive confiscation of wealth by the czars and the Communists; suppression of individual discretion by the communal system and harshly autocratic rule; the Orthodox faith, which teaches humility and blind submission to faith; slavery ending (nominally) only with emancipation of the serfs in 1861; autocratic rulers more than willing to expend Russian blood on dubious foreign military adventures and the grandiose but ill-conceived economic policies; resignation to continuous economic deprivation; and the absence of social mobility
- **Universalist Ethics**—stemming from the absolutism of Orthodox dogma and the unifying fraternal, egalitarian sentiments of *sobornost* and patriotism

ADDITIONAL READING

Management Practices

Bollinger, Daniel. 1994. "The Four Cornerstones and Three Pillars in the 'House of Russia' Management System." *Journal of Management Development* 13(2): 49–54.

Harris, Claudia. 1995. "Cultural Impediments to Economic Reform in the Former Soviet States." *Journal of Management Inquiry* 4, no. 2 (June): 140–155.

Puffer, Sheila. M. 1994. "Understanding the Bear: A Portrait of Russian Managers." *Academy of Management Executive* 8(1): 41–61.

Rubens, Kevin. 1995. "Changes in Russia a Challenge for HR." *HRMagazine* 4, no. 11 (November): 70–80.

Veiga, John F., John N. Yanouzas, and Ann K. Buchholtz. 1995. "Emerging Cultural Values among Russian Managers: What Will Tomorrow Bring? *Business Horizons* 38, no. 4 (July-August): 20–27.

Vlachoutsicos, C., and P. Lawrence. 1990. "What We Don't Know about Soviet Management." *Harvard Business Review* 68(6): 50–64.

History and Culture

Acton, Edward. 1986. *Russia*. (London: Longman).

Belasco, Michael J., and Harold E. Hammond. 1968. *Soviet Russia: History, Culture, People*. (Bronxville, N.Y.: Cambridge).

Billington, James H. 1970. *The Icon and the Axe*. (New York: Vintage).

Davies, Norman. 1996. *Europe: A History*. (Oxford: Oxford University Press).

Diuk, Nadia, and Adrian Karatnycky. 1993. *New Nations Rising*. (New York: Wiley).

Fischer, John. 1946. *Why They Behave Like Russians*. (New York: Harper).

Harcave, Sidney. 1964. *Russia: A History*, 5th ed. (Philadelphia: Lippincott).

Hingley, Ronald. 1977. *The Russian Mind*. (New York: Scribners).

Hupchick, Dennis P. 1994. *Culture and History in Eastern Europe*. (New York: St. Martin's).

Iswolsky, Helen. 1943. *Soul of Russia*. (New York: Sheed and Ward).

Kirchner, Walther. 1976. *A History of Russia*. (New York: Barnes and Noble).

Lourie, Richard. 1991. *Predicting Russia's Future*. (Knoxville: Whittle).

Mead, Margaret. 1951 *Soviet Attitudes toward Authority*. (New York: Schocken).

Miller, Wright. 1961. *Russians as People*. (New York: Dutton).

Pipes, Richard. 1974. *Russia under the Old Regime*. (New York: Scribner's).

Richmond, Yale. 1994. *From Da to Yes*. (Yarmouth, Maine: Intercultural Press).

———. 1992. *From Nyet to Da*. (Yarmouth, Maine: Intercultural Press).

Smith, Hedrick. 1976. *The Russians*. (New York: Quadrangle/New York Times).

Szamuely, Tibor. 1974. *The Russian Tradition*. (New York: McGraw-Hill).

Vakar, Nicholas. 1962. *The Taproot of Soviet Society*. (New York: Harper).

Chapter 9

WESTERN EUROPE

Much of the political map of Europe did not take its present form until
the nineteenth century. A good bit of it was redrawn after each of the
World Wars and yet again since the dismemberment of the Soviet Union
in 1989, and in the case of the Balkans it remains on the drawing board
still. Most European countries encompass a number of cultures within their
borders, and many cultures straddle somewhat arbitrary political divisions.
The two distinct cultures within Belgium, the French-speaking Walloons in
the south and the Dutch-speaking Flemish in the north, are but the most
ostensible among many cultural divisions within Europe. For example there
is more affinity between the industrious northern Italians—the northern
third of the country has a per capita GDP about 40 percent greater than
the southern two-thirds—and their neighbors to the north than with their
more agrarian countrymen to the south, who have more in common with
other Mediterranean peoples. These differences are so great that there is
now a Quebec-like separatist movement in northern Italy. The industrialized, coal-mining, beer-drinking French of Alsace are closer to the Germans
than to their wine-drinking countrymen. The Irish, Scots, Welsh, and English of Cornwall share Indo-European, Celtic origins with the Bretons of
Brittany (westernmost France) and the Gallegos (Galicians) of northwest
Iberia, all of whom were driven westward by the Scandinavian-Germanic
peoples who eventually settled much of continental Europe and England.
There are many distinct cultural groups within most European countries,
some of whom, such as the Basques and Catalans of Spain, still seek independence. The Finns originated in central Asia and migrated westward
into what is now Russia (from which they were displaced northward by
the Slavs) and thus have more in common with Hungarians and Mongols
than with their fellow Scandinavians. Such complications make it difficult
to compare Europeans by nationality. Nevertheless, each country takes

great pride in its perceived uniqueness and superiority, at least on some dimensions. Europeans love to stereotype and caricaturize one another. An example making the rounds during the height of the unification talks during the late 1980s has to do with European conceptions of heaven and hell. A European heaven would have French cooks, English police, German mechanics, and Italian lovers, all organized by the Swiss, whereas a European hell would have English cooks, French mechanics, German police, and Swiss lovers, all organized by the Italians.

Cultural diversity has hampered past attempts to unify Europe. It defied the organizational and infrastructure genius of the Romans, the political and military skills of Charlemagne (whose Holy Roman Empire actually came closest to succeeding in the sense of an economic union, at least in effect if not in intent), the moral authority and power of the Catholic Church, and the military might of Napoleon and Hitler. Not even the Soviet threat could drive all of Europe into the NATO alliance, with France being the most significant naysayer. The Swiss steadfastly refuse to ally themselves with any nation for any purpose whatever, apparently secure in their mountain redoubt. It remains to be seen whether the drive for increased material well-being promised by economic union is sufficient to overcome cultural diversity. Readers will recall that the ongoing push toward a common market actually began with the Treaty of Rome in 1957 but succumbed to nationalistic squabbling and subsided until the success of globalized American and Japanese multinational companies gave the Europeans a wake-up call in the 1980s.

Hofstede examined these differences in great detail for all but the very smallest western European countries. All were found to lie well into the upper half of the individualism index with the exception of Portugal and Greece, clearly collectivist, and Spain, which fell just barely above the center of the scale. Great Britain ranked highest, just behind the United States and Australia, followed by the Netherlands, Italy, and the rest of the Latin, Scandinavian, and Germanic countries, and Ireland, all grouped closely together, except for Austria, which ranked just above the midpoint. Individualism is the most significant departure by European culture from all those that we have examined. The only other individualistic countries found in Hofstede's entire study are those with very deep roots in Europe: the United States, Canada, Australia, New Zealand, South Africa, and Israel. With respect to power distance, most were clustered in the moderately low region, along with the United States. The Latin countries showed the largest power distances, with France the highest and Italy the least high. With respect to masculinity, the Scandinavian countries, the Netherlands, and Portugal were decidedly feminine, with France and Spain moderately so. Belgium and Greece were slightly masculine, slightly less so than the United States, with Austria, Switzerland, Italy, Ireland, England, and Germany all more masculine. Ranking highest in uncertainty avoidance were Greece,

Table 9.1
Cultural Diversity in Western Europe Relative to the United States

Individualism	Power Distance	Masculinity	Uncertainty Avoidance
USA	FRA	AUT	GRE
GBR	BEL	ITA	POR
NET	POR	SWI	BEL
ITA	GRE	IRE	FRA
BEL	SPA	GBR	SPA
DEN	ITA	GER	ITA
SWE	neutral	USA	AUT
FRA	USA	GRE	GER
IRE	NET	BEL	FIN
NOR	GER	neutral	SWI
SWI	GBR	FRA	neutral
GER	SWI	SPA	NET
FIN	FIN	POR	NOR
AUT	NOR	FIN	USA
SPA	SWE	DEN	GBR
neutral	IRE	NET	IRE
GRE	DEN	NOR	SWE
POR	AUT	SWE	DEN

Note: The neutral on each scale divides all fifty-three nations and regions in Hofstede's study. Adapted from Hofstede 1991, pp. 26, 53, 84, 113.

followed by the Latin and then the Germanic countries, and then Finland. Slightly on the weak side, along with the United States, were Norway and the Netherlands. Weakest were Denmark, Sweden, Great Britain, and Ireland. For our purposes, the most useful way to sort out this information is in comparison to the United States, Table 9.1.

Trompenaars's findings on individualism generally were similar to Hofstede's. He found the United States most individualistic and Greece and Portugal but also Italy least so, and that the Germanic countries and Spain followed more closely behind the United States, whereas the Scandinavian countries lagged. As was the case with Hofstede's data however, most were closely clustered and decidedly individualistic, although the primarily Catholic Mediterranean countries (including France) and Austria fell into the middle range. He also found that in an organizational setting, there was a general preference for joint decision making and responsibility, especially in the Germanic and Mediterranean countries. Trompenaars found the Europeans universalist in their ethics, particularly the Protestant countries, but all less so than the United States. The Mediterranean countries, Belgium, and Austria—all primarily Catholic—were only moderately universalist.

He found the Europeans to be achievement oriented—Protestant countries generally more so.

THE CULTURAL SETTING

Europe lies in higher latitudes than does the United States (Chicago, New York, Madrid, and Rome all lie just above the fortieth parallel). However, like the United States, Europe has a very long growing season because there are no mountain ranges situated on a north-south axis to obstruct the flow of the prevailing westerlies that carry the Gulf Stream's moderating maritime climate into central Europe. The extremes of a continental climate, like that of the American midwest, are not encountered until well into eastern Europe. The temperate climate and the generally flat terrain and fertile land of the great European plain have long supported highly productive agriculture. The three southern peninsulas are less productive; Iberia being quite arid and Italy and Greece very mountainous. Access to these peninsulas is restricted by mountains; Italy less so because there are several natural passes through the Alps. There are many fine ports along the entire European littoral, and an extensive system of navigable rivers and canals provides easy access to the sea from many inland cities. The continent is rich in the more basic commodities of industry, including coal, iron ore, building materials, and water power. Although Greece is part of Eastern Europe geographically and culturally, it is included here because of its role as the progenitor of Western Civilization.

The Europeans are a polyglot mixture of the numerous tribes, many of whom invaded from the east, and indigenous peoples, who through migrations and displacement from various causes, have commingled to the extent that, except for very olive-skinned Latins and very fair-skinned Nordics, they are indistinguishable from one another physically. Europe has long been the most densely populated and urbanized continent. Its productive agriculture and mostly temperate climate accommodated rapid population growth and stimulated development of alternative livelihoods to farming. Consequently, Europeans began congregating in towns and exploiting the specialization of labor much earlier and more intensely than did other civilizations. With specialization came interdependence. High population density shortened the distance between towns, which facilitated communication and sharing of ideas as well as trade and specialization. Internal trade evolved into foreign trade, and Europeans began to explore far and wide to meet growing demand and to find new markets for their crafts and, later, industrial products. More than any other continent, Europe's history is one of towns and cities and the variety of activities associated with them as compared to more-rural populations and subsistence economies. Whether it be ancient Athens or Rome, Florence and then Amsterdam during the Renaissance, Paris during the Enlightenment, or London during the industrial revolution, the breadth of participation and the number of advances in politics, the arts and sciences, and other intellectual pursuits are uniquely European. To be sure, Europe has had at least its share of wars and despots, slavery, and other forms of inhumanity, and many civilizations have produced great thinkers, artists, and scientists. European civilization has often been surpassed, at least for a time, by the Chinese, Japanese, Indian, Arabs, Incas, Mayans, and Aztecs, especially during the period between the fall of Rome and the Renaissance. However, the sustained breadth of advance in Europe and then among its offspring in the Western Hemisphere in science, technology, the arts, government, and material well-being is unique.

HISTORICAL FORCES

Hellenism

The roots of western European culture are embedded in ancient Greece. Indo-European migrants from the Caucasus-Caspian region arrived along both sides of the Aegean Sea, that is, modern Greece and western Asia Minor, between 1900 and 1600 B.C. These wandering barbarians, the Hellenes, plundered and destroyed the highly developed Minoan and Mycenaean civilizations (of unknown origin) they found on Crete and the Peloponnesian Peninsula. Lacking any sense of nation, they settled in independent city-states often separated by mountain ranges, many with now familiar names including Athens, Sparta, Thebes, Thessalonica (modern Saloniki), and Corinth. There was enough communication among them so that they developed a common language, literature, customs, and religion. They worshiped Zeus and a pantheon of lesser gods and created a rich array of mythic heroes and villains. They explored and traded on the Mediterranean, built new cities on nearby islands and in North Africa and fought the Trojan War around 1200 B.C.; these were the figures, adventures, and events of the epics of Homer. They fought famous battles on the Plains of Marathon—recall the legend of the Athenian Pheidippides who ran many miles to fetch help from the Spartans—at Thermopylae and Salamis during the Greco-Persian War between 499 and 479 B.C. Had they not defeated the Persian invaders of Darius and Xerxes I, the history of the West might have been very different.

The Hellenes, eventually called Greeks by the Romans, left many great legacies that spanned the entire spectrum of human endeavor. The city-states were monarchies until the seventh century B.C. when the preferred mode of governance became a benevolent oligarchy. Wealthy landowners ruled with a sense of what the French would call *noblesse oblige* (nobility obligates). About the time that Confucius was thinking about how society ought to be organized and governed, the Greeks also were wrestling with this problem. Like Confucius, they recognized the merits of civic duty and professional administrators, but they developed a different conception of the rightful exercise of power. Whereas Confucius thought that demonstration of learning and character justified the exercise of personal power and unquestioning, collective loyalty, the Greeks came to believe that individual people had not only duties as citizens but rights that were sufficiently robust that rightful rule was actually the province of the people themselves. The rights of peasants were codified by Draco in 621 B.C. Thought to be too harsh (that is, *draco*nian), this code was liberalized by Solon a generation later (a name that pundits still apply to distinguished legislators). This notion of rule by the people (*demos*) was called democracy and was firmly established by 594 B.C. It was during this period of emerging democracy that the great philosophers, beginning with Sophocles, followed by Plato and then Aristotle, emerged (the term was then applied to thinkers of all kinds). Athenian civilization reached a peak under Pericles (460–430 B.C.). Art and theater thrived, and the so-called "Western canon" of literature began to take form. Contemporaries of Pericles included, among others, Sophocles, Democritus, Pindar, Hippocrates, Herodotus, Thucydides, and Aristophanes as well as the tragedians Aeschylus and Euripides who, along with Sophocles, did much to define Western virtues and vices. Plato founded his Academy in 387 B.C., which would last until closed by the Byzantine Emperor Justinian in A.D. 529 because he thought it a hotbed of paganism. There was, from the beginning, tension between traditional religion and fatalism and new systems of thought. Sophocles had been forced to drink the hemlock because, at least in part, he was deemed too impious. Not only the philosophers but Greek art and literature took a highly natural, humanistic bent, particularly in sculpture, which sought to portray an ideal human form. The Greeks sought balance in intellectual and physical pursuits, and enjoyed athletic competition; the Olympic Games, first held in 776 B.C., were another legacy. Their morality was stoicism and, like the Confucianists, living by the "golden mean," that is, nothing to excess. Greek stoics Zeno and Epictetus believed in the pursuit of virtue, that behavior should be governed by reason rather than emotion, a strong sense of duty, and training in discipline to overcome pain and suffering (Davies 1996).

Having broken new ground in terms of individual rights and the rule of law—Hammurabi's code, written some one thousand years beforehand, prescribed proper conduct and obligations of classes, not individuals—the Greeks then applied their talents elsewhere. Athens emerged from the Persian War as the seat of a trading empire that dominated the eastern Mediterranean. It exacted taxes and duties from citizens and tribute from subjects and grew rich, which allowed Athenian thinkers to turn their attention to other matters. Whereas some Greeks asked all the great philosophical questions, others pursued more practical inquiry. Rather than accepting without question strictures of faith, the vicissitudes of nature, and the inevitability of fate, the Greeks sought to understand and explain natural phenomena by observation, experiment, and applying the power of reason and to organize and classify knowledge into disciplines. They sought answers in the natural world rather than the spiritual. The stoics' world view was of an orderly universe that functions according to principles that could be identified and understood. Unlike others who sought answers to metaphysical questions in religious terms, the Greeks tried to uncover reasonable explanations. Aristotle set the direction in this regard for those to come like Archimedes, Euclid, Pythagoras, Ptolemy, Galen, and indeed all scientists. Here then, in ancient Greece, lies the origin of rationality, science, technology, and ultimately all modern industry. Here also lies the origin of great difficulty for all those to come who would ask others to accept mysterious events based only on fate and faith. Theologians and the faithful would battle scientists and humanists from that time forward to the present day. Consider this recent example (of many such conflicts through the ages, often with much more tragic results): Pope John Paul II, *in 1984,* rehabilitated Italian Renaissance scientist Galileo Galilei and accepted, on the Church's behalf, Galileo's confirmation, *in 1616,* of Copernicus's theory that the earth revolves around the sun, a view that Galileo had been forced by the Inquisition to renounce.

The Spartans, jealous of Athens' wealth and vitality, began the destructive Peloponnesian Wars in 431 B.C. In the aftermath, northern neighbor Philip of Macedon conquered the weakened city-states and his son, Alexander the Great, extended the Macedonian empire and conveyed Hellenistic thinking throughout most of the then-known world. Hellenism, centered in the intellectual capital at Alexandria, thrived under Alexander and his successors for some three hundred years until his empire fell to the Romans in 197 B.C. The Romans allowed the Greek city-states their independence and learned much from the Greeks.

The Roman Empire

At its peak in the fifth century A.D., the Roman Empire included the entire Mediterranean littoral and all of Europe northward to the North Sea and England where Hadrian's Wall was built to ward off the indomitable Scots highlanders, eastward to the valleys of the Rhine and the Danube, the Balkans, and into Asia Minor and beyond the Persian Gulf into what is now Iraq. The *Pax Romana* unified this huge area under a somewhat centralized rule, a rule of laws, and provided the infrastructure that would allow relatively easy and safe communication and trade throughout. The Roman legal system was grounded in natural law, a stoic system of universal, rational principles that applied to all. It relied heavily on precedent as well as senatorial decrees, and a body of legal scholarship. Conquered people were offered citizenship. The *pax* fulfilled the stoic ideal of a peaceful, universal, unified state with power exercised with an enlightened sense of duty and service (Dawson 1945).

The Romans, like the Greeks, created statutory protection for the lower class, the plebeians or plebs, from the depredations of the upper-class patricians, as early as 509 B.C. The first three centuries of empire saw continual and often successful efforts by the plebs to wring concessions from the patricians. They acquired their own representatives, the tribunes, and an assembly to complement the senate, and eventually could even be admitted to the highest executive position, consul. Also like the Greeks, the Romans were thinking in terms of the obligations and rights of citizens. Unlike a small city-state, however, which might be governed effectively and democratically by direct referendum, the demands of empire made necessary the practice of representative government. When the government acted, it did so as "the senate and people of Rome" (*senatus populusque Romanum* or SPQR, a notation routinely affixed to official documents). This notion of representative or republican government is one of Rome's greatest legacies, alongside its numerous achievements in administration, law, military organization and strategy, the arts and sciences, engineering, architecture, and logistics. Political theorists like Cicero and Marcus Aurelius applied much of what they learned from the Greeks. Though not as clearly articulated as they might be in a modern federal constitution, the Romans put into practice ideas like one man-one vote, separation of powers, and checks and balances. These ideas, like most of classical civilization, would lie dormant for more than a millennium after the Empire fell under its own weight and the pressure of foreign invaders in the fifth century. But arise again one day they surely would.

The primary Roman virtues, articulated by stoics like Seneca, Cicero, and Marcus Aurelius, were *gravitas* (seriousness of purpose), *pietas* (a sense of devotion to family and country), and *iustitia* (justice—a belief in a natural order and law) (Davies 1996, 150). Cicero believed that the law was the best instrument by which government could fulfill its obligation to protect the safety of the people. The Latin word for law, *lex,* actually means "bond," that is, that which binds society (Davies 1996, 173). It is instructive to consider the implication that people require some contrived, abstract instrument to bind them together. Compare this notion to the naturally collectivist orientation, and thus the absence of any felt need for *lex* that we have observed in other cultures. Thus, individualism was well established in Western antiquity—which we should expect, given the view common to both Greeks and Romans that individuals, even peasants, had rights that must be protected. It seems then that government by law rather than by personality or power may be an inevitable accommodation to individualist values. Accordingly, the Romans developed an elaborate system of laws to govern both civil and external relationships and made extensive use of contracts. Classical stoicism would eventually re-emerge in the English "stiff upper lip," French *noblesse oblige,* German discipline, Dutch self-reliance, Swiss circumspection, and American notions of "the rugged individualist" and "fair play." It constitutes an important component of the universalist ethics dominant in the West. Like other universalists to follow, however, and like the Greeks before them, the Romans were quite capable of great cruelty, decadence, and slavery.

Unlike the Greeks, who took to the sea for both trade and conquest, the Romans were more attached to the land. Jefferson's "noble yeoman" appealed equally to Cato the Elder who said that "Tillers of the soil make the strongest men and the bravest of soldiers" (Davies 1996, 150). Like other acquirers and users of land, they sought stability above all, which would explain the highly pragmatic nature of their contributions. Engineering innovations like the arch and dome allowed some improvement on Greek architecture, but Roman art generally copied the Greek, as did Roman religion until the adoption of Christianity, which filled a spiritual void for many Romans. Despite its representative government, Roman society was highly structured and hierarchical. Like other cultures with roots in the land, the *paterfamilias* ruled the extended family with an iron hand.

Germanic tribes migrated from central Europe into the Roman domain in large numbers in the fourth century under pressure from the Huns, who had been driven westward by the Chinese. Their success was such that the Emperor Diocletian moved his capital to Byzantium (now Istanbul) in 331, where the Greek-speaking eastern part of the Roman Empire had been building strength. Portentously, he chose the Balkan Peninsula as the administrative boundary between the eastern and western regions of the Empire. Although the Byzantine Emperors to come would continue to consider themselves Roman, Rome itself fell in 476. The Byzantines' primary contribution to the West was to protect it from Muslim invaders and help preserve its culture until the Ottoman Turks finally took Constantinople (*née* Byzantium) in 1453. The Byzantine bureaucracy also preserved the Roman legal system that was first codified by Justinian.

Prominent among the many Germanic tribes (the Romans called the region to the east and north of their Rhine and Danube frontiers Germania— the land of neighbors) were the Franks who settled much of what is now France and Germany, the Goths in Spain and Italy, the Angles and Saxons in England (Angleland) and the Burgundians and Lombards (long beards), among many others, in the northern European plain. The Lombards also occupied northern Italy, which accounts in part for the differences between the north and south. These tribes were nomadic warriors. Despite their appellation as barbarians, and the collectivist tendencies of tribal societies, they had governed themselves from prehistoric times through democratic, popular assemblies, much like the pre-Islamic Arabs. Some fought under the Romans, often against other Germanic tribes; the final defeat of the

Huns in western Europe, at Chalons in Gaul (now France) in 451, was delivered by a Visigoth army led by a Roman General. After the migrations of the fifth century and the conflict with the Romans ended, the tribes began settling down and converting to Christianity. Clovis, who led the final defeat of the Romans in Gaul, emerged as leader of the Frankish Merovingian dynasty and unified the tribes from the Pyrenees to the Danube. A Visigoth (West Goth as compared to East or Ostrogoth) kingdom was established in Spain. The Byzantines meanwhile were engaged with enemies from the east, Arabs, Persians, Turks, and Slavs, and their influence in the West waned.

Christianity and the Holy Roman Empire

Another of Rome's great legacies was its role in providing the environment for propagation of Christianity throughout much of the then-known world. The *Pax Romana* provided a favorable environment, allowing the free movement of ideas as well as goods, and the empire's transportation arteries, originally developed for military purposes, provided the means. The Emperor Constantine, namesake of Constantinople, adopted Christianity as the official faith of the Empire in 323, and Theodosius outlawed paganism in 381. From then onward to the Reformation and beyond in Spain and the East, Church and state would maintain a constant though not always peaceful or fruitful relationship. The Middle Ages were theocentric, the Age of Faith, according to the teachings of Saint Augustine and, later, Saint Thomas Aquinas (to whom it would fall to reconcile faith and reason); the only rightful purpose in life was to serve God, whose divine will explained all. Medieval art expressed this devotion. The Gothic cathedrals with their ornate, foreboding visages and spires pointing high into the sky symbolized humanity's relative insignificance and devotion to God. Painting and sculpture depicted the glory of God and religious figures.

After the fall of Rome, Europe fell into what has long been called the Dark Ages, what is now known to be a bit of hyperbole, however. The political and physical infrastructure established by the Romans fell apart. The fragmentation of central authority allowed the rise of feudalism and local autonomy. It was a rigidly hierarchical system whereby landowners, in a contractual relationship, surrendered their property in return for the protection of a lord. As tenants, they and their men were subject to levy by the lord for taxes and military service. They retained rights to the earnings from their fiefs of land and control over the serfs who worked it, less a share paid to the lord in return for defense against rival lords, marauding nomads, and bandits. As estates grew larger, these relationships cascaded downward through tiers of subtenants. Feudalism established a multilevel class system and the system of manners and behavior that would set the tone for the proper conduct of interpersonal relationships, the inviolability of the rule of law, property, and the supremacy of the contract. In effect, it preserved the administrative practices inherited from the Romans even in chaotic circumstances of what had become once again a barbarian Europe. Feudalism grafted onto the Christian value system the virtues of chivalry—fortitude, loyalty, integrity, honor, modesty, and the obligation to protect the weak—all very much in the stoic, universalist tradition.

To reestablish order and to counterbalance the rising Byzantine Empire in the East, Charlemagne, King of the Franks, set about building a new empire late in the eighth century. With the power of the Church ceded to the East, the Patriarch of Rome (this office was the predecessor of the Papacy, which would be established after the Great Schism between the Roman Catholic and Greek Orthodox Churches at the end of the thirteenth century) sought the allegiance and protection of the Franks. The alliance was formalized in 800 with Charlemagne crowned as the Emperor of Rome. Unifying most of what are essentially modern France and Germany, Charlemagne extended his rule from the Ebro River in Spain to the Elbe River in Germany and from the North Sea to Rome. After his death in 814, the center of power shifted eastward, where the eastern Franks and other Germanic tribes were converted to Catholicism by monks led by Saint Boniface and established the Holy Roman Empire. The western Franks went their own way and established the kingdom of Francia—the Merovingians became the Carolingians after Charlemagne, eventually replaced by the Capetian and Bourbon dynasties. The Empire would wax and wane, acquiring various European domains according to the abilities of its rulers, dynastic marriages, and the degree of intensity in the struggle for power between the Pope and the Emperor. Under its protection, Roman Catholicism spread beyond the old Roman frontiers into Central and Eastern Europe, as far north and eastward as what are now Poland and Lithuania. Whereas the enlightened Charlemagne, a great patron of education, had assumed the role of leader of the Church in the West, his successors were much weaker and the Empire never established any unity, sustained centralized power, or common language. There was no sense of being European or of nationhood; only of Christendom. The new Empire, led mainly by Saxon kings in northern Germany, reached its peak during the twelfth century when a relative peace descended on Europe following the havoc caused by Muslims in the south, Vikings in the north and west, and Magyars in the east, and Charlemagne's ambitions for political reform and learning began to take hold. Monasteries preserved sacred ritual, as well as the Roman traditions of rule by law, order, and organization, and the learned friars turned outward to teach. Following the example of Saint Benedict in Italy and the Celts in the north, they functioned as ministates modeled on Roman principles. This period saw the emergence of Romanesque architecture and the great universities, with faculties not only of theology, but in secular disciplines such as law, medicine, arts and philosophy, and music, that began developing teachers for new universities. Advances in agriculture such as the plow, the horsecollar, the breeding of the heavy draught horses and the cultivation of oats to feed them, and crop rotation made it much more productive (Davies 1996). This in turn accelerated the rise of towns and specialization of labor. It was also during this period, with a common peace in place but no national boundaries to serve as obstructions, and commerce and trade expanding rapidly, that Europe most closely approached its current intention to form a true economic union. The Italian city-states, essentially independent with the withdrawal of Byzantine political power from the West, came to dominate the Mediterranean and trade with the East, whereas London, Paris, and the burghers of the low-country ports and the Hanseatic League cities on the Baltic, and the textile centers of Flanders, Bruges, Ghent, and Antwerp, dominated the north European plain, accumulating great wealth. It was this wealth that would finance both the creative energy of the northern Renaissance and explorations that created the colonial empires. Much of this progress, a kind of preliminary renaissance that peaked in the twelfth century, subsided temporarily under the weight of wars and the Black Death. The Holy Roman Empire, which Voltaire said was really none of those three things, did not succeed in its attempt to re-create the glory of Rome and establish European unity. Germany in particular remained highly fragmented, and the monastic movement tried to fill the void with considerable success. Instead, it provided the context for many centuries of complex internecine politics, dynastic marriages, and warfare involving such familiar historical names as Medici, Hohenstaufen, Hohenzollern, and Hapsburg. One lasting effect was that it established Roman Catholicism as the dominant religion of Europe and perhaps, because of the common abuses of power by prince and cleric alike, provided part of the provocation for the Reformation. It would last in name until 1806, when it fell apart under the armies of Napoleon, which ended the rule of the Saxon kings in Germany and Austria.

Islam

Arabs first arrived in Spain in 711, bringing with them not only their faith and thirst for conquest but the heritage of Hellenism, which their scholars had helped preserve in the void left by the fall of Rome. They would also bring the scientific and mathematical advances of Egypt and India, many then-exotic commodities, the institution Europeans would call the university, and the example of religious tolerance. By the tenth century, the Caliphate of Cordova (Córdoba) was the richest, most densely populated and most culturally-advanced entity in Europe. Its towns resembled Roman towns at their best and far surpassed the collections of hovels that surrounded the abbeys and feudal castles across the Pyrenees. Its library contained forty thousand manuscripts, and scholars came from throughout

Europe to study the Hellenistic classics during the mini-renaissance of the eleventh and twelfth centuries.

Europeans first began to think of themselves as such when Muslims began their incursions throughout the Mediterranean and from the east. In effect, Europe became surrounded and was forced to look inward upon itself and unite against the external threat. At their peak in the West, Muslims advanced across the Pyrenees as far north as the valley of the Loire before being turned back by the Franks under Charles Martel (grandfather of Charlemagne) in 732. Eventually, Europe's southern mountain spine and the eastern bastion of Constantinople brought about a standoff that lasted until the fifteenth century. It was left to the eastern Europeans to stem the Muslim tide rising from the Balkans at Vienna in 1529 and 1683. In the interim, the Holy Roman Empire and the French and English kings provided the wherewithal for the Crusades against the Saracens—the (presumed inferior) "people of the east." Even though the Crusades did little insofar as their purpose of driving the Muslims out of the Holy Land and relative to the enormous casualties on both sides, there were several important consequences. The Europeans reopened trade on the Mediterranean, setting the stage for the growth of the Italian city-states of Venice, Genoa, Pisa, Florence, and Siena. The cruelty with which these campaigns were waged created a still seemingly permanent divide of hostility and suspicion between Christianity and Islam. The seemingly noble cause (from the Christian point of view) and instances of great heroism imbued European militarism with a strong sense of romance. Campaigns against the Huns and the Saracens in the East and in the Pyrenees and the quest for justice gave rise to legends such as *The Song of Roland* and the Nibelungenlied and heroes like the "knights of the round table," *Don Quixote*, Siegfried, and King Richard *Coeur de Lion*. The pursuit of military glory became the primary purpose of life for crusaders, and romantic militarism persisted throughout the centuries of European history, until finally suppressed by the nuclear standoff of the Cold War. The virtues of chivalry became, along with Christianity, the primary value system of those who would lead western Europe and its institutions.

Worthy of mention is the impact of Islam on those parts of western Europe that fell under its dominion. We noted in Chapter 7 how the Spaniards conveyed many Arab values, some of which we have come to know as machismo, into Latin America. This was the result of the Muslim presence in Iberia lasting nearly eight centuries. Much the same can be said of southern Italy and Sicily, as well as much of the Balkans under the Ottomans. The impact of Islam combined with the barrenness of the southern peninsulas and mountain barriers of the Pyrenees and Alps would impede southward penetration by European culture for many centuries. Spain, Portugal, Southern Italy, and Greece would lag behind their northern neighbors economically and politically.

The Renaissance and Reformation

The Renaissance was a rebirth of classical civilization. It began in Italy in the fourteenth century, peaked there in the fifteenth, and then spread northward during the sixteenth and seventeenth. It was a time of remarkable advances in the arts, sciences, politics, and exploration. Some scholars trace the beginning of the Renaissance to the frescoes of Ambrogio Lorenzetti in the *Palazzo Pubblico* (public palace—a kind of town hall) in the Tuscan trading center of Siena. These two frescoes, very well preserved (Visitors, Beware—a lunch of pizza, salad, and wine for two in a sidewalk café in the town square, opposite the *palazzo,* will cost about fifty dollars), illustrate Lorenzetti's conceptions of the consequences of good and bad government. The benefits of the former are represented in one fresco by smiling faces, hardworking farmers, fat cattle, abundant crops, and a lively town. The other depicts disorder, death, and devastation. For the first time since the fall of the Roman empire and the unfulfilled dreams of Charlemagne, Europeans began thinking of government in terms other than the exercise of power based on military might or the Church.

The advances in the arts and sciences, centered in Florence (*Firenze*), were of course monumental. Dante, Francesco Petrarch, and Giovanni Boccaccio, who sought to emulate the first-century tradition of Cicero, Virgil, Livy, and Horace, set the standard for all Western literature to come. Painters from throughout Europe came to study innovations in media, perspective, portrayal of action, and the beauty and variety of the human form and its relationship to its surroundings. Italian sculpture and architecture emphasized grace, harmony, and beauty rather than the majesty and foreboding of the Gothic cathedral and its fearsome gargoyles. Like the ancient Greeks, scientists sought rational explanations for natural phenomena rather than being satisfied with spiritual ones. Eventually, it would become necessary for theologians to begin accommodating such findings in their teachings. The pursuit of knowledge, aided by development of the printing press, exploded. The prototype comprehensive Western university, encompassing learned professions and liberal arts, was established at Bologna around 1100, followed shortly thereafter by Oxford, Cambridge, Paris, Wittenberg, and Heidelberg. By the fifteenth century there were similar institutions throughout Italy and the rest of Europe. Reports of riches and strange wonders in foreign lands motivated explorers, aided by the compass, the clock (invented by the Chinese but put to practical use by European navigators to measure longitude), cannons, muskets, and pistols (the Chinese invented gunpowder but used it only for ceremonial rockets, not weapons). The development of money and banks and the suppression of pirates and robbers by centralized governments supported expansion of trade.

The Reformation was an attempt to reverse what was seen by its leaders as a departure from the ideals of Christianity. It began in Germany with Martin Luther, a teacher of theology at the University of Wittenberg, posting his ninety-five theses on the door of Wittenberg Cathedral in 1515. Luther did not intend to foment a revolution but was simply posting a call to his colleagues to debate his positions on what served as the university's bulletin board. Luther challenged the Church's insistence that it was the only legitimate interpreter of the Bible, the sale of indulgences (temporal pardon of sins) with the approval of the Church (at least in part to finance the construction of St. Paul's Basilica in Rome), celibacy of the clergy, and the assertion of special powers by priests. Luther advocated faith manifested more in the love of God rather than in fear, and the supremacy of individual faith over dogma. The intellectual foundation of the Reformation was largely the work of the Dutch priest and humanist Desiderius Erasmus. One of the most influential people in European history, Erasmus advocated tolerance, understanding, pacifism, and the exercise of free will. He argued the danger of moral absolutes and satirized in *The Praise of Folly* and *Colloquies* abuses by both church and secular officials. He, like Luther, did not support the revolutionary aspects of the Reformation but became instrumental in its success. The real issue was Luther's belief that faith alone was enough to win salvation, making the Church, its rules, and its bureaucracy somewhat superfluous as the road to salvation became a highly personal one between the individual and God with the Bible and the local congregation as the only essential linkages. Given this threat to its very existence and with the Church commanding considerable political power throughout Christendom, what began as a movement for religious reform precipitated social and political upheaval as well. Although circumstances such as corruption in the Church, depletion of the clergy by the Black Death, and the displacement of piety by fear of a Turkish invasion may well have been propitious for upheaval, it is difficult to overstate the importance and determination of Luther. He persisted at considerable risk (but with the protection of John the Wise, Elector of Saxony) because earlier, would-be reformers, Girolamo Savonarola in Florence, John Wycliffe in England, and Jan Hus in Czechoslovakia in particular, were executed.

One result of this cataclysmic period was the birth of Protestantism, with various sects emerging under the leadership of Luther, John Calvin, Huldrych Zwingli, John Knox, and King Henry VIII of England. The divergence of the two great Christian faiths remains the most discernible cultural faultline within Western Europe. Another was that the Reformation provided an opportunity for those so inclined to assert political independence from the Holy Roman Empire and thus began the momentous transition from empire, religious rule, and feudalism to self-determination, humanism, and the nation-state. They were most often ambitious local rulers supported by those who associated the Church with omnipotent empire and oppression by despotic rulers. Key supporters were the merchants, skilled workers, and entrepreneurs of outward-looking northern Europe who had little or no experience of strong, central rule by caesar or pope, who relished freedom to pursue their livelihoods and welcomed an ethical system that accommodated, not scorned, the accumulation of wealth by otherwise ordinary people. Coupled with the intellectual, scientific, artistic, and exploratory energy unleashed by the Renaissance, the forces were now in motion that would produce Western culture, a value system least like any other in the world. It would also produce economic and military power that would eventually dominate much of that world.

A major figure in the Reformation was John Calvin. A more ascetic man than was Luther, Calvin advocated separation of church and state—unlike Luther, who believed in state religion. Calvin wanted a return to the simplicity and humility of devout faith and a set of behavioral standards that would come to be called the Protestant work ethic. His followers included the Huguenots of France, the Reformed Dutch and Swiss Protestant Churches, the Presbyterian Church of Scotland, and the Puritans of England (and New England). Protestantism became the dominant religion in Germany, Holland, Scandinavia, Switzerland, and the British Isles, except for Ireland. St. Patrick, who had arrived from England in 432, converted the Celtic Irish before the arrival of the Angles and Saxons, and they remained the only bastion of Catholicism in Protestant regions of Europe. The monks of Ireland, which did not suffer the tribal strife of England, preserved much of the classical Latin literature during the so-called Dark Ages, just as the Muslims preserved the Greek classics. The boundary between the two religions conformed closely to the boundaries of the Roman Empire. Historians believe that the tradition of living under Roman law made it only natural to accept the precepts of Catholic Canon Law and therefore much more difficult to embrace the heresy of Protestantism.

Another outcome was the Counter-Reformation, which involved substantive reforms by the Church and an effort to reassert its authority and appeal, led by the Jesuits, a clerical "army" created to restore the dominance of the Church through education and missionary work. The Jesuits were instrumental in keeping France, Poland, Austria, Bavaria, and the Rhineland within the Church and nearly kept England as well. Spain, bypassed by the Renaissance and Reformation and led by the newly-crowned Holy Roman Emperor Charles V, saw itself as the last defender of the faith in Europe and the primary propagator elsewhere, especially in the Western Hemisphere.

Religious warfare, as Catholics sought to defend the faith and Protestants sought to establish theirs, continued though the sixteenth and seventeenth centuries. Even the great universities became religious battlegrounds, particularly those in Germany, where the highly charged debate over Lutheran dogma superseded the objective pursuit of knowledge. They did not recover until the Enlightenment was well underway. The struggle for political power would continue until 1945—the period since the end of World War II is the longest without war of some kind in western Europe. The spirit of the Counter-Reformation was manifested in the art of the Baroque Period, which celebrated the grandeur and majesty of the Church.

The Enlightenment

The endless tragedy and wretched excess of religious warfare gave rise to the Age of Reason. Dogmatism and fanaticism were replaced with rationality, objective inquiry, and empiricism. The Renaissance produced a scientific revolution in the fifteenth and sixteenth centuries that complemented the revival of the natural and humanistic art of the classical period, a renewal of the Greeks' efforts to understand the principles that governed nature. Renaissance scientists, like the Greeks and the Egyptians before them, sought to understand the nature of the earth and its relationship to the heavens. Even as alchemy and magic persisted, astronomy made great strides under the Pole Copernicus, the Dane Tyco Brahe, the German Johannes Kepler, and the Italian Galileo. There were coincident advances in the complementary disciplines of mathematics and physics. When Leonardo Da Vinci, the ultimate "Renaissance Man," was not painting masterpieces, he kept busy drawing sketches of imaginative devices like helicopters and machine guns. These scientists broke the Church's stranglehold on knowledge and paved the way for Enlightenment giants like René Descartes, Baruch Spinoza, Blaise Pascal, Robert Boyle, Francis Bacon, Sir Isaac Newton, Antoine-Laurent Lavoisier, Henry Cavendish, William Harvey, and Gottfried Liebniz, who articulated and perfected the scientific method and expanded the horizons of knowledge by quantum leaps. This foundation in basic science would give Europeans (and their North American progeny) the tools needed to harness natural forces rather than submit helplessly to them.

Social scientists resumed the classical pursuit of the very practical matter of a better way to organize society. Whereas Niccolo Macchiavelli took a more cynical view of the acquisition and use of political power (as would anyone observing the Florentine Medicis in action), Enlightenment thinkers were more idealistic. Notions like individual rights, private property, the "social contract" whereby governments rule only with the consent of the governed, self-reliance, separation of powers, and the ultimate authority of natural law took firm hold, especially in England and France, with the work of figures like John Locke, Montesqueiu, Jean-Jacques Rousseau, Voltaire, David Hume, and Edmund Burke. Individualism was advanced in the economic domain as well where Adam Smith provided the pragmatic rationale for the assiduous pursuit of self-interest. Jeremy Bentham's utilitarianism, which held that the most-righteous actions were those that benefited the greatest number, and Herbert Spencer's Social Darwinism, provided the moral arguments to justify individualism's adverse consequences. Thus rose the basic structure of Western individualism, *laissez-faire* capitalism, and the ultimate "doing" culture. As absolute monarchies (extolled in Thomas Hobbes's *Leviathan*) continued to prevail in Europe, even in the face of these "new" ideas, it was the New World that provided the first opportunity to apply them.

A nineteenth-century countercurrent to the Enlightenment was Romanticism, largely an artistic and intellectual reaction to what was seen as excessive reliance on reason. Led by Germans Immanuel Kant (*The Critique of Pure Reason*), Johann Wolfgang von Goethe, and Friedrich Nietzsche, the movement extended to France, England, Russia, and the United States as well. Much of the great literature of that century expressed a search for absolute truths to fill the spiritual void left by the Enlightenment. Heroic figures like Napoleon and fictional characters like Sir Walter Scott's *Ivanhoe* exemplified such absolutes. Romanticism fueled the rise of the nation-state and patriotism, a kind of revival of European tribalism. The conflict between the materialism, pragmatism, and rationality of the Enlightenment and the visceral emotions attached to Romanticism is still seen in the struggle to unify Europe. Another manifestation of Romanticism is the complaint by German generals after World War II that their army, molded in the image of the Nietzsche's superman and the heroic exploits of Siegfried, Charlemagne, and Frederick the Great, was defeated only by the superior material and economic capacity of the Allies, particularly the United States, and not by superior military prowess (an argument with considerable merit incidentally). The tendency of the French to assert at every opportunity their cultural superiority, political and military independence, and leadership in the European community is another.

It is difficult to appreciate or even comprehend the explosion of knowledge and ideas attending the Enlightenment compared to the relative ignorance that prevailed beforehand. It has been said that any one edition of the *New York Times* contains more information than a typical European of the Middle Ages would learn in a lifetime. The question remains "Why did all this happen in Europe?" The better question may be "Why did it happen first in Europe?" because individualism seems to rise, although perhaps in unique local form, wherever wealth increases (we can establish only positive correlation, not the existence or direction of causality). The role of climate and surplus agriculture, which allowed rapid population growth, more-rapid urbanization, and early specialization of labor, was noted earlier. The most proximate cause of the Renaissance was the wealth accumulated through trade by the Italian city-states, the first to shed feudalism. Their wealth allowed them the luxury of a sense of civic duty and the means and leisure to pursue more-pleasurable endeavors. They, and the municipal rivalries among them, provided the financial support and encouragement sought by artists everywhere. The same pattern would be repeated in the north in the rich merchant cities of the low countries.

Religion

Of greatest significance here is the need to recognize some important differences between Roman Catholicism and Protestantism. Both faiths are found throughout the continent, of course, among others, but Roman Catholicism dominates roughly within the outermost boundaries of the Roman Empire except for Greece and those small areas within the Balkans dominated by Greek Orthodoxy or Islam. Hence, all other Mediterranean countries including France, Belgium, Austria, and the southern part of Germany adjacent to Austria and France, principally Bavaria and the Rhineland, are primarily Catholic. The United Kingdom, Scandinavia, the Netherlands, and most of Germany and Switzerland are primarily Protestant.

The term Protestant in its original usage (from the Latin *pro* = for, and *testor* = give evidence, testify) meant a person who stands *for*, not against, something. That something was the right to reject Catholic teachings and practices seen by the Protestants as inconsistent with Christian values and beliefs as they understood them. It came into use after the Diet of Speyer in 1529 when Lutherans refused to renounce their alleged heresy. Various sects emerged, forming about the leaders of the Reformation. Lutherans dominated in Scandinavia and most of Germany. Calvinists dominated in the Netherlands and much of Switzerland and Scotland; and they constituted a sizable minority, the Huguenots, in France. England became Protestant after the Pope refused to grant an annulment of Henry VIII's marriage to Catherine of Aragon in 1533. Although Henry remained a Catholic, the Episcopal or Anglican Church of England was established in 1549 with the Archbishop of Canterbury as its titular head and the monarch as its protector (a responsibility that still exists and apparently may prevent Prince Charles from assuming the throne following his divorce from Princess Diana). Anglicanism became the "high church" of England; Calvinist evangelicals, called Puritans, were the minority "low church." Some of these same Puritans landed at Plymouth Rock in 1620, fleeing Anglican persecution. Calvinism dominated in Scotland, under the founder of Presbyterianism, John Knox.

One key difference between Protestantism and Catholicism is that the latter is more highly centralized not only in terms of supremacy of the papacy, its bureaucratic structure, and uniformity of dogma but also in its history and propagation as an adjunct to the Roman Empire. Protestantism on the other hand is not only more fragmented by sect but allows much more local autonomy by congregation, perhaps in keeping with the Germanic tradition of tribal democracy. The uniformity and dogmatism of

Catholic teachings, having specified the general characteristics of the requisite behavior and beliefs, do not provide for local deviation but do leave individual Catholics to seek their own salvation as best they can. Protestants place more emphasis on conformance to the moral standards prescribed by Biblical teachings. Each congregation then could be a City of God in Calvinist or, originally, Augustinian terms (an attitude that Catholics thought arrogant). One's personal behavior should exemplify self-restraint, seriousness of purpose, sobriety, piety, and hard work. Those who do are "elected," those who do not are damned. This is part and parcel of the so-called Protestant work ethic. In other words, salvation can begin on earth, manifested in the worldly, material success achieved through honesty, frugality, and energetic application of God-given abilities. Catholics, on the other hand, attain salvation only in the afterlife as a reward for the cardinal virtues of faith, hope, and charity, and avoidance of sin. In effect, Catholics have to avoid certain behaviors but are free to lead an expressive and joyful life as best they can, even if suffering material deprivation. Their relationship with God and their cardinal virtues are highly personalized, and it is possible, if not desirable, to find peace and happiness in poverty. Whereas the Church encourages dependence, especially by the poor, Protestants encourage self-sufficiency. They are free to pursue wealth, but should do so in an outwardly pious, virtuous, and somber manner because their relationship with God is subject to public scrutiny and is supposed to serve as an example. The more ascetic nature of Protestantism stems from its intended purpose to reform Christianity by eliminating the public excesses that precipitated Luther's ninety-five theses.

CORE VALUES AND BEHAVIOR

France

France emerged from the Enlightenment as the richest, most powerful, and most culturally advanced nation in Europe; this was *la belle epoque*. In the early nineteenth century, it nearly subjugated the rest of the continent under Napoleon. It had also become the model of European culture. The French came to think of themselves as universal citizens, that their politics, philosophy, literature, arts, fashion, and values, manifested in the Revolution of 1789, were models for all humanity—recall the controversy so aptly captured by Tolstoy in *War and Peace* when French became the language of the Russian court. Who could argue with the French motto *Liberté, Égalité, Fraternité* as a touchstone for a modern, liberal, civil society? Although this heritage has tarnished a bit with France's loss of economic leadership in Europe to England and, later, Germany following the industrial revolution and its military leadership in the West to the United States after its defeats in the two world wars, France still tries to reassert itself as the leader of the European community and continues to tweak the nose of the United States at every opportunity.

Like other large western European countries, France began as a coalition of independent, largely Germanic tribes. Feudalism reached its most fully developed state here and persisted until the Revolution. Unification, which required centuries of effort, necessitated strong central rule. France remains the most statist, *dirigiste* (managed) nation in Western Europe. There is a strong tradition and preference for centralized control consistent with a long history of domination by the Roman Empire and the Church during France's formative centuries. France had an often oppressive, absolute monarchy (*l'ancien régime*) until the French Revolution in 1789 and relatively powerful central governments since. This conflict was much more revolutionary than the then just-ended American Revolution, which was more a war of independence between an essentially like-minded motherland and its colonies. The French, having a much greater distance to traverse, installed an entirely new social and political order by eliminating, in the most extreme sense of the term, the hereditary aristocracy and replacing it with what was supposed to be a democracy. The First Republic of Napoleon was not exactly what the revolutionaries had in mind, but he served well the French sense of romantic destiny. The result was much the same for the revolutions of 1830 and 1848. Among Napoleon's many legacies was the Napoleonic Code, which, unlike common law systems that rely on precedent and the assumption that what is not forbidden is allowed, takes a much more positivist approach to the regulation of society. It is much more elaborate, detailed, and restrictive. The French have not escaped their statist past, and their democracy remains a much more centralized, mixed economy—a protectionist (Louis XIV's finance minister, Jean Baptiste Colbert, essentially invented the concept as a matter of state policy, and France still practices it avidly), highly-subsidized welfare state complete with five-year plans—than that of their fellow revolutionaries across the Atlantic. This is why Paris still comprises about 20 percent of the population. Full religious freedom and separation of church and state were not enacted until 1795. The French idea of *Liberté* essentially means that one is at liberty to do what one wishes if one can find a way to circumvent the bureaucracy. As in other Catholic, high-power-distance countries, Frenchmen love to break the rules. *Égalité* exists only among those in the same social class, of which there are many—a university might have three faculty dining rooms depending on academic rank. *Fraternité* means little more than that the state will care for the old and unemployed (Zeldin 1982). The proliferation of rules and constraints produces a contravening reaction among the highly individualistic and democratic French, and hence the familiar particularist ethical system that accommodates departures from standards justified by circumstances. In effect, the letter of French law and rules has much more bite than the practice, and French managers are called upon frequently to deal with *le cas particulier* (Platt 1994). This attitude, symbolized by the resurrection of the untruthful bishop Jean Valjean in Victor Hugo's *Les Miserables,* is consistent with the French tradition of highly personalized leadership in which authority rests with the person, not with abstract standards or ideals.

The French, so very romantic and proud of their unique history and grandeur extending forward from Clovis, Charles Martel, and Charlemagne through Henri IV, Louis XIV, the Sun King, the stunning achievements of the Renaissance and the Enlightenment, the Revolution, the triumphs of Napoleon and foreign empire, and the achievements of French diplomacy, science, artistry, and creativity, and a wealth of natural beauty, want to feel unique and respected, which comes across to others as arrogance. It is not by accident that the term chauvinism entered English from the French. The nationalistic pride of the French is impossible to overstate, as is their focus on the grandeur of the past. On an individual level they resist authority and cooperation, even though French society is very hierarchical on an institutional level. They are very private people reluctant to exhibit their wealth (façades of French residences facing the street look much alike, although what lies behind may be quite different, especially on broad avenues in large cities) but are delighted to display their intellect and their style. They rely heavily on somewhat closed networks to share information and support (French managers tend to position themselves at the center of physical arrangements in order to better stay in touch with their inner circle, much like the Japanese).

The French attach a kind of aristocratic status to management, particularly in large firms—about three-quarters of managers in the two hundred largest firms come from wealthy families, compared with one-quarter in Germany and one-tenth in the United States. Education is the primary determinant of status and management potential. Managers tend to be autocratic, aloof, detached, and distant, if not cold and snobbish, toward subordinates (Zeldin 1982). Proper behavior calls for *savoir faire,* formality, order, and finding one's place in the hierarchy. Though normal social intercourse and negotiation among equals tends to be high context (Hall and Hall 1989; Platt 1994), managers can be quite blunt and direct with subordinates (Hill 1992). Business relationships take on the social nature and polychronic lack of concern for time we associate with Latin cultures. Dependence on rationality and precision is extreme, sometimes to the exclusion of common sense.

There is a common perception in Europe that status in the United States derives from wealth, in Germany from the nature of one's work, in England from one's bloodline, and in France from one's cleverness—to be considered as such, or *débrouillard,* is a high compliment (Eggers 1965). Important also are savoir faire, *panache,* and *élan*—resourcefulness, elegance, and style—and an ability to master universal, abstract principles (Zeldin 1982;

Barsoux and Lawrence 1990). In other words, the sense of aristocracy attached to management is a matter more of one's intellect, education, and social grace than the level of one's birth (although access to the most-prestigious levels of education and employment are not easily accessible to those not well connected). The best source of these skills is schooling, preferably in one of *les grandes écoles,* which grant admission to an elaborate old boys' network of fast-track employment in civil service and then a "parachute" into industry, where knowledge of government policy and contacts in this statist society are necessary and welcome. In effect, France's leaders are all chosen from among its top students. However, soon after gaining admission to the fast track, the credential's value subsides, and it becomes necessary to build a solid track record of performance. It is the responsibility of these selected few to preserve the social fabric of society. They are custodians of France's future and therefore feel entitled to respect. The term for manager, *cadre,* is military in origin and implies that managers have a duty larger than their responsibilities to their firm (Barsoux and Lawrence 1990). They cannot allow themselves to become mired in operational details or allow their horizons to be limited. They must seek perfection at any cost. The power to make this happen rests in the view that the state is superior to the firm and the firm superior to the customer (Pitts 1963). Professional training at the *écoles* is generalist and abstract. Training in mathematics, the most-valid evidence of mastery of Cartesian logic, is the preferred discipline; engineering is the most valued profession. Management decisions are too important to leave to subjective judgment. French managers tend to prefer the conceptual to the practical or operational and thus are more comfortable dealing with abstractions like cash flow, investments, processes, and marketing strategies than with products or workers (Barsoux and Lawrence 1990). The French take great pride in the application of inductive reasoning and reliance on first principles to build logical argument, a skill perfected by their countryman, René Descartes. So sure are they of their cartesian skills that after having so reasoned a solution, they find it difficult to accept an alternative. Pride makes direct criticism, individual performance appraisal, and acceptance of training problematical. Another consequence is the tendency to prefer the elegant to the simple solution (Hill 1994). Of such attitudes are bureaucracies constructed.

French firms feature very tall structures and lots of supervision (Zeldin 1982). They are classic bureaucracies characterized by a Taylorist attitude (the "one best way," highly directive) toward employees, impersonal formality, elaborate hierarchical and vertical structures with much compartmentalization, functional isolation and conflict and strata that do not mix, and much political behavior such as exploiting membership in cliques and extensive written communication intended to circumvent bureaucracy and to create paper trails. Decision making is strictly top-down (Hill 1992), and there is reluctance to delegate authority, tight control of information, and little informal interaction between levels. French managers are supposed to know all the answers (Hill 1994). Compartmentalization also applies to a sharp separation between work and private lives, an attitude common throughout Europe. The French like to attend to details in advance and lay out thorough and precise plans, tending to overcomplicate matters, unlike the English who are more willing to let matters evolve. The French management style and value system impose substantial constraints on innovation. The merit of ideas is judged more by their overall impact and broad implications than by their details, but there will be masses of figures held in readiness if needed to make one's case.

Research indicates that the French are least likely among Europeans to accept direction without question and feel little need for explicit direction (Barsoux and Lawrence 1990). These findings appear to conflict with Hofstede's, who found the French highest among Western Europeans in power distance and strong in uncertainty avoidance. Their long history of centralized control, social hierarchy, and proliferation of bureaucracy in all institutions certainly would seem to make the French receptive to large power distance and accustomed to referring to authority for direction in uncertain situations, but it is their intense pride as individuals that makes it difficult for them to accept being told what to do or how to do it. Hence, for French society as a whole, large power distance and strong uncertainty avoidance are thoroughly predictable norms on an institutional level, but on an individual level they are not. This explains Zeldin's (1982) observation that the French feel very comfortable giving orders but not taking them and the impression that they are not good team players (Hall and Hall 1989). It also explains the poor service common in France. As Hill (1994, 59) observes, the prideful French, like the Spaniards, have difficulty distinguishing "between service and servility." France lies just below the neutral point on Hofstede's masculinity index and exhibits a mix of masculine and feminine characteristics. Traditional gender roles typical of Latinized countries prevail (working women reflect badly on the manliness of the husband and provider). Management theorist Henri Fayol himself said management is a man's job because it is essentially rational and deductive and a matter of organizing, directing, and controlling (Barsoux and Lawrence 1990, 142), and traditionally male academic disciplines like mathematics and engineering are most desired. Performance is much more important than maintaining interpersonal relationships except among one's close, personal network. On the other hand, the French are deeply concerned about the quality of their lives, and France is a welfare state (*noblesse oblige*), is relatively permissive, and takes pride in its diplomatic skills. French individualism is most manifest in the workplace in the competitive pursuit of self-interest, including job mobility, and detachment from others.

Germany, Austria, and Switzerland

The Germanic tribes originated in Scandinavia, making their way up the Rhine and Elbe valleys as early as 1000 B.C. Like those they left behind, they were warriors above all. Unlike the Romans, they placed individual rights above those of the state, of which they had no notion. They elected their leaders who demonstrated prowess in battle and believed in equality and communal property. Offenses against the interests of the tribe were considered capital, punished by death or expulsion (a slower form of death because any homeless tribesman could be killed by anyone out of hand). Unlike the mythology of the Greeks or the Romans, Northern gods like *Odin* (Nordic) or *Wotan* (Germanic) were superhuman heroes rather than omnipotent deities. Like *Shinto*, the distinction between humans and the gods was more a matter of degree than kind, and there was no divine law or supreme being. Women, symbolized by the *Valkyries*—handmaidens of Wotan who chose the warriors who would live or die and selected the most heroic for elevation to the hall of heroes, *Valhalla*—played an important role in bucking up the courage of their men who treated them with respect and equality. This practice continued within the German commercial establishment of the Middle Ages where women worked alongside their husbands and shared management responsibility.

A fundamental characteristic of Germany and its history is fragmentation and lack of central authority. Feudalism arrived relatively late and could not be sustained in the absence of a established, quasi-national political hierarchy as existed in France and England. The Holy Roman Emperor was merely first among equals and was in constant battle with the Popes for supremacy in this joint-venture-like Empire. The void was filled at various stages by guilds, state governments, monasteries, and Lutheran congregations or consistories that exercised secular authority. The Peace of Augsburg in 1555, following religious warfare prompted by the Reformation, gave the Electors (secular or clerical rulers) of each of the German states the right to decide between Lutheranism and Catholicism and to impose their choice on their subjects. Most chose the former. This fragmentation would lead to the Thirty-Years War and created a suspicion of outsiders, even those from other cities, that remains in the Germanic countries. Modern Germany was not unified until 1871, an opportunity arising from the end of the Franco-Prussian war seized by the Prussian Otto von Bismarck whose creed was that "blood and iron" will settle all important questions (Blum, Cameron, and Barnes 1966). Being a relatively young state without the more-coherent traditions of France or England, the new Germany assumed that the accumulation of industrial and military power was the appropriate expression of nationhood (Kahler 1974). Its spirit was that of the German philosophers who believed in strong leaders and the positivist exercise of power (Georg Hegel, Nietzsche) but were less certain with respect to being idealists (Kant, Goethe, Friedrich von Schiller) or pessimists (Arthur Schopenhauer) in their expectations of human nature. Among these highly philosophical people, German intellectuals replaced the knight as a romantic adventurer and seeker of truth rather than the holy grail, so well symbolized by Goethe's *Faust* (the Dr. Faustus character, who sold his soul to obtain sufficient knowledge to control the universe, had long been a popular legend in Germany). The romantic German spirit is expressed in the nationalistic operas of Richard Wagner (*The Valkyrie, The Ring of the Nibelung, Siegfried*), Beethoven's *Eroica* symphony, the humanist writings of Goethe, and romantic castles such as the much-photographed Neuschwanstein. Nietzsche's *übermenschen* or superman was not necessarily German; it was more Wagner who helped inspire the extreme excesses of the Kaiser Wilhelm and the Nazis. Germans feel *angst* when torn between their romantic notions, sometimes given to irrationality and spontaneity on one hand, and the need to conform, the Prussian devotion to the state and its power, and the urge to achieve on the other. Adolf Hitler, through expert demagoguery, was able to achieve an additive alignment of these conflicting forces.

A unified German patriotism had begun to emerge in response to Napoleon's defeat of the Prussians at Jena in 1806. Only the diplomatic skill of Metternich, a German serving Austria as foreign minister, prevented unification after the Congress of Vienna in 1815. One dominant tradition of the new state was the heroic militarism of Nordic mythology, Siegfried, Charlemagne (whose seat of power was Aix-la-Chapelle or what is now Aachen, in northwest Germany), the Teutonic Knights of the Crusades, and the Prussian Frederick the Great whom Hitler claimed to emulate (a vote of confidence Frederick surely would have rejected). The Prussian state (what is now part of northeastern Germany and northwestern Poland on the Baltic Sea) was essentially an army with a country. It became a major European power, against the odds given its small size, in the eighteenth century primarily because of the willpower and military skill of Frederick and his victory in the Seven-Years War. Like his near contemporary Peter the Great in Russia, Frederick was an enlightened but top-down micromanager. The Treaty of Westphalia in 1648 that ended the Thirty-Years War gave the electors independence from the Hapsburgs and provided the opportunity for the Prussians to begin to establish dominance. They began the unification process by implementing a pan-German customs union, the *zollverein*, in 1819. Enlightenment ideas made their way into Germany, as they had in Russia, and as did Catherine the Great, the Germans largely rejected them. As a relatively late-born state, it was the post-Enlightenment romantics who drove German thinking and politics.

The Germans are often mocked for striving for structure, exemplified by a provision in their constitution that is to be applied in case none of the existing laws works and by road signs that say "travel on this road is allowed." Hill (1994, 18) cites a French business school professor who finds that unlike the classic organizational pyramid found in France or the very fluid form found in England, German organizations function like "well-oiled machines" with no direction necessary because the rules "settle everything." Lutheranism, like Calvinism, takes a somewhat spartan view of the world and tolerates little deviation (the two were joined in both Germany and Scandinavia as Evangelical Lutheranism in 1817 [Evans 1987]). The German-speaking countries are high in uncertainty avoidance, and the best explanation is a tradition of prolific, even if fragmented, top-down exercise of power that has built a mass of highly detailed behavioral standards. This practice dates from the medieval period when the many independent towns and principalities acted as sovereign governments and considered their residents subjects to be regulated. Monasteries filled political voids and also were quite willing to govern those around them. Kahler (1974) describes Martin Luther as the prototypical German in that he convinced Germans that they owed total obedience to both God and the state, which was God's chosen instrument to exercise his will, even as they pursued their own individual destinies. Lutherans established urban councils that exercised civil authority and expected obedience to rigid moral standards. Consequently, contemporary Germans have a disposition to trust leaders and accept regulation of the most-minute aspects of behavior, such as the proper use of a baby carriage, by one form of authority or another down to self-policing of neighborhoods, which enforces standards for the maintenance of dwellings and the appropriate hours for noisy activities like lawn-mowing. Obedience, work, sacrifice, and duty are important German virtues whether taught by leaders in suits, clerical garb, or military uniforms. Moreover, the rigid strictures of conservative Protestantism constitute a highly universalist ethical system. Germans took their Catholicism more seriously than did many Latins—Luther was appalled at the laxness he found on a pre-Reformation visit to Rome. The Reformation strengthened this attitude. In Latin cities, life centered around the public square, where entertaining diversions might be found. Life in German cities would center on public morality (Kahler 1974).

In keeping with their romantic, nationalistic origins, the Germans have a firm sense of their destiny driven more by emotion and the romantic mood than by rational analysis. It is more important to have and maintain a firm grasp of the whole (gestalt). There is little interest in experimentation as all German institutions share and cooperate in pursuit of this common vision. In the workplace as well, Germans value security, order, structure, and predictability. Max Weber, the father of bureaucracy and a German, thought it to be the optimum form of organizing work because it maximized the benefits of the specialization of labor, used formalized rules and procedures to establish order and maximize efficiency, and rewarded merit according to objective criteria. It was rational and equitable and perfectly suited to the predictable, detached, unemotional process of perfecting product quality. Order and persistence produce precision and unity whether as a matter of military discipline or refined engineering. The Cistercian, Dominican, Franciscan, and Augustinian monks ubiquitous in Germany had demonstrated the dignity of hard labor and self-denial, which would make the Germans more receptive to Protestant asceticism. Unlike clerics elsewhere who often mingled with the nobility, the German monks reached out to common people and taught them the same virtues emphasized by guilds: humility, subservience, and concern for others. Luther taught that it was man's fate to accept one's lot in life in a "fixed and limited area of competence" (Kahler 1974, 240) and make the most of it by hard work. Unlike Luther, Calvin advocated unrestrained competition, with success being evidence of godliness. This view would serve the Prussians well when they built an elaborate military and economic administrative bureaucracy with precisely-defined roles and promotions based on merit.

Once unified, the vigor of the new German nation was dramatic. Although its industrialization had lagged, Germany overtook England early in the twentieth century when it became apparent that military might depended upon industrial might. It did so again after each of the world wars. Spurred by Prussian organizational skill, romantic patriotism, and Lutheran discipline, it built on the traditional communitarianism of the German tribes to develop a national consensus of its rightful place in the world. The strength of this conviction engendered a tradition of cooperation among the state, industry, and labor. Heavy industry took precedence over consumer goods, objective quality and substance over marketing and form. Business was thought to be serious stuff indeed. Precision, solidity, and durability were the most important attributes of products and people. Perfection required application of the best minds and integrative, holistic thinking to coordinate and exploit the best qualities of government, management, and workers.

Consequently, Germans are motivated most effectively by a sense of having done a good job, which for most means having produced a great product that is considered useful and worthwhile by society. Pride in craftsmanship is a cherished tradition dating from the guild system of the early Middle Ages. The Germans of the guild era appear to be the first people on earth to value work as an end in itself. As early as the tenth century, craft guilds in Germany (and Italy) were setting standards for product quality and the qualifications of journeymen and apprentices (Cantor 1993). They protected free trade and the interests of both buyers and sellers by regulating prices and advertising; they preached virtuous business practices (Kahler 1974). Unlike the British or French, the most-talented Germans go into manufacturing, which constitutes about twice the proportion of GDP that it does in the United States. German managers tend to be highly skilled technically and assume that unrelenting and uncompromising pursuit of precision and accuracy produces the quality that in turn provides the security they seek. Management per se is not considered to be an academic discipline or profession, and many top German managers came up through the apprenticeship program rather than universities. There is a direct analogy here to the selection of leaders in the Germanic tribe based on military skill. Like Saxon or Frankish warriors, it is natural for German workers to see potential for their promotion into positions of power as their proficiency improves.

The Germans' small power distance, smaller than that of the United States and the Netherlands and much smaller than that of the Latin countries, may seem inconsistent with the German preference for order and discipline. On one level, it is arguable that the cultural imperative to work hard and to conform is so strong that it obviates the need for supervision altogether. On another level, the Germans have a strong tradition of rebelliousness and independence that predates the forces that produced high uncertainty avoidance, that is, proliferation of local political authorities (both secular and religious), Prussian-Weberian bureaucracy, and romantic submission to the powerful state. The German tribes had from antiquity a strong tradition of democratic decision-making and fierce independence. They contained and then defeated the Roman Empire, defied the Holy Roman Empire, and led the Reformation. Feudalism arrived quite late, and democratic tribalism, free of taxation and bureaucracy, persisted much longer than it did in France and England. Germany under the Holy Roman Empire was a loose confederation of some 300 autonomous feudal states and some 2,500 local and regional authorities, mostly knights who had been granted parcels of land for their service. At the Congress of Vienna it was consolidated into 35 sovereign states and 4 independent cities that still maintained independence until Bismarck's unification.

In keeping with their small power distance, consensus decision-making is the norm, as it is in all Germanic countries including Scandinavia and the Netherlands. Unlike the Japanese version, which requires seeking the ideas and assent of subordinates, this is true participation in the sense of helping make even strategic decisions. This practice is institutionalized by mandatory codetermination whereby labor is represented by a third to a half of the supervisory (policy-making) board, depending on the size of the firm (Randlesome et al. 1993). There is prolific sharing of information across levels. Labor unions are very strong, and labor costs are high, but so are worker skills and loyalty. (Superior unit cohesion and a close relationship between officers and soldiers were among the greatest advantages of the German army in World War II.) Unlike participation in the United States, the German approach is very formal; business is too serious to allow frivolity and casual contact. Seriousness of purpose and a sense of larger obligation cause the Germans to avoid risk and speculation as well as uncertainty because these are deemed not worthy of serious people. (As late as 1987, only 2 percent of West Germans owned credit cards [Hampden-Turner and Trompenaars 1993, 217]). All this *gravitas* produces still more angst.

Nevertheless, there is no more-salient German characteristic than the preference for order and structure. Organizations are hierarchical and compartmentalized with clearly defined lines of authority. Formal manners, ranks, titles, privacy, and personal space are very important; speech is direct; and time is conserved and monochronic. Germanics, the Dutch, and Scandinavians prefer thoroughly prepared, logical, fact-based, straightforward, low-context negotiating styles; whereas the English like to rely on their negotiating skill, imaginativeness, and flexibility; and Latins rely more on social relationships and emotional, high context (Hill 1994). Their firm sense of purpose and methodical processes obviate the need for theorizing or experimentation. In keeping with their high uncertainty avoidance, they (and the Latins) prefer well-defined job descriptions and specialization, whereas the Scandinavians, Dutch, and Britons are more flexible. German managers feel that their first obligation is to serve the common good through the usefulness and reliability of their products and, as a result, job security. Profit is considered a byproduct. There is a strong similarity to the Japanese mentality in this and in taking a longer-term view and thinking more integratively than Anglos (Hampden-Turner and Trompenaars 1993). More communitarian and less individualistic than most Europeans, like the Scandinavians, they enjoy working in groups. This is in keeping with their tribal roots and the tradition of the local religious congregation, an attitude clearly evident in Germanic communities in the United States like the Pennsylvania "Dutch" (*Deustch*).

Switzerland has been officially neutral since 1515. The Swiss are evenly divided between Protestants with close ties to Germany and Catholics with close ties to France, some with Italy. About two-thirds are German speakers. It is a highly pluralistic and fragmented society. There is no uniquely Swiss culture; the Germanic value system predominates. They are hardworking, cautiously independent, frugal, and exceedingly orderly and polite. Austria (in German, *Osterreich*—Charlemagne's "eastern realm") was the Holy Roman Empire's outpost against the Huns and Ottoman Turks. As the Austro-Hungarian Empire, it became much more than that of course (see Chapter 8). It is a German-speaking country and, like Switzerland, it has a value profile very similar to that of the Germans.

England

The British Isles have been the home of Britons (the Romans called them Britannia); Scots; Picts; Celts; Angles; Saxons; Jutes; Romans; Vikings and their derivative people, the Normans; and whatever ancient people created Stonehenge. The Romans completed their conquest of England in A.D. 43, and like their Gallic neighbors, the Britons, Celts, and some Picts and Scots (the last two tribes lived in Scotland) became Romanized, learning Latin, adopting Roman law and dress, and serving in the legions. After the Roman withdrawal, Germanic Angles, Saxons, and Jutes drove the indigenous people into the western reaches of the islands, and England reverted to tribalism. *Beowulf,* the first work of English poetry, recounts some of these struggles. Italian missionaries began converting the tribes in 597 who were later driven westward and south of the Thames by Vikings in the ninth century when the Danelaw or Danish rule was established in the east, called Essex. The English tribes in the west or Wessex under Alfred the Great defeated the Danes in 878 and converted them. From that time, power shifted among the English and Danish tribes and Viking invaders until the Norman conquest.

The Norman King William the Conqueror (so dubbed after the decisive Battle of Hastings in 1066) introduced continental feudalism (with elaborate records kept in the *Domesday Book*) and also the distinctive Norman architecture and an interest in learning into this still uncivilized land, and brought it into the European fold. The conquest set the stage for centuries of rivalry and warfare with France, which continues albeit more peacefully, today. King Henry II introduced common law and the jury system in the twelfth century. Nobles forced the tyrannical King John to sign the *Magna Carta* (Great Charter) in 1215 that subjected the king to the law and set forth the rights and duties of Englishmen (mostly nobles), standardized weights and measures, and established the principle of free trade. This was the beginning of parliamentary government. Oxford University was established in the thirteenth century, as were towns and guilds. An Oxford professor, Roger Bacon, began to apply the scientific method, the beginning of a tradition of empiricism that would make Great Britain the world's most adventurous and innovative nation. The fourteenth century brought serious setbacks, the Plague and the Hundred-Years War with France. The violent Peasants' Revolt produced a new social class, the free farmer or yeoman. In the fifteenth century, the War of the Roses and gunpowder, which made castles undefendable, ended feudalism, and wealth began to shift from the nobles to the towns, setting the stage for the Renaissance to make its way across the channel. In the sixteenth century Henry VIII broke with the Pope and seized the monasteries, which provided the capital to build the Royal Navy that enabled Britannia to defeat Spain and "rule the waves." The British East India Company began building the Empire and, along with the Spanish, Portuguese, Dutch, and French, opening the eyes of Europeans to foreign wonders. The wool trade with the Low Countries flourished, forcing conversion of farm land to grazing land, raising the threat of famine that would one day cause mass emigration. The Church of England was built atop the existing Roman Catholic infrastructure, and Archbishop Cranmer's *Book of Common Prayer* replaced the Latin Mass. The Elizabethan Period saw the English Renaissance in full flower led by William Shakespeare, Edmund Spenser, Christopher Marlowe, and Ben Jonson.

Puritans, known as Roundheads for their haircuts and led by Oliver Cromwell, revolted against the Royalist Cavaliers, the Anglican landed gentry, in the seventeenth century, precipitating the English Civil War. They won the military struggle and seized control of parliament, and they installed Cromwell as Lord Protector with the monarchy in exile. Among the results were a period of stern Calvinist rule, some degree of religious freedom, and—of greatest long-term political impact—the emergence of a two-party system: the Tories, heirs to the conservative Cavaliers, and the Liberal Party, home of the emerging, partly Calvinist, commercial middle class. Here lie the roots of the traditional, upper-class British disdain for commercial pursuits.

The Enlightenment virtually exploded in England, particularly in the political arena, laying much of the foundation for modern Western political and economic systems. The Bill of Rights of Englishmen appeared in 1689. The Puritan John Locke insisted upon every man's right to life, liberty, and property. Manifestations of English Enlightenment thinking included executive power made contingent upon consent of the governed, freedom of individual thought and religion, private property, universal suffrage, contractual relationships between workers and employers, unfettered competition, and free trade.

The industrial revolution, stimulated by the need for arms to fight Napoleon, began with the mechanization of yarn-making and weaving. Scotsmen James Watt and Sir Henry Bessemer developed the steam engine and steel making respectively. Private firms took the initiative in building paved roads and canals. The search for markets for manufactured goods accelerated the spread of the Empire. The ensuing Victorian Period saw England surpass France as the world's most powerful nation, a position it would hold until World War I. England also took the lead in the arts, especially in the literature of the Romantic movement. William Wordsworth, Samuel Taylor Coleridge, John Keats, Percy Bysshe Shelley, Lord Byron, and Sir Walter Scott were just a few of its leaders. Unfortunately, the resulting concern for the humanistic, emotional, and natural aspects of life was expressed more in missionary work and concern for the downtrodden in the Empire rather than for the victims of industrialization at home, so vividly portrayed by Charles Dickens. Reformers like Benjamin Disraeli and William Gladstone were unable to forestall the rise of Socialism and the Labor Party—the old Whigs and Tories had long since combined into the Conservative Party as the commercial class acquired more worth conserving. Labor gained the upper hand just after the turn of the century and retained it until the Thatcher years.

In part because of their insularity, the English tend to see themselves as unique and superior to their continental neighbors. English is the only European language without a word meaning "all other nations but ours" (Shetter 1987). They have generally pursued their own interests, paying more attention to their far-flung empire and then to their American ally than to the affairs of Europe (Barzini 1983). Famous for newspaper headlines such as that proclaiming the continent "isolated" by heavy fog in the English Channel and fear of French rats invading through the "chunnel," their commitment to the European Community still remains uncertain. The new Labor government of 1997 promises to reinvigorate that effort, however. Their many military interventions on the continent were usually intended to prevent any one nation from acquiring sufficient power to pose a threat. Part of their chauvinism stems from immense pride in stoic superiority. It is important to the English to maintain calm in the face of adversity; to set a good example; to avoid ostentation; and to conduct oneself deliberately, resourcefully, resolutely, and with imperturbable dignity. Civic obligation and concern for the weak are important virtues. These values reflect those inherited from the Romans exemplified by the code of chivalry and amplified by Protestantism. Byproducts include a long history of imperialism, a rigid class system, and an extreme divergence between rich and poor, which some observers characterize as the last vestige of European feudalism. Modern manifestations include the hugely wealthy yet hugely expensive royal family, the largely irrelevant House of Lords, and the persistent predominance of landholding and inheritance as the primary vehicles to social status, ascribed primarily to command of the language. One's accent, more than one's wealth, indicates class. One must convey sophistication, wit, subtlety, and understated erudition. Family heritage and schooling and careers in civil service, the learned professions, and finance are more prestigious than management, especially in manufacturing (Critchfield 1990). All this pretentiousness is offset by a great willingness to satirize and laugh at themselves (Hampden-Turner and Trompenaars 1993). Ordinary Britons react to upper-class pretentiousness and overdone subtlety with great enthusiasm for the most-outrageous slapstick comedy and parody of the "swells."

The industrial revolution accelerated imperialism as the English sought bigger markets for their industrial products. The Empire encompassed about a third of the globe at its peak at the outset of World War I. By that time, only about a third of the population was employed in agriculture (Critchfield 1990) as the industrial revolution produced a large middle class with a much higher standard of living, which enhanced political stability. However, beginning around 1870, England began losing its industrial dominance to Germany and the United States as its best talent became more interested in finance and other professions. Today, much of the industrial north of England exhibits all the worst characteristics of a rustbelt, whereas the south, a modern services-based economy, thrives.

England is the home of the modern parliamentary system of government and nurtured the values manifest in the U.S. Declaration of Independence and Constitution. Beginning with the Magna Carta, England is the modern world's oldest advocate of liberalism. John Locke and Isaac Newton were among if not the foremost figures of the Enlightenment. No economist has been more influential than Adam Smith. English (and Scottish) inventiveness and energy, grounded in the Protestant work ethic and a long history of individual independence, essentially created the modern industrial economy. Unlike the much more common Napoleonic codes, the English legal system is based on common law, that is, on precedent. Central to common law systems, like that in the United States as well, is the assumption that any conduct is permitted as long as no law forbids it. The German and French systems take the opposite approach, trying to anticipate any eventuality with a pertinent standard. The former approach is fundamentally expansive and accommodating of change, and thus can be associated with low uncertainty avoidance; the latter approach is constraining and deters deviation from norms, initiative, and experimentation. It is no mystery, then, why England and the United States are such inventive societies and so filled with nonconformists. Combined with achievement-oriented, individualist ambition and a wealth of the requisite natural resources, this explains the English origin of the industrial revolution. It is not surprising, too, that the British value profile is most similar to that of the United States. The most significant difference between the two countries is the class system. Nevertheless, Britain exhibits *smaller* power distance, perhaps due to the more polyglot nature of U.S. society, which is comprised now mostly of immigrants from high-power-distance countries. Unfortunately, English entrepreneurialism succumbed to class snobbery against the self-made man and the malaise that attended the decline of the Empire. Only about 25 percent of top managers have degrees compared to 60–85 percent in other developed countries (Randlesome et al. 1993).

Low uncertainty avoidance remains manifest in a greater interest in strategic management than in Germany and a greater willingness to cut across organizational boundaries to make things happen (Hill 1994). Unlike the Germans, British middle managers tend to consider themselves as scaled-down top managers, as more mobile across functions, and they seek to escape operational responsibilities as soon as possible. They prefer individual accountability to group efforts (Houlder 1994).

Italy

Since the fall of Rome, the history of Italy has been one of a kind of semicontrolled anarchy. Numerous invaders have come and gone, including ancient Greeks, Carthaginians, various Germanic tribes, English, Normans, Byzantines, Arabs, the Holy Roman Empire, Spain, Austria, France, and Nazi Germany (Italy turned against the Germans after the allied invasion and had never been very enthusiastic about its alliance with the Nazis). It even became a prize in the twelfth-century rivalry between Saxon and Bavarian Germans, the Guelphs who favored continued independence for the city-states, and the Hohenstaufen-Prussian Ghibellines who tried to impose an imperial monarchy. This conflict spawned local rivalries that continued long after the Germans' attention was diverted elsewhere. Italy has existed as a unified nation only since 1861. Northern Italy in particular had been a loose collection of city-states, principalities, dukedoms, and papal states that commanded the first loyalty of their citizens. Vatican City and San Marino are contemporary relics of this condition. Southern Italy spent most of the Middle Ages under Byzantine, Muslim, and Spanish domination. The Normans and the English also maintained a presence for a time. When the Ottoman Turks cut the trade routes to the East, the rich city-states of the north began to decline. Italy again became a battleground during the Napoleonic Wars and was a pawn among the dynastic marriages that continually rearranged the European map during the Hapsburg period. Italy's independence from Austria and Spain did not come until the early nineteenth century, and only because of the convergence of the political inspiration of Giuseppe Mazzini, skillful military leadership by Giuseppe Garibaldi, and the diplomacy of Camillo Cavour. Given the lack of unity, tumultuous history, partial isolation by the Alps, and a grave lack of natural resources, it is not surprising that much of the post-Renaissance development in Europe passed by Italy.

Though Italians are intensely proud of their Roman and Renaissance legacy, there is little of the nationalism with its pantheon of heroes or chivalrous romanticism felt so strongly in France, England, Germany, or Spain or much of the sense of social consciousness found in the Netherlands and Scandinavia. The one recent pretender to Nietzchean heroism, Benito Mussolini, was and is reviled by most Italians for the folly of the World War II alliance with Hitler. The Counter-Reformation locked Italy in place and kept out the political advances of the Enlightenment. There was and is little loyalty to Rome—the Empire had found the less-fragmented tribes beyond the Alps easier to govern. There was and is widespread suspicion of central authority, due in no small part to a long tradition of corruption and governmental instability. There is a strong individual tendency to join local groups of all kinds, including the Mafia, as a counterbalance to government authority and to enhance one's ability to work or beat the system—even Mussolini was a draft dodger as a young man (Barzini 1964)—placing a premium on shrewdness and charm. This proclivity to look after one's own interests and bending the rules if necessary is known as *il particulare* (Barzini 1964, 235) and exemplifies Italian individualism and relatively particularist ethics. Italians at once then are quite clannish but individualistic, and the extended family and social connections are an important source of support including providing whatever help they can to work the system. The fragmented *mezzogiorno*, the central and southern regions, has been poor and oppressed by foreign invaders, including long periods of occupation, since the fall of the Empire, and thus uncertainty avoidance is quite high despite the absence of centralized rule through most of its history. Status is attached to power in the south, to achievement in the north. As in other Catholic cultures, there is a tendency toward fatalism created by the stain of original sin that, in turn, engenders a sense of living for today, of enjoying life while it lasts. The contrast with Calvinist Protestantism in this regard is very strong. Mikes (1975) points out the tendency for Germans to look down upon German-Swiss, who then look down upon Italian-Swiss, who in turn look down upon northern Italians, and so on through southern Italians, North Africans, and Black Africans. The underlying link is the north-south transition from a thoroughly "doing" culture driven by the Protestant work-ethic through progressively more "being" cultures; with those at either pole having values totally alien to one another. Barzini (1964) links Italian creativeness in the arts to the poor Italian's need for some form of expression, worldly pleasure, and rebellion against the powerful, including the Church. As an example, he cites Raphael's use of his mistress as the model for his renowned paintings of the Madonna (p. 173).

Italians pride themselves on their independence and self-sufficiency, what Hill (1994, 85) said amounted to each Italian being a "law unto himself." At the same time, however, many would be delighted to have a secure civil service position. This controlled chaos supports opportunism and creativity, and the Italians are the most entrepreneurial people in Europe despite strong uncertainty avoidance. Consequently, small business plays a much more important role in Italy than elsewhere in Europe, whereas its larger companies tend to be dominated by the welfare state (Hill 1992). To the great discomfort of the French, the Italians have emerged as a leader in fashion as well as industrial design.

The industrialized north, settled by Germanic tribes, was actively engaged in trade, dominating the Mediterranean during the centuries before Ottoman expansion and triggered the Renaissance. The origin of southern Italians is less certain, although Greek, Arab, North African, and Spanish influences are present. The Italians of the south tend to be more expressive, animated, open, and emotional than their more serious and businesslike compatriots to the north. Like the Germans, northern Italy has a long history of guilds and pride in craftsmanship but that emphasizes creativity and artistry more than precision, as is to be expected in the home of the Renaissance. The Italians are renowned for the attractiveness of their designs not only for clothing, shoes, and furniture but for industrial products like automobile bodies. There are many small, highly specialized firms in Italy that strive for high product value and uniqueness. Nonetheless, uncertainty avoidance is high, as it is in all Latin countries and for the same reasons.

In addition, Italy has often fallen under foreign domination and been the scene of nearly constant conflict. Unlike the Germans, and consistent with the nature of Italian industry, managers tend to be more intuitive, flexible, and open. Power distance is just above the neutral point, lowest among Latin countries in Europe, reflecting the Italians' alienation from central authority. Traditional Latin gender roles prevail and are reflected in a very high masculinity index.

The Netherlands and Belgium

In the Low Countries the European plain descends into marshland along the North Sea and the English Channel. The principal topographical feature is the delta of the Rhine (*Rijn*) and Meuse (*Maas*) Rivers. This region, originally the province of Holland, encompasses Amsterdam and Europe's largest port, Rotterdam. Like New Orleans, it serves an extensive inland navigation system with the Rhine extending all the way to Switzerland and connecting to many tributaries. This happy convergence of sea and inland trade produced the primary *entrepôt* in Europe that still handles about half of Europe's trade. Much of the coastal area is *polderland,* that is, land below sea level reclaimed and protected by dikes, a process begun in the Middle Ages. Numerous canals connect the rivers and drain the marshland. There is probably no better or earlier example of the uniquely Western attitude that nature, even the stormy North Sea, can be harnessed and even subdued. Consequently, the Netherlands enjoys some of the most-fertile land and most-productive agriculture in Europe. The sea drew the Dutch, who excelled as explorers and mercantile colonialists. They dominated trade in the North Sea and flourished as part of the Hanseatic League and the Baltic trade. The great Flemish medieval cities of Ghent and Bruges dominated textiles and developed a long and mutually beneficial trading relationship with England as importers of wool and exported cloth throughout the world. England eventually saw the value of weaving its own cloth, and these cities eventually lost access to the sea as their estuaries were filled by silt, but their well-preserved beauty ensures their continuing prosperity as tourist meccas. Nevertheless, the close relationship with the English would continue until their colonial ambitions put them in direct conflict in the seventeenth century. In the interim, England was a guarantor of sorts of independence for the Low Countries, primarily to contain France and Germany.

After Europe's external focus shifted beyond the Mediterranean, this region became Europe's warehouse and focal point of international trade, shipping, and finance. The Dutch formed the world's first multinational, the Dutch East India Company, and have built on that tradition ever since as home to such great trading companies as Phillips, Unilever, and Shell. Eventually surpassed by London as a financial center, the delta still ranks at the very top of the world's trading centers. Consequently, the Dutch have long been a very prosperous people. Nevertheless, like the Germans, they were relatively late in industrializing.

The Low Countries—settled by Germanic tribes, principally the Frisians, Batavians, and Belgae—were situated on the northern fringe of both the Roman and Holy Roman Empires and experienced little in the way of foreign rule, although the southernmost Belgae forged a long-standing alliance with the Romans. At the time they reached prominence, they functioned as a collection of mostly autonomous provinces under the Dukes of Burgundy (descendants of the Germanic Burgundians who settled in eastern France). In the midst of Middle-Ages feudalism, they created a professional bureaucracy to govern themselves and formed a republic, the United Provinces of Holland, Belgium, and the Netherlands, in the seventeenth century. These prosperous and progressive merchants, traders, and farmers, who looked with suspicion upon any centralized power that might interfere with commerce, took readily to Calvinism, which advocated separation of church and state and which gave its blessing to material success. Some observers find the Dutch dour and phlegmatic and attribute this to their struggle to reconcile the asceticism of their Calvinist religious beliefs with the material well-being that began accruing to them long before the Reformation at least in part as a result of their geographic good fortune (Shetter 1987).

The Dutch merchants put into practice Enlightenment ideals like personal freedom, free trade, a market economy, the rule of law, and entrepreneurship long before they were articulated by others. Like good businesspeople everywhere, they cherished political stability and the luxury of being left alone to ply their trades. Out of economic necessity they learned how to negotiate and deal peacefully with others and to act as go-betweens. Another incentive for skillful bargaining and pacifism is their military vulnerability due to small size; flat terrain; location amidst three large Western European powers, England, France, and Germany—who have been frequent combatants; and their strategic value as a transportation nexus. This region, especially Belgium, has been the site of many major battles (Waterloo, Ypres, and the Battle of the Bulge being among the most recent) fought primarily by other nations. This history, grafted onto domination by Rome, would explain Belgium's very high uncertainty avoidance. The Netherlands prides itself as a champion of democracy, international harmony, and tolerance. There is little of the romanticism and regret of lost glory and fame that afflict its larger neighbors and no idle, landed gentry to pursue them. Instead they, and to a lesser degree perhaps the Belgians, are more worldly in outlook and seek only tranquility and simplicity. It is not by coincidence that the World Court is located there and that it has been among the foremost proponents of the European Community.

Just as the Netherlands was an important venue for the Reformation

(recall that Erasmus was Dutch), Amsterdam became the northern counterpart to Florence as a center of the Renaissance. Using techniques learned
from the Italians and supported by the wealth generated by trade, the renowned Dutch and Flemish masters painted human figures, typically ordinary people—somewhat prosperous, content middle-class subjects—
unlike their English counterparts who portrayed wealthy, obviously high-
born figures situated in elaborate estates or lavishly decorated rooms or
engaged in foxhunts (Shetter 1987). In keeping with the nature of the *bourgeois* way of life, they usually depicted peaceful pastoral and urban scenes
as well as religious themes but avoided romantic or militaristic images.

The After King Charles I of Spain, a native of Ghent, became Charles V,
Holy Roman Emperor in 1519, he turned his attention to his native land,
which had not only become a hotbed of Calvinist heresy and a principal
center of the Renaissance but, as a collection of semiautonomous provinces,
seemed too unruly and independent to suit the Spanish conception of empire (the entire Burgundian domain had become part of the Holy Roman
Empire by marriage in 1519). It was at this time that Erasmus was criti-
cizing religious and secular authority and advocating free will. Moreover,
Charles's successor, Philip II, coveted their wealth to finance Spain's religious wars and colonial enterprises. He sent an army to subdue the Low
Countries in 1566. They revolted, precipitating a long war that ended in
failure for Spain. These exertions, which included an attempted invasion
of the Low Countries' patron and Spain's colonial rival, England (this was
the famous defeat of the Spanish Armada in 1588), were such that Spain
would never recover its position as the strongest country in Europe. The
Calvinists in the southern part of the region escaped northward when the
Spaniards captured Antwerp in 1585, thereby establishing the separation
between modern, and primarily Catholic, Belgium and the primarily Calvinist Netherlands. A plurality of Dutch today are Catholic, however,
largely as a result of a higher birthrate over the centuries. They live primarily in the southern provinces of Noord (north) Brabant and Limburg,
adjacent to French-speaking Belgium. However, irreligious Humanists, a
term we can trace back to Erasmus, comprise about a quarter of the population and, when combined with the more than 30 percent who identify
themselves as Calvinists, put those with Calvinist views in the clear majority. With Catholics concentrated in the hinterland, the dominant value system in Holland, the historical heart of the Netherlands literally and
figuratively, is Calvinist. The traditional autonomy of Calvinist congregations evolved into local political autonomy, consistent with the long-
established republican government of the United Provinces.

The Protestant work ethic and the humanism of Erasmus drive behavior
in Dutch firms. Consistent with their Calvinist heritage, the Dutch are described as pragmatic, stolid, orderly, polite, modest, frugal, methodical,
reserved, contained and controlled in speech (that is, high-content, low-

context), civic-minded, hardworking, and self-reliant. They value privacy and live as nuclear families. Not surprisingly, the Dutch rank behind only the English in Europe in their individualism. The workplace democracy we associate with Germanic tribal origin is manifested in the requirement for an employees' council in firms with thirty-five or more employees that advises management and mediates between management and labor. Consequently, management-labor relations tend to be very cooperative. The Dutch exhibit the flattest, most-egalitarian, least-hierarchical organizations in Europe (Hampden-Turner and Trompenaars 1993). This we should expect given their small power distance and femininity. Calvinism is reflected in a strong sense of public duty, and service is deemed more worthy than ambition. Speech is sparse and direct; actions impress much more than words. The architecture of the numerous townhouses lining the ubiquitous urban canals, each different from but still similar to its neighbors, suggests individuality in the midst of harmony. A long history of peaceful commerce and the traditional role as middlemen and intermediaries, and a lack of romanticism, would explain its very feminine ranking, which is the only substantive difference between its value profile and those of England and the United States. It is manifested in the workplace by a much greater reliance on consensus decision-making and a more harmonious relationship between management and labor. The affinity between the Dutch and the English has been noted in several contexts. Perhaps the best examples of this relationship are the long-standing and very successful alliances between the two we know as Unilever and Shell.

Long a buffer between Latin and Germanic Europe, the southern provinces, now Belgium, remained allied with Spain, though in reality they much more closely associated with France until Napoleon brought them under French control in 1795. The Congress of Vienna declared them part of the Kingdom of the Netherlands. Belgium rebelled and gained its independence in 1830. Despite being part French and part Dutch, it is dominated by French culture and Catholicism, as indicated by the prevalence of Counter-Reformation Baroque architecture in Flanders, the use of French names for Flemish cities, and the dominance of French in officially bilingual Brussels. Accordingly, the Belgians are more romantic and nationalistic and less resistant to centralized rule than are the Dutch. Belgium was more deeply embedded in both Roman Empires than was Holland, and its history has much in common with France, particularly after the Calvinists fled the Spaniards, which explains its much stronger uncertainty avoidance and much larger power distance, both among the highest in Western Europe.

Scandinavia

Little is known of the Scandinavians, at least those who remained behind when others migrated southward and became known as Germanic tribes, before they burst on the European scene as ninth-century invaders and plunderers. Historians assume that warfare among themselves was the primary pursuit before they found more-hospitable and richer regions to the south. Despite their daunting reputation, the Norsemen (or Normans) who settled in new lands were assimilated readily into Europe. They established the most vibrant culture of the early Middle Ages in Normandy and installed it in England after conquering it in 1066. Visitors to the Normandy beaches or nearby Chartres or Mont Saint Michel should also see the Bayeux Tapestry, which depicts the Norman victory at Hastings, in the Norman town of that name, as well as the Romanesque abbeys and churches and gothic cathedrals throughout the region.

The Reformation spread rapidly into Scandinavia from Germany. The seriousness of Lutheranism gives the Scandinavians, like the Germans, a deep sense of stolidity and moral obligation. Although highly individualistic and achievement-oriented like other Protestant cultures, the rigors of the climate, sparse population, and dependence on trade induce a feeling of interdependent other-directedness. There are many interest and affinity groups and organizations, as in the Netherlands, and there is a long tradition of grass-roots democracy. A good example of this blend of individualism, collectivism, and femininity is the *brug,* a small, somewhat isolated Swedish community centered around a manufacturing plant and totally self-reliant even to the extent that it hires and maintains its own schoolmaster and minister independently of any school system or church hierarchy (Hampden-Turner and Trompenaars 1993).

The Scandinavians are the most-homogenous people in Europe in that they have allowed little immigration and are about 95 percent Lutheran. They also are the most democratic of people anywhere and have the lowest uncertainty avoidance. Aside from Sweden's role as a major military power during the seventeenth and early eighteenth century, when it dominated the Baltic region, the Scandinavians have been content to live peacefully and avoid much of the tumult of European history, much preferring commercial arrangements like their ancient Hanseatic League ties to Germany. Like the Dutch, they are tolerant, socially conscious, but exceptional in their concern for the quality of life. Participative decision-making is very much the norm in keeping with democratic values, and the Scandinavian workplace is the most democratic in the world. It is the home of the self-managed work team, as exemplified for many years by Volvo. Participation in Scandinavia, symbolized by the quality circle and open office design, is much more informal than it is in Germany, land of the closed office door. As good Lutherans, there is a strong sense of duty to others to complement their individualism. There is a tendency toward paternalism and a desire for a leveling in society based on the ideal of moderation or *lagom* (in Swedish), a form of golden mean; hence the high femininity index. This is the basis for the preference for welfare state policies and a tolerance for very high taxes. Its most likely origin is the harsh climate and the traditional isolation of its communities. Scandinavians, very low in uncertainty avoidance, are delegators, comfortable with flat structures, and are very apt to challenge the boss. They enjoy strong social ties in the workplace, and successful performance bears social importance and reflects directly on individual identity and acceptance by peers, but like other Germanic peoples, they value privacy and live as nuclear families (Hampden-Turner and Trompenaars 1993). The vaunted safety of Volvos and SAS's reputation for excellent service reflect the strengths of Scandinavian management practices grounded in their value system, which exhibits extremely small power distance, less individualism than the United States, and strong femininity, reflected in a great concern for the quality of life.

Iberia and Greece

Isolated by the Pyrenees and its Muslim domination and weakened by its role as protector of the faith and by Fascism, Iberia was more North African and Mediterranean than European until Franco's death in 1975. Before the Visigoths arrived in Roman times, Iberia was home to Greeks, Phoenicians, and Carthaginians and was completely dominated by the Romans. The Visigoths had little opportunity to enjoy their hard-won dominion before the Arabs arrived in 711 and occupied most of the peninsula soon thereafter. Parts of the north and west of the peninsula remained Christian under the Celtic Gallegos in the far northwest, the Basques and the Visigothic kingdoms of Asturias, Castile, and Navarre in the north. The Moorish influence was strongest in Andalusia, in the south. The Christian kingdoms began a long, slow *reconquista* that, by the twelfth century, had contained the Moors in the Andalusian region around Granada. There remain strong regional differences in Spain. Like Italy, there is a general transition from a "being" culture in the south to a "doing" culture in Madrid and the north, especially in Catalonia, and its capital, Barcelona, and the Basque country.

Spain became the first unified, centrally ruled state in Europe with the marriage of King Ferdinand of Aragon and Queen Isabella of Castile in 1469, who eventually drove the Moors out of their last stronghold, sent Columbus on his way, expelled all Jews from Spain, and commissioned the Inquisition. Portugal was made part of Spain in 1580 and remained so for eighty years. When Charles I assumed the crown of the Holy Roman Empire in 1519, Spain's rule was extended into central Europe, the Low Countries, southern Italy, and parts of France. With the conquest of a huge and hugely profitable mercantile empire, Spain became the most powerful nation in the world. Its dominance was short-lived as its expenditures on the military campaigns to restore the Church in Europe, especially in the

Low Countries, and the depredations of colonial competitors, especially English pirates in the Caribbean, depleted the wealth extracted from the colonies. Sir Francis Drake drove the Spanish navy from the sea in 1588. The Inquisition suppressed all Spaniards, not just "enemies" of the Church. Lost as well were the artistic and scientific vitality and the trading skills of the expelled Moors and Jews as the Iberian peninsula became progressively more isolated from Europe, including its Renaissance and Enlightenment. The end of the Hapsburg dynasty brought the War of Spanish Succession, which resulted in dominance by the French Bourbon dynasty in the eighteenth century. The nineteenth century brought invasion by Napoleon and a successful revolt in the Peninsula War, aided by the former enemy, England. By 1898, the entire colonial empire was lost, except for some small possessions across the Strait of Gibraltar. By the twentieth century it was a very poor country by European standards, making it fertile ground for socialism. The conservative reaction produced the exceedingly brutal Spanish Civil War of 1936–39 and a fascist regime thenceforth perceived as linked to its Nazi supporters. It became almost a pariah nation (kept out of the United Nations until 1955, for example), and its development was arrested accordingly until Franco's death precipitated a remarkable turnaround that brought Spain into the mainstream of the European Community.

From the Arabs, Spain inherited a fierce sense of romanticism, pride, and machismo. Like other Latins and the Greeks, the Spaniards are proudly independent; have a highly developed sense of personal dignity, manifested in an Arabic capacity to suffer one's fate resolutely; and take themselves very seriously. Likewise, they tend to prefer security to responsibility and see their jobs more as a source of income than satisfaction. Despite their independence, however, they also rely heavily on family connections. Like the French, they admire the engineer's mind.

Although Spain is now developing at a very fast rate, management practices in Spain still resemble more its colonial offspring than those of other Europeans. Most managers come from wealthy backgrounds. The ideal leader is the benevolent autocrat, like the French, highly personalized—*el caudillo*. A sense of chivalry, honor, mutual respect, and equality govern business relationships, which are expected to be intimate and enduring. Whatever time is necessary to conclude business in an amicable way will be taken, as will whatever time is necessary to conclude a meeting, whatever the effect on subsequent appointments. The tradition of the *hidalgo*, a person of importance (literally, a son of an important person), remains, and there is a patina of aristocracy and class distinction attached to management. Proper dress and old-world, formal manners are very important. Like other overregulated and overly bureaucratized Latins, the Iberians seem to be conformists outwardly but enjoy circumventing rules (*Hecha la ley, hecha la trampa* or "Every law has a loophole"—a Spanish proverb [Ames 1992, 34]). Likewise they tend toward fatalism, are highly independent, and lack a sense of community, but networks and extended families still play important roles in business. Hierarchical structures and paternal autocrats are the norm. Seniority determines status and compensation.

Portugal's history roughly parallels Spain's; the greatest difference being that it had little involvement with the rest of Europe. They are more open and easygoing, more sentimental than the Spaniards, more like the Italians. Hill (1992) attributes this condition to the pleasant climate compared to the much more extreme conditions that prevail in most of Spain (Spain's most productive regions lie along the pleasant Mediterranean coast). It lost its colonial empire sooner, has long been a relatively poor, agrarian country by European standards, and also was suppressed by a military dictator, Antonio Salazar, from 1932 to 1968. Its value profile is typical of a culture based on the extended family with a subsistence economy.

Greece joined the East when it became part of the Byzantine Empire and even more so with the Great Schism and the triumph of the Ottoman Turks in 1453. There was no Renaissance or Enlightenment in Greece, despite their Hellenistic origins. It did not regain its independence from the Ottomans until 1830. In 1922 it invaded Turkey to regain part of its ancient empire and took a severe defeat by Kemal Ataturk. Though now ostensibly Western in terms of membership in NATO and the European Community, Greece remains mired in its ancient rivalry with Turkey and its inherent suspicion of the free market. U.S. military intervention prevented a Communist takeover after World War II. Since then Greece has endured rule by military junta and hard-line socialists, squabbled with Turkey over Cyprus and with its Balkan neighbors over Macedonia (which had been divided by the border between Greece and the former Yugoslavia). Greek leaders still seem to dream of a revival of their classical glory (primarily at Turkey's expense) and enjoy flaunting their independence. However, now they must cast a wary eye toward developments among their unstable Balkan neighbors. Greece's economy is dominated heavily by small, family-run businesses—90 percent of Greek companies have fewer than ten employees and about half the work force is self-employed (Broome 1996). Political instability and lack of opportunity in Greece have caused substantial emigration. Modern Greece is a "being" culture which rests on three pillars, the extended family, the Orthodox Church, and the village (Broome 1996). Like Portugal, lacking in resources and still dependent on agriculture and tourism (plus a very large merchant marine), the Greeks have a value profile in the Latin, Mediterranean pattern. Although power distance is quite high and decision making is centralized and top-down, Greeks are very independent and expect a very personal relationship with their superiors (Broome 1996).

CONVERGENCE?

If convergence were to occur, Western Europe should be the place, because a number of cultures have been interacting and have been deeply intertwined here in every facet of human endeavor for two thousand years. It does not appear to be happening. European unification has prompted talk of need for a pan-European management style, or a "Euromanager," to maximize the potential of the common market for European firms, as opposed to Italian firms or Belgian firms. Such a Renaissance Man might exhibit Italian creativeness and entrepreneurship, Germanic discipline and technical mastery, French analytical and diplomatic skills, British flexibility and inventiveness, Dutch teamwork, a Scandinavian leadership style, and so on, and would certainly make a formidable competitor. Given that there are few people who can possess or acquire all these skills and little evidence that the French will begin acting more like Germans or Italians like Britons, some European firms have been well served by a team approach that brings together complementary skills.

Much has been made of a so-called "two-speed" Europe, a "doing" north and a "being" south (for example, Boldy, Jain, and Northey 1993; Bruce 1989). This is an oversimplification, and some convergence is clearly underway, at least in terms of results. Although culture-dependent attitudes toward work, authority, bosses, employees, companies, success, the proper role of the state, appropriate means of expression and communication, time, and the like, will continue to differ among regions within nations as well as among nations, all Europeans are working harder than ever and the lagging southerners are catching up to their neighbors. For example, Pennings (1993) found that more French and Dutch firms are using performance-based compensation despite the former's strong uncertainty avoidance and the latter's egalitarianism.

Europeans, especially those of the northern countries, have value profiles much more similar to that of the United States than to other cultures; specific differences will be discussed in the next section. It appears that the greatest divide is social rather than professional. Europeans, especially the Spanish, French, and English, may cringe inwardly when they hear a U.S. manager boast of his plebeian origins or that he does his own home repairs. Europeans tend to be elitist, respecting old wealth, strong professional qualifications and titles, and prestigious education, whereas Americans admire the self-made man whom upper-class Europeans dismiss as *nouveau riche*. European managers generally consider themselves better educated, more well-rounded, more sophisticated, and better able to deal with diversity than U.S. managers, whom they may consider rather provincial and crude. As Boddewyn (1992) points out, the enlightened and multifaceted conversation and eloquent expression and command of language that might get one labeled an egghead or show-off in the United States are appreciated and expected in Europe. Europeans recognize the achievements and benefits of American egalitarianism, optimism, and inventiveness but are put off by American aggressiveness and impatience. At the same time, however, a self-deprecating American who does not take himself or others too seriously risks being taken at face value by Europeans.

SUMMARY

The uniqueness of Western culture relative to Eastern European, Asian, or African cultures appears to be due to the intellectual energy—artistic, scientific, political, and commercial—released by the accumulation of wealth in cities. The source of wealth might be the spoils of empire, as it was for Athens and Rome; earned through commerce and trade (which in turn depend on surplus agriculture, population growth, and specialization of labor), as was the case for northern Italy and Holland; or a combination of the two, as it was for Paris and London. If such were the case, it would be interesting to speculate how differently history might have unfolded had cities like Byzantium, Novgorod, Tenochtitlán, Timbuktu, Alexandria, or Shanghai not fallen to foreign invaders or tyrants.

The forces shaping Western European culture include

- A physical environment conducive to productive agriculture, population growth, urban development, and specialization of labor
- Hellenism and its attendant humanism, democracy, individualism, stoicism, and rationalism
- The Roman Empire, which established the principle of rule by law; set the precedents for modern democratic, representative government, bureaucratic administration, and the modern state; and created an environment conducive to the propagation of trade and Christianity
- The Roman Catholic Church, which established universal ethical standards and reinforced and extended in time the Roman practice of centralized government
- The Renaissance, scientific revolution, and reformation, which re-established the Hellenic tradition, gave humanity a sense of controlling their own destiny, and established an ethos that accommodated the pursuit of individual self-interest
- The Enlightenment, which made natural law the foundation of Western political and economic thinking; laid the foundation for liberal government, capitalism, and the free enterprise system; and precipitated the industrial revolution
- Romanticism, which accelerated development of imperialism and the nation-state

The core values developed by these forces include

- **Individualism**—Europeans are individualistic but with some qualifications. Southern Europeans, given their relatively late industrialization, still rely heavily on the support of extended families and personal networks seen in many non-western, less-industrialized cultures. The French, though highly egalitarian and democratic, feel a very strong sense of patriotism and national unity arising from their central role in shaping European history and culture. Tribalism, a sense of romantic destiny, and a tradition of local autonomy (both political and religious) engender a more communitarian spirit among Germanic peoples than is found in the United States. Tribalism, local autonomy, and interdependence required by a history of battling the elements and a lack of resources, or battling the sea, does the same for the Scandinavians and Dutch, respectively.

- **Power Distance**—The Latin countries have larger power distances than does the United States, reflecting the more autocratic, top-down, and paternalistic management style found in countries with a long history of strong central rule, social stratification, and largely agrarian economies. Though Belgium, France, northern Italy, and Spain are heavily industrialized, those countries remain somewhat *dirigiste* or centrally managed, and they have very long and relatively recent experiences with feudalism and/or absolutism. Power distances in northern and Germanic Europe are smaller than that of the United States. The long, even ancient tradition of tribal democracy, unfettered by long periods of strong central rule or feudalism, is manifested in highly-developed participative management practices. Although Britain has a long-established monarchy and a strong class system, it began moving in a less authoritarian direction at the time of the Magna Carta and accelerated dramatically during the Enlightenment. British managers, being of the less prestigious "commercial class," are not deeply enmeshed in the class system in any event.

- **Uncertainty Avoidance**—The value dimension with greatest variability is uncertainty avoidance. It is strong in the more-fatalistic Catholic countries (except Ireland, which largely escaped feudalism and much of the tumult of European history), all of which have a long history of obedience to Rome—whether rendered to Pope, to Caesar, or to both. Conversely, it is weakest in those countries most remote from Rome: Scandinavia, the Netherlands, and Great Britain. It is important to note that low uncertainty avoidance in Europe (and the United States) differs from the Asian or African variety. The former is the result of a uniquely Western sense, traced back to the Greeks of antiquity via the Enlightenment and Renaissance, that nature can be overcome through reason and science. The latter is based on the fatalistic assumption that uncertainty is natural and normal but beyond man's control, and thus man must adapt to it. High Germanic uncertainty avoidance is a more recent development arising from a romanticized view of the powerful state, Prussian administrative skill and Weberian bureaucracy, and the mass of rules and regulations generated by a profusion of fragmented governmental bodies both secular and religious.

• **Masculinity**—Europeans are generally masculine; the strongest evidence being an achievement orientation, especially among the Germanic cultures that have always selected their leaders primarily on merit. The Latins tend to see achievement more as a means to advance the interests of their families than as a measure of individual status and worth, prefer high-context communications, and view organizations more as systems of human relationships than as instruments of task performance, but traditional gender roles are also at work here. Although ascribed status based on social class (not wealth), a vestige of feudalism, still looms large in France and England, it is limited to the upper class.

• **Universalist Ethics**—Europeans share with Americans universalist ethics grounded in Christianity's articulation of dogmatic truths and proffered posture as "The Way" to salvation, a posture decidedly different from Asian or African religions. Northern Europeans bear an additional burden in that Protestantism allows no intermediary to interpret God's word or control humanity's access to God. God's commandments are there in the Bible for all to read, are relatively few in number and thus easy to grasp, and are consistent with natural law as interpreted in the West. In contrast, the primarily Catholic countries are more particularist in that a proliferation of constraints, both bureaucratic and religious, promotes deviation in what are also individualistic cultures. Personal relationships with leaders in these more particularist countries are more important because the leader's decisions are less constrained by abstract principles (for example, *le cas particulier*).

ADDITIONAL READING

Management Practices

Bamberger, I. 1986. "Values and Strategic Behavior." *Management International Review* 26(4): 57–69.

Barsoux, Jean-Louis, and Peter Lawrence. 1991. "The Making of a French Manager." *Harvard Business Review* (July-August): 58–67.

———. 1990. *Management in France.* (London: Cassell).

Boddewyn, Jean J. 1992. "Fitting Socially in Fortress Europe: Understanding, Reaching, and Impressing Europeans." *Business Horizons* 35, no. 6 (November–December): 35–93.

Boldy, Duncan, Sagar Jain, and Kristine Northey. 1993. "What Makes an Effective European Manager?" *Management International Review* 33(2): 157–169.

Bruce, Leigh. 1989. "North vs. South." *International Management* 44, no. 5 (May): 20–26.

Burton, Jack. 1989. "Europe's Blond, Blue-Eyed Japanese." *International Management* 44, no. 5 (May): 58–61.

Calori, Roland, and Bruno Dufour. 1995. "Management European Style." *Academy of Management Executive* 9(3): 61–77.

Cox, Charles J., and Cary L. Cooper. 1985. "The Irrelevance of American Organizational Sciences to the UK and Europe." *Journal of General Management* 11, no. 2 (Winter): 27–34.

Eggers, E. Russell. 1965. "How to Do Business with a Frenchman." *Harper's Magazine* 231, no. 1383 (August): 41–44.

Gouttefarde, Claire. 1996. "American Values in the French Workplace." *Business Horizons* 39, no. 2 (March-April): 60–69.

Hill, Richard. 1994. *Euromanagers and Martians.* (Brussels: Europublic).

Houlder, Vanessa. 1994. "The Divide Europe Failed to Bridge." *Financial Times,* September 21, p. 12.

Pennings, Johann. 1993. "Executive Reward Systems: A Cross-National Comparison." *Journal of Management Studies* 30, no. 2 (March): 261–280.

Randlesome, C., W. Brierly, K. Bruton, C. Gordon, and P. King. 1993. *Business Cultures in Europe.* (Oxford: Butterworth-Heineman).

Smith, Peter B. 1992. "Organizational Behavior and National Cultures." *English Journal of Management* 3, no. 1 (March): 39–51.

Tollgerdt-Andersson, Ingrid. 1993. "Attitudes, Values and Demands on Leadership: A Cultural Comparison." *Management Education and Development* 24, no. 1 (Spring): 48–57.

Zemke, Ron. 1988. "Scandinavian Management: A Look at Our Future?" *Management Review* 77, no. 7 (July): 44–47.

European History and Culture

Ames, Helen Whatley. 1992. *Spain Is Different.* (Yarmouth, Maine: Intercultural Press).

Ardagh, Richard. 1990. *Germany and the Germans.* (London: Penguin).

Barzini, Luigi. 1983. *The Europeans.* (London: Penguin).

————. 1964. *The Italians.* (New York: Atheneum).

Blum, Jerome, Rondo Cameron, and Thomas G. Barnes. 1966. *A History of the European World.* (Boston: Little, Brown and Co.).

Brady, Thomas A., Jr., Heiko A. Oberman, and James D. Tracy, eds. 1996. *Handbook of European History, 1400–1600,* 2 vols. (Grand Rapids, Mich.: Eerdman).

Broome, Benjamin J. 1996. *Exploring the Greek Mosaic.* (Yarmouth, Maine: Intercultural Press).

Cantor, Norman F. 1993. *The Civilization of the Middle Ages.* (New York: HarperCollins).

Clark, Kenneth. 1969. *Civilization.* (New York: Harper and Row).

Critchfield, Richard. 1990. *Among the English: An Outsider's View.* (London: Hamish Hamilton).

Davies, Norman. 1996. *Europe: A History.* (Oxford: Oxford University Press).

Dawson, Christopher. 1945. *The Making of Europe.* (New York: Sheed and Ward).

de Madariaga, Salvador. 1952. *Portrait of Europe.* (London: Hollis and Carter).

————. 1942. *Spain.* (London: Jonathan Cape).

Dudley, Donald R. 1970. *The Romans: 850 B.C.–A.D. 337.* (New York: Knopf).

Engellau, Patrick, and Ulf Henning, eds. 1984. *Nordic Views and Values.* (Stockholm: Nordic Council).

Evans, Richard J. 1987. *Rethinking German History.* (London: Allyn and Unwin).

Ferguson, John. 1973. *The Heritage of Hellenism.* (New York: Science History Publications).

Gay, Peter. 1969. *The Enlightenment: An Interpretation,* 2 vols. (New York: Knopf).

Grant, Michael. 1969. *The Ancient Mediterranean.* (New York: Scribner's).

Hall, Edward T., and Mildred Reed Hall. 1989. *Understanding Cultural Differences: Germans, French and Americans.* (Yarmouth, Maine: Intercultural Press).

Hampden-Turner, Charles. 1983. *Gentlemen and Tradesmen.* (London: Routledge and Kegan Paul).

Hampden-Turner, Charles, and Alfons Trompenaars. 1993. *The Seven Cultures of Capitalism.* (New York: Currency-Doubleday).

Hill, Richard. 1992. *We Europeans.* (Brussels: Europublic).

Hofstede, Geert. 1991. *Cultures and Organizations: Software of the Mind.* (New York: McGraw-Hill).

Kahler, Erich. 1974. *The Germans.* (Princeton: Princeton University Press).

Krause, Axel. 1991. *Inside the New Europe.* (New York: Bessie).

Lewis, Flora. 1987. *Europe—A Tapestry of Nations.* (New York: Simon and Schuster).

————. 1992. *Europe: Road to Unity.* (New York: Touchstone).

Marsh, David. 1989. *The Germans.* (London: Century Hutchinson).

Mikes, George. 1975. *Switzerland for Beginners.* (London: Andre Deutsch).

Pitts, Jesse R. 1963. "Continuity and Change in *Bourgeois* France." In Center for International Affairs, *In Search of France.* (Cambridge, Mass.: Harvard University Press): 235–304.

Platt, Polly. 1994. *French or Foe?* (London: Culture Crossings).

Shetter, William. 1987. *The Netherlands in Perspective.* (Leiden: Martinus Nijhof).

Zeldin, Theodore. 1982. *The French.* (London: Collins Harvel).

Chapter 10

SUB-SAHARAN AFRICA

This chapter will focus on Black Africa with an eye toward understanding not so much specific countries but instead the core values Africans brought with them to other lands, including the United States, and the core values that transcend the political boundaries of contemporary Africa. Scholars acknowledge the difficulty of generalizing about so huge an area now encompassing some forty countries and a great diversity of people, nevertheless they have identified some commonalities of history and tradition and, hence, of values.

Only quite recently, in cultural terms, traditional African values have been affected at least somewhat by European colonialists and Christian missionaries who began arriving in large numbers in the late nineteenth century. Thus, the period during which the ancestors of the great majority of African-Americans arrived in the United States as slaves, from the seventeenth through the mid-nineteenth centuries, preceded the European colonization of Africa. Most of these ancestors originated in West Africa, an area stretching from Cape Verde to the Congo basin and including all or parts of such present-day countries as Senegal, Gambia, Guinea, Sierra Leone, Liberia, Ivory Coast, Ghana, Togo, Nigeria, Cameroon, Mali, Niger, Gabon, Zaire, and Angola. Hofstede's research addressed East and West Africans separately but with little difference in results. He found both with moderately large power distance (West Africans slightly more so), both collectivist (with West Africans more so), both with slightly weak uncertainty avoidance, and feminine (with West Africans less so). His research also included South Africans who were found, relative to East and West Africans, to have smaller power distance (though still slightly on the large side), to be less collectivist, about the same in uncertainty avoidance (all three a bit weaker than the United States), and moderately masculine.

THE CULTURAL SETTING

The original home of humanity, perhaps a million years ago, much of Africa is high plateau and savanna, large areas of rolling grass land, lying between the Sahara Desert to the north and the Kalahari Desert to the south. Contrary to a common perception then, Africa is not a "dark" continent in the sense of being mostly dense jungle. The equatorial rain forest dominates only the center of the continent for just a few degrees of latitude above and below the equator. The coastal area around the Cape of Good Hope has a pleasant, Mediterranean-like climate. Very much the oldest continent, most of Africa's mountain ranges have eroded. Extremes of wet and dry weather and the persistence of diseases that threaten both human and beast, particularly sleeping sickness carried by the tse-tse fly, make much of the continent unable to sustain large settlements.

African societies were fragmented, subsistence economies that took several forms depending on climatic conditions. Hunter-gatherers dominated the desert, whereas nomadic herders predominated in the savanna, which was too dry to support many permanent settlements. Where the tse-tse fly and sleeping sickness precluded herding, hardy grain crops provided sustenance. This threat also precluded the use of beasts of burden and, hence, the use of animal-powered, wheeled vehicles, in most of sub-Saharan Africa. The rain forest supported a great variety of crops but only at the subsistence level because the heavy rains leached nutrients from the soil. Where valuable resources were found—iron ore or fertile land, for example—a chiefdom would emerge to control and apportion it.

Access to the interior was limited by forbidding jungle or desert, a dearth of ports, and the threat of disease. Great sub-Saharan rivers such as the Niger, Congo, and Zambezi supported internal trade but falls from high plateaux near the coast or dense, mangrove swamps made them inaccessible from the sea. Thus external contacts were limited to the periphery, and the interior of Africa remained essentially isolated until the late nineteeth century. The temperature and humidity were oppressive to explorers from northern latitudes but were not any more daunting than those overcome in other tropical and subtropical regions in Asia and the Western Hemisphere.

From the thirteenth through sixteenth centuries, major trading empires existed in West Africa, centered on the cities of Timbuktu and Gao, strategically located on the River Niger and at the interface between savanna and desert, in what is now Mali. These cities, advanced civilizations with bureaucracies and institutions such as organized police forces, elaborate legal systems with courts of appeal, import and export duties, banking, and a university at Timbuktu (from which scholars were brought to teach in Fez, Cairo, and Tunis), anchored caravan routes across the Sahara into North Africa until being overrun by Moorish invaders in 1591. Exports included gold, ivory, musk and other spices, ebony, hides, and resins. African slaves were taken in trade by the Romans, ancient Egyptians, Muslims, and Europeans. However, apparently, only the prices fetched for luxury products, or slaves, could justify the hardship of a sea voyage or lengthy caravan journey to sub-Saharan Africa.

Arab traders were established on the east or Indian Ocean coast by the twelfth century. European explorers, led by the Portuguese Prince Henry the Navigator (who apparently never actually left Portugal) and aided by the recent invention of gunpowder, established trading posts on the Atlantic coast in the sixteenth century. They sought access to African gold denied to them by Muslim control of the trans-Saharan caravan routes as well as an alternative route to the East to bypass the Arab, Venetian, and Genoese middlemen of the Mediterranean. Adoption of the triangular, lateen sail developed by Arabs trading on the Indian Ocean in the design of the caravel had made ocean voyages more feasible because the square-rigged European vessels had a difficult time sailing to windward, and thus returning home against the common northeasterlies. Eventually, Portuguese sailors found southerly winds prevailing further to the west and began to take a more circular return route, discovering Madeira, the Canary and Cape Verde Islands in the process. Led by Vasco da Gama, they eventually made their way around the Cape of Good Hope and established outposts at Mozambique and Mombasa (now in Kenya) on the Indian Ocean. The British, French, Dutch, Danes, and Germans followed. Spread too thin by European wars and their forays into Africa, Brazil, India, and the East Indies, the Portuguese were surpassed in Africa and elsewhere, primarily by the British and French. Ghana, in West Africa and once known as the Gold Coast (where Christopher Columbus once sailed before his westbound expeditions), became a principal source of gold for Europe and the rest of the world.

With the eventual demise of the Arab Empire, the Europeans made greater use of the more direct Mediterranean–Red Sea route to more-accessible sources in India and the East Indies, as well as the Western Hemisphere, and the trade with Africa dissipated. The relatively few African ports served more as way stations for ships using the Cape route. Meanwhile, Portuguese planters in Brazil and British planters in the Caribbean and Britain's southern American colonies developed needs for large amounts of labor, and slaves became the primary "export" from West Africa. It is impossible to know the exact number, but perhaps ten to twelve million Africans were forced to endure the difficult voyage to the New World with an estimated 20 percent dying enroute. Adding insult to the injury of slavery, this was much less trade than mercantilist exploitation; Africans generally received only cloth, salt, and other common commodities, trinkets, and obsolete weapons for their slaves and high-value products. All the while, almost all sub-Saharan Africa remained isolated from the rest of the world. It is difficult to overstate the importance of this because, as observed by Maquet (1972), cultures assimilate and learn much more from others than they are able to invent for themselves. Africa, and Africa alone, was denied this opportunity by its physical isolation.

The last half of the nineteenth century brought European colonization to Africa. The Industrial Revolution made many of Africa's more commonplace commodities essential or more affordable. Among them were rubber; palm oil for soap, candles, and lubricants; cotton; coffee; cocoa; and various foodstuffs for working-class Europeans. Whereas the conduct of trade with Africa in the past had been confined to the continent's margins, the economical harvesting of these products of relatively low unit value required a deeper penetration of and more sustained presence in Africa. They required plantations and mines; infrastructure, especially rail transportation; conscription, organization, and supervision of labor; a monetary economy to allow extraction of wealth; and political control to protect it. The discovery of quinine as a treatment for malaria, the steam engine, the Suez Canal, the discovery of diamonds in South Africa, and the missionary spirit all served to accelerate European colonization, made possible by superior weaponry such as the cannon, the rifle (which replaced the musket), and the machine gun. The end of feudalism in Europe had made it difficult to obtain power and amass a fortune the old-fashioned way, that is, by exploiting vassals and serfs—now one had to earn a living. Thus the adventurous and/or the greedy sought more-lucrative opportunities elsewhere. So too the missionaries, sensing the diminution of religious influence in Europe, sought more-fertile ground. With the people of the Western Hemisphere having already achieved independence and much of Asia already colonized, Africa remained the last frontier for mercantilism and proselytizing. Moreover, the then newly-emergent European nation-states were driven by strategic concerns such as maintaining the balance of power, dominance of the Cape passage, and national prestige.

As is typical in agrarian societies, the extended family was the primary economic unit. Land ownership and the social fabric were communal. Traditional gender roles prevailed. African fathers wielded absolute authority over and were revered by their children, even through adulthood. African mothers maintained constant, close physical contact with babies long after birth rather than allowing them to lay alone in a crib and feeding them on demand rather than on a schedule, and were thus a great source of warmth and security. The extended family provided a wide network of readily available help and support. Children were taught from an early age to bond with their peers and were socialized into ritual patterns of behavior and relationships. Children were also encouraged to observe adult discussions and activities such as judicial proceedings. They were prepared as a "class" by elders for arduous initiation rites to signify joint passage into adulthood. In this way, society, in effect, "produced" the individual (Sindima 1990).

Each "class" would provide a lifelong support system for its members and would grow old and exercise more influence jointly. The "class" cut across descent groups, adding another—horizontal—dimension to African communalism. The harsh environment supported only small, isolated settlements and demanded communal effort and interdependence. Arranged marriages established alliances between descent groups. Lineage and kinship were the sole sources of identity, not occupation, class, religion, or nationality, and one's life belonged to one's community and lineage. One held one's life primarily to pass on to descendants for it belonged rightfully only to the kinship group. Kinship ties extended to ancestors and to the unborn. Solidarity of the kinship group was the highest ideal.

Society was stratified by age but highly egalitarian within age groups. Decision making was collegial, and whatever time necessary to achieve unanimity was taken. The opinion of elders was given more weight, and the eldest male of the founding lineage of the clan had the most influence, assuming the foremost position as chief among the heads of families. However, power was distributed among them, and none could overrule another. The role of the chief was to act as first among equals, to advise and persuade, and to pronounce with great solemnity the collegial decision. Once made however, obedient execution of the decision was the norm. Villages centered on the clan were the basic social unit. They were small and widely separated due to the limited fertility of the land. Isolation in the face of a hostile environment induced mutual dependence. Order was maintained by collective pressure—all were known well to one another—and persistent nonconformance or disagreement would lead first to ridicule, then isolation, and ultimately ostracism, which had to be agreed upon unanimously. Outcasts had to then seek admittance to another village, perhaps placing themselves in voluntary servitude. Villages might enslave captives from battles with other villages, but they or their descendants might eventually be taken in and treated as family members.

As the extended family grew larger in number and space, the chief in effect became a king, presiding over a loose confederation of widely dispersed villages—necessary due to the sparseness of the land. In contrast to the collegial administration of the village, African kings tended to fall victim to the same temptations confronting royalty everywhere as they became farther removed from their familial roots. They wielded absolute power; eliminated rivals, even siblings; exercised eminent domain over all property; surrounded themselves with pomp and regalia; established elaborate courts and built provincial and local administration to maintain power; were accorded divine (but not hereditary) right by their subjects; and thus became aloof and isolated. They ruled relatively small states, which were really extended clans. The notion of tribe was a European notion, not African. Thus arbitrary colonial boundaries encompassed many more states than they divided—a common but exaggerated criticism in sub-Saharan Africa—and many Africans were actually stateless in any case.

HISTORICAL FORCES

Slavery

As noted, the taking of African slaves is an ancient practice, dating back to the Egyptians and the Romans. Indeed the early African empires built much of their wealth on a relatively limited slave trade with North Africa and southern Europe. Though historians seem to disagree on the extent and the onset, slavery apparently was common wholly within Africa as it was elsewhere, with anywhere from 10 to 50 percent of local populations in slavery by the late nineteenth century, depending on the peculiar needs of agricutural husbandry in the area. Some scholars (for example, Oliver 1992) argue that Africans learned slavery and the slave trade from Muslims. Africans took captives from war into slavery primarily to help populate the abundant but infertile land and to strengthen and enlarge their households. They were taken into the household, treated with some dignity, and stood a good chance of achieving equal standing eventually, at least for their descendants if not for themselves. The Egyptians, Romans, and North African Muslims took slaves primarily as conscripts for their armies. Muslims also took women and children, as spoils of conquest, to amuse their courts and maintain their households. The Portuguese and Spanish took slaves to row their galleons and to work on plantations in the south of those countries and on various Mediterranean Islands. It was thought that Africans were better suited for physical labor in tropical or subtropical climates. Hence the demand exploded, primarily for males, with the development of highly labor-intensive plantations in the New World in the seventeenth century. The first African slaves arrived in the Western Hemisphere in 1494 and in what is now the United States at Jamestown in 1619. It should be noted that these Africans arrived in large numbers well before most other immigrant groups, including those from Ireland, Scandinavia, and central, southern, and eastern Europe. Most of the earlier immigrants were of English, Scottish, or Dutch origin, with most French immigrants settling in Canada. The practice of slavery and the demand for African slaves were so extensive that some historians question whether the Western slave trade affected only its destination rather than its magnitude.

African chiefs found it convenient and lucrative to sell their criminals and captives into slavery. This was the familiar and highly lucrative "three-way" trade of European cloth, weapons, and metals exchanged for slaves, which were in turn exchanged for American sugar, tobacco, and cotton. Europeans were enriched by both sets of transactions. African chiefs armed with European muskets were then able to obtain more slaves to sell, and then to buy more guns, sustaining the cycle. The Dutch West India Company, formed in 1621, led the way, soon to be followed and eclipsed by the British, French, and Americans. German, Danish, and Swedish traders also participated. The vast majority of slaves were taken to Brazil, the Caribbean, and Central America; perhaps only one-twentieth were taken to what is now the United States (Bohannan and Curtin 1971).

Precipitated by the agitation of missionaries, the Danes abolished their slave trade in 1804, followed by the British in 1808. The British abolished the practice of slavery itself in their West Indies possessions in 1833, and the Royal Navy attempted to enforce an embargo on all slave trading out of West Africa, returning and setting free many slaves taken from ships of various nations intercepted on the high seas. However, the trade continued until the American Civil War and President Lincoln's Emancipation Proclamation in 1863. The South at that point was much more interested in getting war matériel through the Union blockade rather than new slaves.

Historians maintain that slavery's impact on Africa was manifest in an enormous and stagnating drain on the population and in its legacy of a strong bias toward an assumption of inferiority relative to non-Africans in Africa and elsewhere. Others discount the effect on population, however, arguing that the widespread practice of polygyny kept the birthrate up despite a depleted male population.

European Colonization

Whereas Europeans traded only about the periphery of most of sub-Saharan Africa, the more benign climate and fertile land of South Africa attracted Huguenot, German, and Dutch settlers, including employees of the Dutch East India Company, beginning in 1652. These farmers, or Boers, developed their own language, Afrikaans, based on Dutch and Flemish. They raised cattle, grains, and wine grapes, assisted by African slaves. In the wake of the Napoleonic Wars, the British acquired the colony in 1815. Upset by the rates of compensation paid by the British government for their slaves liberated by the British and by the lack of adequate protection provided against incursions by the Bantu people to the north, the Boers tried to establish independence. Continuing tension culminated in the Boer War of 1899–1903. South Africa became independent in 1931, but the Afrikaaners instituted the practice of apartheid that continued until just recently. Instability continues to the present day.

With the end of the Napoleonic Wars, the Congress of Vienna, a rash of revolutions in 1848, and the industrial revolution, a relative stability emerged in late-nineteenth-century Europe with the advent of the nation-state. Rivalry and potential conflict arising from the demand for African lands and commodities caused King Leopold II of Belgium to establish the

International Association for the Exploration and Civilization of Africa in 1876. German Chancellor Otto von Bismarck convened an international conference in Berlin in 1884 ostensibly to organize the protection of Africa but actually to divide the continent among the European powers. The primary instrument of political control was a treaty of "friendship" and "protection" executed with various African kings and chiefs. The primary instrument of exploitation was the royal charter granted to a private company, as the British and Dutch had done elsewhere in their empires, so that the European monarchs, and European taxpayers, would not have to bear the capital costs. The process of colonization was violent in some places and relatively peaceful in others—more infiltration than conquest—in part because some African leaders saw it as an opportunity to enrich themselves by acting as middlemen (Oliver 1992). Generally, African polities were too fragmented to mount much effective resistance. This was just as well for the colonialists because their governments and military forces were quite weak relative to the size of their geographic and human dominions. When force was required, the Europeans would employ Africans to fight Africans.

There was a rush to complete the colonization of Africa after the 1884–85 Berlin conference. The French dominated much of Central and West Africa. Whether because of altruism generated by their own revolutionary experience, a preference for statism, or simple chauvinistic hubris, they set out to assimilate their African subjects into French culture, largely without success. Consequently, they took a more direct and involved role in administering their colonies. The British, more dominant in the east and south, took a more indirect role, allowing more Africans and Indians into administrative positions under British oversight. The slight differences in Hofstede's findings for East and West Africa are consistent with the differences between France and Britain in those same core values (see Chapter 9). The Germans were expelled from Africa after World War I. The Portuguese (primarily Angola in the west and Mozambique in the east) and Belgians (the Belgian Congo—long known as Zaire but just recently becoming the Democratic Republic of Congo, Rwanda, and Burundi in Central Africa) ruled in a more authoritarian manner. Paternalism in the form of looking after what seemed to them to be clearly inferior people provided the moral rationalization for empire, just as it did in Asia and the Western Hemisphere. The Europeans expected gratitude for bringing "civilization," but the Africans reacted quite differently upon recognizing that their chiefs had been deceived and disempowered, their religion mocked, and workers exploited. African workers were treated much worse than their European counterparts, even though the typical African was quite content to maintain a traditional way of life and had no desire to work for the colonialists. Consequently, the Europeans had to resort to conscripted and forced labor—and they paid the workers very little. Revolts were widespread, most notably the Zulu Wars in South Africa and the Mau Mau guerilla movement in British East Africa, now Kenya. Only Ethiopia and Liberia remained free of colonization. Most colonies did not achieve independence until the 1960s.

The legacies of colonialism included arbitrary national boundaries; very strong, autocratic, centralized rule thought necessary to manage radical transformation; supplanting of food crops by cash (export) crops with attendant famines; African arts and literature de-emphasized in favor of European works; education focused on the learned professions rather than on more-practical skills; and socialist bureaucracies on the European model established to "guide" political and economic transition and development. It may have been unfortunate that many African countries became independent during a time when statism reached its zenith in influence not only in the Communist bloc but in the Western European "parents" of the African colonies as well as in as the universities that trained so many African leaders. Many looked to the strong state as an example and for support because the more-idealistic aspects of socialism appealed to the thoroughly communally-minded African. In the event, these leaders generally could not fulfill their peoples' expectations of improved education and opportunity, raised by the colonialists, because of widespread, rapid population growth and a lack of resources. Many abused their power. Continuing political instability was the result. Civil wars, revolutions, and foreign intervention in the context of the Cold War, such as the power struggle in the Belgian Congo and the Cuban presence in Angola, were not uncommon. Withdrawal of Communist support after the demise of the Soviet Union has led to anarchy in some nations such as Somalia. Colonization also forestalled nascent democratic movements begun earlier in the nineteenth century, most notably in Liberia, Gold Coast, and Sierra Leone, either by Africans educated in Europe or by freed slaves returned to Africa from the Western Hemisphere or from slave ships intercepted by the Royal Navy.

Development has been retarded by a lack of native administrative experience because the colonialists occupied the managerial positions or brought in third-party nationals, particularly Indians by the British, to run their bureaucracies and businesses for them, depriving Africans an opportunity to learn these skills. Moreover, many Africans educated elsewhere have elected to remain there, a problem that persists as it does in India. The lack of experience was such that, upon independence, noncommissioned officers found themselves promoted to general and schoolmasters to cabinet secretary virtually overnight.

Despite the colonial experience, traditional African culture remains largely intact. Other than creating an opportunity and expectation of strong centralized rule, the colonialists, whose rule lasted for much less than a century, seem to have had little impact on African values and behavior, limited largely to the elite. Their impact in terms of arresting or at least failing to contribute much to African development appears to have been much more significant. The more-sustained presence and deeper penetration of the "doing" Dutch, Germans, and British in South Africa would appear to account for the differences in values found in Hofstede's research relative to East and West Africa. Nevertheless, black South Africans remain much more similar to other Africans than to the Afrikaaners.

More recently, most African countries fell victim to some of their brothers in the developing world. The oil crisis precipitated by OPEC following the Yom Kippur War of 1973 hit these newly-independent countries very hard. They borrowed extensively to finance development, often much more than they could afford, but encouraged to do so by banks awash in petrodollars. With exceptions such as Nigeria, a major oil exporter, they were faced with rising energy prices simultaneously with reduced demand for their exports because of OPEC-induced recessions. With oil purchases generally payable in dollars, which were soon inflating rapidly, and exports declining, these developing countries found themselves running out of foreign exchange and defaulting on their debts. Recovery is not yet complete.

RELIGION

Though all the major religions are practiced in Africa, the traditional religion was animism. Africans believed that a supreme being created and regulated all aspects of life and, represented by spirits embodied in nature, intervened freely in human affairs, often acting and speaking through departed ancestors. The spirits, nature, and humanity were one. All events and outcomes were spiritually directed, with nature and humanity serving as God's instruments. Hence, there was an enormous dependence upon and submission to nature and a greatly felt obligation to live in harmony with it. Africans thus resigned themselves to their fates, depending upon God for protection and to avenge wrongs. They took pride in humility before God and dignity in the face of adversity. This is not to say that Africans could not be inventive or creative, but that such activity was more likely in response to a threat than in a proactive attempt to bring about change. As a result, life was unhurried and was perceived to proceed according to nature's pace and rhythms. The high risk associated with a bare-subsistence economy precluded experimentation with new crops or alternative livelihoods. The subsistence economy and lack of alternatives to agriculture engendered the "work to live" attitude characteristic of a "being" culture. The assumption of an entirely external locus of control obviated any impetus to identify causal factors and thus precluded developments in science and technology. The little time not spent tending to survival was devoted to leisurely pursuits. The African mind developed as an instrument for experiencing and enjoying life, not solving its mysteries. Nature moved in cyclical patterns with opposite forces ebbing and flowing, much like the Taoist yin and yang. The future held little meaning relative to the past, and time as an abstraction had little value. The only realities that mattered were actual events and human relationships. Life was something to be experienced, not planned. The most desirable outcome of human endeavor was survival, and the primary means to that end was harmony with humanity, nature, and God. Dona Richards (in Asante and Asante 1985, 207) states that what the African valued most was "to live robustly," that is, to live and enjoy life energetically and forcefully.

The African mode of worship was communal ritual, centered on music and dance, which was meant to achieve harmony with God and nature and to express communal solidarity. The rhythmic beat of the drum synchronized, harmonized, and unified behavior and expression. Individuals were expected to participate energetically and were encouraged to be creative and emotive, to develop an individualized style that would demonstrate their fervor. The stylized, rhythmic speech patterns and "call and response" preaching of African-American clergy are rooted in these rituals, as are tendencies toward flamboyance and personalized styles of dress, speech, and behavior such as, according to Kochman (1981), the manner in which an African-American talks, walks, or celebrates. In the same vein, according to Kochman, speech and mannerisms that seem overly boastful, aggressive, or argumentative to others usually are not intended to be so, but are instead the normally more exuberant African form of self-expression.

Rituals were central to African life; they recognized natural events and celebrated human passages. Africans brought them to America. Work songs not only helped pass the arduous days but provided a connection to the solidarity of the African village. They sustained tradition in the face of alienation and provided pleasure and beauty where there was no other. Ultimately, they evolved into the blues and all the musical forms that followed. Who cannot be impressed by the beauty and majesty of the gospel music of an African-American church congregation? The power lies not only in the music itself but in its expression of community among members of the congregation and harmony between the human and spiritual worlds. This joyous, musical celebration is a direct analogue to traditional African religious ritual and remains perhaps the most ostensible symbol of African cultural values in America. However, ritual practice severed from the familiar, cyclical patterns of life in Africa loses much of its meaning.

African religious practice was highly localized, thus it lacked universal truths or dogma. However it was taken quite seriously and, as should be expected given the Africans' total dependence on nature, central to their lives. One commonly recognized virtue was selflessness, reflecting the importance of solidarity and communalism. Individual conduct was regulated closely in terms of fulfilling one's obligations to family and community, but matters of interpersonal conduct, such as marriage, were left to the individual. Evil was manifest in adverse events, presumably triggered by displeased spirits. Though Africans took little interest in scientific exploration, they felt compelled to identify the cause of such displeasure. It was the role of the African priest to identify the source through divination and prescribe the appropriate ritual to placate the offended deity—neglect of the memory of an ancestor being one commonly presumed sin. The priest was expected to maintain harmony within the community and with nature, for disharmony would certainly bring divine retribution. Chiefs were expected as a minimum to provide protection and to look after the common good. Better still was the chief who could demonstrate an apparent connection to the gods, demonstrated perhaps by seemingly magical powers or possession of secret knowledge or understanding of mysterious phenomena.

Today most sub-Saharan countries consider themselves Christian; those on the northern periphery and some on the Indian Ocean are primarily Muslim. However, because most of the schools in Africa were established by Christian missionaries, most African leaders are Christians. Neither religion, in their basic doctrines, differs much from central, long-standing African beliefs such as monotheism, and thus they were assimilated readily but have had relatively little cultural impact. Contemporary African religion is a harmonious blend of indigenous and foreign beliefs and practice. However, there remains less specific behavioral guidance in African religion.

CORE VALUES AND BEHAVIOR

Large Power Distance and Ascribed Status Based on Age and Experience

African leaders are paternalistic and hierarchical. Although highly egalitarian within the age cohort, society is rigidly stratified by age or age cohort. However, power is not wielded with absolute authority (at least at the local level). There is a tradition of participation, at least by immediate juniors, and an effort to achieve unanimity regardless of time constraints and seniority. Nevertheless, elders are deeply respected and revered, and age and experience are the primary sources of authority and status. Approval by an elder is a strong motivator (Dia 1991). It should not be presumed, however, that an individual's authority within one's tribe or village (or work group) will be recognized across boundaries (Saleh 1985). Centralized, authoritarian rule became the norm during the transition to independence. However, there was long-standing precedent for the African monarch, even if more limited in the geographic scope of individual rule.

Collectivism, Femininity, and "Being"

Africans respect individuals but find individualism distasteful (Sindima 1990). In keeping with the importance placed on communal endeavor and solidarity, collectivism is high. Consistent with prevailing, collegial decision-making practices, responsibility and accountability are shared, and tasks are assigned to groups without individual responsibilities (Saleh 1985). Duties to others are one's primary obligation, and individual rights are an unfamiliar notion (Sindima 1990). Beyond survival, social needs become paramount, and maintenance of personal relationships and ritual duties take precedence over task performance and achievement. Economic activity is valued in terms of its potential to advance the welfare of the group (Dia 1991).

Time experienced according to natural cycles is not a resource to be conserved. Considerable time is devoted to maintenance of group solidarity. The need to socialize and participate in rituals and ceremonies puts much value on leisure time. Work lacks intrinsic value; it is a matter of survival and little more. Work is done as part of and in obligation to the family, and work life and family life coincide. Africans working outside the familiy environment subordinate career demands to family needs, and nepotism supersedes merit (Saleh 1985). The development of stylized behavior grounded in religious ritual suggests that the degree of style with which something is done may be more important than the objective outcome (Kochman 1981). In an organizational context, the residual effects of these traditional practices might be seen in a greater degree of improvisation, individuality of dress, emotiveness, spontaneity, and more-forceful expression (Kochman 1981). Equity and redistribution of wealth to equalize welfare within the group are more important than individual achievement and recognition. Accordingly, Dia (1991) suggests that profit sharing and employee stock ownership have much potential in Africa and that Africans make excellent team players.

Low Uncertainty Avoidance and Fatalism

Like other cultures deeply dependent on nature, Africans tend to be flexible and relatively indifferent to the potential stress of changing circumstances. Subsistence economies require little planning and management. Security is the strongest motivator. As is the case with other such "being" cultures and unlike "doing" cultures with low uncertainty avoidance, Africans see little value in attempting to shape events or initiate change, and they assume that changing circumstances may require modification of commitments.

Particularist Ethics

Though there are no research results to support this assertion, the localized nature of religious practice precludes universal standards. Communal solidarity is of course one common ideal, but as we have seen with other collectivist cultures, behavior that maintains collective harmony, protects the family, and preserves relationships sets the standard, and other beneficial behaviors, such as recognition of individual merit, are made subordinate to that standard.

CONVERGENCE?

There is a great gap between African and western culture, eloquently articulated by Kenyan political scientist Ali A. Mazrui (1990, 5). He observed that Africans

> borrowed the profit motive but not the entrepreneurial spirit (and) acquisitive appetites but not the creative risk taking . . . are at home with Western gadgets but are bewildered by Western workshops . . . wear the wristwatch but refuse to watch it for . . . punctuality . . . have learnt to parade in display, but not to drill in discipline. The West's consumption patterns have arrived, but not necessarily the West's techniques of production.

Perhaps we should expect convergence between African-Americans and other Americans because they have been here longer than most. It must be remembered, however, that emancipation did not come until 1863, that segregation remained the norm for another century, and that African-Americans remain a small and largely isolated minority (unlike Jamaicans or other formerly-British Caribbean islanders who were set free much earlier and constitute the large majorities in their countries).

Consider the impact of slavery upon the Africans brought to then-British North America. It only begins with the loss of individual freedom. In addition, each individual was torn from the social fabric of close relationships and a network built and carefully cultivated through generation upon generation, and then placed in a totally foreign and hostile environment. Moreover, Africans found themselves judged by the standards of a culture very different than their own; an emotive, communal, feminine "being" people close to one another and to nature found itself immersed in a "doing" culture based on individuality, rationality, objectivity, and technology and driven by the expectation that it could shape nature to its will. Whereas Africans were unfamiliar with the notion of private property, they now found themselves to be private property. As succeeding generations descended into slavery, much of their cultural heritage was lost, not as a contemporary immigrant and his descendants might have to adapt, perhaps quite gradually, to a new culture, but, rather because the African was forced to modify behavior drastically. They were deprived of their kin, "class," language, dress, and diet; their way of life; their behavioral compass; and ultimately (at least, in the attempt) their humanity. They had no choice but to assume the behaviors forced upon them by masters who sought to condition them to think of themselves as inferior. It is probably impossible for one who has not had or at least learned firsthand of this experience from elders to appreciate the nature and extent of the impact.

African-Americans, after being exposed to the standards of a "doing" culture and provided an opportunity, have demonstrated an enormous capacity for hard work and desire for achievement. This tends to engender a sense of convergence. However, the lack of understanding between Black and White Americans appears to remain great, as was so painfully indicated by their dramatically different reactions to the outcome of the criminal trial of football star O. J. Simpson, accused but found not guilty of murdering his wife and another person in 1996. Such a gulf, which apparently extends across the various socioeconomic levels and seemed to catch many by surprise, suggests that many African-Americans, not just the urban poor, remain a unique subculture, no matter how many may seem to have fully assimilated into "White" and "doing" America. Nevertheless, it is likely that if Hofstede's research isolated Africa-American values and then compared them to more-generalized American values, convergence would be found across the board, except that African-Americans would likely emerge as a haven for the community-minded, which so many commentators advocate as a more humanistic alternative to single-minded individualism, if for no other reason than the continual pressure forcing them to seek strength in numbers and mutual support.

SUMMARY

The forces shaping sub-Saharan African culture include

- Physical isolation that precluded assimilation of the developments and advances of others
- Lack of fertile land, which required the great bulk of human energy to be devoted to subsistence, leaving little opportunity for alternative endeavors
- Animism and dependence on nature
- Paternalism and familial hierarchy typical of agricultural societies
- Geographic fragmentation of society caused by a paucity of natural resources
- European statism

The core values developed by these forces include

- **Large Power Distance**—stemming from recognition of and submission to the authority of age-based wisdom and experience, essential in an agrarian, subsistence economy; amplified by the emergence of authoritarian monarchies and confirmed by the relatively brief colonial experience and the statist influence of European powers

- **Collectivism**—essential for survival in a rigorous environment poor in resources and supporting only small, widely dispersed communities, with the extended family as the primary collective unit

- **Femininity**—essential to maintain harmonious relationships within the collective unit and with supernatural and natural forces

- **Egalitarianism**—reflecting mutual dependence and respect for each individual as a vehicle for nature's life force and the kinship lineage

- **Low Uncertainty Avoidance**—a result of fatalistic dependence on the supernatural and nature, with its unpredictable events and cyclical rhythms of constant change

- **Particularist Ethics**—a result of the lack of universal moral precepts or religious law typical of animistic beliefs

- **Status by Ascription**—based on age and experience, a lack of opportunity to establish measures of merit in a subsistence economy, and the dominance of external attribution

ADDITIONAL READING

Management Practices

Jones, Merrick. 1988. "Managerial Thinking: An African Perspective." *Journal of Management Studies* 25, no. 5 (September): 481–505.

Saleh, Shoukry. 1985. "Western Management Techniques and Developing Countries: The Kenya Case." *Engineering Management International* 3: 91–99.

Sindima, Harvey. 1990. "Liberalism and African Culture." *Journal of Black Studies* 21, no. 2 (December): 190–209.

Sokoya, Sesan Kim. 1992. "Value Orientation and Value Profile of Nigerian Public Managers." *International Journal of Public Administration* 15(8): 1601–1618.

African History and Culture

Asante, Molefi Kete, and Kariamu Welsh Asante, eds. 1985. *African Culture.* (Westport, Conn.: Greenwood).

Bennett, Norman R. 1975. *Africa & Europe.* (New York: Africana).

Bohannan, Paul, and Philip Curtin. 1971. *Africa and Africans,* Rev. ed. (Garden City, N.Y.: Natural History Press).

Chilcote, Ronald H. 1967. *Portuguese Africa*. (Englewood Cliffs, N.J.: Prentice Hall).

Dia, Mamadou. 1991. "Development and Cultural Values in Sub-Saharan Africa." *Finance and Development* 28, no. 4 (December): 10–13.

Kingsnorth, G. W. 1963. *Africa South of the Sahara*. (Cambridge: Cambridge University Press).

Kochman, Thomas. 1981. *Black and White Styles in Conflict*. (Chicago: University of Chicago Press).

Labouret, Henri. 1963. *Africa before the White Man*. (New York: Walker).

Maquet, Jacques. 1972. *Africanity*. (London: Oxford University Press).

Marsh, Z. A., and G. W. Kingsnorth. 1965. *An Introduction to the History of East Africa*. (Cambridge: Cambridge University Press).

Mazrui, Ali A. 1990. *Cultural Forces in World Politics*. (London: James Curry).

McCarthy, Michael. 1983. *Dark Continent: Africa as Seen by Americans*. (Westport, Conn: Greenwood).

McNamara, Francis Terry. 1989. *France in Black Africa*. (Washington: National Defense University Press).

Murdock, George Peter. 1959. *Africa: Its Peoples and Their Culture History*. (New York: McGraw-Hill).

Oliver, Roland. 1992. *The African Experience*. (New York: IconEditions).

Rodney, Walter. 1982. *How Europe Underdeveloped Africa*. (Washington: Howard University Press).

Chapter 11

IMPLICATIONS FOR CROSS-CULTURAL MANAGEMENT

A work of this nature presents great risk over oversimplification and sweeping generalizations for which many exceptions can be found. A meaningful reduction of that risk would require a manifold increase in length or a reduction in scope to perhaps one country or regional grouping. Nevertheless, keeping in mind the need to avoid stereotyping, the mistake of assuming that every Indian, Filipino, Arab, or German we meet conforms to the profiles described in preceding chapters, we can compare behaviors driven by different core value systems and discuss how we might adapt our behaviors to perform effectively in different cultural settings.

No one has studied the practice of management as thoroughly as have we in the United States. Most management models and techniques have been developed in the United States and, as one might expect, have been conceived in the context of its dominant cultural values. This was not the result of a conscious decision to ignore others but simply an inevitable consequence of the individuals involved doing what all people do, viewing the world, their work, and other people through the filter of their own, native, cultural frame of reference. Moreover, the people they studied while conducting the research that led to the development of those models and techniques were also Americans who generally embrace U.S. cultural values. Had Abraham Maslow been Chinese, it is extremely unlikely that he would have hypothesized that individual self-actualization sits atop the hierarchy of needs. Had Frederick Herzberg, in developing his well-known, two-factor, job-enrichment model, studied accountants and engineers in a country with strong uncertainty avoidance, like Mexico, rather than in Pittsburgh, it is very unlikely that he would have found that job security is not a motivator. Had he studied a feminine culture like Scandinavia, it is very unlikely that he would have found that good workplace relationships were not a motivator. All of this may seem quite provincial and unsophisticated to a younger reader, but the simple fact is that international business and cross-cultural management were not important considerations when the bulk of U.S. management theory and practical prescriptions were developed. Indeed it was this very question of the applicability to other cultures of American management practices that lies at the heart of Hofstede's research (1980; 1993).

This chapter will address the practical implications of cultural differences; first from the standpoint of summarizing the major differences from the values that predominate in the U.S., and second by discussing how specific management practices common in the United States might have to be adapted accordingly. It concludes with some final thoughts on cultural convergence and coping with cultural differences.

CULTURAL DIVISIONS

Less Individualism

All cultures are less individualistic than the United States; all but Great Britain and Australia considerably so. All non-Western European and non-Anglo countries are collectivist to some degree. In those countries it is important to recognize the dominant collective unit; in most it is the extended family. There also may be strong tribal ties in Arab countries and in less-developed countries generally. The Japanese, like the French, have strong loyalties to their employer and nation. Whatever the in-group, an individual's identity and self-concept lie more in membership in that group than in a sense of self or self-interest. The greatest adjustment for U.S. managers in collectivist cultures is to recognize that they are no longer managing individuals but instead they are directing and controlling groups. Individuals prefer not to be singled out for any reason, prefer rewards based on group performance, and are more comfortable with smaller differences in compensation between levels. It may be necessary to take into account in-group membership in hiring, promotion, and disciplinary decisions, and nepotism may be the norm. Individuals may feel compelled to act in the interests of the group when those interests conflict with those of the employer. It will be necessary to communicate in ways that do not cause loss of face within the in-group, and shame will be a more effective control device than guilt.

There are some collective aspects to the essentially individualistic western European cultures. French managers feel a great deal of loyalty to their own class, the *cadres,* and have a we-they attitude toward non-*cadre,* whether workers or graduates of less-prestigious schools. Southern Europeans have strong extended-family ties and prefer to work for small companies; the Italians have strong social ties outside the workplace and the family as well; and the Greeks honor their village roots. The Germanic peoples, including the Scandinavians and the Dutch, have a strong sense of community within the workplace reminiscent of their tribal traditions.

Greater and Smaller Power Distance

Non-Latin European and other Anglo countries have smaller power distances than the United States; most others have larger. The largest are in Latin American, Asian, Arab, and African countries. Northern Europeans feel that they deserve to be consulted because (a) they know their jobs and are very good at them and (b) they are conditioned to participate in decisionmaking because of their democratic, meritocratic tribal traditions. Other cultures have long histories of submission to some form of authority whether it be the abstract virtues of Confucianism, a sword-wielding samurai, the Koran, the Pope, or the czar. The United States falls between these two camps because though its origins are Northern European and its basic impulses democratic, its polyglot workforces need some degree of direction to hold them together.

Large-power-distance cultures generally expect managers to function as benevolent autocrats who know a lot about the nature of their subordinates' work. Firm direction with respect both to desired outcomes and methods is the norm. In "being" cultures with large power distance, workers tend to welcome a warm, paternal relationship with their superiors, even if distant in terms of power. A special case is "doing" Japan, where managers are not expected to be autocratic but are expected to build consensus among their subordinates. It is important to recognize the difference between consultation, as practiced in Japan where power distance is moderately large and decisions essentially top-down, and true participation, as practiced in Germanic countries (although Switzerland tends to be a bit more autocratic, reflecting its French and Italian components), where power distance is very small. In these cultures, workers expect little direct supervision, instead preferring only to have expectations clarified and then to be left alone to get the job done. Moreover, they expect to have a say in decisions that affect not only their work but matters of company policy and strategy. Compensation differentials tend to be smaller in these more egalitarian cultures.

The greatest challenge for U.S. managers with respect to power distance is for those who prefer a consultative or participative style and find themselves managing employees with large power distance. Efforts to involve such employees in decision making appear odd to them and might even be seen as evidence of weakness or inadequate technical knowledge. Asking them for advice conflicts with the common expectation among such employees that managers attain their position by virtue of superior knowledge of the task and operational skill. Managers are also expected to act the part in terms of dress, manner, and privilege. Acting like "one of the guys,"

a manner comfortable and natural for many Americans, confuses subordinates. In turn, U.S. managers have to behave with more formality and
deference toward superiors.

Femininity

Masculinity is the most complex of Hofstede's value dimensions because
it has several components that can conflict. Japan is at the top of the scale
because it is highly "doing" and highly male-dominated. The United States
ranks quite high because it is an assertive, aggressive, materialistic, achievement-oriented "doing" culture. Cultures like those of Germany, Austria, or
Hong Kong are masculine for the same reason. Others like Italy, Mexico,
the Philippines, and India are masculine because they have overwhelmingly
strong, traditional gender roles, enough to offset their more-feminine "being" natures. Most Latin, Arab, African, Asian, and some European countries are in the middle range because they combine the two. At the bottom
of the masculinity scale are the Netherlands and the Scandinavian countries
(excluding the more Asian Finland). These very feminine cultures, which
value strong relationships in the workplace, are also "doing" cultures. They
value hard work in large part because it is essential to being a good citizen—it is a felt obligation to others, much as it is in Japan. The difference
is that it is more egalitarian, driven primarily by a desire to maintain relationships among peers and community, whereas the primary obligation
felt by the Japanese is hierarchical, toward one's superior, employer, and
even to Japan itself. The Dutch and Scandinavians, with the rare combination of very strong task and relationship orientations, are ideal managers
in the well-known Managerial Grid framework of Blake and Mouton
(1978) or Likert's System 4 (1967). Because these are "doing" cultures, the
main adjustment for Americans would be to tone down their masculine
behavior; to be less overbearing, authoritative, and assertive; to think less
in terms of rivalry and zero-sum games with colleagues and think more in
terms of compromise, consensus, and teamwork.

The greatest challenge for U.S. managers on this dimension is coping
with the "being" culture. It is important to recognize that "being" people
can and will work hard. It is just that they work to live not live to work.
Work, for them, is a means to an end, not an end in itself. Recall that it
was the medieval German guilds who appear to be the first people anywhere known to value work in and of it itself, suggesting that this is not
the normal human condition. The desired end for "being" people typically
is a whole and satisfying home and family life, and work is endured in
order to maintain it. In practical terms, one should expect "being" people
to be less willing to work long hours or take work home and be more likely
to expect employer concessions to family needs.

The matter of extremely traditional gender roles does not appear to be as much of a concern as it might seem to a U.S. firm considering sending a woman to work in such an environment. According to Adler (in Lane, DiStefano, and Moznewski 1997, 240–256), men from these cultures are aware of differing attitudes toward women in the workplace in less-traditional countries, and most treat a woman in a properly professional manner after they understand the woman's role and responsibilities. However, it is incumbent upon the firm to make that understanding clear.

Strong Uncertainty Avoidance and Fatalism

There are two issues here for U.S. managers. The first has to do with stronger uncertainty avoidance found in all Latin, Arab, and African countries and all mainland Asian countries except India, usually grounded in a lengthy history of strong central rule or elaborate legal systems. The second has to do with the existence of different sources of weak uncertainty avoidance, whether weaker or stronger than the United States, in "doing" cultures like the United States, Scandinavia, the Netherlands, and Great Britain and "being" cultures like Indonesia, India, and the Philippines.

In countries with stronger uncertainty avoidance than the United States, workers desire more structure and order and are less receptive to deviation from precedent or rules and to innovation and new ideas. Things and people that are different are best avoided (remember that uncertainty avoidance is not risk avoidance—people with strong uncertainty avoidance will take familiar risks, and coping measures can be very creative [Hofstede 1991, 125]). There is a strong sense of an external locus of control and constraint on entrepreneurial thinking, and security is a strong motivator. This resistance to change poses a substantial difficulty for U.S. managers who sense intuitively that change is the only constant and, applying their internal locus of control, that they must be proactive to be effective. "Doing" cultures tend to be weak in uncertainty avoidance because they have learned that they can use technology to harness nature and shape events to their liking, at least to some degree. In so doing, they have experienced positive outcomes in their material standard of living and have thus grown to think that change is good. There are many "being" cultures with weak uncertainty avoidance that are very comfortable with change but not because they have grown accustomed to initiating it. Instead, these cultures, typically agrarian, are highly dependent on nature, have witnessed endless changes both good and bad, and have simply become inured to change, which they see as normal, inevitable, but totally beyond their control. This is fatalism, and its implication for managers is that it makes it difficult for people to understand the point of setting goals, developing detailed long-range plans, or taking on major initiatives.

Particularist Ethics and High-Context Communication

Like other countries with Christian and, especially, Protestant roots, the U.S. has a universalist system of ethics, which means that Americans rely on universal truths and principals codified as laws, rules, and contracts to regulate behavior. U.S. businesses will do business with anyone and then sue if a contract is violated. Particularists value personal relationships more than conformance with inflexible, abstract standards and therefore will do business only with those they know and trust. Contracts are statements of general intent and, taking the fatalistic view, will naturally require modification as circumstances change, as inevitably they must. To presume that all changes can be anticipated and appropriate contingencies established beforehand is seen as presumptuous (One mustn't tempt Mother Nature!). The universalist, usually weak in uncertainty avoidance, anticipates that any problems that arise during the execution of a contract can be fixed.

On an individual level, this distinction is felt primarily in the application of situational rather than absolute ethical standards and the way people communicate. Whereas the univeralist is utilitarian in the sense of acting in ways that serve the common interest, the particularist acts in ways that serve more-limited interests. A particularly challenging aspect of this behavior for typically meritocratic U.S. managers is the practice of nepotism or any other form of favoritism that departs from objective standards. With respect to communication, what strikes the universalist as fudging, embellishing, hiding, or otherwise distorting the straightforward, honest, concisely stated, truth is wrong. Particularists not only break rules but violate the "truth" to maintain and promote valued relationships, or to save face in collectivist cultures. Where "face-saving" behavior is the norm, it is more difficult to involve in group discussions individuals who do not want to be seen as representing themselves as more knowledgeable and, at the same time, do not want to risk making an error before their peers. Another challenge is to respond to the necessity to build social relationships when seeking business in high-context cultures. This requires two very different modifications, one behavioral and the other intellectual. The first is patience. The second is to learn about the host culture, its past and present, beyond the business arena and to develop the knowledge base to be conversant on a broad range of topics.

Abundant and Polychronic Time

Some say that it is only the most productive people who are concerned about wasting time because they are so productive. However, many cultures, even some of the more productive ones, do not consider time as a valuable resource to be conserved. It is not that time is wasted but more a matter of different priorities (that is, values) as to how it should be expended. U.S. managers who become frustrated by losing the time necessary to build social relationships in collectivist or particularistic cultures before doing business fail to realize that building social relationships is part of doing business. In effect, they are working when socializing and stroking. Related is the notion of polychronic time, as opposed to monochronic. "Doing" cultures are monochronic, meaning that people do one thing at a time and generally dislike interruptions or diversions. People of "being" cultures do many things at once and do not resent interruptions. The consequences can be maddening for a monochronic person having a discussion with a polychronic person who is constantly taking phone calls and dealing with other visitors. What seems insulting or at least inconsiderate usually is nothing of the kind. The same is true for someone who is constantly late honoring appointments (Hall 1987). The driving consideration is that additional time necessary to cultivate the immediate relationship is more important than the abstract and universalist notion of punctuality.

Ascribed Status

Most Americans take great pride in being "just plain folks" in the workplace—informal, friendly, approachable. Though perhaps overbearing and immodest as tourists, at least with respect to being Americans, at home they tend toward modesty, content to let their achievements speak for themselves. For most, status is very much a matter of what one has accomplished rather than one's family background or even age. Class systems or any other basis for ascribing status violate some very essential American ideals, such as social mobility and the universalist principle of fairness.

U.S. managers confronting ascribed status must be more deferential to age, education, or whatever the basis is for ascription. It must be taken into account in personnel decisions; for example, a promotion based on merit must be considered carefully if the promotion places that person in authority over someone of higher ascribed status, perhaps someone older (as is usually the case in Japan, for example) or of a higher social class (recall that social class and wealth are not necessarily the same). Such a promotion may well be impossible, and that circumstance will be recognized and accepted by others of that same culture.

ADAPTING MANAGEMENT PRACTICES

Leadership Style

A leadership style consistent with McGregor's (1960) Theory X is based on assumptions that workers require thorough supervision, explicit direction, and coercion and derive little satisfaction from their work in and of itself but only from the sustenance and security it provides. This authoritarian style would seem clearly out of place in cultures with small power distance. Conversely, Theory Y assumptions, which hold that workers are motivated best by responsibility, autonomy, trust, and a more open, communicative environment, seem ill-suited for large-power-distance cultures. However, Adler (1991) suggests that a Theory Y style is well-suited to those cultures because workers share common interests among themselves and with management, value relationships, and prefer an egalitarian workplace, that is, the collectivist values that often coincide with large power distance. That coincidence occurs in nearly all non-Western European, non-Anglo countries, suggesting that a Theory Y style has very broad applicability, at least with respect to the leader's assumptions about worker motivation. Workers in large-power-distance cultures would still expect their leaders to make the decisions, clarify expectations, and demonstrate strength and technical proficiency.

Participative Decision-Making and Teamwork

Collectivist cultures should be well suited to participative or consensus decision-making and lateral cooperation, but the typical coincidence of large power distance tends to constrain interaction even when authority figures solicit input from subordinates. The distance literally divides manager and worker; the worker feels dependent upon the manager yet considers the manager unapproachable and not to be challenged even when the manager seeks to close the distance. Moreover, the worker, who assumes the manager to be more knowledgeable, wonders why the manager is asking for advice. Face-saving cultures pose an additional problem because individuals are reluctant to step forward. It may be necessary in such circumstances to seek opinions from selected individuals privately.

The ideal setting for these techniques would appear to be one that combines collectivism with small power distance, but only Costa Rica (the most democratic, egalitarian, educated, and European country in Latin America) fits that criterion. Where participation and teamwork work best is in the Germanic countries, including Scandinavia and the Netherlands, which have very small power distances and, though individualistic, have strong communitarian traditions. Moreover, the Scandinavians and Dutch are feminine in the value they place on relationships, and the Dutch have the added benefit of many centuries of experience as skilled intermediaries and negotiators.

Other than in the feminine Netherlands and Scandinavia, individualism tends to breed competition more readily than cooperation. Therefore, those U.S. managers who do seek to promote cross-functional or interdisciplinary cooperation should find less organizational compartmentalization and rivalry abroad. A major exception is France, where even individuals and departments are chauvinists. Another, though less so, is Britain. Among other individualistic countries, German communitarianism crosses their bureaucratic boundaries very well, and consensus approaches work well in the more "being" Mediterranean countries of Iberia, Italy, and Greece.

The key to encouraging participation, or just a greater willingness to speak up, among large-power-distance subordinates is to build trust. It is important to let them know what is needed from them and why, and there should be an explanation that this is the preferred kind of relationship. Then patience, maintaining a low key, and repeated requests for input will be called for. Any lack of technical expertise should be discussed openly with an explanation that that is less expected in the manager's home culture. An especially tough problem or challenge may be a good, first opportunity, where an "all-hands" effort is clearly necessary. Any contributions should be praised, and by all means no messengers should be shot. Reaction to the first, tentative contributions will be scrutinized carefully by the contributor and by observers and will be communicated rapidly to all others. A decision not to accept an idea ought to be explained.

Strong uncertainty avoidance can cause people to question whether a problem should be accepted as is rather than solved, in effect denying the need for a decision. It also causes a search for familiar solutions rather than innovative ones. Collectivism slows down the decision-making process but makes implementation easier and faster. It also tends to produce "satisficing" solutions rather than maximizing (seizing upon the first mutually-acceptable alternative identified rather than a more exhaustive search for the optimal solution). The holistic thinking typical of Asian cultures results in alternatives being considered at once rather than sequentially.

Communication and Negotiation

Everyone but the Northern Europeans and other Anglos are more high context than the United States. Assertiveness, loudness, butting in, and all the typical behaviors used to make oneself heard in a meeting in the United States are dysfunctional in a high-context setting. This is so even in low-context Northern Europe. It is more productive to rely on written material and objective data to communicate the merits of one's product than upon aggressive personal selling. Boasting must be avoided, and any claim that cannot be supported is likely to be a fatal injury. There will be more attention to the quality of the relationships emerging during negotiations and less to the merits of the facts, which should be available in print to be read by anyone with a need. High-context participants are assessing the long-term viability of the personal relationships being developed. The negotiation must be conducted in such a way that its ultimate results are expected by all to be beneficial for all. The intent should be to maximize cooperation not rivalry. High-context negotiators do not engage in zero-sum games. Confrontation and excessive competitiveness produce disharmony and are thus to be avoided. That having been said, it is important to recognize, however, that Asian negotiators can be very tough even while conducting themselves very harmoniously. This is especially likely when the Asian counterpart senses a favorable balance in bargaining power. Alternatively, shaming may be used by Asians to compensate for weakness. High-context people tend to maintain large networks of contacts that share information, and they like to gather lots of information prior to and during negotiations. High-context people take great pride in their arts and culture and have a deep sense of history. Demonstration of some knowledge and appreciation in these areas helps build such relationships. An educated foreigner may well know more about the United States and its culture than does the U.S. visitor.

Motivation and Rewards

Motivation is an extremely complex issue even when considered only in the context of one culture. Adam Smith assumed that individuals were motivated by the rational pursuit of maximized self-interest or utility. The problem is defining that interest. Smith, and most economists, presume that it is material wealth. However, human beings have many needs and various means to satisfy them. We place different values on those means according to the priority of our needs and the degree to which different means satisfy them. Maslow (1962) arranged our needs in a hierarchy—basic needs such as food, safety, health, and security are at the bottom, followed by social needs, and then psychological needs, esteem, and then self-actualization at the top. He argued that as lower order needs are satisfied, people are motivated to act in ways that satisfy higher-order needs until they reach the point where maximizing individual potential becomes the primary motivator. Thus Maslow might suggest that after people are satisfied with their personal and social circumstances, which most were in his world, all that is left to motivate them is to challenge them with very stimulating work. One criticism of this model is the argument that many people see work only as a means to an end and that they seek esteem and to maximize their potential in family or leisure activities. Another is the likelihood that different needs become more or less salient at any particular time, depending on the circumstances. For example, someone may be working like the devil late in the day to get a report done early primarily to avoid missing an important social engagement later that evening. Taking a broader view, people who are working hard to maximize their potential may eventually find themselves doing so primarily to preserve their job security in a more intensely competitive environment. Notwithstanding the difficulties with Maslow's hierarchy, we have many other models contending to explain motivation in the workplace. Are we motivated by money, and if so, is it to enhance our material well-being or as a symbol of ability and achievement? Are we motivated by challenging goals? an enriched or more whole task? Are we motivated by achievement? power? affiliation? Are we motivated by promotions and increasingly greater responsibility and prestige? Are we motivated by a measure of expectancy that quantifies the relationship between our sense that we can do the job, the value we place on the expected outcomes, and our estimate of the likelihood that promised outcomes will be delivered? Clearly, it remains difficult to determine what motivates people in our own culture. Now we confront the reality that whatever models are thought to be applicable in this culture must be assessed for applicability in another, and then must be modified to adapt to a different value system.

Because values link needs and behavior, motivation is highly culture-specific. The theories of motivation developed and applied in the United States reflect our values. Goal theory (Latham and Locke 1984) relies heavily on the assumption that we are driven by a need for achievement. Job enrichment is based heavily on Herzberg's (1968) hypothesis that motivation is a function of the characteristics of the work itself, whereas contextual factors such as compensation, working conditions, and relationships with coworkers can have, at best, only no effect; they serve only as demotivators if deemed unsatisfactory. Like Maslow's hierarchy, Herzberg's hypothesis has been subject to rigorous challenge in the United States. Consider its validity in a culture with strong uncertainty avoidance where security is very important and the ambiguity associated with variation (for example, job enlargement, enrichment, rotation) in the work will be stressful, or in developing countries where compensation is poor, or in a collective culture where autonomy is less important and even undesirable. Expectancy theory (Vroom 1964) applies only where there is internal locus of control. Incentive or contingency-based compensation requires not only an internal locus but a dominant need for achievement. The need for achievement (McClelland 1961) is subordinate to a need for power where power distance is large or to a need for affiliation in collectivist or feminine cultures.

More-collectivist cultures prefer evaluation and reward of group performance more than individual performance. Collectivists are less comfortable with great extremes in rewards based on performance or position, and with ostentatious perquisites. This also applies in the more communitarian or feminine among individualist cultures. Contingency-based compensation will be less welcome where uncertainty avoidance is strong. Feminine, uncertainty avoiding, and collectivist cultures place more importance upon benefits and working hours and conditions conducive to an enhanced family life. Although all this seems very daunting, many managers in the culturally diverse United States are accustomed to coping with different value systems and motivational drives within their own, wholly domestic work forces. The problem in foreign cultures is more in degree than in kind.

Management by Objectives

Consider the conditions necessary for MBO to work well. Superiors and subordinates must feel that they can communicate, even argue, openly and honestly about what can and ought to be done, levels of attainment to be set, and the existence of and potential solutions for whatever difficulties might emerge (small power distance, high-content communication). The subordinate must internalize the challenge (individualism) and must be motivated by achievement more than by security (masculinity, weak uncertainty avoidance). The subordinate must feel some degree of confidence that the goal can be met and produce a detailed plan and budget that will meet the goal (internal locus of control). The subordinate, particularly for stretch goals, is expected to think and act entrepreneurially and creatively, that is, "outside the box" (masculinity, low uncertainty avoidance, internal locus). It is difficult to imagine a management practice more tailored (even if unconsciously) to the system of core values that dominate business in the United States. Consider the implications of trying to institute MBO in a "being" culture characterized by collectivism, large power distance, fatalism and external locus of control, femininity and high-context communication. This is precisely what Hofstede had in mind when he argued that not all U.S. management practices can be applied universally.

Strategic Management

Those schooled in the European university tradition, including Latin Americans, enjoy arguing theoretical abstractions and pondering contingencies. It is in the implementation of plans and attending to details that they tend to lose interest. The Germans take a more pragmatic approach but also are accomplished holistic thinkers. Asians are known for their focus on the long term. "Doing" Asians, especially the Japanese, take a proactive but simple and straightforward view of the long term. (They served as the model for the concept of Strategic Intent [Hamel and Prahalad 1989], which came to dominate strategic thinking in the United States in the 1990s). "Being" Asians, Arabs, and Africans are more fatalistic and may question the need for a lot of thinking about the unknowable. Hofstede (1991, 170–173) suggests that Taoist cosmology (yin and yang) produces a form of logic much different from that which prevails in the West. For a Westerner it is axiomatic that the opposite of a proposition known to be true must be false. For the Taoist, both can be true. Hofstede argues that this form of logic accommodates more-synthetic thinking compared to the more linear, scientific, analytical Western thought process, and promotes the pursuit of virtue (Buddhism, Confucianism, Shinto) rather than the possession of "truth" (Christianity, Judaism, Islam). There are no absolute truths or axioms in Asian thinking (hence the prevalence of relatively rudimentary legal systems and particularist ethics). Thus, he says, whereas Western logic is best suited to objectivity and science, Asian thinking is superior in matters that are subjective, holistic, and unknowable (like strategic planning).

Organizational Structure and Change

Interventions like re-engineering are suspect in cultures with strong uncertainty avoidance because they challenge basic assumptions about how things are supposed to work and fit together. This is so even though it is the compartmentalized bureaucracies typical of such cultures that normally are most in need of intervention. Also problematic in the face of strong uncertainty avoidance are complex structural arrangements like the matrix that violates bureaucratic principles such as unity of command and single, clearly-defined lines of authority. The same can be said of efforts to build a strong organizational culture and value system, empowerment, and other forms of expanded latitude and discretion intended to supplant the rules and regulations widely thought to inhibit innovation and good service.

SOME FINAL THOUGHTS ON CONVERGENCE

Hofstede's data, the best or at least the most comprehensive available, are nearly thirty years old. Considerable evidence of convergence has developed since; the discussions on this issue at the end of the preceding chapters identified some of the empirical and anecdotal evidence. Even students returning from foreign internships often comment on the apparent similarity of management practices. There is an important aspect of Hofstede's research that is sometimes misunderstood—it is often assumed that he studied only managers, but his data included workers as well, with the intent of gauging their expectations of managers. Thus, if one accepts the presumption that values among the educated or managerial classes of different cultures are more similar to one another than to the values of their respective workers, then it is reasonable to assume that Hofstede's research overstated cultural differences among managers. This presumption is based on the apparent phenomenon that cultural differences are more pronounced the farther one moves away from multinational employers and large cities and down the income scale. Hill (1994, 11) makes this point when he states that cultural differences between classes and generations in the same race are greater than the differences between people of the same class and age of different races. Multinational companies provide a vehicle for melding of values and acculturation. It may well be that there is less deviation among the young in this age of global communication and a kind of universal culture of youth (recall the *shinjinrui* of Japan). Nevertheless, the blizzard of articles and books published in recent years on how to manage cultural differences suggests that there is a long way to go. Culture is embedded deeply, perhaps even more so in very homogenous and very old cultures like Japan's. It is difficult to pick up an issue of the *Economist* that does not report on some cultural obstacle to European unification or a general business periodical that does not refer to some difference between management practices East and West, or North and South. Moreover, we should recognize the possibility that the apparent degree of assimilation may, at least in part, be only simulated out of necessity for newcomers to gain access and acceptance. People can adapt their behavior in order to fit in, but they do not need to and are much less likely to change their values and fundamental beliefs. When we ask people to change their values, we are asking them to modify their own sense of self-identity. Cultural roots probably can be broken or at least supplanted—this is what military training is intended to do—but we do not yet know how long it takes to obliterate them, or whether we should. We may need to be satisfied with simply learning from one another. Although it is assumed widely that those from "being" cultures could do with a little more "doing," it may well be that those from "doing" cultures could benefit from being a bit more "being." The issue of cultural convergence remains very much an open question. About the only safe conclusions appear to be that differences in core values remain pronounced but that there is convergence in practice, at least among managers in the larger companies.

COPING WITH CULTURAL DIFFERENCES

By now readers expecting to find a fistful of magic bullets or cookbook approaches to deal with these challenges realize that they are not going to find any here and probably know why—there aren't any. Cross-cultural management is a challenge to one's determination to learn and even to some aspects of character and personality. The first major hurdle, parochialism and ignorance of foreign cultures, was left behind no less recently than the decision to read this book. Then, anything learned from reading helps clear the next hurdle, ethnocentrism, the tendency to judge people of other cultures according to the standards of one's own. There is nothing to be gained from being judgmental; instead one must recognize and accept alternative value systems for what they are, not better or worse, just different. Familiarity with the roots of these differences helps us understand and accept them. We then can recognize them as artifacts of different histories and influences shaped over centuries, not as indicators of aberrant attitudes or flawed character. An understanding of another culture's core values and whence they came enables us to empathize, to see circumstances as others see them through the filter of their value systems. If, as many say, communication is the most important of business skills, then the ability to empathize may be the most fundamental, for only then can people truly speak the same "language."

Understanding cultural differences is not our ultimate objective, however, but only a means to becoming more-effective cross-cultural managers, colleagues, subordinates, or negotiators. That hurdle is somewhat higher and not all may be able to clear it because to do so requires more than knowledge and commitment. If there are any magic bullets, they are personal traits like open-mindedness; patience; flexibility; humility; consideration and good manners; the willingness to learn, to listen more than talk and communicate interests and needs, and to search for common ground rather than to take bargaining positions; the desire to build lasting relationships rather than to merely collect acquaintances and customers; a related willingness to leave some money on the table and to recognize that making money is not the sole purpose of life; and demonstrating some interest in matters beyond the business at hand and business in general. These values are more common in many other cultures than in the United States, and people of those cultures expect them as the norm in their business relationships. We are still paying a price for having for so long a market big enough to accommodate us. Now that time has passed, and we find it necessary to learn some skills others have long practiced and take for granted. One's behavior and conduct in a foreign setting are more important even than the ability to speak the host's language. Individuals who find it difficult to embrace these values are in for a difficult time in cross-cultural assignments no matter how much they know or how many books like this they have read. There is no intention here to discourage additional study, however. Many very useful practical techniques for coping with specific cross-cultural management problems can be found in the excellent references listed at the end of Chapter 1.

Perhaps the greatest cross-cultural challenge we face is the dilemma of a "doing" manager working in a "being" culture. "Being" must not be mistaken for laziness, indifference, or unmanageability. People of all cultures are willing and capable of hard work, excellent performance, and a cooperative manner. "Being" people simply have different priorities most succinctly captured by the familiar notion "work to live." They typically place family and friends before the employer, derive less satisfaction from their work, maintain great separation, but expect much from the boss, need more structure, and enjoy associations with the work group more than individual achievement. This is the sternest test of the personal traits necessary for success in a cross-cultural setting. It is worth noting, however, that those same traits characterize good managers in any setting. Hence, if one can manage successfully in one cultural environment, the same is possible in any environment, provided that one is sufficiently committed to learn the new cultural "rules" and willing to exercise those same traits at an even higher level.

ADDITIONAL READING

Adler, Nancy J. 1991. *International Dimensions of Organizational Behavior*, 2nd ed. (Boston: PWS-Kent).

Blake, Robert R., and Jane S. Mouton. 1978. *The New Managerial Grid*. (Houston: Gulf).

Hall, Edward T. 1987. *The Dance of Life: The Other Dimension of Time*. (Garden City, N.Y.: Anchor Press/Doubleday).

Hamel, Gary, and C. K. Prahalad. 1989. "Strategic Intent." *Harvard Business Review* 67, no. 3 (May-June): 63–76.

Herzberg, Frederick. 1968. "One More Time: How Do You Motivate Employees?" *Harvard Business Review* 46, no. 1 (January-February): 54–62.

Hill, Richard. 1994. *Euromanagers and Martians*. (Brussels: Europublic).

Hofstede, Geert. 1991. "Cultural Constraints in Management Theories." *Academy of Management Executive* 7(1): 81–94.

Hofstede, Geert. 1991. *Cultures and Organizations: Software of the Mind*. (New York: McGraw-Hill).

————. 1980. *Culture's Consequences: International Differences in Work-Related Values*. (Beverly Hills: Sage).

Lane, Henry W., Joseph J. DiStefano, and Martha Moznewski. 1997. *International Management Behavior*, 3rd ed. (Cambridge, Mass.: Blackwell).

Latham, Gary, and Edwin A. Locke. 1984. *Goal Setting: A Motivational Theory that Works*. (Englewood Cliffs, N.J.: Prentice Hall).

Likert, Rensis. 1967. *The Human Organization*. (New York: McGraw-Hill).

Maslow, Abraham H. 1962. *Toward a Psychology of Being*. (Princeton: Van Nostrand).

McClelland, David. 1961. *The Achieving Society*. (New York: Irvington).

McGregor, Douglas. 1960. *The Human Side of Enterprise*. (New York: McGraw-Hill).

Vroom, Victor H. 1964. *Work and Motivation*. (New York: Wiley).

INDEX

About the Author

JACK SCARBOROUGH is Professor of Management at Barry University, Miami Shores, Florida. He has taught hundreds of international students at Barry, where he developed both the undergraduate and MBA courses in cross-cultural management. A frequent contributor in professional management journals, he has won several awards for outstanding articles.